The Facey Romford Papers.

"Rot the beggar" exclaims Romford.

The Facey Romford Papers.

Days in The Life of the NHS.
An Everyday Story of N£sd Folk.

By Facey Romford, Jr.

With a Preface by Roy Lilley.

With an Afterword & Commentary by
Soapey Sponge VII.

EER
Edward Everett Root, Publishers. Brighton, 2016.

Edward Everett Root, Publishers, Company Limited,
30 New Road, Brighton, BN1 1BN, England.

edwardeverettroot@yahoo.co.uk

The Facey Romford Papers.
Days in The Life of the NHS.
An Everyday Story of N£sd Folk.

Public Policy Series, no.2.

The Text, © Facey Romford, Jr., 2013, 2014, 2016.
The Preface © Roy Lilley, 2016.
The Afterword and Commentary, © Soapey Sponge VII, 2016.
This compilation, © Edward Everett Root, Publishers, Co. Ltd., 2016.

Hardback ISBN: 978-1-911204-02-2
Paperback ISBN: 978-0-954-2075-26
eBook ISBN: 978-0-954-2075-88

Dust-jacket illustration from a 19th-century *papier-mache* box in the author's collection.

Frontispiece illustration, *"Rot the Beggar", exclaims Romford"*, by John Leech, from *Mr. Facey Romford's Hounds* (Bradbury and Evans 1865 edition).

The portrait of Facey's predecessor shown on the title-page, from *Mr. Sponge's Sporting Tour* (Bradbury, Evans 1853 edition).

Typeset by the author in Times New Roman.
Designed by Pageset Limited, High Wycombe, Buckinghamshire.
Printed and produced in England by imprintdigital, Exeter, Devon.

TO

THE HONOURABLE LADY 'LIZZIE' OF UCKFIELD,
MBE
THIS VOLUME IS INSCRIBED
BY HER
OBLIGED AND EVER FAITHFUL SERVANT
THE AUTHOR.

AND TO A CLOSE AND MUCH
MISSED FRIEND DR. BILL PICKERING.

"Think about it. Instead of manipulating people, why not *empower* them? Let them know what we're up against. And have that drive our collective will." – Hugh Howey, *Wool* (2013).

"The spirit of self-help is the root of all genuine growth in the individual; and, exhibited in the lives of many, it constitutes the true source of national vigour and strength. Help from without is often enfeebling…

"Whatever is done *for* men or classes, to a certain extent takes away the stimulus and necessity of doing for themselves; and where men are subjected to over-guidance and over-government, the inevitable tendency is to render them comparatively helpless…

"The highest patriotism and philanthropy consists not so much of altering laws and modifying institutions, as in helping and stimulating men to elevate and improve themselves by their own free and independent individual action." – Samuel Smiles, *Self-Help. With illustrations of Conduct and Perseverance.* (1859).

"Whatever you can do, or dream you can do, begin it. Boldness has genius, power and magic in it."- attributed to Goethe.

"There are many who give up, and many who procrastinate, but there are some who go on." C.S. Forester.

"The point of research, always, when writing fiction, is to bring the imagination to the point at which it can make up stuff so like reality that we can't tell the difference." – Philip Pullman.

Acknowledgements

As my good friend Roy says in his very generous *Preface*, the essays in this book first appeared as a regular column in 2013-14 on his absolutely essential nhsManagers.net e-letter – which everyone concerned with public policy finds indispensable. Roy is, of course, *the* leading commentator and analyst of the British healthcare system. He is a former Chairman of an NHS Trust, the progenitor of the NHS Confederation, and the author of essential books on the management of the NHS in the interests of patients. I am deeply grateful to him for finding space for my work originally on his site, and for his friendship and unswerving support over many years. I much appreciate his contributing his inimitable *Preface*. I am indebted to Brian Aird, too, for his help with his special computer skills when publishing my columns.

As a reader, I am much indebted to the great novelist Robert Smith Surtees and his timeless illustrator John Leech, in course.

As a commentator I am also most especially indebted to my close friend, the late and much missed Dr. Bill Pickering – whose work was distinguished by his advocacy of an Independent Medical Inspectorate, which is still much needed. The dedication of this book to him and to Lizzie of Uckfield acknowledges much. Bill was the most thoughtful and reflective doctor and the most politically aware medic I have ever known. He was enormously well read, wonderfully independent, with a vivacious, warm, witty and original mind. And suitably politically incorrect, too. Lizzie's devotion and support have always helped me time and again in more ways than I can capture in words.

For the production of this work I am also especially grateful to Nigel Austin of Pageset Limited of High Wycombe for his expert and invaluable advice. Nigel designed the book jacket too.

I owe thanks to many other good friends in the NHS, notably the late John Simmonds, the late Dr. Gerry Doherty, Mrs. Margaret Dann, and to other supporters – several of whom no doubt would prefer to remain entirely anonymous, like Mr. Romford! After all – in a world which has nurtured Sir David Nicholson, the Silent Communist Knight of N. Staffs – you never know who is listening….

Meanwhile, it should be no surprise that the author still prays for *any* government which genuinely empowers the individual by passing money into their specific hands. And which declares explicitly and argues constantly for a liberal and competitive market economy of adaptive change, consumerism, social mobility, and resulting in a better life for every individual taking self-responsibility. The radical personalisation and individual control over your own health, education, and personal choices would be transformative indeed. Let's have it!

This book is, of course, a work of fiction. Names, characters, places, and incidents are either the product of the author's imagination or are used fictitiously. Any resemblance to actual events or locales or persons, living or dead, is of course entirely coincidental.

FR, Jr., 27 July 2015.

PS: NHS Manager Stewed Bludgeon says "I will *not* resign!"

PPS: Lord Oakeshott says…[*who he?- Ed.*].

PPPS: Mr. A. Birdnumb, MP says "My policy is…."

PPPPS: Professor A. Hampster of The Klingfilm Fund, London says "I have some points…on the one hand…on the other…."

PPPPPS: Apology for absence: Lord Alascooke of Smugdominion.

NB: *The Editor* notes that Facey Romford Jr. is the *nom-de-plume* of an experienced NHS non-executive and former government adviser. [Name & address supplied].

Contents

Acknowledgements vii

Contents ix

Preface by Roy Lilley xiii

Dramatis personae xv

Episode 1. Days in the life of the NHS: An everyday story of N£sd folk. The Story Begins 1

Episode 2: Cleanliness next to Godliness…The West Boggleypool-on-Sea scandal! 7

Episode 3: Win a Postcode! 13

Episode 4: Five "Andrew Marrs" in the A&E queue, and three "Jackie Ashleys" 17

Episode 5: Those new peerages, and why we're here at all 21

Episode 6: The Richmond House Revels, Scene 1 27

Episode 7: At Your Expense…The NHS & The Economics of Politics 33

Episode 8: Docs, drugs, and rock and roll 43

Episode 9. The Spectres of Health Policy to Come…a Warning from The Nether World? The Richmond House Revels, Scene 2 47

Episode 10: On Doctor's Orders.The Practice of General Practice. Part 1 57

Episode 11: On Doctor's Orders.The Practice of General Practice. Part 2 65

Episode 12: On Doctor's Orders.The Practice of General Practice. Part 3 75

Episode 13: Obesity-Class in the NHS. The National Anti-Obesity Campaign…Part 1 .. 81

Episode 14: The NHS Merry-Go-Round. Round and round we go! 89

Episode 15: Obesity-Class in the NHS. The National Anti-Obesity Campaign…Part 2 .. 97

Episode 16: Enter Lord Ironsides. N£sd Musical Chairs, and a New World? Part 1 103

Episode 17: Obesity-Class in the NHS. The National Anti-Obesity Campaign... Part 3 109

Episode 18: Enter Lord Ironsides. N£sd Musical Chairs. A New World, Perhaps? Part 2 115

Episode 19: Enter Lord Ironsides. N£sd Musical Chairs, and a New World, Perhaps? Part 3 119

Episode 20: "The System." Little Dorrit and the Bradford Child, Little Hamzah Khan. Or, 'Nobody's Fault' 125

Episode 21: Who's for Wilful Medical Neglect or Negligence then? *Wilful*, indeed? Neglect, or *Negligent?* And so to The High Court, 5-years in the Clink, or Transportation? We Ask Away! 131

Episode 22: Obesity-Class in the NHS. The National Anti-Obesity Campaign.... Part 4. Being the charming [?] winter tale of Mrs. Gobble, and her three young plumpy but not very jumpy children, Goblitup, Goblthelot, and Gobblygook 137

Episode 23: The Richmond House Revels. Scene 3: Part 1. How Unknown N£sd Doctors Practice. Or Courting Disasters. What you are not allowed to know 143

Episode 24: The Richmond House Revels. Scene 3, Part 2. How Unknown N£sd Doctors Practice. Or Courting Disasters. And Patients requiring tickets for prompt emigration to Uzbekistan? Apply here. The dramatic text...as promised 149

Episode 25: Our Wonderful NHS. A Seasonal Ode to Hopes 155

Episode 26: The impending Bugginsturn North By-Election. The Nation Reveals All. A forthcoming and seasonal New Year's Entertainment 159

Episode 27: A Job Application [or two?]. We see into the N£sd future, and reflect. Is it bye-bye Cameroon and Cluggy, hello the FREE Kid? The Hunted Fox satirically reveals some of all 165

Episode 28: The Richmond House Revels, Scene 4. A mistaken but "expert" voice on a mysterious N£sd telephone call. A Christmas Pantomime Jollification 171

Episode 29: Collector's Corner. The Age of the NHS Postcard 175

Episode 30: Snakes and Ladders. Or how the NHS so carefully guards scarce taxpayers' money. And, *Redundancies Ahoy!* 181

Episode 31: Facey's Frightfuls. As noted in My N£sd Diary. Extracts, to be read on train when Oscar Wilde Diary is finished. Part 1 187

CONTENTS

Episode 32: Facey's Frightfuls. As noted in My N£sd Diary. Extracts, to be read on train when Oscar Wilde Diary is finished. Part 2 193

Episode 33: Britain to Teach the World How to Improve its Cancer Care. Major new PM international initiative. NHS to lead radical cancer care changes in ex-Soviet Republic of Muckitupkistan. Part 1 199

Episode 34: Britain to Teach the World How to Improve its Cancer Care. Major new PM international initiative. NHS to lead radical cancer care changes in ex-Soviet Republic of Muckitupkistan. Part 2 205

Episode 35: Where there ain't a will, there's definitely a way! Or waiting list? What waiting list? Part 1 211

Episode 36: Where there ain't a will, there's definitely a way! Or waiting list? What waiting list? Part 2 215

Episode 37: Old rope for money? The British Doctor proposes innovative ways to fund The N£sd 221

Episode 38: Just Call 999 – if your Budgie is sick! Culture, Effort, & The Great Educated British Public after 65 years of the NHS. Or a quiet evening on 999 – and in A&E, too 227

Episode 39: Cameron launches NHS Inter-Galactica. "World's Best Service" – Now to Serve Space. Astonishing N£sd Venture... 235

Episode 40: How To Be Top. "Total Management" – The Bergkamp and The Arsenal Way 241

Episode 41: Shock Horror Tory & Labour Disasters At Bugginsturn North By-Election 245

Episode 42: Lord 'Owzat's Corner of NHS Wonders 251

Episode 43: The PM & The N£sd 'Reforms.' An Early Extract From His Memoirs, Part 1 263

Episode 44: The PM & The N£sd 'Reforms.' An Early Extract From His Memoirs, Part 2 273

Episode 45: The PM & The N£sd 'Reforms.' An Early Extract From His Memoirs, Part 3 279

Episode 46: The PM & The N£sd 'Reforms.' An Early Extract From His Memoirs, Part 4 283

Episode 47: The PM & The N£sd 'Reforms.' An Early Extract From His Memoirs, Part 5 287

Episode 48: The PM & The N£sd 'Reforms.' An Early Extract From His Memoirs, Part 6 291

Episode 49: The PM & The N£sd 'Reforms.' An Early Extract From His Memoirs, Part 7 303

Episode 50: The PM & The N£sd 'Reforms.' An Early Extract From His Memoirs, Part 8 311

Facey's Holiday Postcards 319–345

Afterword & Commentary by Soapey Sponge VII 347

Preface, by Roy Lilley

The author of this book's ingenuity, creativity and power to entertain knows no bounds!

His unique approach to writing and grasp of character and narrative make him a joy to read.

Nowhere are his talents better showcased than in the tales of Facey Romford, Jr.

I know this to be true for two reasons.

First, he entertains me and manages to make me laugh out loud and that's not easy!

Second, he had the same effect on the thousands of readers of my nhsManagers.net eletter where much of this book first appeared as a regular column. I know that to be true because readers wrote and told me so!

The author holds up a mirror to the NHS and public service, its foibles and peculiarities. He shines a light into the dark recesses and makes us think, entertains us, pokes fun and encourages us to do better.

His characters are a delight and his stories grasp the issues of the day and sets them out in a new light.

I am thrilled that this whole body of work can, at last, be found in one place. It is a work of genius. Enjoy it, rip through it. It is a breathless read but you will never think of the NHS in the same way again!

RL, 2 July 2015.

Dramatis personae

The living and the dead, the real and the imagined, all jostling together in the Gilbert & Sullivan 'Topsy-Turvy' World of the N£sd.

The reader will meet the following fictional and non-fictional characters (and be required to tell the difference):

Dr. I.I. Addio. Trained in Edinburgh, he is a senior GP in Soccertone-on-The-Blink, Chemslfton, Essex. He spends his weekends mending old wheelbarrows and garden tools.

Mr. [then Sir] H. Applebird, OBE, Assistant Under-Secretary of State for Hadministrative Affairs, Leytonstone Marshes House, Walthamstow, E. Then Permanent secretary.

Professor A. Applecore, Chief Astrologer, The Klingfilm Fund, London

Dr. Sydney Avogotta-Nohidea CBE, President, Woyal College of GPs.

Mr. Edth Ballth, MP, a Labour politician. *[Not elected in 2015].*

Ms. Poloddo Barnstormick, B.Sc., LL.B., of the Crown Prosecution Service.

Lord Betwell of Epsom Downs, odds-maker and adviser to government.

Mr. Andy Birdnumb, MP, Labour politician.

Mr. Syd Bishop-McHancox, JP, Chief Executive of The Square Peg National Exceptions Hospital Trust at Bicknoller in the Quantickle Hills. Before that he was trained as a Janitor and Night Watchman at The Lady Macbeth Personal Injuries Centre, Forres in Scotland. He was, until recently the Planning and Development Director at Oddsbodkins Rural Care Services Trust, Snafflebridge, Fife. He likes to think of himself as "a very practical bloke."

The Rt. Hon. Tony Blair, PC, the former successful Labour leader.

Mr. Stewed Bludgeon, an NHS Manager in SE England. ["I will not resign!"]

Mr. T.U.C. Lord Bob Crowcouncilhouser, MBE, JP, Hampstead magistrate and council tenant.

Professor Philip Booth, the real and distinguished British economist. Editorial & Programme Director, Institute of Economic Affairs, & Professor of Finance, Public Policy and Ethics at St. Mary's University, Twickenham.

Baroness Bottomley of Headhunt, formerly Secretary of State for Health, Conservative Fabian politician.

Sir Richard Branson, venturesome space entrepreneur &c.

Dr. Alexis Brooksnubbra, a GP. Trained in Austria, and at King's, London. Head of the urban general practice in Pubsvale, Chiselhurst-on-Wash, Suffolk. He owns a cat called Lord Lucan. He is 46.

Mr. G. Brown, MP, the alleged PM. *[Left House in 2015. Seat then lost to Scotnats].*

Ms. Actressii Rosie Bruford, MP, JP., a Hampstead magistrate.

Ms. Bernice Camden, formerly a leading amateur wrestler, is Chief Executive of the Hoop-la and Hula-Hoop Women's NHS Hospital Trust, Wiggers-on-Acveon, Soomersetshire. She is a key adviser to the Institute of One Idea at Monologue House, London, and to the IT'S ALL FREE Party.

The Rt. Hon. D. Cameron PC, MP, Prime Minister. Subsequently ennobled as The Duke of Notting Hill and Chipping Thompson, KG, OM, FRSPR.

Lord Carpetking, retailer and adviser to government.

Peter Carter, OBE, General Secretary and Chief Executive, the Royal College of Nursing.

Mr. Ian Clownlives, Medical Director of The Bit Parts of England NHS Trust, West Midlands.

Mrs. Lesley Crooper, an extremely unpleasant, semi-literate, and impatient patient.

Mr. Andy Cunningham (1910-2010), crooked Old Labour politician and jailbird, close associate of John Paulson the rascally and jailed architect and property "developer."

Mr. Sid Daley, an NHS archivist.

The Rt. Hon. Mr. D'Arcy Plantaganet Cromwell, PC, MP, a one-time Secretary of State for Health.

Lord J.C.B. Digger, industrialist and adviser to government.

Admiral Albert George Quincy Lascelles Vernon de St. Valery, Lord Ironsides, the new Chair at Chessingfield-on-Soke NHS Trust – now renamed The Edmund Burke NHS Trust. A major local land-owner of aristocratic descent, and a former head of the Fleet Air Arm. He is aged 60 [in 2014]. But looks a very vigorous 50. And acts accordingly.

Nursie Nursie Dixbungle, Chief Executive, The Great British Whitewash Company PLC.

Ms. Petronelli di Champagni, an Italian hospital administrator who is an Exchange Visitor from Roma. She is presently a Secretary in Sir Crank Lamparde's Private Office at Richmond House.

The Rt. Hon. N. Clegg, PC, MP, Liberal Democratic politician. *[aka as Clugg or Cluggy – Ed.]*

Grandmaster The Worshipful Sir Peter Coquille Albert Perceive Aloysius Gravities Cooke-Praster, CBE, a leading surgeon.

DRAMATIS PERSONAE

The Duke of Notting Hill and Chipping Thompson, KG, OM, FRSPR. Politician, and formerly Prime Minister.

The Rt. Hon. Iain Duncan Smith, PC, MP, Conservative politician and welfare reformer.

Sir Vinnie Earns, house builder and founder of RunEmUpandRun PLC, adviser to government.

Professor Brian Edwards, CBE, distinguished former NHS manager and contributor to nhsManagers.net eletter.

Ms. Jane Ellison, MP, a government health minister.

Mr. Nigel Farage, MEP, leader of the UK Independence Party.

Dr. Angela Findlater, GP in Halstead Hill, Durham.

Lord Fogelstumped, journalist, editor, and adviser to government.

Mr. Nick Gibb, Conservative MP, Minister of State for Schools after the 2015 general election (having held the same post between May 2010 and September 2012). Very bright, rising star. Future Sec. of State.

Sir Jeff Goodglesnetspacer, technology entrepreneur and adviser to government.

Dr. Mark Goldman, formerly controversial NHS bureaucrat in Sutton Coldfield and Solihull, Birmingham, now a significant NHS pensioner.

Dame Fannie Gonebarkers, B.Sc., D. Univ., NCSC, DBE, Quangoite; socialist bureaucrat.

Mr. A. Gorbachuff, interviewer at Sheffield Hallam City Job Centre. Ex-Sovietite.

The Rt. Hon. Michael Gove, PC, MP, leading Conservative politician.

Professor A. Hampster, of The Klingfilm Fund, London. ["On the one hand…on the other hand…."]

Lord Ralph Harris of High Cross (1924-2006), British economist, General Director of the Institute of Economic Affairs, London, 1957-88, and then fund-raising Chairman.

Ms. Polly-Esther Harty, nutritionist.

Mr U. Heap, a City of London solicitor and adviser to Lord Patterer of East Asia. Irish office: PSD. Porson, Shilleto, and Dobree.

Mr S. Higbon-Ballcock, temporarily Chief Executive of the West Boggleypool-on-Sea NHS Hospitals Trust, Snape Street, Suffolk.

The Rt. & Very Rev. Dr. B. Hogbin, GCSE, Bishop of St. Just, religious adviser to The

Independent Labour Party. Related to the Hoglebin family of Chessingfield-on-Soke and to the Hogblinkered family. Anti "change."

The Very Rev. Rural Dean Dr. W. Hogblinkered, GCE, his relative, and a religious doctor. Similarly "progressive."

The Rt. Hon Mr. Jeremy Hunt, PC, MP, genuinely likeable Tory politician, Secretary of State for Health, etc.

Professor Sir Brian Jarman OBE, was Professor of Primary Health Care 1983–98, Imperial College School of Medicine and President of the British Medical Association from 2003–4. An important modern doctor.

Mr. Augustus Melmotte-Jobber-Johnson, a 'political' doctor and long-term Woyal BMA activist. Now aged 91 (or possibly more). Widely known in the profession as "Jurassic Johnson." A leader of current GP contract negotiations. Collects oceanic cruise-liner menu cards.

Mr. Merfyn Merffyne Jones-Jones, LL.B., a Clerk to the Court, Hampstead, N. London.

The Rt. Hon Mr. V. Kable (or Cable?), PC, MP, then a government minister. *[Not elected in 2015]*.

Ms. Barbara Keeley, Campaigning Labour MP for Eccleston and Worsley South.

Professor Sir Ian Kennedy, quangoite *[is he real? -Ed]*.

Sir Bruce Edward Keogh, KBE, British surgeon and physician, specialises in cardiac surgery; Medical Director of the NHS in England since 2007, and National Medical Director of the NHS Commissioning Board (NHS England) since 2013.

Sir Snuffle Kettledrum CBE, President, Woyal College of Surgeons.

Lord Klinnockles of Brevity, a life-peer.

Lady Gladyss Klinnockles of Income Augmentation, a life peeress.

His Very Distinguished Grand Eminenceship The Lord High Grandmaster, The Worshipful Sir Pweeter G.G. Knatchbull-Bullknash, CBE, The Very Hon. & Very Distinguished Surgeon and Very Life President of The Royal College of Vested Interests.

Mr. U. Knowitmakessense, MEP and MP, UK Independence Party.

Ms. Lynda Lamentable, a 'famous' and often self-mentioned NHS 'activist.'

The Rt. Hon. Andrew Lansley, PC, MP, a civil servant who became hapless Tory Cameroonesk politician and Secretary of State for Health and then demoted to be 'leader' of the House of Commons. *[Left the House in 2015]*.

DRAMATIS PERSONAE

Ms. Jennifer Knott-Necessary, Secretary to Lord Patterer of East Asia. Her father is the well-known contractor Lord J.C.B. Knott-Necessary

Sir Crank Lamparde, the Permanent Secretary at the Department of Health. Graduate of the Henry VIII Matrimonial Enhancement College, Cambridge. Studied Arch & Anth. Greek Major Scholar. Son of Sir Evenkrankier Lamparde, former Labour High Commissioner to Dominican Republic. Sir Crank – when merely Mr. Crank – was formerly a local health authority chief executive. Collects old match-box labels. He is aged 63.

Mr. Brendon Lewis, MP, government minister.

The Rt. Hon. Dr. Julian Lewis, MP for New Forest East since 1997. Defence expert and author. In June 2015 elected to the Chair of the Commons Defence Select Committee.

Mr. Paul Lewis, freelance journalist, regular BBC commentator and money expert.

Mr. Roy Lilley, the leading national commentator on NHS management and culture. See his regular and indispensable nhsManagers.net eletter.

Sir John Major, PC, KG, very dull Tory politician; close friend of Mrs. Edwina Currie, former Tory MP.

Mr. Mansfodler Mansfodler QC, a dodgy left-wing fully-employed lawyer.

The Rt. Hon Reginald Maudling (1917-79), PC, MP, crooked Tory politician and candidate for Party leadership in 1965.

Mr. Damien McBridge, Consultant Orthopaedic Surgeon at The G. Neville NHS Hospital Trust, Burton-on-kickemharder-at-Tweed.

Dr. Jim McCeltic, GP and Chief Executive of Hull-on-the-Wye Health Authority.

Stephanie Rose McGovern, an English business journalist for the BBC and the main business presenter for BBC Breakfast who also sometimes co-hosts the show itself.

Professor Martin McKee, Professor of European Public Health, London School of Hygiene and Tropical Medicine/ Director. One of the 'Twerpy Twins.'

The Rt. Hon. Alan Milburn, PC, formerly successful Secretary of State for Health; now Chairman of the Social Mobility and Child Poverty Commission.

Professor Ralph Miliband, Marxist pro-Soviet political academic.

The Millkibar [or Millkiband] Kid, PC, MP, Labour politician.

Dame Jennifer Susan "Jenni" Murray, DBE, a British journalist and broadcaster, best known for presenting BBC Radio 4's 'Woman's Hour.'

Ms. Nevermindthemanagementfeelthedosh, MP, long-term acolyte of Mr. G. Brown, the alleged PM.

Dr. Jeff Neville, GP and Chief Executive of East Harley NHS Trust.

Sir David Nicholson, Communist Knight, an NHS employee, now a major pensioneer-in-chief. *[Cf, Mid-Staffs, www.].* The Silent Knight!!! A.k.a. as Sir D. Nickolodeon

Sir Extrasmuchsatisfied Perceval Nowtdunne, CBE, President, Woyal BMA.

Lord Oakeshott [*who he? Ed*].

Kevin O'Grady, Chief Executive of the Coleraine St. Fortescue Veterinary Hospital, N. Ireland. He is an old – and very shrewd and street-wise – friend of Mr. Barney Wells, with whom as a student he regularly went on short canal boat boating trips in Ireland. He was formerly a government adviser on community care.

Mr. Jamie Oliver MBE, leading British TV chef and restauraunteur.

Councillor Orioglu Maintenanchance JP, a Hampstead magistrate.

The Rt. Hon. George Osborne, PC, MP, Chancellor of The Exchequer.

Lord 'Owzat, a Government Health Minister.

Mr. John Paulson (1910-93), crooked architect and property developer, and close associate of T. Dan Smith, the N.E. England and similarly crooked Old Labour politician.

Mr. Jeremy Paxman, fierce TV interviewer, and author.

Mr. G.A. Petrified-Grey, a leader, The Royal College of Vested Interests.

The late Dr. William Graham Pickering [died 5 February 2015, aged 63], trained at King's College Hospital, he was later a hospital doctor, then a GP, and a noted expert-witness in legal cases concerning the NHS. A real friend to better care. Independent advocate of a National Medical Inspectorate. See William G. Pickering, 'An independent medical inspectorate', in D. Gladstone (ed.), *Regulating doctors* (London: Institute for the Study of Civil Society, 2000).

Ms. Serpentine O'Privilege, long-time "associate" of Lord Puggy Pointsdarn, known to him as "Popsie." She was formerly a horse-jumper at trials. She is a comfort in his distresses.

Lord Chrissie Patterer of East Asia, a distinguished professional non-executive director, who is widely employed in the City of London. He is a senior member of the new NHS Board of Control. He is also a prominent Freemason, a City of London Liveryman, a private yachtsman and a fervent cricket fan.

Mr. Alfie Peach, a recently [but regularly] redundant senior NHS manager, is a new applicant for welfare-support and re-settlement by the NHS Re-Settlement branch, Recompense House, Elephant & Castle, London, SE.

Lord Puggy Pointsdarn, the former left-wing ex-mariner, a noted "expert" on this, that, and the other. Sometimes. Usually. When telephoned. However, he has no known

DRAMATIS PERSONAE

previous interest in the NHS but he is the non-executive Chairman of Co-op Theatres and Circuses PLC, the leisure division of The Woyal Bank of Overlegs, Little Fiddlestown, Essex.

Ms. Jessica Pottlegun-Wedgwood-Benn-Tyza CBE, Chair, Socialist Medical Congress.

Dr. V.P. Rooney Porke. Trained in Mainchance-Mannheim, East Germany, now a GP in Paddle-on-Down, Essex. He is a member of the GP's renegotiating committee on the existing GP's contract. He spends his week-ends on a jet-ski as often as he can.

Mr. Nick Robinhoode, an unusual and independent-minded [?] BBC reporter.

Dr. Arthur Seldon, CBE (1916-2005), British economist and joint-founder President (with Lord Ralph Harris of High Cross) of the Institute of Economic Affairs, London, where he directed academic affairs for 30 years. Father of Sir Anthony Seldon.

Lord (previously Sir) Stuart Rose, Baron Rose of Monewden, who Facey calls 'Sir Roses.' British businessman, executive chairman of Marks & Spencer (annual salary of £1,130,000.) Following the appointment of Marc Bolland in May 2010, Rose stepped down as executive chairman at the end of July 2010 and remained as chairman until early 2011 when he was replaced by Robert Swannell. Knighted in 2008 for his services to the retail industry; created a Life Peer in 2014.

Shami. [*Unidentified. Apparently a left-wing figure.– Ed.*].

Baroness Sitting Bull of Emertonii, an appointee of sorts.

Ms. Anna Soubry, MP, a government health minister, and, from 2015, Small Business Minister who also attended Cabinet.

Major-General J.J. Slopkins, MM, MC, CBE, etc., Chairman of The Tower of London NHS Trust. He is a retired cavalryman. He is aged 82. He lives at Coggeshall in Essex. He collects old military trench-maps and 18th century ceramic pot-lids.

Professor John Spiers, radical free-market commentator, long associated with the Institute of Economic Affairs, London. Author of *The Invisible Hospital and The Secret Garden. An Insider's Account of the NHS Reforms* (Oxford, Radcliffe Medical Press/London, Institute of Health Services Management, 1995); *Patients, Power, and Responsibility: The First Principles of Consumer-driven Reform* (Oxford, Radcliffe Medical Press/London, Institute of Economic Affairs, 2003), *Who Decides Who Decides? Enabling choice, equity, access, improved performance and patient guaranteed care* (Oxford & New York, Radcliffe Publishing/London, IEA, 2008), and *Coming, Ready or Not! The Present and Future of the NHS* (Brighton, Edward Everett Root, 2015). *[– that's a rather special Christmas hamper you owe me now, John! – Ed.]*

Ms. Maisie Spry, a 999 operator at Broxbinge, Hertfordshire.

Mr. Simon Stevens, NHS England Chief Executive from 1 April 2014; Labour politician, health care manager, political adviser to Tony Blair, and to Alan Milburn. The Lord Stevens of Bexhill-on-Sea-to-be.

Sir Cyril Squoffington-Squogg, OBE, JP, Chief Executive of The Tower of London NHS Hospital Trust, London, E. He is aged 67 [2013]. A retired senior civil servant, Department of Pensions & Nicholsons. He is also a noted amateur biographer, having written lives of P.B. Shelley, John Keats, John Masefield, and the early 19th century publisher Henry Colburn. He is at work now on a new book on Walt Whitman. He collects 19th century' railway library' fiction, called 'yellow-backs.'

Lady Bernice Squoffington-Squogg, his wife, is Chairperson of The Wiltshire Artists Benevolent Fund. They live during the week in Sloane Street, Chelsea and at weekends at Wobblybottom Towers, Minceyglade, Wiltshire. She is a former ice-skater. She is aged 39 [2013].

Paul Bristol Squoffington-Squogg, their son, is a nature writer on the *Financial Times*, and writes the popular weekly column 'Splashing About Happily.' Often compared with Mr. Boot's famous column for *The Daily Beast*, 'Lush Places.'

Mr. Mike Stickit, MA, Chief Executive of The Two Counties and Twin Piers NHS University Seaside and Downs Hospital Trust, Squivington-by-the-Thames, Sheppley, Kent. He collects coloured silk weekend jump-suits, and was a co-owner of a racehorse, *Fergietime* [out of *Knighted-in-Error*, by *Bullyrefs*]. The horse was initially entered for the next Aintree Grand National. However, unfortunately it ran very inadequately at Lancaster Gate in the Transfer-windows Stakes. And although it was allowed an extra 6 minutes in which to finish it still came in last, behind the winner *Wenger-Ahoy*. The previous classic winning horse *Jose Ole* was placed third, over-burdened with one-liners. The distantly placed colt *City of Moneybags w*as an undisciplined poor fourth. The untried youngster *Spur-you-on-but-going-down* was scratched at the start. The trialist *Astonished Villa* was fifth. Mike was previously a Senior Ticket-Officer at Loggoland.

Ms. Gloria Swansong, MP. Formerly Secretary of State for Health, and still Labour MP for Haringey-in-Drugbonk. Formerly a Senior Case Officer with the National Campaign for Increased Immigration. Trustee of Expand Police Complaints Commission. Holidays in Bonkidorm, Spain.

Mr. Taxitt Spendyerwaytosecurity, Labour MP, Special Adviser and Ministerial PPS, and long-term acolyte of Mr. G. Brown, the alleged PM.

Mr. Jeff Thomas, a senior nurse at Broxbinge NHS Hospitals Trust, Hertfordshire.

Mr. Edward Timpson, MP, Tory politician. Minister of State for Children and Families at Department for Education from May 2015. A rising star.

Mr. Nick Timplekins, *Financial Times* Chess correspondent with an interest in the NHS.

Mr. Percy Tistleton-ffolkes, an unfortunate patient, and his wife, Edwina.

Ms. Jessie Tompkins, civil servant at the Department of Health, and Minutes Secretary to the Ministerial National Anti-Obesity Advisory Group.

DRAMATIS PERSONAE

Mr. Spanner Unworksit OBE, Chair, Woyal NHS Alliancers.

Mr. Pierrot Carlossa Urugluee, an especially arrogant A&E consultant at Bugington, Sussex.

Dr. Pedro Ventura. GP. Trained in Portugal and in Belfast. Head of the rural general practice in St. Squids, Cornwall. He is godfather to Dr. Alexis Brooksnubbra's children. He is 49. His Mother is in a care home in Suffolk, near his friend's practice.

Sir Harry Verney, CBE, a retired GP. A Cornishman (born in Tremoutha Haven on the north coast) and the founder in 1960 of the now large general practice at Tinsdale Weir, Suffolk. A scholarship boy, who became a distinguished GP. From a working-class coastal-fishing background. Knighted for services to botany, ecology and the environment. Prize-winning author of five books on these subjects. Still a regular on the Andrew Marr and other 'news and opinion' programmes. He is 72.

Mr. Valentine Vox CBE, Head of the NHS Re-Settlement branch, Recompense House, Elephant & Castle, London, SE.

Ms. Janice Waldegrave, an A&E reception nurse at Broxbinge NHS Hospitals Trust, Hertfordshire.

Ms. Ali Walolah MP, head of the Tory-Women-To-Be-MPs group.

Mr. George Washington, a Senior Investigator with the Suspicious Expenses National Audit Office. He is engaged full-time on enquiries within the NHS. He is an economist trained at the London School of Economics and at George Mason University in Virginia. He has also previously worked for four years for one of the big five accounting firms in the City of London. He is married with three young children, and is aged 35.

Mrs. du Maurier Weeknees, a very glamorous and stylish patient in Suffolk.

Mr Barney Wells, BEM, Chief Executive of The Arthur Scargill Memorial Hospital, Chessingfield-on-Soke, which has recently down-sized to Units 7-34 Karl Marx Industrial Estate, Lubyanka Avenue, Chessingfield-on-Soke. He began his career as an accounts clerk in the S. E. Regional HQ of the NHS. He has also played hockey for Bexhill-on-Sea Deficits, the leading local club. He is aged 56. He is the father of nine sons. All are employed as trade union officials. He collects books on pigeon-racing.

Mrs. Rita Wells MBE [*nee* Rita Hogleblin], wife of Mr. Barney Wells, she was Chairperson of The Arthur Scargill Memorial Hospital, Chessingfield-on-Soke NHS Trust. Then became Labour's Parliamentary candidate for the 'safe' Westminster seat of Bugginsturn North, in the by-election there. [For results, see below]. She left Downhills-on-Soke comprehensive school aged 15, with one GCSE. She is a local Unite Trade Union official. Previously contested four parliamentary seats for Labour, but without success. She collects old copies of '*Peg's Paper.*'

Brenda When, a North country woman and Secretary/PA to Mr Wells. She is a graduate of the University of Kent at Canterbury, and a working Mum. Her friends often liken her to Donna, Josh's brilliant assistant, in the *West Wing*. She is now studying part-time for an

MBA. She often makes key points, and is widely thought to have executive potential.

Mrs. D. Willitzers, MP, a government minister. [Later Baroness Havant of Banks].

Lord Robert Winston, Blairite Labour luvvie doctor. One of the 'Twerpy Twins.'

Mr. Youknowwho, Senior Surgeon, The Bit Parts of England NHS Trust, West Midlands.

Mr. Youguesswho, Chief Executive, of the same.

Apology for absence: Lord Alascooke of Smugdominion.

EPISODE 1

Days in the life of the NHS: An Everyday Story of Healthcare Folk.

The story begins.

By Facey Romford, Jr.

Dramatis Personae:

Sir Cyril Squoffington-Squogg, OBE, JP, Chief Executive of The Tower of London NHS Hospital Trust, London, E. He is aged 67. His wife, Lady Bernice Squoffington-Squogg, is also Chair of The Wiltshire Artists Benevolent Fund. They live during the week in Sloane Street, Chelsea and at weekends at Wobblybottom Towers, Minceyglade, Wiltshire. He is a retired senior civil servant, department of pensions. She is a former ice-skater. She is aged 39. Their son, Paul Bristol Squoffington-Squogg, is a nature writer on the *Financial Times*, contributing the popular weekly column 'Splashing About Happily.'

Major-General J.J. Slopkins, MM, MC, CBE, etc., is his Chairman. He is a retired cavalryman. He is aged 82. He lives at Coggeshall in Essex.

Mr Barney Wells, BEM, is Chief Executive of The Arthur Scargill Memorial Hospital, Chessingfield-on-Soke. He began his career as an accounts clerk in the S. E. Regional HQ of the NHS. He has also played hockey for Bexhill-on-Sea Deficits, the leading local club. He is aged 56. He is the father of nine sons. All are employed as trade union officials.

The Chair of The Arthur Scargill Memorial Hospital, Chessingfield-on-Soke is Mrs. Barney Wells, MBE, a local Unite Trade Union official. She left Downhills-on-Soke comprehensive school aged 15, with one GCSE. She has contested four parliamentary seats, without success. Very Old Labour. [Later, elected as a Labour MP.]

'Brenda' When. A North Country lass, is a secretary to Mr Wells. She is a graduate of the University of Kent at Canterbury, and a working Mum. See below.

Our sources:

We can reveal the following telephone conversation as Mr .Wells, an admirer of the Rt.Hon. Anthony Wedgewood-Benn MP [The Viscount Stansgate], is in the practice of recording his conversations. He acquired this habit when hearing that Mr Wedgewood-Benn did likewise. However, there is within his office someone who does not approve of him. We will call her 'Brenda.' She will appear from time to time in this everyday tale of NHS folk. We will also, in later reports, draw on correspondence and e-mails, where available.

***

THE FACEY ROMFORD PAPERS

Telephone conversation recorded by Mr. Wells on 2 July 2013.

[*Telephone rings*].

Brenda: Sir, it's Sir Squoffington-Squogg. Shall I put him through?

Barney: Yes. Right away please.

Sir S-S: That you Barney? Just rang to congratulate you. Though it WAS a bit risky, that caper!

Barney: Hello. What's this then Squoffy?

Sir S-S: Those new A&E signs, that's what. I know about it all. I have my sources. I have my reports. I know, and you know I know, and you knew I'd know I know. So come clean. Right now! Stop your finageling!

Barney: *What me?* Those big blue and white signs on every road 5 miles out, do you mean? Those signs with RAC-type lettering? The ones saying "Your nearest A&E is in Derby Road, Stoke-on-Trent" ? *Those* signs?

Sir S-S: Yes, Barney, indeed those! Bloody Derby Road is 30 miles from your A&E, and going in entirely the wrong direction!

Barney: Well dunno anything myself about them. Mea no culpa. Mea innocenti. Mea incognito. Me know nuffink. Me in-the-clear!

Sir S-S: Oh, come off it Barney. You've had all those signs put up directing people miles away, to some other poor bloke's A&E. So your A&E isn't full. I know it was collapsing. I know you are being investigated. I know there are no consultants there from 5.30 p.m. on a Thursday until 10 a.m. on a Monday.

Your MRI isn't working then is it? No scans? No proper examination of x-rays? Only junior docs? And a steep rise in your death rates. As to morbidity, you have no idea, do you? You don't record it, do you? No-one does, do they? Now you are having it easy! But be careful. You'll get done for it.

Barney: Well, I confess that on my way into work when I saw those signs they were all in French and English, like those signs 'Drive on the Left' at Dover. *a gauche* and all that. And I – I mean, someone unknown – has had 'Made in Belgium' stamped on the back. They looked like official signs to me.

Sir S-S. Well, Barney, once again I have to tell you the real solution. We know that A&E represents about 55% of all NHS hospital work. We know that even under the Blessed Margaret's *regime* we all just got paid directly from the Treasury for A&E work and none of that mobile GP Fundholding business. We know we can predict A&E work – how many injuries, what kind, how many drunks and druggies etc, how many pub fights, which days and peak times. We've got good data over many years. So we *can* do something real about it. We *could* easily require every voter, by law, to insure for A&E use. This would pump billions into the system, enable us to expand facilities, pay the consultants more...

Barney: *More!* GOOD LORD!

Sir S-S: Yes, more. Economic incentives. Works. ....and would solve the problem. Otherwise, deficits as deep as the Grand Canyon. Mortality rates higher and higher. More political bullying from up there. More and more Trust failures, collapsed Hospital Trusts, Special Measures, you name it.

Barney: Hmm. You know at Brighton once, in the early 90's I think, the big hospital there put GP's into A&E. They saved a lot of money. Fewer referrals into beds. Fewer drugs prescribed. Happier patients. Less Saturday night violence. That might work?

Sir S-S: Would certainty help. But that experiment got squeezed out as the Region didn't continue the budget, I think. Short-sighted.....

Barney: Well, got to go. But just one more thing. Seen this report of Trusts letting lawyers advertise for actions on injuries caused by clinical errors, on hospital notice-boards?

Sir S-S: Yes. Totally amazing. Like a supermarket having a notice on the way in which says, "Insure here in case our sausages give you salmonella!" Or a petrol station advertising "If our petrol blows up and kills your Mum, insure with us first."

Barney: Well you should take it up with that health minister, who was he, Lord L.B.W. 'Owzat, who opened your sponsored Costa coffee-shop last week?

Sir S-S: Don't bring that one up, please. I'm in trouble because the coffee price has risen and I've also had to squeeze out the volunteers who did it all for free. Big fuss in the local *Chronicle*.

Barney: Oh! Well, got to go! But just one more thing. My chum Sid Daley, you know, works in the NHS archives? Just sent me the following old Sir Humphrey stuff. Nothing changes, does it???

Bye for now!

***

A Message from Sir Humphrey Applebird, from the NHS Archives.

My Dear Bernard,

Yes, of course I did see that Editorial on the R. Lilley site about somehow allowing voters to have their hands on our tax budgets. I am surprised that you should have been reading it however, and not doing your work. I see everything. Do not think I can't be everywhere. I am. Yesterday, today, and tomorrow. I am all-seeing. I am all-listening. I am all-knowing.

And, yes, I have also seen the convoluted advice note from the Minister's teenage Special Adviser about trying to reduce 'noise' about the NHS and its alleged "systemic difficulties." AND I have noted the Minister's annotations, insofar as they were legible.

As to the note from the Minister's Special Adviser, by all means refer it to the DoH longer-term study group. But I would think an appropriate target date for its consideration would be in 2019. A new coalition may have coalesced by then. I do not expect another majority government.

As to the specifics for action today…

1. By all means let us retain the Friends and Family interview project – just launched. So to see what people say, lying in their hospital beds (but with the doctor or nurse listening carefully close by, of course). BUT DO NOT GIVE PATIENTS CONTROL OVER THE MONEY.

2. Let's have some more community consultations about reform plans, closures etc, led by local Chief Executives (with an eye on their pensions)…

…BUT DO NOT GIVE PATIENTS CONTROL OVER THE MONEY.

3. Let's give local councils a bit more of *a say*. Perhaps. Sometimes. To be considered. BUT DO NOT GIVE PATIENTS CONTROL OVER THE MONEY.

4. Let's form some more committees of patients and GPs in local commissioning, perhaps testing this on car-parking provision. No budget, alas, but let's think about it. Talk to Mr. Wiezel. BUT DO NOT GIVE PATIENTS CONTROL OVER THE MONEY.

5. Let's talk more to some "expert-patient groups." We could begin in the Scilly Isles. Usuaul suspects. We appoint. BUT DO NOT GIVE PATIENTS CONTROL OVER THE MONEY.

6. Let's issue more leaflets, guides to services [open and closed], information on bus routes, long-distance weather reports, paint-cost futures, etc. BUT DO NOT GIVE PATIENTS ANY CONTROL OVER THE MONEY.

7. Let's encourage more NHS read-to-old-ladies volunteers, tea-ladies, car-park assistants, notice-board aides, A&E light-bulb changers, board-room dusting staff, and emergency porters – many more much needed, I know – BUT…BUT… BUT DO NOT [*NOT*! **NOT***!* NOT! *NOTALOTNOTTYNOT*!] GIVE PATIENTS ANY [*ANY!!!]* <u>ANY</u> CONTROL OVER THE MONEY.

Tax-based individual healthcare funds indeed!

People exercising individual financially empowered choice, indeed!

Taking their mobile tax-based fund to a co-operative, 'democratic', mutual purchasing organisation to bully providers to do what individuals think they think they want, when and how they want it, indeed!

Such a notion would play merry hell with what is after all a very proper state monopoly. Not even Andrew Lansley thought such ideas appropriate.

As to any choices, *we* made those in 1947 with Mr Bevan, and so we should let well alone.

Well. ALONE. If we encourage such ideas there will be a general election about it, and who knows then what might follow? Bernard, do not venture your toes onto thin ice. Not ever. I hope I make myself clear, Bernard? *Very clear?*

Yours, with my usual helpful and careful guidance, I trust.

[signed]

Sir Humphrey Applebird, KCMG.

***

And...two days later...

Bernard,

Come and see me at 1.12 p.m. precisely today. You will not require lunch.

I have your note in reply to mine of the last inst.

Bernard, why are you sending me such thoughts when you should by now be well ahead with the detailed proposals for the new State Directed Food Warehouses, which will replace Tesco's, Sainsbury's, Morrison's, Waitrose, M&S Food Stores, The IceLot, etc when Mr Milkkiband is elected shortly. We must make progress promptly with the plans for these vital improvements in the locations of food stores, their stock, quality and price. I have already approved the opening hours of Monday to Wednesday, 11.30 a.m. to 2 30 p.m., and we have drafted the Order in Council. I ask myself why we spent all that money sending you to North Korea in Mr E. Balls' party if you are not now making the necessary progress in your work. Bernard, you must do better!

As to your suggestion that it is "their money to start with" concerning the electorate and the funding of the NHS, I do not see how you can have reached such a weird conclusion. Surely you have read your Beatrice Webb diaries? Please be reminded that WE are the "experts." WE know what is best for people. WE [and only we] can be trusted to make the right choices. They cannot. They shall not. They will not. Indeed, some are even supporters of the club which I believe is known as Moaners United! Surely this in itself is sufficient guidance for you?

You will now shred your copy of your note and of this note, remove it from your computer, and do not cc anyone else with it.

Bernard, I still have high hopes for you and your career. You do not, after all, really wish to apply for a transfer to Coleraine and to the Liaison Committee with the Provisional IRA at Gerry Adams House, do you?

Be prompt at 1.12 p.m.

Yours, very sincerely,

[signed]

Sir H. Applebird, KCMG.

PS. DO NOT....

***

Facey adds: "Let the Guilty be known!"

EPISODE 2

Cleanliness next to Godliness... The West Boggleypool-on-Sea scandal!

Dramatis Personae:

Sir Cyril Squoffington-Squogg, OBE, JP, is Chief Executive of The Tower of London NHS Hospital Trust, Traitor's Gate House, Embankment, London.

Mr. Barney Wells, BEM, is Chief Executive of The Arthur Scargill Memorial NHS Trust Hospital.

Mrs Barney Wells, MBE, Chair of The Arthur Scargill Memorial NHS Trust Hospital, is a local Unite Trade Union official.

Brenda When, a North country woman, is Secretary/PA to Mr Wells.

Today's Guest appearances: Mr. Percy Tistleton-ffolkes, a patient, and his wife, Edwina. And Mr S. Higbon-Ballcock, who is [temporarily] Chief Executive of the West Boggleypool-on-Sea NHS Hospitals Trust, Snape Street, Suffolk.

***

[telephone call transcript].

Sir S-S: Morning, Barney. I see that today is declared "Save A&E Monday!" *Lovely day, anyway!*

I'm sitting here reviewing the 'papers. Got to go on to my local commercial radio later today, to take calls. Seen the announcement by the PM of £500 millions extra for A&E. Bailing out the duff ones yet again. Why don't we just let them close? Daft to go on giving bonuses to those at the bottom of the class. But all these crises may actually be just what we need to force some real, deep thinking and some proper reforms!

Barney: Yep. *Maybe.* Gordon spent all them billions. Stuffed those doc contracts with gold. More money for less work, big drop in productivity. *Very* progressive! No needed changes. So, is this at long last the last-chance saloon?

My Secretary Brenda calls the £500m bail-out Cameron's A&E-lection fund!

And I see that already the Emergency Docs are whingeing about it. Usual: "Won't be enough-too-little-too late, no one asked us, etc." They don't seem to mention Brown's new doctor contracts much, though. Or weekend work. Personally, I'd spend it all on social care and home help. Oblige GPs to open, too. Got to stop the flow into A&E. Or even employ some of those extra French Border Guards! The BMA to blame for there being too few A&E consultants, of course. They control the training and so the supply.

Sir S-S: YES! 'Course, the PM – the Duke of Optimism in a Trollope novel – goes on declaring how wonderful everything is. But that isn't politics – it's spiritualism, religion, faith without facts. The bourne from which no PM returns!

But, heavens above, Barney, have you seen the story about West Boggleypool-on-Sea? That bloke Higbon-Ballcock is for the high jump there, and no mistake As they say, "What a mistaker ta maker!"

Barney: Nope. Haven't seen it. But don't read the *Health Service Jungle* any more. Too glum. No job ads suitable for me. Don't know anyone who does read it. Well, apart from the Unite lot. For the job ads.

Sir S-S: Well, Barney, it seems that what happened was that a very well-founded local Solicitor, one Percy Tistleton-ffolkes, was taken ill at a taxi-rank in Bogglepool.

There he was, off to the 7.03 a.m. train to Liverpool Street – bowler hat, pin-stripes, furled brolly, black leather briefcase, *FT*. But suddenly taken a bit queer.

Faints. Ambulance arrives. Into A&E. Admitted for observation. An old mixed ward, but with a plastic curtain divider. Wakes up mid-afternoon. Disgustingly appallingly, really awful, almost burstingly dreadful smell under the bed. Stank, rank. Gets out of bed, slowly, and takes a look. There he finds a huge, grey, putrescent, rotting, maggot-writhing, long-tailed, much swollen RAT. Clearly very dead. Very smelly. Very nasty. Very long-time long gone. Presses emergency buzzer. Red and puffy in the face. Holding nose, trying not to breath.

Almost bursting with rage. Fifteen minutes passes. Then a very surly nurse comes in, "Yes? *What?*" The said Tisleton-ffolkes draws her attention to the rat. She vanishes. Not a word said. Five minutes pass. Then said patient is hurriedly wheeled away by a grim-faced uncommunicative porter, no name badge, into another ward two floors up.

Anyway, Tistleton-ffolkes turns out to be OK. So is sent home that evening. Next day he takes the entire day off, and writes the most furious letter. But then nothing happens. No acknowledgement. No reply. No action taken. Three whole weeks pass. Getting angrier now by the day. About to write to the Sec. of State, local MP, local 'paper and radio station, cc to everyone he knows. Actually has traditional '*Swan*' ink-pen in hand when the postman comes.

"Knock, knock." Wife, Edwina answers, and then calls out to hubby, "Percy, Look at this! Special delivery! Signed for! Lovely, cream, embossed envelope! Has West Bogglepool Hospital crest – a Cuckoo in a Holly Bush, resplendent, vert – on the front. Has 'From the Office of the Chief Executive' embossed in black and gold on the back. Must be an answer to your letter!"

Percy, apparently, just grunts. "About bloody time!" But opens it up with his butter-knife.

"Well then, read it to me Percy", urges his wife.

So he does:

CLEANLINESS NEXT TO GODLINESS…

"Dear Sir,

I have received your extremely distressing letter with the utmost shock, astonishment, appalling-ness and surprise. I am entirely bewildered as to how to reply. I have been an NHS manager for 27 years. I have never, on any occasion, ever, seen or heard of such a thing. Never before in all my experience. Not ever. *Appalled!*

Certainly, here at West Bogglepool NHS Hospitals Trust we are deeply committed to the cleanest, most hot-water washed, permanently Dettoled, re-scrubbed, rub-a-dubbed, brushed, dusted, filtered and especially watered, 100% antisepticised wards.

We have received a John Major National Chartermark six times for this achievement. Our wards are widely recognised for their absolute cleanliness. Eat your dinner…etc. And so you may well imagine my utmost horror when I received your letter. Our wards are noted as being even cleaner than the lavatories in Motorway cafes.

So I do take this immediate occasion to tender my most humble and deepest regrets and apologies on behalf of my colleagues and staff for this extraordinary lapse. We do all hope, however, that your health is much better now, and that this truly ghastly experience is in the past.

Thank you for writing to me.
With all my sincerest apologies, I remain your humble doormat.

[*Signed*] S. Higbon-Ballcock, Chief Executive."

Mrs. Tistleton-ffolkes then apparently said to her much mollified husband, who was by now smilingly proud of an Executive Reply to his letter at last: "Well, Percy, what a nice letter. You must be happier now?"

Percy: "Yes my love, that sorts it properly."

"BUT", says his wife," what's this clipped to the reply? Oh, it's your *original* letter", she says.

"Some filing clerk's mistake, I suppose", says Percy.

"Yes", says his wife. "But look, there's something else written at the top of your original letter!"

Percy: "What is it then?"

His wife responds, "In pencil, there's written 'Send him the rat letter'."

Barney: Cor!

Sir S-S: But don't get me started on the messages of the day! That is, the messages of the environment that Higbon's reply sums up! Management by walk-about, but entirely unseeing. No-one taking personal responsibility for anything. No proper directions to anywhere you need. "Information" months out of date. The permanent NHS Sellotape

Culture. The attitudes towards patients which our incoherent signs on doors give out. Our crummy buildings. Our "cleaning." Our peeling paint. All cultural and aesthetic messages. And letters to patients telling them in response to their complaints, why things must be the way they are. What did that sociologist Brenda Case Scheer call it? "The culture of aesthetic poverty." Tells the patient who matters, and who doesn't, eh?

Barney: Yep. Have struggled with all this myself, without success. Head bashed on walls, and all that. Given up. Breed my pigeons instead now.

[*Brenda interjects:* And no answer to the old question "What does it take to get sacked round here?" And, Mr. Chairman, I saw again today that that Dr. Ah-me has again put a hand-written sellotaped and peeling old notice on a door as you come into reception: "Dr. Ah-me's Clinic is now in Workhouse Building 3, Room, JPj907." When I asked him about it he called me a Racist!"].

Barney: By the by, Squoffy, my old mate Sid Daley in NHS Archives just sent me another little exchange between that Bernard and that Sir Humphrey. Lovely one, this. He *does* dig them up!

***

Dear Sir Humphrey,

Thank you for seeing me at 1.12 p.m. precisely on Wednesday last, and for your much valued guidance concerning those perplexing funding issues.

I have studied the files, as you directed me so to do.

I am forwarding for your attention a copy of a Memorandum to the then Secretary of State which you wrote in July 1988, and which you may like to keep.

Yours, as ever.

Bernard.

***

[*Here is the Memo*]:

Dear Secretary of State,

<u>The Study Group on Health Insurance Payments by NHS Patients.</u>

As you directed, I have now completed the study work on the possibility of revising (or supplementing by top-ups) the funding basis of the NHS. For example, to assess any requirement for every individual to hold a personal health-care fund, drawn from taxation or created by tax-transfers to the poor. Or to consider moving the system towards a European-style insurance model.

You made the point that the Swiss Healthcare system has been proved by the OECD to be the best in Europe in terms of access and outcomes. And that this is an insurance based system. Accordingly, we did set in place a series of comparative studies. May I say that the young economist, seconded from the Treasury, Mr E. Balls, has been particularly helpful in this work. I have recommended him to Mr G. Brown as a recruit to his office. He may have a bright future in Vehicle Licensing at Swansea.

We do not accept the OECD findings, however. As the attached detailed 3-page report shows, a change in funding arrangements is not in our view tenable, even if it were desirable, which as you know I have previously questioned.

Your initial view was that the economy was changing rapidly, and that there was and would be much more discretionary personal spending. In addition, people would wish to express personal choices by using this money. Our analysis does not, however, endorse this perspective.

For example, the Healthcare Funding Group which you established has carefully studied the market for these new mobile telephones, as Mr. Edwards in Derbyshire asked us to do on your behalf.

We find that this market will be negligible. There is not the money in the economy which will enable private individuals to purchase or run these instruments. Nor is there ever likely to be under present Monetarist policies. We expect their sales to be very small, and restricted to people like AA and RAC mobile repair-men. They will be like the hula-hoop, a five minute wonder. We dismiss the idea, too, that children will want these, almost as toys. We find this idea to be derisive in the extreme. The hint, from your Japanese banking friend, that they may even become cameras or some kind of personal wide-ranging electronic message and networking devices (or even miniature televisions) is surely cloud cuckoo-land.

In addition, I have before me the report of the Illegal Drugs Surveillance Group of the Home Office. Again, although there are some individuals using these mind-changing drugs we do not forecast any substantial growth in this market. It will remain small. It is a marginal issue. Nor do we believe that the suggested change in public house opening hours, proposed by Mr Blair, will increase teenage drinking. We reject the idea therefore that such funds could be invested in a personal healthcare plan. Again, the economy will not support this. We do not therefore find support for the idea, that such a personal plan would make costs very visible to the individual, and help to change personal behaviours. We have thus rejected the submission from Mr Arthur Seldon CBE at the Institute of Economic Affairs.

Therefore, our chief recommendation is that since there is no prospect of private individuals making their own funds available for mobile telephones, illegal drugs or more alcoholic consumption, there is no question of these expenditures being an alternative to funds being available for individual health insurance.

We find the suggestion that a healthcare fund could be paid for through taxation, with top-ups from personal funds, to be unfounded. There is not, nor will there be, the funding in the economy to support any such healthcare insurance projects. People, individually, will not be able to afford insurance, or even small top-ups, just as the markets for these mobile telephones will not enlarge.

The separate report [attached] by Mr Millkiband on the future of the new World Wide Web takes the same view. This will remain an investment of major government Defence Contracts only, and not go further than that. In addition, the experience with the early BBC computers indicates that these will remain an expensive personal toy for the very rich.

Therefore, we do not find any support for Mr Tebbit's suggestion that "there is plenty of discretionary money in private hands, and that the economy will grow such as to increase these funds" [Speech to Social Market Foundation, London, 3 June 1987]. Indeed, Mr Millkiband's work on this suggests that such funds will fall back.

We are not persuaded that the potential for mobile telephone usage, or further increases in illegal drug usage, or personal computing exists. What may work in Oregon and in Washington State – both, very queer places – will not translate into other economies.

There is just not (nor likely to be) the money in the economy. Nor does the Bank of England forecast that the economy will grow more than one-half a per cent per annum for the next 12 years. The Treasury is not persuaded that Mr Milton Friedman or his Centre for Policy Studies and IEA acolytes have made their case at all. For completeness, we have attached the dissenting note from Mrs D. Willitzers in the Treasury, together with a note from Mr J. Ridewood at No.10. However, we do not endorse these obscurantist views.

I have therefore accordingly directed that the files and working papers be lodged at the 'Out-of-Date Archives' in Wookey Hole, Somerset. I trust that this action will meet with your approval.

Yours faithfully,

Mr H. Applebird, OBE, Assistant Under-Secretary of State for Hadministrative Affairs, Leytonstone Marshes House, Walthamstow, E.

EPISODE 3

Win a postcode!

Dramatis Personae:

Sir Cyril Squoffington-Squogg, OBE, JP, Chief Executive of The Tower of London NHS Hospital Trust, Traitor's Gate House, Embankment, London, EC. He is aged 67.

Mr. Barney Wells, BEM, is Chief Executive of The Arthur Scargill Memorial NHS Trust Hospital, which has recently removed to Units 7-34 Karl Marx Industrial Estate, Lubyanka Avenue, Chessingfield-on-Soke. He is aged 56 and the father of nine sons, all of whom are employed as trade union officials.

The Chair of The Arthur Scargill Memorial NHS Trust Hospital is Mrs. Barney Wells, MBE, a local Unite Trade Union official. She has contested four parliamentary seats, without success.

Brenda When, a North country woman, is secretary to Mr. Wells. She is a graduate of the University of Kent at Canterbury, and a working Mum. Her friends often liken her to Donna, Josh's brilliant assistant, in the *West Wing*.

***

[telephone call transcript].

Barney: Hey, Squoffy, I've had this brilliant idea. *Really brilliant*! Though I says it myself. *My* idea! Can't think why it's never been thought of before in the entire NHS! Half a century old, and just wasted!

Sir S-S: Yes?

Barney: It will be a national sensation!

Sir S-S: Yes?

Barney: It will be all over the media!

Sir S-S: Yes??

Barney: *Everyone* in the NHS will be talking about it!

Sir S-S: *Yes???*

Barney: That Prof. Hampster bloke at the Klingfilm Fund will have another of their regular socialist study-days on it.

Sir S-S: As bad as that is it?

Barney: No! But I don't know if it can be done.

Sir S-S: Yes??? Well, *what is it*? Come on, spill the beans!

Barney: My lottery! My way to sell thousands of tickets! My wheeze to add some real money to my budget. MY solution to waiting-lists! My way to get people to get their op. quicker.

Sir S-S: Barney, WHAT is it? I'm a patient man, as you know. I'm sitting quietly. I'm all attentive. *But what is it*?

Barney: *Win a postcode!* In my lottery!

Sis S-S: Eh?

Barney: Here's the idea. Any of my local patients will be able to actually win a postcode! Just for a pound! Or six tickets for a fiver! I pick, say, a few clinical conditions with long waiting-lists. You know, hips, cataracts, dialysis, transplants. Or much under-funded, like mental health care. Then I get a few NHS Trusts in other parts of the country more favourably funded than my Trust, and with some spare capacity, to join me.

We all sell tickets in my lottery – "Win a Postcode!" If you get a lucky ticket you get to go to the Postcode somewhere else in the country – probably in your posh patch in London. You then go where there is a good provider, with proven quality and a shorter wait-list. You actually WIN A POSTCODE! The patients gets the necessary. My local commissioners pay the costs. Down come our lists. We get the lottery income! Everyone's a winner, that's no lie! Bingo!

Brenda in my office says that if you the individual patient could take the money where they wanted, it wouldn't matter what your home postcode was. And she asks me how poor providers are to be incentives to improve if they don't face losing customers and income to better providers. Well, bit radical that. But what's the answer, then?

Sir S-S: Barney, you truly are an innocent, aren't you? Where *have* you been? But, believe me, they'll shoot you and her for ideas like that. And for notions like WIN A POSTCODE! Pronto. Or Richmond House will have you sent as an opposition observer at one of Mugabe's polling stations. Or they will hide you away in a deep dark cavern, full of Vampire bats. Or NHS England will un-person you. Or Monitor will vapourise you. Or Dean Royles at NHS Employers will send in his bailiffs. Your GCSE's will even be revoked. And you'll never get any facility trips, not even to the Yemen. They'll *never* allow your idea and currency! The best you'll have to hope for is to be put in charge of Obesity Alert.

Win a postcode indeed! My friend, it's a one-way route to career oblivion! So I do sincerely hope you haven't even whispered this to anyone yet. Not a whisper? You haven't, have you? Not even my own chairman, the old Major, would have thought of such an idea. And in NHS terms he *is* a radical!

Barney: Nope. Not said a single word. Has been all my own work. All on the quiet. No one consulted. Said not a word. Not a hint. Not to a dickie-bird. Not a tweet. Not to my barber. Not to Jorrocks, my lovely wolfy doggie. Not even to my Chair, her indoors. I'm still thinking out the details and the timing. Doing it all myself. But you think it might be a *bit* dodgy? Just a bit? Needs more thought, perhaps? Bit more detail?

Sir S-S: Barney, I *always* have to tell you the facts of political and management life. Yet again! Usually about economics and incentives. Or politics. Or the management of professionals. Look. IF you want to try to take forward a national agenda which will really liberate patients from all the old NHS bureaucratic noggin go and have a look at the eye-care market. That clearly shows people individually financially-empowered to make their own choices. That has worked wonders. I've told you this before. Or go and study the effects of giving people in social care their own budgets. Another huge success. Indeed, I can't understand why this present government isn't building on that. That's the way to extend real choice, and give patients the financial influence they lamentably lack. Without starting another war, either. Milburn would've had it spread everywhere by now.

But, "Win a Postcode?" NO! Not even me, who doesn't vote for your chap, would try that one on. No-one wants to admit there is anything called a postcode lottery in the NHS. Still not. The very words are "unhelpful." No-one…no-one wants to own up to the idea that there is varied access to treatment. And to quality. Or that there are surprisingly varied outcomes. Or admit that it takes a very dedicated doctor to go and work in some of the grimmest places. Or that it matters at all where you live – let alone how you speak. So, Hampstead and McNorkville-on-Clyde, all the same, d'you see? We've all still got to make out that the NHS service is identical everywhere. Me, too. That's what we're paid to do. Must even be in the regional contract somewhere. The financials all tell a different story, of course.

Look at drugs denied in some places, but get them a few miles away with a different PCT. Still, no-one wants to face up to the facts of economic life. So some patients are still not getting the same access to vital drugs and treatments as their neighbours. But, sshh. You'll have seen that report on all this. Still sshh! Seen that in Knowsley on Merseyside, they spend £118 per head on cancer treatments? But in Ealing in west London, they spend just £47? Apparently ghastly Middlesbrough spends £167 per head on circulatory diseases, including heart disease. Yet compare that with £76 by Southwark, near me in central London. How can that be just? Does this lead to higher death rates in some areas? A *national* service? Pull the other one.

Put human faces on the reports. You'll recall some famous cases, like that chap – Colin Ross, was it, a cancer sufferer – who was told he would not survive the autumn unless he received the cancer drug 'Revlimid.' Took his case to the High Court. A sufferer of multiple myeloma – cancer of the blood cells – but denied the drug, cost £4,000 a month. West Sussex PCT said "No go." Even though a top cancer doc described him as "eminently suitable" for treatment. The drug was thought to be able to prolong his life by 3 years. Geography, again.

A mile-and-a-half away from his home in Horsham he'd have come under a different PCT and been more likely to get the drug. Then there was that Jane Tomlinson. I've got a cutting here on my desk. Dead now, sadly. Similarly, denied a drug that doctors believed could prolong her life. Although neighbouring PCTs provided it, hers wouldn't. She did eventually receive it as part of a clinical trial. NHS finding a technical wheeze to stop the noise. The fuss helped her. But we both know that some PCTs spend more than 9 per cent of their budget on cancer care, including drugs, but some spend just 3.6 per cent. Same snags with circulatory disease. Same with mental health problems.

On top of it all, I've never have understood why patients haven't for years past been allowed to buy their own drugs, as a "top-up", by the way. Or why we've done nothing to ensure much more personal responsibility for your own health. That's got to be linked to tax-based money, an insurance excess, or something like it, of course.

Then there's staff. We've no real economic incentives to get people to staff some of the worst hospitals. And we are great at denial. Look at all the denials about those varied death rates, and all the excuses. Results startlingly varied there. Of course, just for beginners, a seven year old kid knows that if you can't vary wages by region you'll not attract or keep the best people – who otherwise mostly go south. BUT, if you try that lottery idea, oh dear, all the old fuss about the NHS being a post-code lottery will burst like world war one shrapnel into the clear blue sky above you. You'll never hear the last of it.

But, look, Barney, sorry, but I've got to go. I'll arrange our lunch at the Ath when you're down here to talk over my private document on managing waiting lists. But I've got to scoot now to my social meeting at that modest little BMA HQ building near Euston. Seeing my old BMA chum "Jurassic" Johnson.

Barney: As up to date as that was he?

Sir S-S: *Now now Barney!* That's enough of your naughtiness for one day! Go and do some proper work! And don't let the Nicholson Thought Police catch you talking in your sleep!

EPISODE 4

Five "Andrew Marrs" in A&E queue, and three "Jackie Ashleys."

Dramatis Personae:

Sir Cyril Squoffington-Squogg, OBE, JP, Chief Executive of The Tower of London NHS Hospital Trust, Traitor's Gate House, Embankment, London, EC. He is aged 67.

Mr. Barney Wells, BEM, is Chief Executive of The Arthur Scargill Memorial NHS Trust Hospital, which has recently removed to Units 7-34 Karl Marx Industrial Estate, Lubyanka Avenue, Chessingfield-on-Soke. He is aged 56 and the father of nine sons, all of whom are employed as trade union officials.

The Chair of The Arthur Scargill Memorial NHS Trust Hospital is Mrs. Barney Wells, MBE, a local Unite Trade Union official. She has contested four parliamentary seats, without success.

Brenda When, a North country woman, is secretary to Mr. Wells. She is a graduate of the University of Kent at Canterbury, and a working Mum. Her friends often liken her to Donna, Josh's brilliant assistant, in the *West Wing*.

***

[telephone call transcript].

Brenda: Welcome back, sir! First 'phone call from London. It's Sir Squiffy... – so sorry, I mean Sir, well, you know! Here he is.

Barney: Hello Cyril. Nice sunny day! Hope you had a good time in Barbados. We went in the caravan to Whitby. Great place. Every year since 1979. Already booked for next year. But I've come back to another real shocker! Need your advice, as ever. Urgently!

Sir S-S: Well, *that* didn't take you long! I was ringing up about Postcode Lotteries. But what is it now Barney?

Barney: Well, I've got five "Andrew Marrs" in my A&E, and three "Jackie Ashley's." Beats me!

Sir S-S: Barney. I am a patient man. I am sitting down. I am sitting quietly. I am not easily excited. I am calmness itself. A Nobel Prize for it is, indeed, overdue. But just tell me the whole story. *Slowly*, please...

Barney: Well, when I came in today – all relaxed and jolly – the duty manager buzzed me and said he had five "Andrew Marrs" in the A&E triage. AND two of them are Indians, one is a Somali, one is a Vietnamese, and one is a Glaswegian. Then there are three "Jackie Ashleys" there too. Two are over 75, both retired teachers. The other one is a 30 year-old taxi driver. *He* is Welsh. Argumentative, too. One of the ladies is Norwegian. The other one won't say.

Sir S-S: Doesn't sound as if any of them are related then?

Barney: What? No. Probably not. But that's not the point. Not at all.

Sir S-S: Well, what is? Out with it man, for gracious sakes.

Barney: Well, I've discovered what's happened. The Chessingfield-on-Soke Heart & Stroke Patient's Expert Group went, *en bloc*, to the Deed Poll Office in Nottingham. And they have all changed their names. All either to Andrew Marr or to Jackie Ashley.

Sir S-S: Hmm. Did they get a bulk discount?

Barney: Eh? What? Mmm. Didn't ask. But here's the point....

Sir S-S: Barney, just let me tell *you* the point. I can guess the story for myself. I am always having to point out to you the real reasons why, on any policy or management issue. And what to do about it, whilst keeping your head and your job!

First, let me say for the record that I am a great admirer of Andrew Marr. I very deeply regret what happened to him. Good on TV. Good historian. Always very pleasant to meet. His wife, Jackie Ashley, is also a good soul. I met her Dad once at the Cambridge Union debate when he was still the Labour MP for Stoke-on-Trent. In 1966. Really good chap. She's interviewed me on the BBC a few times, too. You probably read her very sensitive piece recently in *The Guardian* about how she's coped in the terrible crisis that befell Andrew? Felt for her. Deeply. We all hope they will both come back stronger for it all, of course. Gracious, he was damned unlucky. A stroke at 53. But, as Jackie wrote, he's had "brilliant support from doctors, nurses and physio-therapists." He's back on his feet, and returning to work. Thank goodness. Some success there.

Barney: Yes, but...

Sir S-S: *Don't interrupt.* Not now. *No buts yet.* The doctors' saved his life. Clearly so. And the physios have got him back to strength. BUT – and here's the explanation of those extra "Andrew Marrs" and "Jackie Ashleys" in your A&E. "Ordinary" people (if we can put it like that) all want to be sure that they get the same attention and treatment as Andrew Marr or Jackie Ashley, even if they are nobodies. So...

Barney: Well, makes you think....

Sir S-S: Yes, but *listen*. Even with the good work done in that hospital Jackie Ashley herself said the system is staggeringly inflexible. Un-coordinated. Hospital care, if you are lucky, can be very good. But what then? Where's the support after that? Be lucky. Whistle. Hope. Pray. Ask nicely. But...

Barney: Well...

FIVE "ANDREW MARRS" IN A&E QUEUE, AND THREE "JACKIE ASHLEYS"

Sir S-S: Listen, Barney. *Just listen, please.* All those "Andrew Marrs" and "Jackie Ashleys" of yours just want the support and treatment which they suspect the middle-class get, and that they often think they don't or won't get if they don't throw the same social clout. We both know that accent, dress, address, attitudes, contacts all matter. *They do.* Shouldn't. But they do. Always have. Probably always will. The middle-classes support the NHS, too, because they get the best of it. And a stroke victim must have daily intensive physiotherapy. Occupational therapy. Help with exercises. Neurological examination, and check-ups later. Without which…you know.

So your extra named-patients in your A&E are right. It's why they changed their names. Costs us in A&E. But shows, too, that people will go to A&E if they think that's where the services are. And with GP's closed all weekend, can well see why they turn up in A&E as they do.

They and their supporting relatives soon learned from Jackie Ashley's experience, too, of how demanding the role of the carer is. Every year 150,000 people suffer a stroke – it can come out of a clear blue sky, no warnings. Often does. And a third of them are of working age. Relatives don't know what to do at first. Smashes up the economy, too. So they all want to be Andrew Marrs.

Barney: What should I do then, Squoffy?

Sir S-S: Here's what, Barney. Treat every patient as if they *were* Andrew Marr or Jackie Ashley. Every one counts, whether muddy, grubby, ignorantly idle or not. Whether brilliant, famous, on the Tele, ex-editor of a national 'paper, married to a peer's daughter or not.

Barney: Yes. Just what I thought. Just what I always Say! 'Course, I know what you are going to say next! That if they all had that tax-based individual mobile cash fund we keep hearing about they could make sure they got it all, couldn't they? Their purchaser – what's it to be called, a Patient Guaranteed Care Association? – would insist on it, wouldn't they? No funding, no patients, without guaranteed quality care! Providers to jump pronto, or leave the stage. The lot. Makes you think. Does. Even me, an old Labourite. If you could just take your tax-based money where you wanted it, it wouldn't matter what your local NHS was like, or what your home post-code was, would it?

Sir S-S: Yes. Quite so. All those think-tanks on about it all the time. Read that ex-Brighton Chairman bloke Spiers's book, *Who Decides Who Decides?* He's got it right, seems to me. All the basic principles are there. All the details, too.

Barney: Well, I'm starting to think so, too, about the funding ideas, yes. And how it could be directly linked to better, self-responsible behaviours, too. Did you see the *Sunday Times* report of the NHS Information Centre's information on the obese, with the 20-stone 10 year-olds? Frightened me, I can tell you. We'll never cope….not unless people take care of themselves first. Not stuffing, boozing, drugging, living off burgers, no exercise – all that. And imposing such life-styles on their kids, too.

Sir S-S: Dear me Barney, incentives and self-responsibility! Funding and incentives! *Economics!* And behaviours! Bless me, my old friend, you're not turning into a believer in the market are you? Don't you let your wife hear it!!

You know that I always say that it's the free market which has improved food, water, housing, education, travel, leisure and everything else – save for state monopoly services, which have been immune from free choices. Like the NHS! Like local-government run schools! But, bless me, Barney, have I begun to persuade you too? Or is it down to experience? What happens at work on Monday morning, and all that?

Barney: Well, it just so happens that our little Grandson, Wayne, is starting secondary school soon, and I've been wondering about those Free Schools…

Sir S-S: Well then, read Gove's stuff, Barney. *He's* the boy! Got to go, Barney. *Duty* calls!

EPISODE 5

Those new peerages, and why we're here at all.

Dramatis Personae:

Sir Cyril Squoffington-Squogg, OBE, JP, Chief Executive of The Tower of London NHS Hospital Trust, Traitor's Gate House, Embankment, London, EC.

Mr Barney Wells, BEM, is Chief Executive of The Arthur Scargill Memorial NHS Trust Hospital, Chessingfield-on-Soke.

Major-General J.J. Slopkins, MM, MC, CBE, etc., is his Chairman.

The Chair of The Arthur Scargill Memorial NHS Trust Hospital is Mrs Barney Wells, MBE, a local Unite Trade Union official. She has contested four parliamentary seats, without success. However, she has now been adopted as prospective parliamentary candidate for Bugginsturn North, a Labour seat since 1906.

Brenda When, a North Country woman, is Secretary/PA to Mr Wells.

***

[Telephone call transcript].

Sir S-S: Busy today, Barney, but wanted a quick word. Just to touch base. I've been worrying my head for answers to the question 'Why we are all here in the NHS at all?' Thoughts prompted by these new peerages, and what my Chairman said to me this morning.

Fortunately, I've now got into your insidious habit of pressing the "Record" button, so here's what we said.

[transcript].

The Major-General: No peerage for you this time then Cyril? What, what?

Sir S-S: No. The price has gone up. And no HP any longer. Next election is too near. They need cash now. But it's the usual Gilbert & Sullivan cast-list all the same. Just look…

Lord Ringszatill [Lab./convenience foods].

Lord Balti [Lib./spicy dinners].

Lord Clique-Claque [Cons./Columnista & Osbornista].

Lord Rizla [Cons./Smokers Alliance].

Lord Brandshatch [Cons./Motor Racing Tobacco Congress].

Lord Bigmuddigger [Cons./PM Old Etonian industrial chum].

Lord Quorum [Lab./SDP/Cons./Ind.].

Baroness Buydalabourvote [Lab.] – deserving lady, but a cynical ploy still, I say.

Lord Doshiedashie [Lib. Dem/fund-raiser].

No Mr. Andrew Howdonebe included yet, but I suppose he'll be Lord ToldyouwhatReform next time?

At least, there is one genuine comfort there: no Lord Nicholson of Mid-Staffs. Nor ever likely now. No sleep lost over that one, eh?!

But there's still that rumour that they still plan to erect that new statue over the door at Richmond House. Copy of the Old Bailey golden lady of justice. But a carving of a blindfolded Mid-Staffs manager! Nickoldeon, perhaps, will model for it? Would charge a fee, in course!

Major-G: Quite so, quite so, what what? But a "No, no." But yet surely the Tories are missing a big trick on this peerage business? IF it is a business, that is. They could do much better, I've no doubt. Add up the numbers properly. Keep in mind Maundy Gregory. And the Welsh Wizard, eh? what, what?

Here's how. Tell you a story.

There was once a rather rough cockney house-clearer who had a stall on the Farringdon Road in London. Just after the last war. I used to walk past there from Carthusian Street. Not long after I got back from Burma. I was still collecting old maps then. This chap had been a window-cleaner. He knew nothing about old books, but he had got hold of a lot of them. Somehow. I suspected at the time looting, myself.

At all events, each Saturday he started trading at 8.00 a.m., with the loud cry "Every book on this stall is £2,000". The experts in the antiquarian trade who really knew their books were gathered round. They snatched up everything worth that or more. The market decided. He didn't have to know anything. And it was very profitable to him. Probably got most of the books for very little. Probably got a decent price for most of them. A few incunabula perhaps got away too cheaply. But he still did very well. Bought a football club later.

Anyway, at 8.30 his cry was "Every book on this stall is £1,000." And, again the books with that value quickly sold. And so on. "£500." Then "£250." Then "£100." Until by 5.00 p.m. he only had the rubbish left. He then sold that for a few shillings and pence. I got a few really choice old things for not very much. Still have them, what what?

As of today just imagine the PM trading there, in proper Regimental style! "Every peerage on this stall is £5 million." He'd get a few fast takers, eh what? No questions asked. None of that committee approval nonsense. Then, an hour later, "Every peerage on this stall is

£3 million." More quickly sold. And so on. General election paid for in one morning. I suppose at 5.00 p.m. he'd be down to CBE's! Shillings and pence. Eh? What, what?

Sir S-S: Mr Chairman, sir, very droll!

***

Barney: Not as droll as the report from *my* Chair! Her cousin Alice in Sunderland rang 111, just to see how it works. She got a recorded message: "Hello, you've reached Lesley at 111. I'm doing my nails at the moment, but will ring back in a few minutes. Please take an aspirin while waiting." Apoplectic she was. I got the "We should move to Bulgaria" speech all over again at supper from Her Ladyship.

Sir S-S: Yes, Barney, my sympathies. I heard that one woman in Port Vale rang 111 and was put through to an Indian lady in Pondicherry in southern India, who gave her the local weather report! S'why they all still go to A&E.

But THE real and serious point about all this peerage business, of course, is that we have always to ask of any public service, "Why are people doing this? What are they in it for?" Think about our NHS itself. Why are our people working in it? For the knighthoods? For peerages? For the money? For the status? Hardly, surely? None of that. So, why?

Tell you a personal story. You know that I took this job when I left the civil service. Told you this when we first met at that IEA lunch in Lord North Street. YOU were the token leftie there then! I'd been asked by Sir Jethro, my old chum from Trinity College, to consider running this Trust. I know I'd got my K. already. But that just came with the rations at pensions.

My reason was that I've always kept in my mind all the time what the NHS did for my Mother in the 1940s. We weren't always posh, you know. She was a widow, and had very little. She was frightened and very fragile. She had two little boys to care for, and no money. The NHS found her breast lump, and dealt with it quickly. She was saved, and lived on until she was nearly 70. Another 30 years of life. We could easily have lost her in the 1940s. The people there then showed her real compassionate and competent care.

I suppose care then was still a bit primitive. I don't suppose she was offered any choices. Radiotherapy doses very hit and miss. No sympathetic chats or advance explanations. But they saved her life all the same. She was a wonderful woman, from a very poor Hoxton background in the East End. Her Father was born in the Workhouse there. He was blown to pieces, a volunteer in the Middlesex Regiment, near Ypres in July 1915. She was one of four children. She was born with a damaged leg. One of her brothers went blind with measles. They were very disadvantaged. Our Nan only kept the family together by scrubbing school and pub floors. When the NHS came along in 1948 they breathed sighs of relief. Before that they'd been helped by charitable hospitals and doctors. But the whole social situation was very different then.

Anyway, that's why I took this job. And it's why I am trying now to help shift the care axis so radically so that we can go on doing the job well and for people like my Mother. Indeed, much better than we do now. So I attack the complacency and the self-interest when I find it. So I oppose and expose the vested-interests. So I try to give individuals much more power. So I argue that it's giving people control over the money – and only that – which will do it. That's why I've had those bumper stickers done – *"Think User!"* And why I've had them put up on all the pipes in the boiler-rooms, on the interminable draughty corridors, on operating theatre walls, in the car-parks, in staff lounges [including the docs!], and on the cars we run too! Maverick? Maybe. But that's why.

Barney: Well, must be right. Must be. Got a lot of hard-working, conscientious NHS people, even if some scroungers. More good apples than bad though. But it's getting worse. More stress. More demands. Higher Expectations. New drugs we can't buy. Too few beds. Too much political interference. Hopeless links with community care. Social care threadbare. Long hours. Exhausted staff. Bluff-barmy Union demands even I can't fathom. Nicholson's £50 millions or is it billions? – gap. Worse to come. And new cures to keep everyone living to 100. Second new hip at 80. Third at 90. Fourth at 100. And don't you dare discriminate on age or capacity to benefit!

Sir S-S: Yes, Barney, the same here, too. But the key point is not to demonise all these people in the NHS. Just like the patients, they are trapped in a failed system. It's this which needs to be changed. Give them all a better chance, and a better life. If I can be colloquial, it's time we totally dumped all this 1940s ideology. It's NHS-Spiritualism: Keep The Faith, Never Mind The Results. The original Default Position, but with all its faults.

Staffing, too. Certainly we need to change who we hire. Recruit many more people with the right kind of empathy, human sympathy and intuitions about people. And not just those who are technically competent. We want to clear out those docs brilliant at college but bastards at work. And the duff nurses who fiddle the weekend rotas to suit themselves. Rude porters. Off-handed desk staff. I've got them, too. Need to totally change not only the clinical quality, but the day-by-day patient experience. We need good management, there, of course. Read what that Professor Brian Edwards writes so well on that Roy Lilley site. It's Pure Gold!

And we desperately need to learn from the best airlines and other firms who rely on willing individual revenues and individual preferences. *They* demonstrate what really good customer service and care actually comprises. We're light years behind. And this NHS thing is huge, complex, and needs proper, careful, and creative local management. Only get it if there are economic incentives to reward the good and encourage the bad to do better.

Barney: Well, you've convinced me. And Brenda here keeps nudging me, too. She says that we certainly do need to liberate everyone within what even I can see is more and more a failed system. Worse for me than for you in posh London, of course. I'm an old Labourite, I admit. Only wanted Blair back when we saw how awful Brown was! And here in the north we've had to remove to a perishing Industrial Estate, down-sizing. We've just got into those Units because of our budget problem. You're lucky, you don't live in the Socialist State of Chessingfield! Try dealing with this lot here!

But one bit of good news – whisper, whisper; hush, hush. Her Ladyship, The Wife and Chair, has just got the Labour nomination for the Westminster seat of Bugginsturn North. Been Labour since 1906. So, she's "in." Liberal was second last time. One Ms. Leticia Lynkseye. But they'll lose their deposit now. No student votes. I 'spose Clegg will make

Lynkseye a Viscount, or whatever the feministic equivalent of that is. Course, I've got to find a new Chair. Search is on. Region might have to pick a Tory. Then there'll be ructions here! I'll keep you in touch on that.

Sir S-S: Right Barney. Rather you than me! But it's not enough always to be right, you know. On these issues, though, we *are* right. And we have to get the political leadership based on that. That's why I've been privately trying to persuade Ministers to face the real fundamentals – you know, individual healthcare funds; competitive purchasing; insurance and agreed excesses for bad life-styles; economic incentives for better personal life-styles; tax-incentives for top-ups.

Barney: They surely can't go on making Andrew Lansley's mistakes of fighting over peripheral issues, losing the battles, being damned for it, and throwing away years when the fundamentals could have been tackled – and for the same political price. They could get so much more, if they did the thinking first, set out first principles, planned a strategy, and constantly pointed out to the Great British Public why things are as they are, and how they could change for everyone's benefit. Then refer every NHS event to those first principles. And build wide public support for change. Then get into office, and be in actual power. I'm writing a long memo to the SofS about this. Have done so to three past Secs of State, too.

[Brenda interjects: Can't see why politicians are so apolitical. Don't they want to win the next election?].

Barney: Hmm. More your pitch than mine Squoffy. You dine in those Clubs. You know those nobs. You've roamed Whitehall for your whole career. You get to those country houses. But don't forget to mention us when the blue moon comes and the pigs fly!

EPISODE 6

The Richmond House Revels, Scene 1.

Dramatis personae.

Sir Cyril Squoffington-Squogg, OBE, JP, Chief Executive of The Tower of London NHS Hospital Trust, Tower Hamlets, London, EC.

Lady Bernice Squoffington-Squogg, his wife, is also Chair of The Wiltshire Artists Benevolent Fund.

Mr. D'Arcy Plantaganet Cromwell, MP, is the new Secretary of State for Health. He is 37.

Sir Crank Lamparde, Permanent Secretary at the Department of Health.

Ms. Gloria Swansong. MP. Formerly Secretary of State for Health, MP for Haringey-in-Drugbonk.

***

The Richmond House Revels...

Lady Bernice: Here, Cyril, your morning coffee, Cyril. And a crispy digestive. What are you working on?

Sir S-S: Christmas is Coming! It's Later Than You Think...so I'm writing my usual script for The Richmond House Revels.

I've written the first scene already. Based on an old joke.
Lady Bernice: Tell me.

Sir S-S: OK. Here goes:

A new Secretary of State for Health arrives into his office on the first day after the General Election. Name of D'Arcy Plantaganet Cromwell, MP. He has been rapidly promoted. Was Junior Shadow Wind-Farms Secretary in opposition. Before that, was a research assistant to Lord Oakeshott [*who he? Ed*]. Graduate of Trinity College, Dublin [Ancient Icelandic Geography & Media Studies: 2.2]. A convert from the Labour Party, then from UKIP. Formerly neighbour of Sir Nigel. Chief hobby grouse-shooting. Once noted by weekly *Health Service Jungle* as "a coming man." Came, and went.

He enters through the DoH entrance in the original house, standing still at right angles to the new entrance to Richmond House on Whitehall. His new Private Office staff clap him in. He sits down in that big room, with the Permanent Secretary, Sir Crank Lamparde. Under the big new portrait of Baroness Bottomley of Headhunt by the fashionable Italian portraitist Linoleum Ogg.

THE FACEY ROMFORD PAPERS

Permanent Secretary, Sir Crank: The initial business of the day concerns the papers left behind by your predecessor, sir. The Urgent First Business. Also, SofS, here are the Three Envelopes.

SofS: Three envelopes?

Sir Crank; Yes, sir. Left for you by your predecessor. Traditional.

SofS: No time for that now. Let's deal with the immediate issues.

Sir Crank: Right. Here is an analysis which we have prepared for you, SofS. And the limited policy choices, as we envisage them. Also, our recommendations, which we expect you will prefer to adopt. No need to read all of this material. Just initial the first sentence and we will do the rest.

SofS: But the first sentence just says "I agree."

Sir Crank: Just so, SofS.

SofS: Well, first let me read this document on the top, "The Twenty 'Most Urgent' List [in order of priority]":

[Stage direction: Scans rapidly...].

1. Interviews with National press health correspondents.

2. Media training weekend at Vocalists House, Esher.

3. Ministerial Hair-styling advice. *Most* urgent.

4. Selection of Ministerial drivers and motor vehicles, from approved list 3, DoH, 2012, [g].

5. Richard & Judy TV appearances.

6. Ministerial holiday-rota, personal preferences.

7. A&E and 'Winter Crisis.' [Traditional].

8. GP much improved new contract, 2014-19.

9. Drug denials and post-code lottery, expansion thereof.

10. Social Care budgets: proposals to restrict.

11. Bed blocking. An enquiry by Nurse N. Dixon to be established. MBE for same.

12. Dr. W. Pickering's appointment as Head of new Independent National Healthcare Inspectorate. Knighthood for same.

13. Incorporation of existing Hospitals & Care Inspectorates to above. Appointment as

THE RICHMOND HOUSE REVELS, SCENE 1

Ambassador to Washington of Professor Sir M. Richards. Peerage for same.

14. The Christine Oriohogu case [Moscow].

15. Close of General Medical Council, and compensation budget.

16. National conference speeches. Non-participation of SofS.

17. National NHS Sports Day. Participation of SofS.

18. Consultants A&E Hospital Car Parking. Improved facilities.

19. Foreign Aid budgets and Hospital Twinning Programme. Expansion.

20. Nurses and use of WWW in work-time. Additional merit payments

SofS: Right, Mr. Wiezel and I will take this away now, and study this material, together with my first red boxes.

Sir Crank: Thank you, sir. You have all my telephone contacts. Do call if you need me. This afternoon I will be at the Orang-Utan project at London Zoological Gardens, but can be disturbed of course. My text and call sign is 'Spandex.'

FURTHER:

[Director's notes: Noises to be provided.... The very next morning, total bedlam! In comes SofS in purple-fury. Mr. Wiezel running to keep up. His driver smirking [cf, 'Solihull Project."] SofS's feet hardly touch the ground. Slam, bang, doors! Private office staff cower at desks. Huge wallop of files and red box onto floor. Echoes all over building. Huge roar: "Sir Crank! Get in here!"].

SofS: Can hardly believe it! First, 95% of these files are written entirely in Latin! Second, full of acronyms! Third, the important stuff was at the very bottom of Red Box 7. AND what the devil is the GNTBITBP?

Sir Crank: "Great Not To be Informed Trusting British Public", sir.

SofS: Humph!!! And what the devil is "OL&MBMA"?

Sir Crank: "Our Lords and Masters, the British Medical Association, sir."

SofS: Humph!!!! So what for dear Euclid's sake is "DNGTPACOTM?"

Sir Crank: "Do not give the patients any control of the money", sir. Three absolutely fundamental policies, ever since 1948. Our Holy Trinity, sir. Always been All-Party agreement, too, sir. No dissent.

SofS: Well, Sir Crank, all that's as maybe. But do please explain to me in English words of half a syllable, how can – HOW CAN! – there be such chaos. How? *Such* chaos! And all those extra billions you've got. Heavens, we claimed it was as bad as this in opposition. *As* bad!

Our equivalent of JFK's 'missile gap.' But we were only half-right! Golly, it's just hopeless! All those billions. But services collapsing everywhere! And no competition in a market. No-one to go bust. No-one to be sacked. No failed providers. No incompetent purchasers. Six figure NHS Trust Chief Executive salaries, and whopping pensions, indexed too. Gongs galore. And cars. No-one ever actually sacked in disgrace, but just quietly moved to another job.

As to medical results, no systematically collected and published morbidity data, either, despite Dr Foster's good work. And all those NHS executive staff golden parachutes. Indexed pensions. Long contracts paid out in lump sums. Tax-free lump sums, too. And then Honours. CBEs and all that. Golly, they do as well as footballers! But for me, talk about a bed of nails! Why didn't he give Sir George Young this job, instead of me? And, Sir Crank, what do you propose to do about it all?

Sir Crank: Well, Sir, I am here to advise only. I would suggest the traditional and approved route. You have to open THE FIRST ENVELOPE.

[Stage direction: SofS therefore opens draw, pulls out the three envelopes, unties ribbon, breaks wax seal. Inside is the message. Reads this aloud...]

"You will encounter absolute and unexpected chaos on day one. Go immediately to the House of Commons. Denounce your predecessor fiercely."

This he does. In very angry, vicious, often un-parliamentary tones. Back-benchers love it. Speak of him as possible future Leader. The speech denouncing his predecessor provides some short-term relief, both from the media and from the gesticulating and snotty PM's new 'Get-It-Done-Now' office, fronted by Sir Alf Grarnett.

BUT a month later, the situation is even worse. Trade Union strikes. GPs demand for three-day week. Consultants demand for increased 'Merit' payments. Nurses demand for personal 'Samsung Tablets' provided for digital leisure work while on wards. Refusal by overseas hospitals to twin with NHS facilities. Turkey excepted. Foreign Aid budgets tripled, with funds withdrawn from hospital bed-unblocking project. Waiting lists growing rapidly. NICLE enquiry into necessity of pharmacies in High Streets or not reports early with recommendation of widespread closures.

The SofS is in despair.

SofS: It's not working, Sir Crank. *Even Polly Toynbee likes me!* What do I do, Sir Crank? *Come on! Advise!*

Sir Crank: Well, sir, the tradition is that this is when you open THE SECOND ENVELOPE.

[Stage direction: So SofS does so. Inside, the message: "SET-UP AN ENQUIRY." He does so, very promptly. The Wiilliam Walkaway Commission, advisory deputy director Baroness Sitting Bull of Emertonii].

THE RICHMOND HOUSE REVELS, SCENE 1

BUT this enquiry moves at a snail's pace, or what the NHS calls Vegetable Speed. Three months later, all GP commissioners report "No money left." Hospital referrals cease entirely. Six out of ten A&E emergency doctors on strike. Bishop Hogbin, GCE, denounces SofS from pulpit in St. Just, Cornwall. National conference of BMA sets date for all senior consultants to go entirely private, in cells, like barristers. GMC decides to meet in public regularly, and to publish minutes. Nurses, forbidden to use WWW at work, announce 'National Turn Up To Work Nude' day for following Thursday. SofS really now in total despair!

SoS: What *do* I do, Sir Crank.

Sir Crank: Nothing else for it sir. You must open THE THIRD ENVELOPE.

[Stage direction: He does so. Inside he can read the message: "Prepare Three Envelopes."]

Curtain comes down on scene one. Music played by Mo Foster and the Rockets band: "For he's a jolly good fellow," but to the tune of *Mikado* overture.

Lady Bernice: Golly! Just can't wait for Scene Two!!!

EPISODE 7

At Your Expense…The NHS & The Economics of Politics.

Dramatis personae:

Mr George Washington is a Senior Investigator with the Suspicious Expenses National Audit Office. He is engaged full-time on enquiries within the NHS. He is an economist trained at the London School of Economics and at George Mason University in Virginia. He has also previously worked for four years for one of the big five accounting firms in the City of London. He is married with three young children, and is aged 35.

Sir Crank Lamparde is Permanent Secretary at the Department of Health.

Lord Chrissie Patterer of East Asia is a distinguished professional distinguished non-executive director, who is widely employed in the City of London. He is a senior member of the new NHS Board of Control. He is also a prominent Freemason, a City of London Liveryman, a private yachtsman and a fervent cricket fan.

Ms. Petronelli di Champagni is an Italian hospital administrator who is an Exchange Visitor from Roma. She is presently a Secretary in Sir Crank Lamparde's Private Office at Richmond House.

Ms. Jennifer Knott-Necessary is a Secretary to Lord Patterer of East Asia. Her father is the well-known contractor Lord J.C.B. Knott-Necessary

Mr. U. Heap is a City of London solicitor, advising Sir Crank Lamparde and Lord Patterer of East Asia.

[Telephone rings].

Secretary at Richmond House: *Pronto!* Iz speak Petronelli di Champagni. Sir Lamparde Crank office. 'elp you? *Che cura fa*?

Mr. George Washington: Good morning. Not about my health. But thank you. I'm fine. My name is George Washington. From the Suspicious Expenses National Audit Office. Am I speaking to Sir Crank's Private Office, please?

Sec: Iz di Champagni. *Parla Italiano?* Spikka Italian? *Respiri profondamente…*

GW: No. No need. I'm fine, as I said. But sorry. English only. Well, a few words in Italian. And schoolboy French. But good morning anyway. *Bon jour.* May I speak to the person who handles Sir Crank's expenses please?

Sec: Yessa. S'is OK. But dependi. What thissa concerni?

THE FACEY ROMFORD PAPERS

GW: Expenses claims. Sir Crank Lamparde. Official Audit.

Sec: Oh. Notta OK. Notta mea. You needa dother office. Me sendda you. Transferz di calli.

GW: OK. Thank you.

Clicks on telephone.

Switch: Yes?

Sec: Thissa caller. To extender 999, thissa caller, pliz.

Switch: Transferring you now, sir.

Another line rings.

A male, voice: 'ello. Wot?

GW: To whom am I speaking, please?

Voice: Wot? Wot you mean? It's me.

GW: Ah, but who is me?

Voice: Who is you? Surely you know, dontcha? Owerwise, can't 'elp yer.

GW: Oh dear. This is not proving easy is it?

Voice: Innit? Not my fault. You made the call. Wot you want, anyway? I'm busy signing monthly Hospital Consultant's Clinical Merit Awards cheques.

GW: Yes. No. Let me explain. I am from the Suspicious Expenses National Audit Office. It concerns an important suspicious expenses claim.

Voice: Ah. Hmm. Do I need my solicitor present then?

GW: No. Not you. Not so far as I know. No. But I do need to speak to whoever it is who deals with Sir Crank's expenses.

Voice: Ah. Not me then. You need Christabel Harrods in CELSO?

GW: CELSO?

Voice: Chief Executive's Life Style Office.

GW: Can you transfer me?

Voice: Will try. 'old on.

More telephone clicking noises.

AT YOUR EXPENSE…THE NHS & THE ECONOMICS OF POLITICS

Telephone rings at another extension. No reply. Then recorded message: "You have reached CELSO. Leave a message. Our legal advisers will return your call."

Nine days later, Mr. Washington's telephone rings.

GW: Hello, Washington. Can I help you?

Mr. U. Heap: This is Mr. U. Heap, from Deny It, Wasn't there, and Alibi Always Available, Solicitors, Cheapside. We represent Sir Crank Lamparde. How can I help you?

GW: Ah, yes please. This is George Washington. From the Suspicious Expenses National Audit Office. It concerns Sir Crank's recent expenses claim.

UH: Yes? What about it?

GW: I need a meeting. I need to go over the recent figures with someone in authority.

UH: Oh. Not me then. Too high up for me. You need Lord Patterer of East Asia. He's the NHS man in charge there. I will get his Secretary to call you.

Another nine days later…

FJ-B: Hello, may name is Miss Fruity Juicy-Bath, Lord Patterer's PA. How may I help you?

GW: Thank you for calling me. Yes, if you will help me, please. This is George Washington of the Suspicious Expenses National Audit Office. I need a meeting with Lord Patterer to discuss Sir Crank Lamparde's expenses claims.

FJ-B: We deny it all. And haven't you received our Press Release? We have denied this 19 times already. I will e-mail the papers to you. Your e-mail, please?

GW: g.washington@suspexexes.nao.org All lower-case.

FJ-B: Thank you. On it's way!

Five days later, the papers are delivered by bike messenger, to be signed for.

Eventually, some weeks later, a meeting is arranged, at Lord Patterer's offices in Nine Elms Towers, White City.

JK-N: Hello, my name is Jennifer Knott-Necessary, please come in. We spoke on the telephone. Lord Patterer is waiting for you.

Lord P: Morning! Welcome! New chum, eh? Might be on a City Board together some day, eh? Pleased to see you. Come on in. Coffee? Biscuits? Brandy? Cigar? Caviar? No? It's the good stuff. The best Russian. No? Well, allow me. You're quite sure you won't? Me, I always do at this time of the morning.

[Munches away…].

35

Do sit down. Make yourself comfortable. Best view in all of London from here. See all the way to my home in Surrey. Park your Roller OK for you did they? Chauffer accommodated downstairs with coffee? What? Came on a bus? Lawd! Not been on one for 47 years! I drive a Byford Mark £1m GTR myself. Really goes!

Now, how can I help?

GW: Well, it is a rather delicate matter, my Lord.

Lord P: Please, not the Lord lark. No need. Just call me Chrissie. Everyone does.

GW: Yes, your lordship. Thank you. Chrissie.

As you will know, the NHS is under tremendous financial pressure. A&E chaos. Bed-blocking. Endless pressures. Many new demands. Collapse of General Practice. Everyone living to 99. New hips, new knees, diabetes, all of that. Every penny matters. VERY hard times.

Lord P: Yes. Heard something about it at the Garrick.

GW. Well. Sir. We are trying to ensure to the utmost that no money is wasted. It's a very big job. We've had to expand our staff 350 per cent this year, just to check expenses claims for Richmond House, let alone other NHS facilities.

Lord P: Yes. I see. Very difficult for you. My own expenses have been queried too, over at Moby Dick House. But I'm on 29 other boards, so I spread my claims around, you know.

GW: Yes, Your Lordship. Chrissie. I see. Well. Can I just ask you about Sir Crank?

Lord P: This isn't a trivial enquiry, I'm sure. But it's not, either, a matter for the NAO, is it? Nor for the Serious Organised Crime Agency. Nothing like that. Not at all. He's a good man. Totally honest man. Known him years. Cambridge together. Same College. Same year. Same staircase. Same regiment. Lunched with him at the Venice Lido last summer. And so far I've seen no papers. No paper trail, I think they call it? Quite new to me, of course. I've not talked to Sir Crank about this, either.

But we might have a brief word, informally, you and me, you know, just between us, however. Otherwise we will need the lawyers here. And that's expensive, as you know well enough. See what we can sort out privately, eh? On the QT.

GW: Well, Your Lordship. Chrissie. If you like. At least as a first step. But I can make no commitments on behalf of the Office or for our Chief Executive, Sir Harold Hardip.

Lord P: Hardip? Oh!

GW:...but can I just suggest some lines of enquiry and some related general issues we might wish to pursue, then? Very informally at this stage.

Lord P: As you wish. Yes. But there is to be no minute, you understand. And I may not be able to comment at all.

AT YOUR EXPENSE…THE NHS & THE ECONOMICS OF POLITICS

GW: I understand, your Lord…Chrissie.

Lord P: Yes. Of course. Well, no. No. Certainly not able to say very much. I have had no discussions with him, with Sir Crank, you see, about this subject. All new to me.

GW: But your office, apparently, has issued denials?

Lord P: Has it? Indeed. Ah, well. Can't expect me to know everything, can you? Busy man! And this isn't *High Noon*, you know. Sir Crank has issued no detailed statement, has he? Only an initial, initial denial?

GW: No. Nothing. Not yet anyway. May be waiting for the call to the House of Commons again.

Lord P: *Again?* Has he been to the House on this already then?

GW: Actually, Lord Chrissie, he did appear before the Public Affairs Committee last year. They then quizzed him about his expenses totalling a big lot then. Some many thousands! But there does not seem to have been much of a change in the first quarter of this year, does there?

Lord P: Don't know anything about that. But I'm perfectly sure that everything claimed is proper and correct. He is an honest man. Gross insensitivity to public concerns, you might want to say. Might have to agree. Perhaps. But not theft. Nor is this like that BBC Severance Scandal, you know. 'Course, nothing to do with me, that, you know. All those payments of £369 million to those 7,500 departing staff. I know nothing about it. Know nothing about the average severance pay of £164,200. Nothing about the 150 managers paid-off. Nothing about what contractual entitlements were.

Never met that Caroline Thomson, former Chief Operating Officer. Nor that HR woman accused of lying. Never knew her either. Never knew that CT's salary was £330,000 but paid £670,000 to go. Never met that Jana Bennett, who was paid another £700,000 to go. Nothing known about the £1m paid to that other fellow, either. Well, I'm only guessing at the figures, you know. But something like that anyway. Just making that clear. BBC is very popular, too, you know. Has 26.8 million subscribers. Or so I'm told.

GW: *Subscribers?* Well, not exactly. The TV license is compulsory, isn't it? And government decides its level, doesn't it? Not exactly an open consumer's market!

Lord P: Surely you are not suggesting, are you, that decisions made by individuals on how they spend their money can make a difference to what happens, are you?

GW: Well, many might…

Lord P: Anyway, thousands of them treat the TV license as voluntary, anyway don't they? Just like the road-tax, road-insurance, MOT, and their council tax!

GW: Again, a big topic….

Lord P: Well, just another of my little jokes!

And getting back to what you say about Sir Crank's expenses. Not dangerous, is it, like texting drivers? Not operating on anyone, is he? And we don't know the full story, do we? He has yet to appear before that dragon Margaret Hodge and the Public Affairs Committee at the House. This year, anyway, as you say. Or before that Keith Vaz's Home Affairs Committee. Need his explanations. Give the man a fair go.

Not been there, has he? I'd have known.

GW: No, sir. Not appeared. Committees all too busy with the BBC scandals enquiries.

Lord P: Ah. I see. Anyway, where do you get this expenses information?

GW: It's the official published data. Check it if you like.

Lord P: I will, of course. Yes.

GW: Lord, Chrissie, you do know, don't you, that Sir Crank's expenses amounted to more than plenty, you might think, on food and travel etc in the first quarter of 2013? And this at a time when he is exhorting the very hard-pressed NHS to make very big efficiency savings. Billions to be saved. Everything being squeezed very hard. And this when A&E staff shortages and chaos fill the news every day.

Lord P: Quite right. Save public money So they should. Doesn't grow on trees, you know.

GW: No. Comes from taxpayers. Ask the Taxpayers Alliance.

Lord P: No! But thank you! So, what is he supposed to do then, to do his job? Travels First-Class? Quite right, too. Has got to work quietly. And all the docs, the consultants, travel First-Class class to meetings, don't they? Always have, since 1948. And someone else has to do their work then in clinics and operating theatres, too, don't they? So, all quite normal. And the chap has got to eat, too.

GW: Seems like a terrific lot of very good dinners, doesn't it? And in top places?

Lord P: Well, don't want him meeting patients, do we! My little joke!

GW: Hm. Well, his chauffeur-driven car prevents that, doesn't it? Has no encounters like that of Gordon Brown with that very angry woman in the street in the last election. Car has prevented him from meeting patients. Well, did until he stopped using the government car recently. Cost us all some thousands for the first three months this year, still. Travels anonymously on the tube now, I suppose. Or in a second class quiet carriage.

Lord C: Probably, yes. Keep in mind, too, that he only has a small pension pot. What is it, a couple of million? Take that into account, if you will. Chap has got to live.

As to efficiencies, we do have a 'Turn Up On The Day' policy. Very efficient. Pay that day's price. Can't start fussily pre-planning and pre-booking train tickets. Waste of important time. Can't start the office at Leeds holding tickets in readiness, bulk buying. Can't be at the game of predicting scheduled diaried meetings in advance.

Can't have BR sandwiches or a messy lunch box, either. Salmonella risks. Not good enough. All too difficult. Can't have all our meetings in London, either. A lot of VIP bureaucrats at Leeds involved. Huge capital cost of Leeds Centre too. Got to be used. And so much cheaper to send the Chief Exec to Leeds once a week.

GW: Can read claims for negligence concerning the NHS on the train then, too. And the numbers are rising there, as you know. Doubled last year.

Lord P: Ah. Very alert chap, too. Was wide-awake, wasn't he, during all that hospital deaths fuss? Wide-awake, our Sir Crank.

GW: Well, I might remind you, very sadly, that a lot of patients died unnecessarily then. He's not a doc, of course. But he was the Chief Executive of one of the nearby chief local health authorities then, wasn't he. Wide awake? Well. Maybe.

Lord P: Well, he did get hired as Chief Executive of the whole NHS, didn't he? And knighted? Says something, doesn't it?

GW: Alas, yes, Lord Chrissie, it does.

Lord P: Well, seems to me to be a lot of fuss about nothing. But I suppose you'll witch-hunt him now, will you?

GW: Not at all. But it's our duty to watch out for anything which anyone might consider suspicious. And to enquire within with some care. Evidently you don't think so?

Lord P: Hmm.

GW: May I make some wider points before I leave today?

Lord P: Yes. Go ahead. By all means.

GW: This is a very clear example of what is called "the economics of politics." That is, that bureaucracies serve themselves first. And that they collaborate with politicians and vested-interests – the docs, the public service unions – in keeping the public out of decision-making, so far as they can. When I was a student we were told by the Profs – James Buchanan, Gordon Tullock – that…

Lord P: Economics of *what*, d'you say?

GW: Economics of Politics. Gordon Tullock's collaboration with the later Nobel Prize winner Jim Buchanan. This produced *The Calculus of Consent: Logical Foundations of Constitutional Democracy* (1962). A seminal work in the new field of public choice theory, as it's called. Applies economic theory to all sorts of non-market phenomena, especially in the realm of government and politics. What's called 'rent-seeking.'

They were both there at George Mason University when I was there. In Fairfax, Virginia. You'd probably want to look at Tullock's work *On Voting: A Public Choice Approach*. Came out in 1998, but still current.

Lord P: What's 'rent-seeking' when it's at home, then?

GW: 'Rent-seeking' is when a monopolistic firm – or a professional vested-interest, like the docs and the BMA or the other Trade Unions here – use their financial position to lobby politicians in order to create legislation with the intent of increasing their profits, or their incomes, or their powers. This can lead to moral hazard when politicians make policy decisions based on the lobby instead of the efficiency of the policy.

Lord P: Academic munbo-jumbo, then?

GW: Well, no, actually. Very directly applicable to how the BMA dominates governments on the NHS, and halts all intelligent debate. Would threaten their privileges. And the cosy deals between them, governments, TU's, docs, and the bureaucrats like Sir Crank. And it's why the PM runs so scared, too.

But if I can move on....secondly, what is it that Sir Crank does that is so special? And how can you justify a salary of £210,000, a vast pension pot, and all those expenses? In the old days in the '60s the official story was that civil servants were clever people, and could earn much more in industry than in the public service. So, by way of compensation, they got social status, an honour, and a decent pension. And then many of them still went onto City boards and earned more once they were 60. Yet here is Sir Crank, vastly overpaid. Huge pension pot. NHS can't go bust. No competition. Captive patients, in the main. He leads a sheltered life – well, until recently – as do most top civil servants.

How is his pay package and huge pension possibly justified? He can't say he has to fight his corner for the DoH to get more funding, can he? The politicians can't wait to stuff too much public money into the NHS, can they? Never stops. Won't listen. Do it, even without any required management changes.

Lord P: Well, I do not wish to offer any answers today. I must consult.

GW: My Lord, is this then a case of you being in the lovely position of being in charge of something but being responsible for nothing? Just like that old John Majorite whose name sounds similar to yours, that Lord Patten, the Chairman of the BBC Trust?

Lord P: No relation of mine. And the BBC? Now don't get all arty-farty with me!

GW: Big issues there, too, actually. As London Mayor Boris Johnson wrote the other day in the *Daily Telegraph*, if payment of the BBC license fee was voluntary we'd soon see the BBC get itself into the real world. Same, too, for the NHS. If all NHS health facilities had to earn willing revenues and in competition, we'd soon see big changes. What's the saying? "Money Talks, and Preference Walks."

Lord P: Now, I have said already, don't get all arty farty and economiksacomical with me!

Lord P stands abruptly: Well, thank you for coming to see me, Mr. Washington. I will take this on advisement. I will speak to Sir Crank. Can you find your own way out? Thank you.

GW leaves.

AT YOUR EXPENSE...THE NHS & THE ECONOMICS OF POLITICS

Lord P picks up intercom: Miss Knott-Necessary? Has that dreadful man gone? Yes? Good. Do come in please. Bring my recent expenses claims file with you, please. And a calculator. Thank you. And get Sir Crank on the 'phone will you? Try his mobile. He's at Ascot today.

EPISODE 8

Docs., drugs, and rock and roll.

Dramatis Personae:

Sir Cyril Squoffington-Squogg, OBE, JP, Chief Executive of The Tower of London NHS Hospital Trust, Traitor's Gate House, Embankment, London, EC. He is aged 67. His wife, Lady Bernice Squoffington-Squogg, is also Chair of The Wiltshire Artists Benevolent Fund. They live during the week in Sloane Street, Chelsea and at weekends at Wobblybottom Towers, Minceyglade, Wiltshire. He is a retired senior civil servant, Department of Pensions. She is a former ice-skater, aged 39. Their son, Paul Bristol Squoffington-Squogg, is a nature writer on the *Financial Times*, contributing the popular weekly column 'Splashing About Happily' – regarded as the successor to Mr. Boot's 'Lush Places.' *[Due for Fact-finding trip to Ishmaelia? – Ed.].*

Major-General J.J. Slopkins, MM, MC, CBE, etc., is Chairman of The Tower of London NHS Hospital Trust. He is a retired cavalryman, aged 82. He lives at Coggeshall in Essex.

Mr. Barney Wells, BEM, is Chief Executive of The Arthur Scargill Memorial NHS Trust Hospital, Units 7-34 Karl Marx Industrial Estate, Lubyanka Avenue, Chessingfield-on-Soke. He began his career as an accounts clerk in the S. E. Regional HQ of the NHS. He has also played hockey for Bexhill-on-Sea Deficits, the leading local club. He is aged 56 and the father of nine sons, all of whom are employed as trade union officials.

The Chair of The Arthur Scargill Memorial NHS Trust Hospital is Mrs. Barney Wells, MBE, a local Unite Trade Union official. She left Downhills-on-the-Soke comprehensive school aged 15, with one GCSE. She has contested four parliamentary seats, without success.

Brenda When, a North country woman, is secretary to Mr. Wells. She is a graduate of the University of Kent at Canterbury, and a working Mum. Her friends often liken her to Donna, Josh's brilliant assistant, in the *West Wing*. She often makes key points.

***

[telephone transcript].

Brenda: Mr. Wells, sir. I've been thinking about the A&E signs which were done. You know, sending people somewhere else. All that. No-one really knows where. Sir, it does strike me that a lot of terrific creative ingenuity and energy went into that wheeze. And that there is all that genuine quality in good people working in the NHS. But the system just crushes it out of us.

I know that what you call 'the third-in-line mafia', the business managers, are a talented gang. But they spend their lives chasing their tails. We could do so much more for patients if we were really allowed to concentrate on our job, and not on the politics. I know I mustn't mention "markets" to your wife, our Chair, or Tescos – though she shops there, doesn't she?. But if we'd been able to put all that ingenuity into doing more for patients, instead of gaming the system, well....

Barney: Yes, Brenda. You are right. As ever. But alas it's the way it is. What's next?

Brenda: Well, sir, telephone call for you. Sir Squoffy...on line 1.

Barney: Hello Cyril. 'Fore you start, have you seen NHS Circular 786VJNHS/Nicholson? Oh, not that again! How the billio am I supposed to get my Top Docs in on Sunday mornings at 5 a.m.? How does that dopey old rope Sir D think I [or anyone!] can get Junior Docs to phone the top docs in the Casino at Bournemouth? I ask you. Oh, 'arry Redknapp to that! Ha – what a reference Junior docs would get then after their 6 months training placement here at Scargill's. And I'd be 'No Confidenced' pronto, too. Well, I suppose there is some hospital work on lighthouses in Orkney? They do say, too, that the Gambia is nice in November, too.

But I wanted to raise another point that's really worrying me. Drugs and doctors. Stuff done behind the hand. Stuff no-one is supposed to notice. Drugs conjured into nowhere. What we are not to mention. My real worry is a rumour that some docs may still be prescribing drugs for their own families, and for themselves. What do you know about this? A difficult problem for management or a Chairman to tackle. But the cost was said – privately – to be something like £20,000 per annum to the individual hospital budget 20 years ago. What is it now? Multiply that up across the country! It's a lotta money, as 'arry Enfield might have said.

Sir S-S: Ah, Barney, more take-care-territory! *Quicksands – beware!* This is all politics, of course. Oh, I know that when the BMA meets in conference it's a highly political body. But that's a given. We both know, too, that the docs look after their own interests very carefully locally. They don't think that any rules made by management or by politicians are necessary, relevant, or apply to them. My lot, I know, have no regard for the rules. Consider the one asking them to live within the required radius of the hospital, and so being rapidly on call. Drugs? That's a biggie!

Barney: So, what do I do? Advice, please!

Sir S-S: Barney, once again I have to tell you the real facts of life. That's definitely 'Don't light the blue touch paper, and don't stand anywhere near' stuff. Get as clear and as far away as you can. Don't touch that one. Don't. *Just don't.* It's lethal. *Keep well away!*

Barney: Just what I thought! But it is a lot of money....

Sir S-S: Barney, you should by now have learned that important fact about British life: that doctors are untouchable. It needs plenty of courage to challenge them at all. Our masters above, the politicians, don't have it. And to tackle them locally you must have national political backing. The few efforts we've seen to try to get some change have proved this key point about contemporary Britain. That you get a big black mark if you have a go locally. Even Sir Brian, even with a K, even a Prof. and internationally respected, one of the best docs in the country, just look at the struggle he had to get any hearing in Whitehall or at the BMA about the publication of varied surgical death-rates.

Look at the whistle-blowers in nursing and medicine, and what happened to some of them.

Look at some non-execs. Shot on duty. Shot in the dark. Gone! Abused! Denigrated! Try to tackle any of this – then you are labelled eccentric. A maverick. A loose cannon. It's a losing gambit. That is, if you want a continuing career. Of course, this system is itself a kind of terrorism. You pay for your words. But, you have to ask yourself, where would we be without the independent-minded mavericks? And without their moral courage. They are the ones who bring ideas into play and which can eventually change policies. Without them? Going backwards always, we'd be without them. But, there is, alas, no such thing as painless change.

Barney: Mmm. But what about the politicians? Where is *their* leadership? Why have *we* got to do it all? What are *they* for?

Sir S-S: Too early in the day for me to start laughing, Barney! Keep in mind the words "state monopoly"; "fear of the voters", and "Politician's Peerages ahead." But, as my good old friend the late Arthur Seldon always insisted at the Institute of Economic Affairs, the politician's job is – or should be! – to lead and to educate. Read your Hayek! And the boundaries of the 'politically practicable' are always shifting. But you'll never do it by yourself. And anyway, the docs will always have power. They do things for us which we can't do for ourselves. No patient in an ambulance ever says, "Take me to your manager!"

Barney: Yes. But the drugs business? What to do?

Sir S-S: Nowt, my friend. Nowt. That drugs issue. It's a real one. But just write a memo to yourself and get Brenda to bury it!

Anyway, got to go. My Roller's alarm has gone off. Got to see about it. No minion here to send. Makes a terrific racket – which is the point I 'spose.

However, docs and drugs – BEWARE!!! *No CBE's in that!*

EPISODE 9

The Spectres of Health Policy to Come… a Warning from The Nether World? The Richmond House Revels, Scene 2.

Dramatis Personae:

Sir Cyril Squoffington-Squogg, OBE, JP, is Chief Executive of The Tower of London NHS Hospital Trust, Tower Hamlets, London, EC.

Lady Bernice Squoffington-Squogg, his wife, is also Chair of The Wiltshire Artists Benevolent Fund.

And an unlikely [?] spectral crowd make a first "appearance"….

***

THE RICHMOND HOUSE REVELS, Scene 2.

Lady S-S: Cyril, here's your morning coffee, dear. It's that *Costa Rica* blend, the strong one you like. And a mint cookie. Help take your mind off of all those awful stories.

Sir S-S: Yes, dreadful batch of NHS cuttings this month.

Lady S-S: Seems to be worse every month. And the most distressing thing is this decision by the GMC. How can the public ever trust again that doctors will ever be accountable? And surely the level of proof that the GMC requires cannot be so high that no action could be taken? Astonishes me. No-one having any action taken against them. Well, except for the one doctor earlier struck off for financial irregularities.

Sir S-S: Yes. And patients don't usually die from financial irregularities, do they? Die from other kinds of doctor and nursing incompetence. And management ineptitude, too. A terrific number did – and still do? – don't they?

Sir S-S: Well, certainly seemed so at the big enquiry. I suppose we must face the fact that self-regulation is no regulation, and there is damn all we can do about it. State institutions are a no-go area for 'quality', which is awful. And how can patients trust us?

Lady S-S: What it needs is for some rich folk to test it all in court. Someone should sue the GMC for failing to make doctors accountable at Mid-Staffs. I think the law might prize a door open – but who will take them on? Why not the Sec of State himself? And the Department of Justice? Or both!

Sir S-S: Hmm. Well, THAT would work! 'Course, Gordon Brown increasing the pay so much in the NHS was senseless while he kept all those people there who were not doing it in the first place. And you have to wonder – if we've got all these Chief Executives paid £220k or more and all these high-earning hospital consultants and GPs – why they are *still* not getting it done?

Lady S-S: Well, my love, you've done your best, haven't you?

Sis S-S: Yes, but actually, *understanding it* is the easy part. *Making the changes happen* is the hard part. And my humour for the Christmas Revels show can't and shouldn't hide the continuing snags. They are fundamentally endemic. Actually, *The Richmond House Revels* is intended to offer some real lessons about it. You, know, "Make 'em laugh, make 'em cry, make 'em go home thinking!" You'll see.

The real answer, of course, is that if real performance was tied to real individual and mobile healthcare funds then the consumers and their collective, co-operative purchasing agency would decide who their purchasers would talk to, who they would buy from, what results they would try to demand. Quality and access central. Costs, too, would be much more controlled. Not all in the hands of the self-interested docs. But without price signals you will get nowhere.

Lady S-S: Yes my love. What was that old Everly Brothers song? "*All I Have to Do is Dream*"? But are you writing again, Cyril? I can see all those new notes….

Sir S-S: Yes. Working on Scene two of the *Revels*. Christmas *is* coming. I'm making a point about the GMC. Very plainly. And I'm also very fearful for any real changes being stultified if that Mr. Millkiband gets in. So, trying to shock them all at the Christmas Revels show. It's just a draft. But do take a look. You are always my best first-reader…

She reads aloud.

Stage directions:

The setting: a massive old but very private 19th Century Woolly Processing Warehouse – the National HQ of The General Medical Whitewash Company [GMWC].

The main entrance: a sandstone-carved archway, lettered "The Advanced Sir Nicholson NHS Hospitals Pensionable Trust & GMWC Out Relief Centre. Abandon hope…."

At the main gate, the noted NHS Staffordshire folk-songsters, 'The Completely Innocents' [backed by the percussionist quartet 'No Case to Answer'].

They are gathered together to chant the traditional professional psalm "Thank You O Lord for Our Private GMWC." Conducted at the rostrum by Nursie Nursie Dixbungles, to the tune of the aria "There's No Evidence! No, There's Not! So There." Same tune as 'Old Macdonald Had a Farm.' Rhythm: 44 not-barred-heart-beats to the minute. Sotto voce.

We see a long line of black-shrouded patients' funerals and large black hearses led by black plumed horses as a continuous backdrop against the Mid-Staffordshire landscape, echoing out into the far and even infinite distance. And a huge pile of new white blankets, marked "Reserved. For Cover Ups Only."

THE SPECTRES OF HEALTH POLICY TO COME...

The backdrop: a barren moorland waste and an ancient bleak burial-ground. The entrance itself leading under a dark and lofty canopy. Iron gates, overrun by tall grass and dank weeds. A howling, eerie wind. A large, red and black tent, shaken by the weather.

Seated at a round oak table under a tallow candle spotlight, a very old Sibyl. Rough stone steps lead up to a Gothic carved seat before her.

A visiting figure, a Mr Taxpayer Ordinaryperson, takes up a blazing torch and enters the centre of the space before him.

Even with the torch in his hand the air is bitterly cold.

The Sibyl waves her sleeves. This is Medusa's poisoned cloak.

The forlorn visiting figure is beckoned forward by the Sibyl.

She cries out: "Sit!" The figure does so.

She cries out, "Cross my palm with a PFI contract." The figure leans forward, earnestly.

The Sibyl gazes into her huge crystal ball. She says, in a croaking voice: "I see through cloudy smoke. I see the future...I see...I see...I see some dishevelled figures in white coats. I see them foreshadowing certain grim ends. I see them gathered at an ancient oaken desk – this is labelled THE LODGE. Are they gypsies? Are they tramps? Are they the undead? Are they the denizens of purgatory?"

A chorus of shadowy, sight-less monks replies: "No! No! Alas, No! This is the Future That Yet Might Be. This is the spectral healthcare policy board meeting of the Independent Labour Party."

The Sibyl cries out: "Oh! Oh! Catastrophe and Coalition is awaiting! At your own shoulders, my visitor, are the three awful ghosts of NHS Policy Past, NHS Policy Present, and NHS Policy Yet To Be." The Sybil cries out "Ask, Is It Too late for Conscience? Too Late for Regrets? Too Late for Correction? Too Late to Dispel the Shadows I Will Show You? Or will there be Hell for Ever and Ever, and No Amen?"

She then vanishes suddenly, in a sharp lightning flash and a puff of purple smoke. Only ashes remain at her Gothic seat in this infamous resort. Instead the audience sees the following...

An important Independent Labour Party [no connection with adjacent TU cheque-books] health policy top-level political meeting.

In attendance [including observers]:

In the chair, a Mr. Ed Millkiband, Minor – an MP ["The Great Independent Leader."]

Ranged round the dark oak table, we see seated the ILP Politburo Policy Board :

Edth Balth, MP [Treasurer].

THE FACEY ROMFORD PAPERS

Lord Klinnockles of Brevity.

Lady Gladyss Klinnockles of Income-augmentation.

Lord Cunard-waiter of Spellcheck.

Lord Corkscrew Oakeshott of Seagrovebog (Jenkins Claret Party; prospective-coalition observer) [*who he? V. Cable*].

Lady J. Cumerbund (Chief Patroness, Consulting Inc. PLC).

Professor J. Applecore (Socialist Worker).

Dianne [Daily Attendance Fee: £1,750] Abbgotbottle MP.

Ms. Harriet Hardwood, MP.

Sir D. Midstaffs [In attendance to receive the Award of Socialist Hero of Labour].

Various NHS Dis-Trust Medical and NHS Dis-Trust Clinical Directors [optional; pensioned].

The Rt. Rev. Dr. B. Hogbin GCSE, Bishop of St. Just [religious adviser].

Mr. Andy Birdnumb, MP [Shadow].

[Proceedings].

Mr. Millkiband: Welcome, dear Comrades. Welcome to The Long March. And to Healthcare Policy. Which we need to finalise. Fourth-with. I'm calling it HS2 – Health Service 2. Seems very catchy! Fits on the rails! Rattles along! Costs more! Just the ticket!

Mr. Balth: 'ere, 'ere. But that's my missiles Department, Werner Von Braun told me…and I'm still in five minds…

Mr. M: Now, today. Yer Health. Referred back to us at Brighton conference. Er? Yes? NHS. Er? Yes. Er? Sort it today. Er? Like. Y'know. See what I mean? I'm no speaker, but *[consults large white prompt-cards]*…

But 'scuse me, though. Where is Lord McDuffski of Cashbond? Not here?

Lord K: No, Comrade Chair. Apologised. In France. Studying how to manage improved industrial relations. Spending his time with the French Communist Party, Trade Unions, and massed sheep farmers. B&b at Calais…

Mr. M: Ah. Good. Useful lessons for us too then when we're in government again. His cheque still came in, though, I hope.

Now, you all have the, er, minutes, like. I have previously signed them. Like. Know what I mean? Like. We have already previously agreed, er, Like, the following, Like:

THE SPECTRES OF HEALTH POLICY TO COME…

- The manifesto title: *Our Manifest Destiny*. Preface by Lord McDuffski of Cashbond.

- Our theme campaign tune: *We Are Family*.

- Our Motto: *By, For, and Of the Unions*.

- Our key-words and ever-strategy: *Tax More! Spend More! Do it Now! Today, Tomorrow, and Forever!*

All agreed.

- Bigger, bagglier government!

- And more FREE EVERYTHING, too!

But we now have to decide on a basic additional set of new taxes…I mean, new policies, for health reforms. We are talking about our most precious national resource and the very futures of our precious and beloved children…*Votes!*

So, draw nearer, Comrades. Take a close prospect of the papers before you. They are the yield of many steady hands. They are drawn from our latent spring of Millkiband-Leninist-Marxist Theory. They are the product of much good out of evil. For we cannot just produce policies out of a hat. Ours are the result of much diligent preparatory work. Klingfilm Fund, and all that. "Knowledge the wing wherewith we fly to heaven." That's from Shake-speare you know.

With these policies we can now achieve the required absolute order and enshrined beauty which we require from the confusions and intrusions of recent 'reforms'. "Onwards to the People's Revolution!" That's from my Dad, you know.

For ours is a metaphysical, an ideological, and a practical litany. And it's the detail which will bring it all most fully to life. With these policies we can win the next election. And the one after that too.

Lord K: Point of order. Comrade Chair. "The one after that too…" ? Shurely, not so. When we made sthat agreement with Mr Bruzzshnuv, one election shwas to be shufficient. No more would then be needed. We were going to shign that sphecial prothection shagreehment…

Mr M: Yes, yes, quite so.

Lord K: Move next business then, Comrade Chair.

Mr Birdnumb: Well, my policy is….

Mr M: We will move on. No tapestry needs to unwind. No need to debate again our holistic beliefs. No need to restate the obvious. What was agreed is agreed.

Now, on health-care…

Mr Birdnumb: Well, my policy is…

Lord K: Move next business, Comrade Chair.

Mr M: Yes. But seriously. We come to the basic competition – pardon that word – the quiz. Our Healthcare reform proposals have now to be selected from the following list.

You each have before you a voting form. As usual, a big prize. You know the usual mobile and text charges. You are asked to number these policy proposals 1 to 13 in the order of your preference. We will adopt the first lucky 13 policies selected out of the 13 offered. The winner of the competition will receive a 20% discount at Lady Gladyss's Health Spa in the Turks & Caicos Islands. Oh, yes! *[Uses bulldog's voice from Churchill Insurance ads]*.

Lord Cunard-waiter of Spellcheck *[very loudly]*: CARD VOTE!

Lord K: Oh, very good! Very good! VERY good! Oh, reminds me of Conferences past, present, and future! But, Turks & Caicos. S'loverly there, too, my mateys! Yes! Right on! See Gladyss's pay-up site: www.incomeaugmentation.co.uk *[Waves his arms wildly in the air]*.

Mr. Birdnumb: Well, my policy is….

Mr. M: As I said, I will read my list – the magic pontoon, or 13 points:

THE NECESSARY PROGRESSIVE 13 SAVE-THE-NHS POLICIES:

1. Introduce an indexed salary premium for all TU members, also to be computed into indexed pensions. Very urgent.

2. Merge all Unite Trade Union local offices with NHS Trust boards. Saves subscription costs. Priority policy.

3. [and socialist sub-sections]. Introduce Mr. Balth's New Fiscal Measures [one indissoluble package]:

    i) Instant: 'Opportunity tax' on all shops selling clothes worn by Duchess of Cambridge.

    ii) Union Jack 'stamp' charge on flags used in public events or sold to by-standers.

    iii) 'Windfall' charge on all new mortgages and small business loans.

    iv) Shopping-mall entry charges.

    v) Credit card charge for use of Motorway emergency telephones.

    vi) Car-park tax at supermarkets.

    vii) 'Exit' charges on bus, tube and railway usage by passengers.

viii) Tax on every click on public library computers.

ix) Premium charge on rural bus stops.

x) New license charges on health clubs and weight-watching clubs.

xi) Distribute acquired funds as wages. Alongside 'Free' policies [various].

4. [and socialist sub-sections]. Our additional 'shout louder' proposals for new funding sources for NHS:

   i) New prescription charge on anti-obesity drugs. Big fund-raiser.

   ii) Halt free prescriptions for over 70's – "have had their share."

   iii) Expand the late Mr. Robin Cook's Investigation Commission, to query doubtful new NHS industrial processes, query efforts to lower costs, query so-called improved innovation strategies and capitalist competitiveness. Builds modern economy.

   iv) Reduce unnecessary protection on unnecessary copyright drug patents to 3 years maximum. Serves them right.

   v) Ban all foreign car imports, to protect British Leyland [deceased]; create new UK car maker, the BMV [British Motor Vehicle], on "people's" lines of German VW [prop. A. Hitler, 1932-45. Carmaker]. Creates industrial revival. Pays for wage/salary increases.

5. Open large new NHS Hospitals Trust at Sangatte, N. France, to process new patients via lorries into Kent and Sussex Hospitals. Enable these potential new Labour voters/patients – to sample UK care, ready for transfers to other UK counties with marginal seats. Chair, Dame Fannie Gonebarkers, B.Sc., D. Univ., NCSCC, DBE.

6. Immediately end all NHS Sunday working. Save on electricity, etc.

7. Close dangerous and destabilising social-care Direct Payment personal budgets scheme, and close down by Ministerial Order the Independent Living Association. Also, close so-called Health and Well-being Boards. Improves access to A&E.

8. End independent contractor status of GPs. Improves morale.

9. Rename all Nurses as Senior Sociologists. Expand compulsory sociology degree programmes for "nurses." New grants for full-time Ph. Ds in sociology. Enhances on-ward care.

10. Merge NICE [National Institute for Clinical Evasion] and NICCA [National Institute for Cost Control Avoidance] with new NITUC [National Institute of Trade Union Control]. Chair: Lord McDuffski of Cashbond. Requires new budgets.

11. Merge health, social care, and education ministries with transport and employment

ministries. One new expert Control Commission, Sov-com-educ-hea-trans-employ. Short title, Sovduffgov. Chair, Lord Cunard-waiter of Spellcheck. Political adviser, Lord Oakeshutt [*who he? Ed*]. Enhances popular appeal.

12. End free-for-all in eye-care. Compulsory acquisition of high street eye-care premises. Convert to local Independent Labour Constituency Party charity shops. Improves High Street trade viability.

13. Merge former healthcare socialist charity Klingfilm Fund with new Millkiband policy Department of Frankfurt Skool of Marxist-Leninist-Millkibandism at Gateshead railway goods-yards. Chair: Lord K of Brevity. Chief Executive: Professor A. Hampster. Chief car-park attendant, Nursie Nursie Dixbungles, B.Com. (Graduate, Huey P. Long University of Our Lady of The Anguished Nation's Conscience, Bama, Tennessee, and Jesuit Collegia Innocenti, Roma). Produces "Reports."

Mr M: So, in summary: *Sed quae non prosunt singula multa javant* – 'But many things are helpful which singly are of no use' – as Sir Humphrey said to me recently.

[Chortles to self. In room, bewildered silence reigns. Audience shuffling sounds, of many early leavers…].

Mr Birdnumb: My policy is…

Mr M: Yes. Well, we can close now then. A good meeting dear Comrades!

Lord Cunard-waiter: Just wanted to say, Comrade Chair. Congratulations on your opinion poll ratings being up as far as "dire." Big boost from Brighton conference. Well done! Your new health policies must have done it. People just want to pay more in taxes, and no need of outcomes data or management changes at all.

Mr M: Just so. Justice so. Just-a-minute so. And, as our…*my* Daddy used to say, the primitive, falsely-conscious electorate is in a state of necessary socialist and theoretical pupilage. But we will teach them yet! *Just won't we!*

We will now collect your completed forms. You too, Mr. Birdnumb, when you can. Ms. Hardwood will make an announcement on the *Today* show soon. Three-line whip for you all to listen at my Mansion House in Kilburn. No need to text in your replies with your entry fee of £100 each. I take Paypal.

[Telephone rings. Mr. M. answers this. Stands to attention as he takes the call]:

Mr M: *Yes, SIR.* Yes, Prime Minister. **Yes, Sir.** Consider it done! Yes, Sir. Yes, Gordon, *Sir*. Yes, Sir, absolutely Sir. Yes. Yes, we will. As agreed, Gordon. Yes. Of course, **Sir**. All in hand, Sir. Your Will Be Done. YES, Gordon, SIR. Thank you, Sir. SIR."

The Rt. Rev. Bishop Hogbin, GCSE: Amen!

The meeting then closes. The ghostly figures instantly vanish into smoke. An awful stunned silence follows.

THE SPECTRES OF HEALTH POLICY TO COME...

Mr Taxpayer Ordinaryperson *advances to front stage.* Asks aloud, like *Hamlet* in his soliloquies:

"But was this all just a ghastly dream? A ghostly projection of my mind, due to a piece of Dickens's undigested cheese or fragment of underdone potato? A pickled onion running awry? A difficult and disturbed malevolent slice of beetroot? Avoidable if we change our ways? Or an awful premonition, a dire warning of things that might yet be?"

"Were this dreadful Millkiband figure and his gnomic gang a clutch of real creatures, real spirits in a dark valley, transported to me as a gesture of despair to come? Or a warning of Policies That Are Yet To Be? Like a shrivelled fingering tree, a threatening shape out of the black-forested *Grimm's Fairy Tales* themselves?

"It was certainly a strange, exotic, unnerving experience. But it was **surely** no more than a childish echo of something from a fairy tale, or my present mind merely playing obscure, gloomy, midnight tricks?"

Mr Taxpayer Ordinaryperson *starts to leave the tent, his legs trembling beneath him, STAGE RIGHT.*

But then a spectral supernatural skeletal figure, STAGE FAR LEFT, calls aloud that he must first wash his hands in hallowed water.

He is handed a small ivory bowl and a towel. He is then handed a tiny small printed booklet by a black shrouded and aged phantom figure, with bony hands in black gloves. "Take this. Treasure this. Read it most carefully", says the hooded monk at his elbow.

Mr. Taxpayer Ordinaryperson *takes the booklet. Pushes it quickly into his pocket. He then moves to front stage before the footlights, to make his closing speech:*

"Well, I awoke. Restored to consciousness. Sweating heavily. Terrified! Not sure if I was dead or alive! But what a relief! I found myself in my own safe bed at home. My own bedposts. My own pictures on my own walls. My own chair at the bed-side. My own books. My own family photos. My lovely wife next to me, asleep. The birds singing outside the window. Sunlight. Sweet fresh air. The fields full of wild, living flowers. So it *was* indeed all a dream. Just a bad moment in the night. An insomniac horror, lawless and demonic, the shadowy side of our daily existence. But swiftly cleared by the fresh-morning air. A dread future from which we can all *still* escape. A new awareness of the threats all about us...."

"*Alive! Safe! Awake!* These spectral, gliding ghosts, these demented phantoms, merely a Gothic fantasy of the early hours. Surely so, yes? And still life left in me to change it all!

"A dream. Ah! And now all gone! Still time to erase the Future that Has Not Yet Come. Still time for kind words, for kindnesses reciprocated, for more consideration for others, for a new life guided by different policies indeed! [*And for some Economics! – Ed.*]. Still time to erase a Pinched and Twisted Doomladen Future. To do so for ourselves, procuring real change. And in the living years.

"But then, still in my dressing-gown later that same morning, I put my hand into a side-pocket. And I was very surprised indeed to find a small crumpled booklet there. It wasn't there when I hung up my dressing gown last night. Definitely not.

"The booklet? Titled *The History of Dr. John Faustus, Showing How He Sold Himself To the Devil to Have Power To Do What He Pleased For Twenty-four years. Also Strange Things Done by Him and His Servant Mephistopheles. With An Account of How The Devil Came for Him....*"

*[*Mr. Taxpayer Ordinaryperson *holds up the little booklet. A large version is projected onto huge screens in the hall for all to see. It is printed in Gothic type and in red ink. Hollow laugh of Mr. Balth clearly resounds and re-echoes in the hall. CURTAINS!].*

Scene closes to music of *Tom Hark*, words sung aloud by nun chorus, "You have to laugh or you'd cry."

Lady S-S: But *will* the voters take the warnings? You know, self-deception is still rife. The NHS is still a comfort-blanket dramatisto which people cling, no matter the results. We see things as strange as anything in the *Arabian Tales*. And yet the cold light of truth is still unwelcome. People too often prefer the mummeries of the world.

Sir S-S: Well, Francis Bacon wrote in his *Novum Organum* "For what a man had rather were true he more readily believes."

That great intellect said many other wise things. "The end of morality is to procure the affections to obey reason."

But, as we consider the NHS, recall that he wrote in *The Advancement of Learning:* "As it is a principle in nature that the best things are in their corruption the worst, and the sweetest wine maketh the sourest vinegar."

Still, I'm an optimist, as you know. So let's keep in mind what he says in *The Rape of Lucrece*: "Time's glory is to…unmask falsehood and bring truth to light."

I'm now thinking about Scene 3 of *The Revels*. Going to be about the BMA's plans for new NHS fund-raising...will bring the house down!

EPISODE 10

On Doctor's Orders…The Practice of General Practice. Part 1.

Dramatis personae:

Dr. I.I. Addio. Trained in Edinburgh, he is a senior GP in Soccertone-on-The-Blink, Chemslfton, Essex. He spends his weekends mending old wheelbarrows and garden tools.

Dr. V.P. Rooney Porke. Trained in Mainchance-Mannheim, East Germany, he is now a GP in Paddle-on-Down, Essex. He is a member of the GP's renegotiating committee on the existing GP's contract. He spends his week-ends on a jet-ski as often as he can.

***

The problem of a re-negotiated GP's contract grips the nation.

Meanwhile, in the General Practice in Soccertone-on-The-Blink, Chemslfton, Essex Dr. I.I. Addio is on the telephone to Dr. V.P. Porke, a GP in Paddle-on-Down, Essex.

An unrepresentative discussion, no doubt…

Dr. A: Just got my copy of the new *Pulsate*. See that the front page story says you are on the new BMA Committee to renegotiate our contract. Chairman old "Jurassic" Johnson. So will be a crusty affair, won't it?

Dr. P: Well, I'm listening and I'm learning. And earning from it, too, in course. But most GPs – however they're organised in these new plastic outfits – seem just like us. Been enabled by the new contract to do less work for more money. And keen to hang on to that deal.

Dr. A: Right up our street, that!

Dr. P: Yes. I'm having none of the changes some people want. We're paid for what we do, and what we don't want to do either! I'm hanging on to the purse. And I'm not going to work my weekends either. How can they make me, eh AB?

Internal telephone rings: Switchboard, "Your 10.00 is here, sir."

"Thank you Jane. I'm in a meeting."

Dr. A: Well, we'll see what the talks offer us, won't we? Any real changes likely, d'you think, to the contract?

Dr. P: Well, very unlikely. Government too timid, as ever. And old "Jurassic" is proposing that one trade-off should be that the government allows us to do private practice, too.

Could then open at weekends for private patients. Earn some more. But they aren't likely to wear that. So, no go all round, seems to me.

Dr. A: Might open up half an hour later on Wednesdays, perhaps?

Dr. P: Maybe. Ha. *Might*. Might not. Not a swallow in my summer! How about you? Still doing all you can to reduce the work-load?

Dr. A: PV, you're going to hell! But, yes. And at the same time trying to protect our jabs-income. Best earner we've got. And the screening. All those government incentives. Lovely jubbly!

Dr. P: Yes. I'd say so. The patients need the jabs. You should see what I see on a Monday morning. You, too, I'm sure. Many more are drunk, more drugged, more addicted, more obese, chain-smokers, less interested, less responsible, less sympathetic. Much more demanding. Much less patient. Often aggressive, too, with internet stuff. Many of them long-term welfared up to the gills. Rude, insulting, some shocking language. Kids just as bad. With the nurses, too.

Dr. A: Well, old Squoffy says in his article in the *Health Service Jungle* that as there are no direct economic incentives for patients to take care of themselves, it won't change. That's at the root of it all, of course. Then there's the old and ageing, the warfarinised, the frail, the falling apart, the Altzheimer's and Parkinson's…bit late to incentivise them?

Dr. P: We get all that here, too. But leave out the frail for a moment. Just look at the rest. The supposedly young! Many of them with no idea of how to be a patient, let alone a parent. Kids who turn up here effing and blinding. Turn up at schools, Jenny says, at age 5 and don't even know their own name, or how to wipe their bottoms. At 15 can't or just won't read or write. Grow up – if that's the word – in families where no-one has worked. Or even tried to work – and for three generations.

You see their future in their already hardened faces, these unlucky bloody awful kids, when they are only a few years old. Ear-ringed. Crew-cutted. Tattooed. Illiterate. As likely unemployable forever. Will grow up, but won't have any skills. Oh, so help me! And then come in and tell us "You're the bloody doctor. You fix it!" And "Gimme me benefit chits!"

Dr. A: Yep. So help me, Monty! Not like that in the Far East, I'll bet? We'll end up making T-shirts cheap to sell to Asia!

Internal telephone rings: Switchboard, "Your 10.15 is here, sir."

*"Thank you Jane. I'm **in** a meeting!"*

Oh, meant to ask, have you decided against calling your new practice centre 'The Sharp Needle Centre' then?

Dr. P: Yes. Puts them off, even if we need the jabs-income. So calling it 'The Anti-biotics Centre' instead. Produces enough demand for us to earn well. 'Course, don't give them any anti-biotics. Just offer jabs instead. "Nice little earner."

Dr. P: Yes, but joking apart, you're quite right to restrict access to anti-biotics. Not just on cost, either. This loss of effectiveness of anti-biotics is really serious. I've just read the new book by Dame Sally Davies, Dr. Jonathan Grant and Professor Mike Catchpole. Bloody terrifying, actually. Penguin book, *The Drugs Don't Work*. Shows how we are fast losing the battles against bacteria. Grim prospect when antimicrobial drugs won't help us. We'll be back where we were decades ago. Go and get a copy. And give copies to all those hospital docs who don't wash their hands properly. As a general habit, as well as between handling patients on the wards!

Dr. A: To *all* of them who don't wash their hands? Will cost me a Lottery winnings!

Dr. P: Still, we're lucky. We can live a lot in our own private worlds. Good pensions, too. We've also slipped the ropes on the rules a bit. I've just got a new contract to provide well-man and well-women health checks and employee screens for BSDuyu Bank PLC, and that Dutch lot Netherthere PLC. Next stop will be special cover for accountants, lawyers, and the Good-e-veg greengrocery chain. Greg wants us to open up a private occupational health clinic in the City, too. Do it with the pharmacy chains. Should be a decent little earner.

Dr. A: Isn't that a bit offside?

Dr. P: No. I'm not interfering with play….

Dr. A: Well, as Bill Shankly used to say, what are you doing on the pitch, then?

Dr. P: Aha! Got me! But I don't think the politicians or the general public have any real understanding of what we have to put up with. The job, frankly, is a bore. I have nightmares every Sunday night about what's waiting for me on Monday morning. Drunks. Druggies. Hypochondriacs. Loonies. And *Art critics*! I could bash some of them with my bricka-scope. Can usually tell, too, who is to be HM's guest next in the High Courts. Most people declare themselves, inadvertently or openly. You can smell the killers!

Dr. A: Well, unless you're a social worker. Look at child abuse. The most evil parents can be the most plausible.

Dr. P: Yes. Right. Just look at this Coventry case. The social lot say that something "happened" to that unlucky little kid. Look at that poor kid. His bloody parents starved him to death. Bloody wicked! And it didn't "happen", as the "experts" say. It was *deliberately* done to the poor mite, the poor murdered kid!

Dr. P: Yes, and how's it possible for all those so-called "agencies" – including half-awake so-called under-paid school teachers – not to notice a starved kid who was rifling through dustbins at school for food, with broken bones and bruises all over him? Four years old, a stone and a half. Terrible.

Dr. A: The whole lot of them should be prosecuted, and given long jail sentences. And on short-rations, too.

Dr. A: Makes you think of all those sociology-nurses up at St. Hilda's. Too *busy* to notice patients! Or to give them a glass of water!

Dr. A: Yep. Really frightens me, too. This new rule about nurse numbers. Well, yes, want it. But if they're duff to start with?

Dr. P: I know. No-one wants to ask that, do they?

Still, I see you've moved into your new place. Progress? What's it like practising in an old windmill?

Dr. A: Yep. Any port in a storm. But it's a bit windy and a bit noisy. Like in that wonderful old Will Hay film *Oh Mr. Porter!* But a lot of them can't get up the stairs. So deters a lot of the expensive oldies. Helps the budget. Keep them on the paid-for-list, but don't see them. They just go off to A&E instead.

Internal telephone rings: Switchboard, "Your 10.25 is here, sir."

"Thank you Jane. I'm in a MEETING!"

Dr. P: Well, we're still doing our best to get the receptionists to deal with patients.

Dr. A: Not let them anywhere near you, you mean?

Dr. P: Put them onto the nurses, if we can. Sort out a lot of people we never need to see. Actually, probably better medicine!

Dr. A: 'Nuff said.

Got your new receptionists yet then?

Dr. P: Nope. Still interviewing. Hard job it's proving to be. Having to stay after 5 every night. Well, have hired one. Rumanian. Speaks hardly any English. Speaks very slowly. Hard of hearing, too. Sufficiently cantankerous, we think. Name of Roskovilliovichski Slobodono Bonomonodoggiovichiski.

Dr. A: Takes her a bit of time to spell her name to callers, then?

Dr. P: *The very idea!* Indeed! How can you say such things! You *are* the devil!

Dr. A: Only hired one so far, then?

Dr. P: Yep. A lot of replies to the advert, but all too nice. Too friendly. Too competent. Too quick on the uptake. Too eager to help. Just can't seem to find the kind of naturally nasty, sufficiently angry, appropriately rudely obstreperous and especially off-putting people we used to have and still need so much now. Indeed, more so than ever. But still looking. New advert in *Swop & Dregs*, local give-away Friday 'paper. Might produce a recidivist or two. Quite keen to give ex-prisoners a chance, you know. Can't all go to cut keys in the High Street, can they?

Dr. A: Here, we've put in the Premium 'phone lines, meanwhile. Earning us a bit already.

What's happening about the e-doc project you mentioned at the Bournemouth conference, by the way?

ON DOCTOR'S ORDERS…THE PRACTICE OF GENERAL PRACTICE. PART 1

Dr. P: Well, if at least half of our patients were seen by a computer instead of a GP, would help us a lot. Just like the public libraries. No books there now, just DVDs, CDs and computer terminals. Good model for us. Am waiting for the BMA sub-committee to report.

Dr. A: But what about the existing problem of DNA's, meanwhile? You're on that Royal College study group with old Petrified-Grey, aren't you?

Dr. P: Ah. One of my nurses had an old bloke who DNA'd 10 times! Now, if we could charge £25 for every visit to the practice, put a stop to it. Would, wouldn't it?

Dr. A: Well, might. But not sure how we could do the charging. Receptionists are already overwhelmed. Never a dull moment for them. 'Phone never stops. Might charge on credit card, or Paypal, I s'pose. Register those details when you first register a patient.

Dr. P: Would impact on all the unnecessary visits to us, surely? People would surely say to themselves "I'll just see how I get on with this sniffle." And then get well naturally? Anyway, told the nurse to double-book that DNA blighter, and if he ever turns up, just keep him sitting there a bit. That's what they do in out-patients up at Scargills.

Dr. A: Hmm. That would work, yes. My dentist's e-mails or texts to remind me of an appointment, couple of days in advance. We should do that.

On another hot topic, what are you doing about all this pressure to annually examine the 'well elderly'?

Dr. P: Eh? Not me, old chum. Different strokes…busy enough already.

Internal telephone rings: Switchboard, "Your 10.40 is here, sir."

"Thank you Jane. I'M IN A MEETING!!!"

Dr. A: D'you know, what, though, old chum?

Dr. P: No. What?

Dr. A: One of our nurses was heard in the loo yesterday, talking about doctors. Said that some of us aren't caring at all. Just in it for the money. Or because Daddy was a doctor. Or because our Grandfather was. That we just wanted the status, the power, and the cash. The networks and the contacts.

Dr. P:…and to meet Mrs. Weeknees!

Dr. A:…and that a lot of us didn't care about people at all. Technical and scientific at school, same at College, never read a novel, never been to a concert. Some with totally hopeless personalities.

Dr. P: Oh, reminds me of the tale of that bloke at the Brighton hospital who was said to think that Mozart was a German beer? Didn't some other bloke there also think that Ruskin's *Modern Painters* was a works manual?

Dr. A: Austrian, actually, the beer. And he was a manager, wasn't he? Don't know about the second bloke. Was he an NED? But very believable story, that.

Dr. P: Oh!! A Manager!! Sorry! Enough said!!

Dr. A: But that nurse! Good lord! No? You can't be serious? However did she get into your practice? Who hired her for gracious sakes?

Dr. A: That silly old sod, our previous practice manager, Patrick Ondafiddle. Him that should have been sectioned. Retired now, thank goodness. Nurse now gone, too. We discovered that she was only a summer locum. Back in Huddersfield now. Apparently a descendant of that Labour bloke Harold Wilson. The pipe-smoker. You know "The pound in your pocket…"

Dr. P: One of us, then, really, eh?

Dr. A: Aha!

Internal telephone rings: Switchboard, "Your 10.50 is here, sir."

*"Thank you Jane. I **AM IN A MEETING**!!!"*

Dr. A: S'pose you got the Royal College questionnaire this week on why you became a GP in the first place?

Dr. P: Yep. Usual stuff to tick boxes on how became a doc because you wanted to help people. But no room for saying came into it to make some good money. Can't see why not.

Well, my motives were a bit of a mix really, actually. Bit of both. But the money is lovely. And a lot nicer than the actual work! Even nicer these past few years with much more money for much less work! A lot nicer than many of our patients these days, too. Well, apart from that Mrs. Weeknees, that is!

Dr. A: Aha, the green-eyed sex monster again! You *will* go to hell!
Still some basic problems, though, aren't there? Almost all of our money is still earned from the taxpayer. All through the government. Got to explore all these new ways to make extras. Una Coates's ideas, and all that. Lot of good wheezes there!

Dr. P: Well, old "Jurassic" will have to trade something for these extra sessions. Got to do private work, in exchange for weekend consultations.

Dr. A: Weekend consultations? What *every* weekend?

Dr. P: Seems likely. I've seen a draft of what the government is proposing. We're being asked to staff casualty departments one day a week. Or a couple of sessions. Hunt says that in that way we can put our medical knowledge to use. And that if we spent time in casualty we'd soon realise what it's really like out there. Says we don't know because we shut our shop at weekends, diverting the accidents and the emergencies along with all the other crap – drunks, druggies, all that.

And that the nurses take the strain – some see 40 people a day. Seems to think we're an idle bunch.

Dr. A: Well, we're not going to want to know about all that, are we?

Dr. P: Well not me, that's for sure. And old J has already said to Hunt, show us the colour of your extra money and we *might* talk!

Dr. A: Good lad! *Might!* Usual delaying tactics, of course.

Internal telephone rings: Switchboard, "Your 11.00 is here, sir."

"Thank you Jane. I AM IN A MEETING!!!"

Dr. P: Yes. Last thing I want to do is to see the patients in A&E that I might have seen in General Practice. No bloody fear, thank you very much! Might be the decent people that George Eliot said all go to unmarked graves. But not for me. And definitely not when I could be on the yacht on Sundays.

Depressing stuff, all that, all the same. Not like that with that Mrs. Weeknees, though, eh?

Dr. A: Aha! *Mrs. du Maurier Weeknees!* Now, there's a… she was in here first thing this morning. Just a summer cold, actually. But crispy rustling white linen trouser-suit, lovely blonde hair, perfectly turned-out. Full make-up. Scarlet shoes, with silver buckles. Steel-tipped high heels. Terrific poise. Those curves, too. And *that* voice! Absolute class. Makes me tremble! When she's here I can't help but think about those Aubrey Beardsley drawings! Long consultation essential, of course. Will need an early recall. Only comfort of this job is that you *do* see a lot of attractive women. And sometimes you can have an interesting discussion with a middle-class patient who reads. Chap came in the other day with a new book on tree-pruning. We talked for ages. Only had a few waiting out there.

Dr. P: Well, it can't all be stress and troubles then, can it? But it's just awful when you have to tell someone the worst news. And how much sympathy and empathy have any of us really got inside us? It's not an endless store, is it? Just how many times can you say to a patient, "Oh, I'm so sorry, but it's a very difficult diagnosis. It's the big C." Wracks me, anyway.

Dr. A: Wish I could avoid offering a final diagnosis. Terrible business, giving out that news. Much better to refer on to a specialist. Then tut-tut at the reply. But in the end you've got to help people live with their condition, however awful it is.

Dr. P: At least the nurses are good at comfort, advice, sympathetic shoulders. Not all automata, though they're so often accused of being so. Best of the bunch, our nurses here. Wish we could keep them more than a few months at a time, though. Expensive, these locums.

Internal telephone rings: Switchboard, "Your 11.15 is here, sir."

"Thank you Jane. I am very busy. I am in my meeting. Send him through to Dr. Jackson,

the new locum, please. I'm over-booked."

[Alarm bell rings]. Oh! Sorry, Addie! Got to go! That's my wrist-alarm. Time for me to go to my AA meeting. Tootle-oo! Or should it be Oodles, too?!

As he leaves, the radio in his new scarlet Mercedes sports-car plays Bobby McFerrin, 'Don't Worry Be Happy.'

EPISODE 11

On Doctor's Orders….The Practice of General Practice. Part 2.

Dramatis personae:

Dr. Alexis Brooksnubbra. Trained in Austria, and at King's, London. Head of the urban general practice in Pubsvale, Chiselhurst-on-Wash, Suffolk.

Dr. Pedro Ventura. Trained in Portugal and in Belfast. Head of the rural general practice in St. Squids, Cornwall.

Sir Harry Verney, CBE, a retired GP. A Cornishman (born in Tremoutha Haven on the north coast) and the founder in 1960 of the now large general practice at Tinsdale Weir, Suffolk.

Mr. Augustus Melmotte-Jobber-Johnson, a 'political' doctor and long-term BMA activist. Widely known in the profession as "Jurassic" Johnson.

Episode plays in to the tune of Brian Adams, 'Everything I do, I do for you.'

Dr. AB: Hello, PV. Just wanted a few words about the negotiations on our contract….

Dr. PV: Hello AB. As it happens I'm just sitting here shooting the breeze on that very thing with Harry Verney. I'll put you on speaker.

Sir H: Hello Alex. Things good in Pubsvale? Moving up in the BMA, I hear!

Dr. AB: Harry. Grand, glad to say. We miss you a lot though. It's like *The West Wing* without Jed Bartlett and Leo McGarry! Not the same without you around. But, like you, we're very anxious about the renegotiation of our contract. So, not so grand, actually. Bit hellish, really. Must admit.

Sir H: PV, I'm glad of a plain word.

Two big things to discuss:

First, what are you doing about Obesity in your patients?

Second, what are you doing about the renegotiation of the contract?

So far as I can see, the answers are not obvious to most of us. But the first issue – Obesity – is the one that matters the most.

Alas, though, most GPs don't know much about economics, only about incomes! And that despite all the new super-structures and mysterious acronyms under which GP practices now hide!

But, PV, you are on the new GP Contract renegotiating committee, aren't you? With old "Jurassic" in the lead?

Dr. PV: Fact, fact, fact. Fun, fun, fun!

Sir Harry: So you've got a lot of serious responsibility. Just as we all have the responsibility to try to make this country a better place.

Dr. AB: And, as you always used to say, the same night awaits us all!

Sir Harry: So let's set out some guiding principles. Then bring together the various strands. It's about deciding what's right. You can't do it on auto-pilot. Thinking caps, please!

Dr. PV: Usual seminar then, Harry! Just like the old days!

Sir Harry: Yes. 'Fraid so. So I'll get my 7 poster-points up first!

- Don't waste a good crisis, as Winston said. Use it creatively, for fully integrated and continuing care.

- Don't try to solve the contract problems with cosmetic-changes.

- Go for real economic incentives as the basis of a new model of stability and resilience – pivoted on much better self-care by the individual.

- Get the demand-side sorted out, as well as the supply-side.

- Address the fault-lines that produced this staffing and coverage crisis. All – GPs and hospital docs to work a rota: five days or nights out of seven.

- Get maximum use of capacity; encourage the necessary traffic; control costs.

- Work from day-centres and places where the patient traffic is in their ordinary lives, and adopt all those electronic-contact ideas that Roy Lilley has proposed.

And act on the old Cornish motto, "A long pull, a strong pull, and a pull all together." Do that, and you'll nearly be there!

Dr. AB: So, Harry the key question...

Sir Harry: Is OBESITY! Costing the NHS £5billion a year, and a further £27 billion to the whole the economy, Sir Crank tells me.

And a lot of the most difficult challenges here arise from a big historical change. We family doctors used to have to deal with the consequences of poverty. Now it's the consequences of prosperity – and stupidity. Once there was not enough food. Now there's too much. Vast amounts. The wrong sort, too. It's turned all that we have to do on its head. Sugared and stupified, they are.

What to do about it? Direct economic incentives for life-style changes. Much better continuing care. And you can't do it if you are closed As far as patients are concerned at weekends your surgery is derelict. Yours is near the station, Pedro, isn't it? Might as well rename it 'Bewildering Junction' then.

On the issue of hours, rotas, evenings and weekends, that's actually the easy part. Can be fixed. We can negotiate it. The really challenging part is the *creativity* needed to give much better continuing care. And to restructure the whole NHS with proper, direct, individual economic incentives for patients to take responsible care of their own lives.

We desperately need reforming market liberalism. Economics. There's no other way to do that. We've got to get the balance right, of course, between the stultifying stagnation of monopoly controls and the adaptive creative dynamism of competitive growth. We've got to make clear, too, that much of what we see in the NHS has nothing to do with better care. It comes from the short-term tactics and strategies of the political parties.

It was Henry James who said that "to live over other people's lives is nothing unless we live over their perceptions, live over their growth, the varying intensity of the same – since it is by these they themselves lived." That's our challenge.

Dr. AB: Harry, you are an intellectual!

Sir Harry: Yah! And as to time and rotas, that's the easy bit. You just have to offer 5 days out of seven. Flexible rotas. Some of your time in A&E. The hospital docs have got to do 5 days out of 7, too. Rotas, the same. As to the daft idea that out-of-hours care can somehow be kept away from the core work of general practice is ludicrous. It must – and promptly – be returned to the core of GP practices, and to hospitals. Any other idea is just plain dopey. Whoever believes differently should be fed to the crocs!

Dr. AB: Wasn't that daft notion suggested by someone at that Richmond House meeting in August? You know, the one for which nhsManagers.net had the minutes? [*See nhsManagers.net, DoH meeting with SoS, 6 August 2013 – Ed.*].

Sir Harry: Well, talk about Brian Edward's "dark corners of the NHS"! Reading those minutes was hardly inspiring. If the idea not to enfold out-of-hours care into the core work was from Ben Dyson [NHS Head of Primary Care, England] or one of his side-kicks, they should be sat in the corner with the Dunce's Cap! Same if it was from Mike Dixon [Chair of the NHS Alliance]. Or one of the Royal College people.

Dr. PV: Be a very crowded corner!

Sir Harry: Yes! Would be. Who was it who was there? One was old Petrified-Grey? Once President of our own College. Now the Chair of that substitute for giving patients control over money – the so-called "National Patient Participation Group." All that *greater say* malarkey! Means poffletoft! No real levers joined to real wires. Pull – and poof! Well, I ask you! Most of them at the DoH seemed to have not the slightest clue about economics or incentives. No imagination. No creativity. No spark.

Dr. PV: Yes. Thought so, too. All captured within the failed assumptions of the existing system. My opinion, anyway. The lot of them, 'Clueless in Seattle' And *they* are advising the Sec. of State!

Sir Harry. Yes. Bit like walking in front of an oncoming roaring express train, waving a little red flag! Naïve. I don't get any sense that that supposedly "expert" committee realises how radical the necessary changes actually need to be.

And, anyway, where did we all get this curious language in the first place about "in" and "out" of hours?

Who decided what were "in" and what were "out" hours in the first place?

We've lived in a 24-hour society for ages. And who decides which are "in" and "out" hours for ambulances? And, tell me, too, when and how are we going to measure and judge our own, the GPs, performance? No progress there that I can see. This isn't a freight railway line. You can't just measure wagon-miles-per-engine-hour (or day).

Dr. AV: Well, they've started inspecting hospitals now. But not yet any of the new GP Collisioning Groups.

Sir Harry: Yes. Hospitals only. But my mate Dr. Bill Pickering....

Dr. AV: What, the bloke who wants unexpected inspections of everything in the NHS?

Sir Harry: Yes. That mate. Gets the palm for the clear mind. He has worked as a hospital doc, as a GP, and as an expert-witness. Good botanist, too. Knows his stuff. He's right. Sent me an e-mail about it. Let me bring it up on my laptop…yes…here it is:

"It's important that politicians don't confuse large 'inspections' of hospitals with accountability. It is one thing to go in en masse (as I heard on R4 whilst driving), guns blazing, widely reported, everyone thinking 'ah, this'll do the trick', when actually, it's largely a publicity stunt. You don't have inspections of large numbers of drivers. You have traffic police who stop you when you cross a red light, straight away, and points or fine. THAT is accountability. It's laughable that there is one chief inspector for UK. There needs to be one or two in every district (small beer really, when one considers how many employees in the NHS). One man in a police car. Also, note this 'Inspector' doesn't address GPs at all. Why? Because in its present form this Inspectorate can't. This takes some thought, and they've refused to countenance that!"

Dr. AV: Spot on, of course. The current new approach is just another cosmetic Christmas Charade! They must believe in Father Christmas!

Sir Harry: These aren't side issues. They're the determining factors for general practice now. But indelibly, mark my words, the umbrella of a new contract won't be enough. You need a great, new, all-enveloping structure, a proper and earth-bound new building. Needs to be named Self-Responsibility House. So don't botch the design.

It's a fight over the question itself. It's about who will serve the public best, and how. It's about which structures will deliver good continuing care best. And it's about economic incentives to prompt the individual not to eat and drink themselves stupid – the problems of junk food, drink, drugs, couch-potatoes, all that.

Your key daily job is diagnosis, referral, and then continuing care. And a lot of the latter. You are well trained, and that took a lot of work and devotion. So you are entitled to earn properly. But it's not all about money. Your aims and approach must be ethical, not financial. And economic – which isn't just about your own incomes – as I keep saying. GP is the word: Get Practical!

It's about how you and the government together can focus a very direct impact on the towering tsunami that's going to overwhelm them and you. These issues of the lack of self-responsibility. Far, far too many patients have abandoned self-responsibility. Obesity, diabetes, cancers, you know. So much of it avoidable illness. But it's going to swamp us all. We need to build an acute new individual awareness and positive emotions. I know it won't be easy. You are working with human behaviour. But economics does bite, you know. And not much else does.

This is not, actually, really a political problem at all. It's an economic problem. You've only made it political with that loopy new contract you all signed in 2004. It's fundamentally an economic issue. How to use direct incentives to improve our own practices, as well as the behaviour and the life-styles of patients. Fundamentally, you can't coordinate anything properly without price signals! If this is the only point I get across before I die, that's it!

Dr. AB: Well, Harry, makes me wonder...

Sir Harry: Not yet, AB. Not just yet.

We've got to use economics and incentives very directly. Only thing many really get. So, price, tax, excess on premiums in an insurance model. Can see no other way, myself. So, price and vouchers. People need economic incentives to look after themselves. So use tax-based individual healthcare funds with regular MOT's for everyone. Premiums go up if you take no notice of MOT advice from your doc. And we can put in relevant and persuasive incentives: hit your agreed targets (less tobacco; alcohol intake reduced; exercise) and you get a season ticket to your exercise club – or even your football club. A lot cheaper than the huge cost per person per year for 20 years because of diabetes.

Dr PV: An individual patient MOT twice a year? Annually? Bi-annually? We'd need to think about the impact that work would have on us. But I agree that printing leaflets doesn't do it. Doesn't increase self-responsibility. Advisory websites galore don't do it. Hectoring doesn't do it. It's to economics, incentives and price that we must all turn now. You're right.

Dr. AB: Well, makes me wonder what percentage of our list we do see even once a year? Seem to see a few people a lot. But a lot never come near us. Or only come when it's too late...

Sir Harry: Well, we *ought* to be in contact with our list. And if they had to have an MOT that would do it. This is the time for creativity in general practice, too. So we can try to guide it. It's one with enormous new potentials.

But people have got to start paying properly for it. Taxes alone can't do it anymore. Have to have top-ups, like a single charge for seeing a GP. £25 a time is about right. Do it in France. And tourists pay it. Then people need a tax-based, individual healthcare fund. And that can be the pivot to provide economic incentives to live better lives. They can use savings or pay out of current cash for extras. But the basic will be universally covered.

If you stay in the existing box, you can't win. And nor can government. So get together on all this, come on! You all need shock therapy – doctors, ministers, and patients.

Dr. AV: I'm signed on, Harry!

Sir Harry: Let me also make two other absolutely fundamental points on this contract negotiation. First, that any campaign you mount has got to be based in your value system, and your work culture. You are here for the patients. Not just for the money.

Second, context is critical. Everything has a history. First thing any of us do with a patient is to take a history. Context is all, for the patient, for the GP, and for this big debate too. We all know that the GP's relationship with and knowledge of the patient can and does make all the difference. But it's a shattered mirror right now! So what's your bumper-sticker? Surely not "We want the money, but not the work!"

Surely, be tough in the talks with Hunt. Be authentic. But be on the side of the consumer. And win back local respect. This is where your momentum must come from. And, by the by, Hunt is on the side of the consumer, too. Just watch Hunt. He comes on quietly. But he's a major figure. A real heavyweight. A Cameron protégé. But when Cameron is gone Hunt will still be there, one of the three or four big players. Gove, Osborne, Hunt, perhaps Hammond, IDS, and Haig. Gove number one. Energetic, engaged, transforming education already. Practical, tackled Education department heads-on, ignored obfuscating Sir Crank's and the dithering Tories too. Real Tories just can't wait for him to be in No.10. And without Real Toryism they have no hope of bringing back the Farage vote into their camp. Barmy conferences or not.

Dr. PV: Don't know what you're drinking Harry. But it must be powerful stuff!

Sir Harry: Well it's the booze of experience talking. I'm not some junior Ministerial special adviser hack who has never had a proper job. I've been in medicine since before you were born. And in medical politics as far back as John Moore and Ken Clarke.

So let me try your patience with two other big points.

First, you now need real national leadership. You need someone who is a natural communicator. A connector who can interpret the profession's views to the public, and take the fullest account of the public's views. Be persuasive to Ministers and the civil servants, too. An exceptional person.

But there's no sign, alas, of anyone like that at the BMA. Or in the Colleges. Produces too many old-gang medical-political-careerists. Not leaders. And they can't win this one for you by fighting a fierce battle in defence of GP's privileges. You don't have public sympathy and support. And it's obvious to all that a special-interest that tries to manipulate government will lose. This time, anyway. The old Bevan solution of them deciding how much money there is and you spending it as you like, that's gone for a Burton.

Dr. AB: Oh, oh….make mine a Large Martini!

Dr. PV: VERY large, please!

Sir Harry: Now don't die on me, AB. Give him an 'Aspro', Pedro!

Second, my other big point. If you don't come forward with solutions then they'll be *imposed* on the profession.

The worst possible solution is to have changes imposed on us. Because that will leave all the credit with the government, all the credit for the adoption of improved practices to our critics. It will be clear that the initiatives came from Ministers. And that you had no choice but to comply. Then your case will go by default. Do you want to be defeated in plain sight? As a solid, sinister selfish phalanx, and losers too? Good job *Punch* is no longer published is all I can say!

Dr. PV: Oh, Sir Harry. Hurts! What's *in* that coffee?

Sir Harry: I ask you both. How does the BMA and the Royal College approach differ from corporate lobbying?

You all signed that barmy new contract. But why didn't you see all this coming? You've let yourselves down, all of you. Recklessly. And you've let down the patients. Badly. And you've thrown away all that goodwill, community respect, family affection.

As to the BMA, it does medieval princely-drama admirably. All that theatrical make-up and tears. But remember, in those old Tudor plays the stage was always littered with dead bodies at the end. And Hunt has the power to impose any changes he wants. He's not an aged dug-out. Coming man. No good behaving with him with off-handed arrogance, like some DGH managers I remember from the 1990s.

Dr. PV: Like that Stewed ["I will not resign!"] Bludgeon bloke?

Sir Harry: Yes. Quite. Hunt would prefer to have you on board more willingly, I'm sure. He's got public opinion on his side. So watch yourselves.

Remember, too, that your constituents aren't in that room at the BMA. They are sitting out there in your waiting-rooms. The public has had it with an approach of you openly being determined to secure your own ends, whatever inconvenience that might cause to them. Especially in a situation where there is no competition.

Real solutions demand imagination, as well as sincerity. And we all know that the market is a much better problem solver than government or special interests, including our own. So we need to be really radical and support real change. Economics. Incentives. Price. After all, if it's quite OK for us to sell our services to government – and to private patients, when no-one's looking – why not directly to patients holding taxed-based state-funds individually?

You have to say "Yes" to these things. Old Squoffy is right. Let's have these mutual, co-operative, member-owned Patient Guaranteed Care Associations to buy the services, too. Including GP services. We can run that set-up, you know. The competition between different PGCAs would do us all good too. The patient's would have their cash-fund. And that would be mobile. So these PGCA's would compete for support. Much more democratic. Much more in the tradition of self-responsibility and self-help and local mutuality. And, by the by, a much more likely model for linking how people live their lives to their health outcomes.

Dr. AB: So you really think that we can run these local organisations?

Sri Harry: Yes. Who else could do it? See who makes it all a much better service then. See the chance to have much more time in which to see patients. Have more empathy. Time for real follow-ups. Stop running the thing just as a machine for handling parcels and receiving money.

Dr. PV: Have to be easy for patients to move, of course. So the individual health savings accounts would have to be mobile? Could move every other year? Promised by statute? Have to be real differences between the PGCA's, too. So that it would make sense to choose one or the other. Some specialised in elderly care. Some specialised in young family care. You know...

Sir Harry: Yes. Quite right. But not unneighbourly relations, although there'd have to be some similar competing PGCAs, too, otherwise there'd be no real choice. So no 'non-aggression agreements' on the QT in the golf club!

One other thing. If there were these health care savings accounts for individuals – tax-based, of course, as you say! – there could also be mobile, digital, record cards. They could carry them with their credit cards or their Tesco Club card. Be very valuable if they were picked up by an ambulance, or went to A&E themselves. Or were ill on holiday. Just scan the data. Stop the scandal of people in A&E with no notes, no history. No way to tell us their ailments or allergies otherwise.

Dr. PV: Hmm. And if the ambulance had a scanner, they could send the data on to the hospital, and take the patient to the most appropriate facility, too.

Sir Harry: Patients should own their own records, their own data, anyway.

Dr. PV: Ah, yes. But would stop old Simpkins and his codes, wouldn't? You know, writes in the notes "FLK", funny looking kids; "FLP", funny looking parents?

Sir Harry: Yes. But if they saw that he'd just make up a Latin expression to cover it!

A few last words. I know you've just added a handsome conservatory to your house. Well, go and read Sir Henry Wotton's 1624 book, *The Elements of Architecture*.

He says:

"The end is to build well.

Well building hath three conditions,

Commoditie, Firmenes, and Delight".

Which, by the by, is no more than an echo of his master, Vitruvius. Commodity, or your service. Firmness, or your commitment. Delight, or your outcomes.

Want it in Latin? *Haec autem ita fieri debent, ut habeatur ratio firmitatis, utilitatis, venustatis.*

Dr. PV: Sorry, Harry, we'll have to break off. I've got a patient to see. But back in a bit. Soon. Have to take a break…

Sir Harry: Fine. But when you get back we must talk about how important FAITH was, the old belief in what we could do for patients. What the ancients meant, when they thought about the idea of awe and holiness and timelessness and healing through believing. And what's been lost there…all down to that contract, and to the shift from deference to "me, me, me"….

[To be continued….].

EPISODE 12

On Doctor's Orders….The Practice of General Practice. Part 3.

Dramatis personae:

Dr. Alexis Brooksnubbra. Head of the urban general practice in Pubsvale, Chiselhurst-on-Wash, Suffolk.

Dr. Pedro Ventura. Head of the rural general practice in St. Squids, Cornwall.

Sir Harry Verney CBE, a retired GP, the founder in 1960 of the now large general practice at Tinsdale Weir, Suffolk.

Mr. Augustus Melmotte-Jobber-Johnson, a 'political' doctor and long-term BMA activist. Widely known in the profession as "Jurassic" Johnson. A leader of current GP contract negotiations.

***

Sir Harry: Seen that patient, Pedro? All done? Good. Let's get back to this contract business then. I can't stay here all day!

Dr. PV: Well, going back a bit to your big points. As they say on the BBC: "So what you are saying is…." that everything has a context. And we need to rewind the film, with that in mind? Be creative. Find new ways to work. Deliver a much better, personal, 7-day service. All of you – GPs and hospital docs – to do proper five days and nights out of seven. Tackle patient Obesity as a priority. Give all our support to direct economic incentives to encourage self-responsibility in patients. 'Course, with 30% more doctor time, have to find ways to pay for it. So if taxes can't do it…

Sir H: Got me, PV! Take another sip! Need to talk all the funding ideas through, and honestly, with the public. AND tackle obesity with direct economic incentives…

The key – we all know it! – is to eat well, live healthy lifestyle. Take in 600kcal a day than most people are used to. Weight loss. And exercise. But losing weight takes HEFFORT, commitment and encouragement. So, economic incentives!

Patients need to recover faith in us, too. The healing-faith that people had in Dr. Finlay in the old days. *Dr. Finlay's Case book*, family doctor, and Dr. Cruickshank, I'd go back to that like a shot. Look at the difference it makes when the patients know you, and you know them. Know their full history. Know their full family history. When there is mutual trust and respect.

Many of my patients had a GP, like me, who delivered them into this world. Who knew their childhood illnesses. Saw them through, to the delivery of their own family. Many I'd know all their lives. Quite literally. Knew their history. Had effectively lived with them. Knew whether the Father was a drunk. Knew the cancer that killed their Mother. Or whatever. Much more easily diagnosed them. Spotted problems quickly. Referred them swiftly and effectively to specialist care. Now they look on the internet, instead of a chat with a GP. And a lot never see the same doc twice.

Not like my time now, is it? Some practices are very very good. Some GPs quite outstanding. Could name dozens. Just look at Jerry Comfort over at Cockleton. Absolutely outstanding. His patients ask to see him and they see him, not some locum. Knows his people. There for them.

Dr. AB: Yes. That's so. But Jerry's is a tiny practice. Little rural shop.

Sir H: Principle still applies. Up to us all to organise ourselves that way. Even with 10,000 on our list, like this fast-growing urban practice you've got here. Get some more women partners in, too, while you are at it. Just look at us talking. Three chaps. Where is Dr. Simpson? Seeing patients! Mary is overwhelmed. Only female doc in the practice. Can't spare the time to talk with us. So you should re-organise for her, and others like her, to work full or part-time. And there are a lot of overseas people here now, too. Cultural barriers there. Many don't even register with a GP. Somalis and so on. What to do about that?

As for the contract, sort out your negotiating platform. And get rid of old "Jurassic." Lead the majority. You are the skilled minority.

Try to put back what has always been vital. Faith. And it's impact on healing.

What have we got instead? Now they look up information on the internet. Don't believe what we tell them. Suspicious. Untrusting. Faith in us worked wonders once. When we gave advice, they believed. That in itself cured many of them. Now that's gone. Hunt's right to say that our links with patients have been "fatally undermined" by the 2004 contract deal. And the absence of "after-hours" appointments.

That's a big part of why they turn up in A&E instead. Not rocket science, is it? 'Specially when we're closed at weekends. Out-of-hours care will have to come back. Laurie [Dr. Laurence Buckman, Chairman of the BMA's GP Committee] can yell blue murder all he likes about more funding. Will need more people, of course, to get proper cover. But he's got to face the truth. The BMA was just spouting rubbish itself, accusing Hunt of "talking rubbish"! Made no sense at all. More than a million more a year attend A&E than three years ago. Rising population, true. But a lot of those should have been seen by you, shouldn't they? No escaping it, is there? And if there is to be more home care for acute cases and much better continuing care, who is going to provide it? You know who! And we've seen that Hunt now wants every older patient to have a named GP responsible for their health. More home care, for you and community staffs to provide.

Dr. AB: Yes. I can see all that is inevitable. What we should be doing, all along. When I read the stuff by Buckman I thought that the BMA needed a nappy changed!

Sir Harry: Mm. Yes. So, boys, it will be a big job now to shift your stance. But you've got to re-align, got to line up with public opinion, got to try to get back to Dr. Finlay. And to faith, too. That A.J. Cronin knew his stuff. Then you can put the NHS back where it ought to be. The critical factors. Real and very flexible care in the community. Preventive care. Tackle obesity, good diagnosis, specialist care referral, and much better mental health care. And the rest. But at the moment all your arguments are below the fold.

Dr. AB: So, Harry, re-pivot everything on our work?

Sir H: Well, isn't it still the case that 80% of every care intervention happens in a general practice? So, why ever not? If you all go on refusing to re-negotiate the contract you'll find that it's a bigger blood sport than that. You and the government. *Not* what I'd recommend.

As for me, well I got the K. Long-service gong. But I grew up in that caravan in Cornwall and then on Canvey Island. And I've still got my roots. I just know that Joe Public is not going to stand for the collapse of A&E and the withdrawal of GP services. There'll be a revolution in December.

The key is to get back to mutual respect. You'll only do that if you actually open up and provide the services at the time that people want them. And if you negotiate along my lines, rather than chuck a hand grenade round the Minister's door. He's clearly seen by the voters as on the side of the working poor, and on the side of the hard-working, self-respecting, independent Brit too. Taxpayer Man, not Top Doc Man. So you've all lost that one.

The media have rumbled, too. They've seen that GPs (just like hospital docs) are an interest-group, jockeying for their own interests, not for patients. And the hospital consultants. They're worse than you!

There must be many other unexpected consequences still to come. Next thing is they'll end your private contractor status. Then where will you be? You can only earn a crust by doctoring. Can't see you driving a crane-lift in a wood-yard, PV, or flipping burgers! They might make many more conditions tied to the government paying for doctor training too. So even threatening to go abroad and leave the NHS might require a special visa, and paying-off a big training debt. Six figures. They might well also give existing private practice a bashing, with the hospital docs in that firing line. So, some crucial renewal of battles supported by The Auld Enemy! Want *them* on your side, do you? Me? I'd find another trench!

Dr. PV: Do any of that and there'll be no applicants for medical schools at all.

Sir H: That's not what you want, is it?

No? Well, in my view you need a Lincoln to lead you, not a failed Confederate General.

Dr. AB: Actually, Harry, on this money thing, we GPs are innocents in the nursery. Compared with the hospital docs, anyway. Look at this *Sunday Times* report. Senior hospitals doctors claiming more than £150,000 a year in overtime. Potential annual earnings of £300,000 or more. Triple-time hourly rates! One doc at the Lancashire Teaching Hospitals NHS Foundation Trust got £167,750 in overtime in 2011-12 alone. The best rewarded consultants can get an extra £250,000 on top of the max basic of

£101,451. And a clinical excellence award of more than £75k. We GPs are just tadpoles in the pond. We've hardly even grown legs!

Dr. PV: And the consultants are just swimming in bank-notes!

Dr. AB: You can quite see then why the consultants ganged up in secret and got rid of that radical Chairman bloke at Brighton, in 1994 was it? He was said to be trying to get their salaries linked to performance, and to clinical outcomes. To really get control of them. No wonder they knifed him.

Sir Harry: Years ahead of time, he was. But on a tough beat then.

Dr. AV: And what did that John Major and Mrs. Bottomley do then? Remind me....

Sir Harry: Hid in the bushes. Eyes wide shut. Gave no support for local change. Poked the fire to start with, and then doused it with water. The consultants ran the whole show.

John Major should have said that "We, Ministers, appoint Chairmen, not the docs." Those changes were needed. AND Even now, we're struggling with it all, with a hardly changed culture. If they'd tackled the doctors then, we'd have had managers in charge, not doctors.

Barefaced they were. BMA led from London. All that helped to build up to where we've all landed up now, of course. Did another Chairman at Derby, too, didn't they? But, go on to 2003. The new consultant contract then was even more damaging than your own. Labour just bought the consultants off, didn't they? Great deal for them. Very weak deal indeed for the taxpayer.

Dr. AB: And let them go home on Friday nights, too, for a happy long weekend, too! Consultants, that is.

Dr. PV: Quick enough to come back for the overtime, though, eh? "On call", of course.

Dr. AB: Yes, well, maybe. Just like old Mr. Stephen Sweetnerz, the cardiologist at Scargill's – "on call" on his mobile 'phone in Paris!

Sir Harry: Well, that lot are the most arrogant of the lot, aren't they? Earn huge private incomes. Some more than £750,000 privately. And that's a big under-estimate! Anyway, Hunt will just have to insist that he gets proper consultant cover at weekends. And soon, too – winter is already in the hall. Seven-day working critical.

But...always a 'but'...we're talking about non-emergency work, as well as 'on call' work. For that you need a proper deal. And you need more people. If you want that kind of cover. There, at least, Buckman is right. Hunt will end up fixing a maximum payment for any extra work. And changing the contract to ensure non-emergency cover at weekends. Proper staffing levels.

Dr. PV: Yes. But – a 'but' of my own! – Paul [Dr. Paul Flynn, Chairman of the BMA Consultants' Committee] can wriggle all he wants. As elegantly as he likes. Go off like fizz-pop as often as he wants. But he can't set aside the real situation that the lack of staff is causing. Nor discount the death rate rise at weekends. What was it, a 20% rise in 2011-12 at weekends in hospitals?

Dr. AB: Well, Bruce [Professor Sir Bruce Keogh, NHS England Medical Director] says he'll fix it.

Sir Harry: Let's wait and see. Does he really carry the guns? And I really wonder whether NHS Employers can get the changes that we all need.

Dr. AB: If I was the PM I'd be rid of this ridiculous cluster of extra NHS central bodies. Have just one boss.

Dr. PV: Not that Sir Crank, either.

Sir Harry: No. Not him. No. Let's hope that Hunt just makes the changes. Throws down the gauntlet. Let the hospital docs challenge him if they want. The public will be on his side. And, boys, please *do* learn the lesson yourselves from all this disgraceful consultants' money-grubbing. Get to the job again yourselves with creative changes to your own services. Away from the "case" put by the BMA, that is. Or, as Dickens would have called it, that "confused phantasmagoria."

I know I sound like Father Noah out of The Ark. But I'm not just mumbling old stories. So fix your responsibilities in real values. Deal in ordinary things, not the lurid and the wild. And observe what's happening to the patients too. It's a sacred trust, a legacy, a responsibility to the nation. Don't give yourselves a shabby legacy instead.

So…go and tell "Jurassic" to make a positive offer to Hunt. *Take some initiatives.* You'll have to agree to help staff casualty departments one day a week. Even a couple of sessions. And you'll have to do much more in the wider community. But you do want to do work that helps people, don't you? 'Course you do. That's why we came into this to start with. Me, anyway. Zillions of years ago now, I know.

Dr. AB: So it's not about giving away the store then, is it? Use the new contract conversations as a new opening, as a new opportunity? By all means focus on money? But use it as leverage, as the power to open up a more individual, more personalised, more market-based system? Well, they'll have to pay us for it. More, too. I'm not giving up what I've got now, either. Can't afford to do so. Not with Simon at Winchester, and Gillian at St. Paul's.

Sir H: Well, you've got to try to use these negotiations as a genuine opportunity for gains all round. Mutual. You should be the entrepreneurs. Creating new services. Being creative in the market. And remember that Matt Santos speech in the *West Wing* when he got the Democratic Presidential nomination? He reminded us all that we – none of us – have lived perfect lives. We're all flawed.

We're all broken in one way or another. Remember, too, that there is no single truth. There are many necessary perspectives.

And that it is cultures which shape who we are, too. There we can do a lot more to set the terms of engagement. It's cultures which form how we give service. And how we respond to calls for help, how we structure what we do, and why. We have got to do more to influence all this. Economics. Your new contract can set an entirely new tone, a new culture, a new direction. Don't waste it!

Dr. PV: We don't want the US system…

Sir Harry: On, not that old chestnut again!

It won't be that. And you both know that it won't. We'll guarantee universal coverage, through the tax system. And the poor will do better, too. They'll have guaranteed tax-transfers into a personal fund. Guaranteed voluntary membership into a local PGCA. And if they stop stuffing with junk food – conscientiously carried off in plastic bags costing them 5p! – They'll be much better off.

Every patient is different, of course. People *are* all different. No way to get away from that. The PGCA they choose would be voluntary. Let them choose their purchaser and see what happens. We've just got to cope somehow. *We're individuals, too, of course.* We both deserve respect, us *and* the patients. And we both should have to *earn* IT! And none of us can get to the right answers unless we ask the right questions first. Still, I was ever an optimist…and I've still got some of my hair left! Well, just a bit! Still, I've got to go. But on the way here on the bus I was reading some poetry. Here are a couple of final thoughts for you both to mull over:

First, Wordsworth. *Sonnet on Steamboats, Viaducts, and Railways.* The last six lines:

"In spite of all that beauty may disown
In your harsh features, Nature doth embrace
Her lawful offspring in Man's art; and Time,
Pleased with your triumphs o'er his brother Space,
Accepts from your bold hands the proffered crown
Of hope, and smiles on you with cheer sublime".

Or, if you'd prefer Tennyson, from *Locksley Hall*:

"Let the great world spin for ever down the ringing grooves of change".

And:

"As we surpass our father's skill,
Our sons will shame our own;
A thousand things are hidden still
And not a hundred known…."

Bye, boys! **Make me proud!**

EPISODE 13

Obesity-Class in the NHS. The National Anti-Obesity Campaign...Part 1.

Dramatis Personae:

Mr. Barney Wells BEM, Chief Executive of The Arthur Scargill Memorial NHS Trust Hospital, Chessingfield-on-Soke.

Kevin O'Grady, Chief Executive of the Coleraine St. Fortescue Veterinary Hospital, N. Ireland.

Sir Cyril Squoffington-Squogg, OBE, JP, is Chief Executive of The Tower of London NHS Hospital Trust, Tower Hamlets, London, EC.

Various business-people and some of the usual NHS suspects on the new National Action on Obesity Advisory Group, including Lord J.C.B. Digger, Lord Carpetking, Lord Fogelstumped, Lord Betwell, and Sir Jeff Goodglesnetspacer. MPs are represented by Ms. Ali Walolah MP, head of the Tory-Women-To-Be-MPs group. And some hard-nut Bradford ex-textiles men and women and some actual surviving Brummy metal-basher and building entrepreneurs, including the hod-carrier who built the enormous housebuilder, RunEmUpandRun PLC, Sir Vinnie Earns.

Also: Sir Snuffle Kettledrum CBE, President, Woyal College of Surgeons; Dr. Sydney Avogotta-Nohidea CBE, President, Woyal College of GPs; Mr. Spanner Unworksit OBE, Chair, Woyal NHS Alliancers; Mr. Augustus-Melmotte-Jobber-["Jurassic"]-Johnson, formerly President of the Woyal BMA; Nursie Nursie Dixbungler, Chief Executive, Great British Whitewash Company PLC, and Jessica Pottlegun-Wedgwood-Benn-Tyza CBE, Chair, Socialist Medical Congress.

And: Sir Harry Verney, the retired GP; Dr. Angela Findlater, GP in Halstead Hill, Durham; Jim McCeltic, C/E of Hull-on-the-Wye Health Authority; Jeff Neville, C/E of East Harley NHS Trust. And the nutritionist Polly-Esther Harty. And Sir Cyril Squoffington-Squogg, C/E of The Tower of London NHS Hospital Trust, Tower Hamlets.

Also added late: Professor A. Hampster and Professor J. Applecore, of The Klingfilm Fund, London.

Apology for absence: Lord Alascooke of Smugdominion.

Kev: Morning Barney. Oi, what's that great music I can hear in your office?

Barney: Johnny Restivo. Old 50's rocker. *The Shape I'm In*. Great rockabilly. That track's as good as Elvis. I'm still an Elvis fan, 'course.

Kev: *Isn't every one?*

Barney: Yep. None of that Crustacean Richards 100th LP *Send-Grannie-to-By-Byes* junk here.

Kev: Congratulations! Anyway, I've got some totally amazing news of my own, about this huge new National Anti-Obesity project. The National Anti-Obesity Campaign. It's got a posh motto, too. From Francis Bacon. "His own health ought to be the first study of every man." From his *Natural History*, apparently.

Kev: Got that from Old Humpy, I bet. Now what's all this about? Got the details yet?

Barney: Yep. Well, some of them at least. RUMOUR is that the NHS is to be divided into 4 classes! First (for docs), Business (for the middle-classes), Coach or Economy (for the working-classes). And the OBESITE Class (for the fatties). New class of citizenship. Leastways, as regards access to services.

No one wants to admit it, but actually the real NHS is already effectively divided up into 4 classes.

Kev: Recognises realities, then? Just like the two Ronnies and John Cleese…I look down on him…I look up to him…I have a stiff neck…!

Barney: Yes. First Class especially – or where the docs know where and to whom they'd send their daughters!

Kev: But won't tell us….Or won't send their daughters at weekends!

Barney: The SofS's Advisory Group is still sitting in secret, apparently. Still very hush-hush. So all this is 'tween you and me only. Got it from Jessie Tompkins at the DoH. She's the Minutes Secretary to the Advisory Group. Very old chum of mine, as you know. And is usually very reliable. Government's going to tackle THE OBESITES. S'what they are now to be called in *every* reference from now on. Tackled head on. Being pressed hard on it by JH, and by his new whipper-snapper….

Kev: Whippet snapper!

Barney: Yes. That Jane Ellison, the northern lass. Says that Fat *is* a Political and an Economic Issue.

Kev: Shades of that Susie Orbach, then? Ellison has just taken over on public health from the delicious Anna Soubry, hasn't she?

Barney: Aha! Yes. *Will miss her.* Dee-dee-dee-light-full!

Anyway, the key new policy is all economic. Direct economic incentives. Health Savings Accounts, and insurance, and co-payments. Everyone is to be seriously encouraged to do something about their life-style, diet, weight, exercise, all that. Or else. Those with unacceptable BMI to be given some real economic and social incentives. Get a proper biffing, actually.

Kev: Shape up, quite literally then?

Barney: Yes. And, as we know, the emphasis has got to be on exercise as much as on diet. So we've got to do much more on getting them into health clubs, and then that they actually attend regularly. Follow an agreed programme…

Kev: Well, they'll have to come up with real and imaginative incentives. Use tax, direct them via their benefits, even cut them off from priority care if they ignore the advice? Tricky Nanny-State stuff. Moral as well as practical issues.

Barney: Yep. But we've got to follow the methods, haven't we, which circumstances force upon us?

Anyway, the word is that everyone is to have a Health Savings Account for starters. Tax-based. To be personally managed. Everyone then to join a mutual purchasing outfit – calling them Patient Guaranteed Care Associations. Everyone to top-up with compulsory private insurance and catastrophe-insurance, too. So, much more cash in the NHS, and in social care too. And with how you live directly connected to visible costs. With incentives to save as much as possible, to live much more healthily. And then the savings can in part be carried into individual elderly care funds too.

Kev: Saved? Nicely ambiguous! Magic gong, eh?

Barney: Well not use up the HSA foolishly. Be less demanding. Be much more responsible in how you live, and the calls you make on the healthcare system. Be aware of costs, charged to your account.

Kev: Like in Singapore? Like the proposals from Professor Philip Booth at the IEA [Institute of Economic Affairs]?

Barney: Yep. Best approach I know about anyway. And if we don't adopt it, then, in my opinion, it's all U.P. with the NHS.

Kev: Can I read it up in detail, the Health Savings Account?

Barney: Yes. Read Booth's stuff. And see that book by Spiers, *Who Decides Who Decides?* Just saw in *The Times* letters, too, that Dr. Mike Dixon [Chairman, NHS Alliance; President, NHS Clinical Commissioners] stressed that co-payment "should not be a taboo subject." Look at the sucesses in Australia, too. Miles shead of us.

But I saw that the Twerpy-Twins, Prof. Martin McKee and that Lord Winston, objected.

Kev: Yep. Dixon wants to sustain equal access where medical intervention can make a significant difference. And that takes money. Which the NHS won't have if we just rely on taxes. Saw that. But what happens with HSAs if you are terrifically demanding, and the money runs out?

Barney: Well, quite an incentive to demand sensibly, is that! If individuals managed properly the money would not run out. Works well in Singapore. Lot of lessons for us there – if only we'd look. Alan Milburn started to do so. But silence reigns with the Tories. There will be cover for catastrophic care, of course. State-funded. But for more ordinary care, it's up to you to manage your fund, your demands, and how you live.

Kev: *Quite* an incentive then, if the money *will* run out! Maybe the Tories should switch Milburn onto this now. Seems quite a work-horse. Brilliant report on social mobility. Keen on meritocracy, too.

Barney: Yes, should do that. Alongside the HSA you would also be required to insure privately for other cover.

Kev: … and not rely on *Taxpayers Ahoy!*

But I just saw in *The Times* that it's to be the end of bike sheds in schools [*The Times*, Letters, October 21, 2013]. So where will free-market Tories who want serious economic incentives, Health Savings Accounts, the encouragement for private insurance and cash top-ups in the NHS now be shot?

Barney: Nice one!

Kev: Quite.

Barney: And the plans are the biggest changes since 1948. There are to be several parallel policies. IF you manage your Health Savings Account well, and IF you insure privately for other cover, you'll be helped to reduce weight and change your life-style. And get good access.

But IF you don't, you'll effectively always be in the 4th class, that of The Obesites Only. So this effectively puts you at the back of the queue for being able to benefit from any treatments in out-patients, A&E and cold-admissions. If you improve your condition, you can effectively promote yourself to the 3rd class – or higher, depending on your own 'class' – and avoid all the disadvantages that obesity entails.

Kev: So, loads of economic incentives to make the Obesites take responsibility for themselves?

Barney: S'what I'm being told anyway. Don't know if it's true that Ministers want all this. But it seems to me that we are getting behind the curtain now. HSA's have been on the horizon for a long time. But only the Professor Philip Booth IEA, that Spiers book, and the Adam Smith Institute have put the case properly in the UK.

Anyway, this anti-Obesite campaign is going to apply to all NHS services. And then to other key providers of services.

Kev: One big stone, many waves in the pond?

Barney: Quite so. Jessie, though, says what she's been able to tell me already is tame compared with what's coming from the Ministers next! Even so…

After the HSAs have been established, and the encouragements to private insurance, too, we'll get even more drastic changes…

Ah, here's Sir Squoffy. Welcome!

Sir S-S: Just came from the Advisory Group meeting. Catch you up.

OBESITY-CLASS IN THE NHS. THE NATIONAL ANTI-OBESITY CAMPAIGN...PT 1

First, THE AIRLINES.

They are going to make a start with the airlines. Be a big symbolic statement. They're to be required to charge all passengers by weight. Adding luggage and the weight of the individual together. Trains and buses, too, later. Then the policy will be extended to cover entry to all supermarkets, and then to other shops. You'll be weighed on entry! All to be Anti-Obesite. Fatter you are, harder to be admitted. Proposed by Ms. Ali Walolah. Very keen on this idea.

Kev: 'Bout bloody time too!!! I'm 12 stone 6 lbs. Why should I be charged on a flight for a few extra pounds in my luggage and some big fat slob who flows over into two seats next to me not be charged for his or her weight? Should be special seating. Double-seat rows, the rows of shame, too! And loaded on last, and from the back. By crane, not up a stairway.

Sir S-S: Second, ALL OTHER PUBLIC FACILITIES, including private ventures, will offer only very limited entry for Obesites to soccer, rugby, cricket, tennis tournaments, and holiday venues. There will be BMI-controls. Too fat, can't come in. There they'll only serve health food, and just plain water. Weighed on the way in. Shut out if too fat. A real big bang push to tackle it all, at last.

New car and lorry number-plates will be introduced, too. Use the letters FAT with a number. Will be digitally treated so can only go into NHS facilities and supermarket car-parks in the Obesites section. And from there only get access to facilities by Obesites-only entry doors. To be a special digital ID card, so can only go where that card allows you.

Kev: So, a real bite-'em in the bums Anti-Obesity programme, eh? Want it to actually get done? Then should put Duncan Smith or Gove in charge of it.

Sir S-S: Quite so. IDS has done the welfare job. And that despite the civil servants. Gove started to sort the schools, too. 'Course, like on a lot of these basic NHS issues, no-one in government ever wants to step up. They have a great fear of the slightest mis-step. You can see why. But you can see why they must step up now. We can, anyway. We're at the sharp end. We should be the foot-soldiers for change. Not the victims of timidity in Whitehall.

Kev. But it does look as if the SofS is on the case now? And if we're ever going to get any real solutions for the NHS the PM has to push every limit on this. Whole structure and rationale has to change. Can't leave the machine in charge of itself. Can't let the fatties swamp everything. Can't go on adding to the £3b annual bill for alcohol-related illnesses. Can't tolerate the situation where some people take in a quarter of their weekly calories in alcohol alone. And these are the people who live on that. Burgers, pizzas and chips. Otherwise PM fails us all.

Sir S-S: Yes. We need to clearly define what winning means, too. It's about real action on these big issues. It's not just about getting any particular politician into office.

Brenda: We all know that any real move to tackle the Obesites, just like empowering other patients with money, is going to be controversial don't we?

Barney: Can take that as read. To do something serious about the NHS – and about obesity

– the special interests and the Hypochondriac Poverty Think-tanks [*sic – Ed.*] are all going to make a big fuss.

Barney: Yep. Klingfilm Wonderland! Squeal away! Hampster and Applecore. And the public service unions, the docs, the nurses, and the poverty action mob will all yell blue murder. But it's about the patients and the consumers of services. It's not about the politicians, the charityites, the unions, and their careers. And it's time government stopped just putting up with the costs the Obesites cause. And stopped pandering to the Poverty-mob, the Joseph Rowntree Trust, all of them.

Kev: It's too easy to tell special interests what they want to hear. You know, Milton Friedman's 'Iron Triangle' – professionals, bureaucrats, and Ministers. Instead, we need reforms which help everyone else. But governments will live in fear until the day when they really make the case. 'Course, at elections they might campaign in poetry, but they govern in fear.

Barney: Source of all this Obesity.... Old Harry Verney is right on all this, you know. No exercise; too much of the wrong food. A lot of it arises from a big historical change. Family doctors used to have to deal with the consequences of poverty. Now it's the consequences of prosperity – and stupidity. Once there was not enough food. Now there's too much. Vast amounts. The wrong sort, too. It's turned all that we do on its head.

Sir S-S: It's true that these people have done it to themselves. Of course, it's the price of successes: the enormous new availability of all this rubbish food, and of higher incomes, which has made it possible. When everyone was poor, it wasn't possible.

But, think of it – a lot of what they call poverty now is a form of hypochondria....

Only got a *small* car. *Only* have *one* foreign holiday a year. *Only* got a *semi-giant* plasma tele. Can't afford the *full* Sky package. Council will *only* give me a 5-bedroom house, and I've got 10 kids and no job. Never had one. Struggling to get by on £40,000 of benefits, p.a. All that. Many just want more. They just want it. They think they deserve it. A right! Welfare-state and all that. Academics tell them they are poor – with all sorts of complicated global references. Marxigook academics...

Banrye: And Klingfilmites!

Kerv: Yes. Them, too. Academics – paid for by the taxpayer! – tell them they are suffering, disadvantaged, and victims of endemic inequalities. As I've heard it said by that gang. So we are all to join hands together and cross the finishing line joint last!

Course, they don't talk like that in Singapore, China, Vietnam, and all points to the east!

Barney: Which is why the globe is tipping sideways towards them and away from us! David Green, David Marsland and Peter Saunders have got all this right, if you read them. Course, *The Groggyian* op.ed. pages won't ever mention *them!* And Cameron has got it wrong too, trying to look like More Compassionate Than Thou!

Kevb: Yep, Meantimes, it's us who are the victims of Kinnockles-Brownite-Milkiband-Academogorok-Marxigook-Webbian lefty ideology, again!

Barney: But, you know, very many of the so-called poverty-liners *have* got the resources to shop, cook, eat and live more sensibly. And they've got the time. If they could be bothered. But bone idle. Ignorant. Uneducated. Uneducatable. And all the welfare incentives are to stay like that too!

Just look at the hours they spend on bling-jewellery tele-shopping channels, for example. Could exercise and eat well, if they could only be bothered. Plenty of dosh. Many of 'em anyway. Either earned, or from welfare benefits. But no notion of how to be self-responsible.

I'd be glad to help the single-Mums in real difficulty. There *is* some genuine poverty there. And it's not always the fault of the poor. But I won't help the Burger Body Boyos, if they won't help themselves. They have both hands in welfare and social worker pockets, in course. Asking for bigger and free Welfare Seeker's Allowances! S'why they turn out and vote Labour.

Kev: Yep. Just so. Lot of loony advice about definition of poverty. Well-meant, but hopelessly unrealistic. All goes back to academic nuisances like that Prof. Peter Townsend, of course.

Barney: As to the Burger Bodies, not much good, is it for Squoffy telling fat and guzzling kids to keep a record of snacks they eat, and the time they spend watching TV instead of getting any exercise. Some hopes!

Kev: Dreamers, those bureaucrats. Live in a well-cushioned Klingfilm Wonderland, as you say. A lot of the fatties don't care, won't listen, aren't interested. Even though a third of kids are overweight or obese already, and four out of five teenagers will become obese adults. Try telling a lot of them to take up aerobics and stop playing computer games. None of that will work without direct economic incentives. It's the idle and the ignorant parents who we have to motivate, too.

Barney: Well maybe we'll see some progress. But be warned: it's all politics.

See what the great man Surtees says in *Ask Mamma*. Here it is! "If a man wants to be thoroughly disgusted with human nature, let him ally himself unreservedly to a political party. He will find cozening and sneaking and selfishness in all their varieties, and patriotic false pretences in their most luxuriant growth."

Kev: Well, political parties have no monopoly there, do they, as we both know from those we have to deal with the NHS day-by-day! But it sounds like the new anti-obesity policies will stir 'em up!

Barney: Got to run, Kev. Chairman's office calls. Ring me next Monday. I'll have some Minutes by then. But given the Sir Cashmeup Digital KGB thereabouts Jessie can't send them safely by a scan. So has to be hand to hand. I'll pick them up from her in St. James's Park....unobserved, I hope!

Kev: *Careful!* A telescope from the back of the Treasury building is trained on those walking paths, night and day. And I suspect listening devices are also placed conveniently in the trees, too!

Barney: Sounds just like the 1950s Spy Days in MI6, eh? Pity no one was listening in Mid-Staffs, eh?

Kev: Yep. But the Centre, *a la* Moscow, is very Len Deighton and John Le Carre! George Smiley's world! But be careful, all the same.

Tara for now!

My hot chocolate awaits!

NB. "And as we are in for a burst, let us do the grand and have a fresh horse."

EPISODE 14

The NHS Merry-Go-Round. Round and round we go!

Dramatis personae:

Mr. Barney Wells BEM, is Chief Executive of The Arthur Scargill Memorial NHS Trust Hospital, Chessingfield-on-Soke.

Mr. Kevin O'Grady is Chief Executive of the Coleraine St. Fortescue Veterinary Hospital, N. Ireland.

***

Kevin: Hello, galley-slave! And what's up with you then?

Barney: Well, feeling a bit like the old joke about the Commie Soviet Union, actually. "How are you Today, Comrade?" Answer: "Better than Tomorrow!"

But I'm missing Jackie, in accounts. Causing me a lot of extra work. Iced towel on me head!

Kev: She still on that international exchange visit at the Thabo Mbeki Aids-Caused-By-Toothpaste Centre in Lusaka, then?

Barney: Sadly, so. Got that fancy-money Gordon Brown Young Over-Spender of the Year Scholarship.

Well, I want a word with you about Millkiband, his Marxist Dad, and the *Daily Mail*. Topic of the day. Especially if he is going to be the next PM and take us back. To the even bigger spend NHS, to let it rip, to no need of changes in management, to hand the trowel to Lord VAT, to trade union bossidom again. And all FREE.

We're a long way, as a society, from the Marxist USSR, of course. But we should keep reminding ourselves of what that society was like. You know, an all-powerful state enforcing a monopoly system on behalf of so-called political values. And in the interests of some larger theoretical good. But political values which no one wanted, 'cept the Bolsheviks. Millions murdered arbitrarily; concentration camps; show trials; no free press; elderly and young alike starving in the streets; shot if the bosses felt like it. The lot!

We're not where the Commies were, thank goodness. It's not just a matter of scale or of degree. We're different. But they had the fundamental Communist assumption that the sacrifice of human beings didn't matter in the achievement of some future (but long postponed!) human happiness in 'Building Socialism.' And that itself only done by brutal force and mass murder.

Kev: But we've still got such a terrible wastage of substance and energy. And that in a democracy! A state monopoly system is always just one great deception. Conformist mediocrity. Endless repetition of a few prescribed and over-simplified ideas. But no bold investigation of new ideas. Imagination? Curiosity? Adaptive ventures? Trial-and-error initiatives? Action by people with executive ability? New ideas? "Dangerous" – is all that is.

Barney: But The Millkibar Kid will, no doubt, soon propose a Five Year Plan!

Kev: And Four for the Four Years Taken! Trains to run on time. But otherwise the perfection of nothingness. As to his Daddy, well you've got to respect him for defending him. But what a wicket, eh?

Barney: Come in, Uncle Joe, all is forgiven!

Kev: And history shows us that in Marxist states socialists have always been keen to sacrifice lives for a cause. And usually other peoples too.

Barney: But we mustn't mention his Dad, must we! Or the *Daily Mail*! So I won't!

Kev: Well, just let me say this. *Joking quite apart.* Anyone – *anyone at all* – who considers actually listening to Millkiband defending his Dad should read the most frightening books I know. Read Robert Conquest's *The Great Terror*. Concentrate on his Dad's ideas, not the man. And indisputably these ideas *were* dangerous to democracy. Communism *is* terror.

Then read the book by the American Communist and serious journalist Eugene Lyons, who worked in Moscow for years and saw the reality of Marxist-Leninist life after the 1917 coup by the Bolsheviks. The years of arbitrary terror. The squalor. The lies. The torpor. The Gulag. The cruelty. The hopelessness. The mass starvation and the mass murder. The Bolshevik ruthlessness. The bottomless hopelessness. Imposed on millions – if they lived! – for 70 years.

The book's called *Assignment in Utopia*. Published by George G. Harrap & Co. Ltd. Terrifying book. Makes you sick at heart. You'll find it hard to believe how anything could be so awful, or so deliberate. *But it all happened.* Compare what Conquest and Lyons carefully document with the romantic guff put out by Millkiband's Marxist Dad.

Barney, do get a copy. It's a riveting book. And a terrible warning about Marxism, however fuzzy at the edges some advocates try to make it. "Never been properly tried", and all that. Total bollocks! And Lyons's transparently honest account is a terrible warning, too, about people like that academic and deliberately blinkered theorist Ralph Millkiband. And those who rationalise about him. Him a democrat? Well, then Stalin was our tea-lady!

Kev: Yep. But all part of the Romantic Conception of State Planning as a Magic Formula.

Barney: Ah. "Building Socialism!" And FREE! More important to publish good wishes than to provide a good product. All that Commie dreamland stuff. 2 plus 2 equals five. Or not, as it turns out. But we at the sharp-end know too well that it transcends logic. And mis-states human nature. However Millkiband's political showmanship might try to dress it up in his statistical contortions. Whatever Unite…

Kev: …and Lord VAT!

Barney: …say about protecting the public.

Barney: From the truth…

Kev: Just breeds bureaucrats, draws up fine plans and fine promises, irrespective of costs or quality. But don't actually deliver very much. And the economic buck? Passed to others.

Barney: *Taxpayers Ahoy!*

Kev: Whole thing is a snarl of contradictions. Great aspirations, but structure won't ever deliver. We've both tried our utmost for years and years. N£sd Shortages, ineptness, lack of proper incentives, whole thing politicised. Pitiful investment in preventative practice and after-care. No economic incentives for patients to be self-responsible. Gaping gulf becoming more and more obvious, between aspirations which we both had and the practical applications locally. Big difference, too, between the care for the upper few and the gray swarms – that's particularly startling.

Barney: And just look at the sacrifices made by suffering patients. The NHS as it's become now is a postponement of what we might have instead, not a solution.

Kev: High-minded, of course. And a lot of wishful thinking still. But everything over-crowded. Dangerous. Unhygienic hospitals. Haphazard management. Accumulating shortages. Debt. Deprivation. Rationing. Denial of services. No basic human right to be certain of necessary services.

And the imbalance is paid for in immediate suffering, higher costs, and ultimately an economic machine which is going to stall.

Will collapse under the weight of the frail.

Barney: *And* the obese!

Kev: Them, too.

And remember that so many listening to Old Labour and Millkiband now know nothing of what the Communists actually did to Russia, and to Eastern Europe. We need to keep those experiences alive. And to bat away pronto any suggestion that people like that academic Daddy had some sort of truths to tell us. *[- Or Corbynliner! – Ed.]*

Barney: Meself, I can't see any progress in the NHS, even without Marxism making it worse. Back to being a political football. General Election nigh. And the Tories just won't see political – and cultural – sense, and make themselves *the* party of the consumer, and of the liberal free adaptive market.

Kev: That would mean giving us all a chance to encourage self-responsibility in the individual! By the means of introducing individual and personal Health Savings Accounts. Key instrument for change. On the Singapore model. Tax-based, but with excess charges to the obese individual so we can encourage responsible living. And with tax-incentives to top up with private insurance, too.

We've got somehow to get patients to take seriously the impact of their ways of living on their health. Just like driving cars. An excess for bad diet, no exercise, ignoring a target with your GP for weight-control and life-style changes.

Barney: And an extra premium to pay if you are deliberately and irresponsibly unfit?

Kev: That's it! *Be* unfit if you like. But don't pass the bills to the taxpayer.

The Tories should have done the work on this approach in opposition, and introduced it the day they came into office. The very day. That's what Cameron's Downing Street Garden chat should have said. Not all that guff about being Clegg's Siamese twin.

Barney: Yes. Should have set out first principles of HSA's, and self-responsible healthcare. Then explained why the NHS can never work without individual self-responsibility. And why there'll never be improvements without competition. As well as why there will never be enough money if we only get it from taxation. So need incentives for private-insurance and top-ups, too. Health Savings Accounts a key part. Could have used the success of personal budgets for social care as a prelude and an example. Cameron should then have referred to these first principles every time there was an NHS issue. And showed how we'd go forward.

Big missed opportunity.

Kev: Which was and is every day!

Barney: Yep. Every day. So the Tories did have masses of chances to get the public on-side.

Kev: But Cameron hasn't, has he?

Barney: No. His needle has never pointed to the pole, has it? The thinking just not done. Just gave us the usual chitter-chatter: "Have-faith, it's wonderful, spend more." All that guffy-stuff. No sensible discussion about money, even since. Even if Jeremy Hunt has awoken like the Kraken and started to raise the issues. Like his piece on the family today. And why a care home should be the last resort. *The family should be the first resort –* that's the point!

Kev: Quite right. You've said so for ages, too. Cameron should have got the public thinking on healthcare. On social care. On pensions, too. Just as Gove is trying to do on education. Even if he is prescriptive and a centraliser, on which I'm less keen.

Barney: Energy prices, too. Making prospects worse. Cameron getting a terrible kicking from The Millkibar Kid on that one, too. Don't they *want* to be re-elected? Don't they *want* to have market pressures driving absolutely necessary NHS change? Don't they *want* the elderly – who vote – on their side? Why don't they WANT to be the party of the consumer? AND of individual self-responsibility in society?

THE NHS MERRY-GO-ROUND. ROUND AND ROUND WE GO!

Kev: You may well ask!

Barney: Anyway, enough of that. Doing anything much?

Kev: Nope. Slow news-day, I see. "Suarez bites dentist." "The Millkibar Kid Prettifies Marxism. Daddy a Real Teddy Bear!" "More shock horror NHS...." Usual blurgie stuff on the A&E crisis.

Barney: Oh yes! Gawd! Never ends! Most of the customers there are *neither* an accident nor an emergency. Can hardly blame them, though, if docs just won't work weekends. And if they can't understand what all these NHS alphabetic mysteries and puzzle-words actually mean. PCTs and all that. And even Monitor doesn't understand them!

Kev: Ah! Why ever they can't make changes so that they recognise where people want to be treated I just don't know. Why not have all services in one place? GPs in A&E. Proper triage. "You are a GP patient. Corridor A. You are an A&E patient. Corridor B." Job done!

Barney: Yep. But the only sense we get from Richmond House is non-sense! And what we all want is greater productivity, lower-costs, and higher value outcomes. Get none of that without higher morale, more time for patients, and a mature debate about patient charges and Health Savings Accounts. Changed attitude to private health care necessary, too. Should be tax-incentives for private care insurance. Need to deter all the rubbish in A&E and in General Practice, too. Start with charges for GP appointments. Works well in France. And in Oz.

Kev: Absolutement! Personally, I know what the right courses of action usually are. I listen very carefully to that Lord Winston...

Barney: The Old Labour Islington luvvie?

Kev: Yes. Him. And I then do the opposite!

Barney: You are a snake-charmer!

Kev: And as to the usual *Guardian* stuff, we know all about "advanced" liberal intellectuals with kind hearts and fuzzy minds. And who really believe the voodoo cry that the NHS is the "best in the world." To them, believing is more attractive than thinking.

Barney: I calls it "Polly Toynbee-ism", myself. Divorced from realities....seeing a structure which doesn't actually exist! Safe and snug in their congealed leftie heritage. All make-believe. Just like her indoors, Mrs. Bugginsturn!

Kev: Saw that Anna Soubry, Tory junior health minister, on the BBC. Seems quite good. Bit of a looker, education, &c is essential in a modern democracy, too. But no mention of prices, markets, or incentives. Or of HSAs or private insurance incentives or individual cash top-ups.

Barney: Now, *there's* a surprise!

Kev: You'd think a *Tory* minister would know that there's no substitute for market knowledge. And that without prices you've got no chance of regulating demand in anything. Key signals. But without tackling that they know they needn't bother to change the other basics. There's no requirement. Price-less system cuts us off from real knowledge of what people would prefer, though – and would be prepared to pay for. Cuts us off from sorting what people really think is important. Cause of most of our problems. You know, if it's free, I'll have the lot mate.

Barney: Or two! 'Course, not free, is it? *Taxpayers Ahoy!*

Kev: Yes. But not for the benefits-lot. Don't pay a brass bean. And even paying taxes doesn't give you command over a necessarily intimate, personal, timely service, does it? Voting don't do it, either, do it? And it's no help either to the poor blighters up there working in A&E that we can't control false demands.

Barney: Old Squoffy says he still can't see why we can't go for individual compulsory insurance for A&E services for everyone.

Kev: Why not, indeed for everything? Give tax-incentives to do it. And impose an excess charge on the obese, the drunks, that lot who behave just as they like and give everyone else the bill. Would bring in billions…

Barney: And change demand too. As well as behaviour, perhaps. Economics. Incentives. You know. But "markets" a Forbidden Word. Uncameroon. Shot at dawn behind the bike sheds if you say it.

Kev: Humph! Key things to do obvious enough about A&E, anyway. GPs and consultants actually doing their jobs 7 days a week on rotas. Us sensibly running the hospitals, too. Fewer patients shoved out too soon, only to come back double-quick. Fewer patients in A&E, more staff for real emergencies, better social care outside. Outrageous that the docs won't turn out at weekends. Not all about money, either. It's attitudes, too. And more money is always equated with better services. Not that poverty is much fun, either. But we need to do more than put in more money. More money does not necessarily make it any better, anyway. Look at the new GP and hospital doc contracts dished up by Gordon Brown. Made everything worse.

Barney: Well, the GP contract is a key. So, too, are consultant's contracts. Big road-blocks. But there's no such thing as an employment contract that you can't renegotiate. Be difficult, noisy, expensive. But GPs or our hospital docs aren't going to move on it voluntarily, are they? Even Cameron seems at long last to have realised this. But have the docs? And will he really tackle it all?

Kev: Up to a point, Lord Copper! Or, possibly. Or, maybe. Or not, as the case may be. His conference speech says he will act. So will chuck in billions more as an Elastoplast. But that's just a fudge.

Barney: Meanwhile, A&E's full of frightened, frail elderly, with no hope of a GP appointment. Worst place for many of them to be, too. But they go there as they know they'll be seen by someone, eventually. And, as well, who is asking why the families of the elderly aren't doing more to support patients at home, instead of just demanding a blue-light ambulance and shoving them in?

THE NHS MERRY-GO-ROUND. ROUND AND ROUND WE GO!

Kev: Well…nobody much. 'Cept for Hunt, this week. Family life? Ah. Not so much of that about as there was, is there? And even when a family is together in one room, one of them is watching TV, three are texting, two others are on their tablets typing away, another at least is boozed to gonnery or drugged to their eye-balls. And Grannie fast asleep too. As to sons and daughters, they say "Why isn't *the State* doing something!"

Barney: "So, bye-bye, Grannie. Just sign the will first." Bloody awful people, a lot of the don't-care families.

Kev: As to the hospitals and performance info, still no morbidity data issued, I see.

Barney: Docs don't have none. Won't get none. Don't want none, either.

Anyway, Kev, I've got some really major news. About our new chair. Going to be such ructions!!!

Ring me on Monday. Will tell you then. For the mo, all hush-hush! But you'll be *very* surprised at the news….

Kev: *I'm a valid consumer*!

Barney: *Taxpayers Ahoy!*

*And now, having accommodated the reader with a second horse, perhaps we may be allowed to take a fresh pen and finish the run in another chapter…

EPISODE 15

Obesity-Class in the NHS. The National Obesity Campaign…Part 2.

Dramatis Personae:

Mr. Barney Wells BEM, Chief Executive of The Arthur Scargill Memorial NHS Trust Hospital, Chessingfield-on-Soke.

Kevin O'Grady, Chief Executive of the Coleraine St. Fortescue Veterinary Hospital, N. Ireland.

Sir Cyril Squoffington-Squogg, OBE, JP, is Chief Executive of The Tower of London NHS Hospital Trust, Tower Hamlets, London, EC.

Brenda When is PA/Secretary to Mr. Wells.

***

Barney: Well Kev, I've got more from Jessie on the National Obesites Campaign. Share it with you, now.

My personal good news is that at least we at Scargills are not to be the national pilot place for it! I'm glad to avoid all that aggro. The entirely new David Copperfield NHS Trust at Whitstable is to get it. There's a steering group, too, for the National project. So that will be under the All-Seeing Eye!

Barney: Yep. I've got Sir Squoffy and Brenda with me here. Squoffy's on the Group, of course. Chatting it all over now. Putting you on speaker….

Sir S-S: Top of The Morning to you, Kevin! As to the Obesites, I'm keen to hear your views. I'm taking a very active part, mostly behind the scenes, with Sir Crank.

Kev: Well, my main point for you is that they stuff themselves stupid because we let them. Economics, as you say. If you want change, use price, use tax, use incentives. Bring in Health Savings Accounts. And compulsory top-up private insurance. Some serious economics, please. And more action like that you've already proposed on the Airlines, too.

Barney: I agree I never used to think so, but I'm convinced now that only markets can sort it out. So we've got to get the Obesites to the tipping point by making some new rules. That's the key lesson. Force-feed the alternatives.

Kev: Pawn to King Four!

Barney: Or is it Prawn to King Four?!

Sir S-S: Well, you're both quite right that the FOOD INDUSTRY should have been tackled long ago. Utterly basic. By strict regulation, and by forcing prices up with really heavy taxation on junk-foods full of saturated fats. We could even ban the Muckburgers from opening up in the High Street. And from drive-ins at petrol stations too. Anyway, got to stop the over-packaged, nutrient-lite, additive-dense stuff being sold at all.

Kev: And ban the supersizing they offer in Muckburgers and Wodgiegung and Chips-With-Every-Saturated-Fried-Chicken.

Brenda: Ban the TV ads too, as was done with tobacco. No more sloganising. No more "I'm Stuffin' It" on those adverts.

Kev: Ban junk-food on railway stations, too? And on trolleys on trains and buffets? The rail firms are making big profits from that stuff. So are the sports stadiums. All serving up oodles of pizza, chips, coke, and fizzy drinks, along with the booze they sell.

That all needs action. And give people on benefits 'Good food Vouchers' exchangeable at good food shops only. *Instead* of benefits.

Barney: Yes, but they'll probably not eat it, the better food. Will just flog the vouchers instead! Still, that Jamie Oliver's Ministry of Food centre in Leeds Kirkgate is giving anyone on means-tested benefits cookery classes. A great step to take. Now don't let anyone leave school without a cookery GCSE. Keep them there into the 20s if they won't do it. Gove might do that next? He's the very boy.

Kev: When I see what people load into their trolleys in the supermarkets I grieve for sanity. Can't say they haven't been told, can they? So I say no more peerages, either for the food manufacturers who do the damage! No more Lord Balties and Lord Saltie-crisps.

Barney: Yep. Otherwise, what chance have we got to do a better job in the NHS? Fat as sacred cows too. Who's to pay for that, eh?

Kev: *Taxpayers Ahoy!* And just look at what's out there. Extraordinary how so-called parents haven't a clue. Kids arrive at primary school not knowing their own names, can't wipe their own bottoms, haven't had any breakfast. But get cash to nip out somehow and buy crisps and fizzy drinks. Obese at 5 years old. Their Mums and Dads expect to work for 5 minutes in 30 years, and then live on benefits in old age, too. Look at that couple in Bournemouth, picking up £32k a year in benefits, with a 10th kid on the way and demanding a bigger house from the Council. What have we come to as a society?

Sir S-S: Well, very sadly, a lot of them won't ever get there into middle-age, of course. I saw a report recently that there's more goodness in cat food than in what a lot of those people choose to eat! And the burger outfits still make those junk foods laced with stuff which makes people crave more. Salads and coleslaw should be healthy. But they lace it with special fatty sauces to encourage more demand. Eat it and you're still hungry. So eat more of it. And still no satisfactions in it.

Kev: Regulation is obviously needed. But I'm usually against over-prescriptive policies. Bit of a quandary here.

Sir S-S: Yet within a very few years three-quarters of Brits will be struck down by obesity-linked illnesses. Hastening their own deaths by cramming themselves with these fast routes to heart disease, diabetes, the lot. And by their own choices.

Kev: Yes. Igliotas all.

Barney: And if they vote, they vote Labour, of course. So they can get even more welfare benefits. The Millkiband Kid's 'Vote Labour to Grab Even More' campaign slogan seems likely now.

Brenda: Well, we know that one in five deaths is down to obesity in the USA. We're next. We can't say we haven't been told either. But the patients ignore the facts, and just pass the bills onto other people.

Barney: ...AND it's no good the patients saying that they pay their taxes, so never mind what they eat. A lot of them bloody well don't pay *any* taxes!

Kev: Yes. But that's a problem with the idea of an insurance excess, too, isn't it? If the benefits office just pays it, there's no incentive for the sluggards and the Obesites.

Brenda: Except early death. And 10 years of chronic misery first.

Kev: Yes, and very expensive misery for the NHS it is, too.

Sir S-S: Well, I'm to consult with the leading UK economic expert on insurance schemes, Professor Philip Booth at the IEA, and report back to Sir Crank on those points.

Brenda: Did you all see that Centre for Workforce Intelligence report in August? They said that we'll be some 190,000 nurses short within three years, let alone in the medium-term. So who will care for these patients?

Barney: Not their hopeless families, I'll be bound.

Kev: ...AND the people who just say, well, send the obese to the back of the queue don't help us at all. The bloody obese *ARE* the queue!

Barney: Right. It's NOT "the other half" we're talking about. It's the 90 per cent. And the lack of self-control produces many of the cancers we have to deal with. Junk food, booze, drugs – cause many avoidable cancers. Breast cancer risk for teenage drinkers made worse by it. Younger they start, greater the risks. Cancers of the liver. The mouth. The throat and oesophagus. Drink triggering hormone-receptor-positive types of the disease. Three in four adults now likely to suffer heart diseases or diabetes by 2030. And so it's bloody daft to ignore the evidence!

Sir S-S: *Is* education the answer?

Kev: Well, it *should* be. But I doubt it. All those so-called progressive teachers, running go-wild, no-structure, no-discipline, do-as-you-like "classes." So many of the kids there don't get any education. Don't want any either. Don't read. Can't read. Can't write. Can't add up. Ignore good advice. Don't read the papers, even those who can read a bit. Can't spell. Only texting. All that ow-r-u stuff. Not interested in culture. Just boozed to buggery. Another brick in the wall? More like another thicko in the junkyard. But we get the job of doing something about it. And they curse us for it, too. Turn up drunk and violent in A&E. All that crap.

Barney: Yep. Don't look in here at 2 a.m. Saturday nights/Sunday mornings. Like World War 3, on booze tsunami.

Brenda: Still, some people are still trying new things. I see that in Pittsburgh they're introducing cameras that measure the calories in a meal.

Kev: But some hopes of any of that lot taking any notice here! And a lot of shops won't even list calorie info anyway. Even then, only the already aware will be aware. The unaware fatties will never even see it.

Barney: And just look at those huge numbers of families where no one has *ever* worked. More than 200,000 Brit families. *All* living on benefits. A lot just don't intend ever to work. And what are *they* eating? You can guess. Even though good food is cheaper than junk. But they can't be bothered to prepare it or cook it.

Well, it's true that these people have done it to themselves. Of course, it is only the enormous new availability of all this food that has made it possible. When everyone was poor, it wasn't possible. But, think of it, what they call poverty now is a form of hypochondria. They've got the resources to live more sensibly. If they could bother.

Brenda: Still, in this Anti-Obesite thing there's talk here, as you say, of economics. That's what can lead to generational change. Relying on education won't do it. We've got to enforce [encourage!] exercise, too. One idea is make them chase their money. Not being able to get your giro in the post any more.

Kev: Have to go *in person* to an office?

Barney: Yep. Walk! Step by step! And if your BMI is wrong, you can only get to the distant local Giro office by walking or by going on an Obesites-only bus, to very out of town offices with no public car parks. So must walk, or use that bus and pay £2 each way. Not very frequent buses. Likely to be long delays, too, as it would be an unpopular staffing slot for GMB members. Obesites-only lines. So long delays. No parking within a mile for the bus, either. No dropping off zone. So a walk back at least a mile each way for the Obesites. Giros to be recoded, too. Reduced to pay for Weightwatchers and/or Health club memberships vouchers, not otherwise encashable. Non-transferable. Finger-print coded.

Kev: As the GP Dr. Jeff Neville told me on that, the numbers of cars nicked will jump! You'll see. And I s'pose there will be jaw-wiring on the NHS next, too!

Barney: Not bad! Sir Crank will probably propose it! He agrees with the British Dietetic Association proposal to ban Junk Food at supermarket checkouts, too. Would probably ban production completely! Lower in salt-contents; clearer labelling; less fat in foods. All OK. But still marginal. Need some 'real-wallop' policies.

Sir Squoffy: Soonest I can probably give you, very privately, more details of the Anti-Obesites plans. As Housman says, "With the great gale we journey…." So tune in again…

Barney: You two! All this Likerichure! I'm not Irish, but what I want is what that other poet, George Russell, wrote. In his poem "On behalf of Some Irishmen not Followers of Tradition." I want what he wants: "The golden heresy of truth"!

Now, just pass me those lovely looking grapes, please!

And we now request the company of the reader to the following part 3, due shortly.

EPISODE 16

Enter Lord Ironsides. N£sd Musical Chairs, and a New World? Part 1.

Dramatis personae:

Mr. Barney Wells BEM, is Chief Executive of The Arthur Scargill Memorial NHS Trust Hospital, Chessingfield-on-Soke.

Lord Ironsides, no less. The new Chair at Chessingfield-on-Soke [in succession to the Old Labourite Mrs. Rita Wells MBE] is a local land-owner of aristocratic descent. Admiral Albert George Quincy Lascelles Vernon de St. Valery, Lord Ironsides is a former head of the Fleet Air Arm. He is aged 60. But looks a very vigorous 50. And acts accordingly.

Kevin O'Grady is Chief Executive of the Coleraine St. Fortescue Veterinary Hospital, N. Ireland.

***

Kev: Ringing you as promised! The supply of gossip and the spy data does not keep up with the demand! Should be a daily *Guardian* supplement. So, under the new Complaints System…Upsides old matey, have you got your new Chair yet?

Come on, fill me in. I'm already hearing stories. Some very strange rumours and odd tales. Leprechauns ring me. I hear Chinese whispers, too. And eerie echoes from dark caves….

My Irish mates are everywhere Barney! All whispers lead to me! All drums beat! Hearing some dark echoes, too! Every sound speaks. So, Barney, come on, *whatever* has happened? Whatever *is* going on over there?

Barney: Well, yes, we've got a new chair. But what a shock it is! Can hardly believe it myself. Will turn the whole kaboosh upside down! Just you watch – earthquakes…

We're to lead the way as the national exemplars of how to get more hospital mergers done, duff the present competition laws, play bigger regional role for biggest DGH in the North, get new A&E monopoly, re-organise funding structures. And then they are to make us deliver on demands for much better, safer, cheaper care. And focus on the patient experience and outcomes…AND get economic incentives, face the Obesite problems, awaken self-responsibility…doctors at weekends… give the game a chance…

Urgent Agenda gets bigger every day!

Kev: Big regional monopoly by amalgamations? Well, they'll get resistance from the Right. For sure. I see that the Tories say that the water industry and the fuel firms need sharp competition. But we seem to be below that wire…

Still – and BUT – as Sir Squoffy will tell us, no doubt – successful organisations welcome change rather than resist it. "Change and development being the essence of life. The unadaptable go to the wall."

Competition, regulation, whistle-blowing and publicity – *especially that* – are the only things which have driven any improvements and revealed abuses.

The spotlight, combined with proper inspections. And a better competitive provider in the wings.

BUT, again, these principles will always be called into question by The Royal Academy of Vested Interests. The particular applications of good principles for radical change will always arouse trade union, local and sectional hostility. And the Judges won't allow the SofS to downgrade hospitals now, either, if Lewisham proves to be a precedent. Unless they bring in a new Public Law No.1 on mergers, and double-quick too.

Barney: That's just the plan, I'm being told.

Kev: BUT – for the third time – the NHS can no longer be secretive about its affairs. Squoffy told me at that Torquay conflab that in healthcare information is of another order from most data. It touches every individual personally. Hospital institutions cast a long shadow in their community, too. So tinker at your peril.

BUT – fourthly – the public is catching on to how bad some of them can be. And that, despite the so-called British way of doing things. Some very shady chapters, alas, being revealed. They're starting to discover how many Dr. Deadwoods there really are. And covered up, too, by the docs, and for years.

Barney: Well, yes, still at it, too. But now being watched a bit more. And criticised accordingly.

BUT – I says – JH will have to face all that. He's subject to regulation by statute, subject to challenge in Parliament, by the press, and by individuals and patient groups. All heating up.

Kev: Yep. So is the State going to manage the NHS, or the NHS to manage the State? *Dat be de question, your honour.*

Barney: Well, I've already been told that the new Chairman thinks he's here to give leadership. And to be strong and tough (but fair!) on the key issues. To challenge! And to RUN THE PLACE! Got some powerful medical chums, too. Seems he's known Sir Mike Richards for yonks. Met him at a Christmas drinks party at Prof. Eric and Dr. Karen Caines's when he lived in Oxted. That radical reform pair Roy Lilley and John Spiers there, too. Knew Mike before he got his first stripe as the Cancer Czar. Long before he got this so-called Top Inspections job.

Kev: Strewth! Might be very helpful with the senior docs then? Sounds like he's going to need the backing. But he's evidently not like the usual nonentities.

Barney: Nope. Keynote is LEADERSHIP! The lot! Ironsides by name, Ironsides by nature! Put in on us to really sort the fish from the shrimps. Cue the music from *Jaws*. Oh,

ENTER LORD IRONSIDE. N£SD MUSICAL CHAIRS, AND A NEW WORLD? PART 1

cripes! Wave of the Future. Chairmen to be put in to really get a job done. No more just sitting there, safe hands, keep quiet, wait for the CBE. What a change that will be!

Kev: Unions going bananas, then? Docs too? Leadership usually means TROUBLE!

Barney: S'why we don't get any. At the core of what the new chairman calls "THE NHS PROBLEM."

Kev: His voice, and in CAPITAL LETTERS!

Barney: Oh, yea. The word is that they *really mean* to make these new reforms stick. And that there are really radical things to come, including these huge new mergers and changes to the competition laws.

Kev: Very interesting. SofS is going to ask for new powers to overbear local opinion and inertia, is he? Roll-em-over, eh? But surely that's contrary to the way popular opinion is now running, isn't it? Very different from asking outside managements to tender to deliver and manage services? For A&E, for example. As we should do for such monopolies. Big new mergers and far-reaching monopolies will be very different from bringing in agents, and increasing competition? No grist, and no mill, eh?

Barney: Well, meself, I thinks there's a sea-change in public ideas about the relations of the State to the great utilities of production. Including the NHS and services within it. BBC, too.

People are much less interested now in who has the ownership. Much more interested in what services are actually like. What the doc's results have been. New chairman keener on free competition if it is properly regulated and can produce real efficiencies, which seem beyond many NHS facilities. Need regulations and controls, naturally enough. Check how it's run, and if it's genuinely competitive. Coverage and access. Financial practices. Safety of operation. Costs. Do the right hernia. But it's about the quality of service at the end of the day, and who can best deliver that, isn't it? That's what Tommy Atkins wants, you know.

Kev: Wants to survive, too.

Barney: Well, her Indoors – Labour's next MP for Bugginsturn North, so help us – will never agree. She is incandescent. Unspeakably furious. Lit up at the ears! Smoke and flames from her nostrils! Terrible oaths to curdle witches breaths! Curses, and blessings that would freeze a polar bear! She's astonished. *None* of her relatives even short-listed for the Chair here.

Kev: *None? Not even short-listed?*

Barney: Not one of them. So we've got Admiral Lord Ironsides! Imposed by DoH. No choices. Fate-o-comply!

Kev: *Admiral* Lord Ironsides! *What*, the Falklands Islands bloke? *That* Admiral? *Your* new Chair?

Barney: Yep. Very same. Him in person. Or is it him in poison? We shall soon see. And the timbers be shivering us! And there's big waves and earthy-shakes to come with more like him, right across the NHS if I'm not mistaken in the fennel in my fingers! First of a new succession of real heavyweight Chairs who really mean to get things done, it seems.

Squoffy says that they're going to push on with integrated care and reconfigured services. With real economic incentives that will work at the local level, to motivate patients and managements. All that IEA-dom stuff. And to deliver what they are calling "real service change for better patient outcomes." How to pay docs be part of it, too, it seems.

Kev: Y'mean align local quality and outcome results – and payments – with national policies?

Barney: Yep. Just listen to this. From the *FT*. Cutting from Jubilee Year, when the new Chairman got another gong:

"Lord Ironsides is a man of the people, despite his aristocratic ancestry. He is a great believer in a free society, and a keen disciple of Adam Smith and of Milton Friedman, the Nobel-winning champion of the free-market and of individual self-responsibility. A modern Eminent-Churchillian and IEA supporter, he believes that the best basis of social advance is for the aggregate of decisions taken by individuals in a free market to enable the best kinds of creative, trial-and-error, dynamic progress. Much more so than through the centralised decisions of government, and of Mandarins."

Kev: *Mandarins?* Very *FT* lingo, that!

Barney: And…"He is also noted for having told a succession of senior Ministers – several of whom were at Eton with him – that the mistakes made by governments are much harder to correct than any faults of the free-market. He is an exemplar of measured efficiencies, in getting the job done, and without fuss or focus on himself. He is a sceptic of the idea of politics perfecting mankind and human society. And so he is an advocate of the invisible hand, not of political Masterplans."

Kev: *Watch this space!*

Barney: Yep. S'alright for you. He had me in his office this morning. Already got his books on his shelves. Also, an ancient Italian violin. Apparently he plays for fun.

He said to me that we will make music together in the Trust. "A hospital is like a violin. Responds to the environment. Can be frisky and warm, hostile and cranky, moody and jealous. Wood, strings, grip all very changeable and need to be nurtured. It's imagination which is the crux of who we are, and it's acts of kindness which must guide our work. We must play upon the musician's bow. A pride must be taken by all our staff in democratic acts of decency."

Kev: Cor!

Barney: Looked him up in the *Doubleimupshire County Guide & Hare-Hunter*. "Pop" article by The Hon. Penelope Percy:

"Lord Ironsides lives in the vast and handsome great sandstone pile Keeble Hall, built for Ralph Ironsides in c.1580. It has huge crenulated towers. A drive 3 miles long. Deer all

ENTER LORD IRONSIDE. N£SD MUSICAL CHAIRS, AND A NEW WORLD? PART 1

over the rolling meadows. Coal-mines under everything. Black gold. Family owns half the county. Been on the right side in every big conflict. Great man in a red coat with the hounds, too. Father and Grandfather famous MFH's. Uncle Jauncey runs The Quorn still. The Admiral rides like a Sioux Indian."

Kev: Goodness gracious gogglefoggles! A real intellectual *and* a practical man, then? Could be a dynamic combination. Real dynamist. Not a statist at all. And we certainly do need real leadership, don't we, if the service is to survive? Someone who does not regard the necessary as "the impossible." Who can push the vested-interests and their bureaucrats aside...

Barney: Sounds like us! But can't be right, can it? Not very Camerooncleggie, is it?

Kev: Ho, ho, Barney. But you know it makes sense. Shake up the docs, too. And bring a sense of pace and urgency with him. With him in the field I can quite see how and why Mrs. Bugginsturn didn't get her favoured bloke, her cousin, old fuzzy Hogleblin.

Barney: Nope. Not a shoo-in, after all. Biggie surprise. All gone a-kybosh, it has! A right turn-up! And we did it all the right way, too. Four big ads in the *Health Service Jungle*. Usual inexpensive four-column ads. for 8 weeks in *The Guardian*. Official notices in local papers. Local radio interviews. Big ad, worded by DoH itself, in the *Sunday Times*. And yet just look at what we've got! THIS bloke! Gawd to Murgatroyd!

Kev: But didn't Mrs. Wells make up the short-list, and then make it work for you? Speak to Gerry at Region? Advice from that Stewed ["I will not resign!"] Bludgeon. Get old what's-his-name, Jeff O'Allagreed, as independent assessor? How *long* have you two been at this game? Know how it works, don't you?

Barney: Well, you'd have thought so. But, oh 'eck....

Kev: Ah...sounds *very* ominous, from one point of view, but very promising from another, doesn't it? Heard as much anyway about him getting the job. But just couldn't believe it, given the stranglehold the Hogleblins have had over there. *No* Hogleblin family member of any kind chosen? Not one? *None* of them? *Unbelievable!* Been running the show, successive Chairs, for years. Like the Jacksons, in Evelyn Waugh's great novel *Scoop*.

Barney: Quite so. One of my own favourites. But we'd all expected to just pass on the job, of course. And the fees. Safe sailing. Then me to be in post until retirement date. Then I'd be made a non-exec at a PCT. Useful extra cash, too. But evidently them days really are over. Did my best to get one of those Golden Goodbyes, y'know. One of those £200,000 payouts, and then promotion, re-employed, to another higher-paying job too within the N£sd. But missed out. So now I've got to deal with this Golden Hello Lark instead! And we're *all* going to get new Chairs who mean to do something, it seems!

Kev: 'Course, on the brighter side, the Admiral *is* a local man?

Barney: Yep. But that won't help me! Never comes to the Working Men's Institute. Never seen at the dart-board in the *Squirrel and Dolphin*. We plebs left in the rainy fields, slaving at the spuds.

Kev: And for him all canons loaded, all the time! In the firing line? Bang!

Barney: Seems the case. So no more inside-out and outside-in, whispers behind your hand fix-ups. You know, good old long-standing Attlee-arrangements. Joe-sent-me, proper coded knock on the door, rubber-stamp deployed, everyone happy. Hand-shaker in the consultant's Lodge at St. Hilda's. Start your new job on 2 May. But, nope, not now. No 'jobs' like that now. No longer a world of no boats a-rocking and all a-calm and a-happy at The Front. No more 'let's not bother with all these re-organisations and reforms.' No more bed-pans dropped and bust but no-one hears them in Whitehall.

Kev: If you've got any bed-pans, that is….

Barney: Well, this bloke is the real Admiral. *Shoot first. Aim next. Ask questions last!*

*NB. Obesa Cantavit. But the regular reader may be confidently advised that there is much more to be said on what Lord Ironsides actually does…as will follow shortly….That distant music that you hear? It has to be the '*Marseillaise*'.…*

EPISODE 17

Obesity-Class in the NHS. The National Anti-Obesity Campaign...Part 3.

Dramatis Personae:

Mr. Barney Wells BEM, Chief Executive of The Arthur Scargill Memorial NHS Trust Hospital, Chessingfield-on-Soke.

Kevin O'Grady, Chief Executive of the Coleraine St. Fortescue Veterinary Hospital, N. Ireland.

Sir Crank Lamparde, Permanent Secretary at the Department of Health. Cambridge.

The members of the new National Action on Obesity Ministerial Advisory Group, as previously listed.

***

Barney: I've just got those Minutes, of the National Action on Obesity Advisory Group. It's startling stuff!

Kev: *Be careful then!*

Barney: Yep. Very hush-hush. Handling it with thick gardening gloves. Jessie over in Richmond House can only send the papers once there are many copies, so hard to trace to her. The Midstaffer KGB is everywhere. Still, we do get from her info on some potentially dodgy policies when they're still in the chrysalis stage, before they emerge into the butterfly state of existence.

Kev: Meanwhile, seen that report of the study for the British Heart Foundation? Taxes on fizzy drinks – good one, that.

But I'd want it much bigger than the suggested 12p a can. That'll make no difference to the OBESITES. Will just pay and grumble. Look at what they do when the Chancellor puts a bit more tax on ciggies. Sales fall for a day and a half. Back up again then, pdq. I'd put a quid on every can, myself. And another 50p refunded on return of the can. Course, the government can't have it both ways. If price change works, health costs will fall, short and long term. Great! But so will revenues fall for the Treasury. They'll have to cut waste and woeful public spending, won't they? More off benefits for the idle, all that. So, good policy that way, too.

Barney: But a big hike in tax *would* cut obesity, type 2 diabetes, cardiovascular disease, and dental caries. The report said that people between 16 and 29 drink an average of 300ml of sugary drinks a day. Just beggars belief, with all the public health info out there.

Kev: Don't see it, do they, the Obesites. Hello Co-op Funeral Parlour, here we come!

Barney: But not before they've cost the NHS a burglar's fortune, and over many years.

Kev: Gotta go for far bigger tax rises then, haven't we? Whack 'em in the wallets. It all needs *action*. If you please, Sir, NOW! Not just more Cameroonishcleggie-i-chatter.

Barney: And did you see that The Millkibar Kid is on about giving more and more things out FREE? School dinners...*Taxpayers Ahoy!*

Kev: Yes. Saw that. The Kid and the TU's to give out more free-school meals. Galore. But the nippers will just take the free meal, and then top-up on the way home with crisps and coke! See them every day as you drive about. And then chucking the cans and crisp-bags down in the street.

Barney: Who pays the billios there then? As per usual. *Taxpayers Ahoy!* How are you, anyway?

Kev: Well, still holding onto my dream. Of The Moaners being relegated....

Barney: To the second division.

Kev: Can't be long now, can it? Successive relegations? Might even be three?

Barney: *Would* be nice! Would show that kick 'em and rush don't work any longer. Nor special pleading for extra-time by The Great Gum Chewer.

Kev: And thrower of the wrappers onto the ground!

Indeed. Got a good story for you, anyway. Apparently The Millkibar Kid was at St. Struggles in Bradford. Visited the new Northern Safe and Sound Chubb's Care Home in Station Road. One of those very carefully quite accidentally announced totally unexpected unannounced, polish-the-light-bulbs, paint-the-kerbs, Queenie-coming, hide-the-bad-staff-first, unannounced but inadvertently press-released and spotlighted-in-advance shock surprise inspections that they do. Surprises us all, in course!

Kev: Ah, yes...as they do. Policy to catch them doing everything right. That is, until the *Daily Mail* reveals all, and shuts 'em down with big neglect scandal...

Barney: Well, The Kid walked all round. And on the way out he came across a dear old lady half asleep in a wheelchair. Spoke to her. No reply. Spoke to her again. No reply. She then stirred, but only very slightly. Spoke to her yet again. Dear old lady opens half an eye. Looks at The Great Leader himself. The Kid Millkibar: *"Do you know who I am?"* Old lady: *"No. But if you ask Matron, she'll tell you."*

Kev: Love it! Great story. Heard it before, though, about that Kerr bloke, and about Virginia Bottomley too. Always gets good laughs.

Barney: Well, I've *some* good personal news about this Anti-Obesity Campaign.

Kev: You being weighed then? Dieting?

Barney: No! But I'm on the escapees list. Glad to say we're not after all to be the national pilot site. Going to Kent instead. I'm glad to avoid all that aggro. Got my hands full as it is with these mergers here.

Kev: Heard that, too. The new David Copperfield NHS Trust at Whitstable is to be the first place for all the new stuff to be tried. They're equipping an old Victorian Oyster Warehouse for it. Rumour is that they are going to give the Chair to the ancient Baroness Sitting Bull. Dunno why. And that Prof. Applecore is to be Chief Executive.

Kev: Both Socialists, aren't they? How will that work then?

Barney: Search me! The ways of Sir Crank are never entirely clear. Are they? But not intended to be, either. Confusion the best path to change, eh?

Kev: Very Camerooneshk! Probably just figureheads. Or fall-persons. They will be under the All-Seeing Eye!

Barney: And the mysterious peace of the Lord knows no understanding, and all that.

Kev: Be an interesting side-show, anyway. But first, tell me who's on the Advisory Group.

Barney: Well, good group of GPs, with the business people too. Includes Lord J.C.B. Digger. Sir Vinnie Earns. Lord Cartpetking. A lot of people who have built firms, risked their own money, been successful entrepreneurs, responded to ever-changing markets, actually run something competitive where they have needed to attract willing revenues in the real world. High-powered lot. Apparently Sir Crank calls them the 'sound sensers.' That's where the power will be. So must mean it. We'll see what Hunt has to say about it in his big forthcoming 19 November "Off We Go" speech. To tell the nation his response to all the recent reports, scandals, disasters, special pleadings by the Royal College of Vested Interests, all that…

Kev: But I heard that the group includes old "Jurassic Johnson" from the British Medical Army [BMA].

Barney: The famed "negotiator"!

Kev: The very same!

Barney: And that Jessica Pottlegun-Wedgwood-Benn-Tyza CBE, Chair of the Socialist Medical Congress.

Kev: What, the SWP Trot woman?

Barney: Her, indeed. Ex-Liberty supporter? As they deign to call it now.

Kev: The renamed old hard-leftie National Council for Civil Liberties as was? Very-leftie lot?

Barney: Still took the CBE though, one of 'em did, didn't they? Be Damed next! Ha! Also I hear they are to add to the Advisory Group that Professor Martin I. Muckuup from the Woyal London School of Haywhine. And Professor A. Hampster, Director of The Klingfilm Fund in London.

Kev: The socialist intellectual?

Barney: If you says so.

But also they've got Sir Harry Verney, the well-known GP, and Sir Squoffy from the Tower Hamlets Hospital Trust.

Kev: *Some* sense then. Your mate, Squoffy. Ex-civil service, isn't he? Knows his way around Whitehall then. Old pals with Sir Crank, I'll bet. Just like Humpy and Jumbo. Usually knows the meaning of things. Reads the codes. And knows whose shoulder to tap on.

Barney: Yep. A lot of good sense and experience there, in that group. Dr. Jeff Neville is there, too.

Kev: The GP who is now a Chief Exec? Good man. Trying to get Dr. Sybil Benjamin, too, I heard. Top GP in Cumbria. But very busy in her practice.

Barney: So it's all going to be about direct economic and social incentives. That's what can produce behavioural change.

Only that, too. The new E-RAND study said so, anyway. Repeats what they did 35 years ago. No change. But no-one listened then. See what happens now. Relying on education or leafleting won't do it. Got to *enforce* change. S'what Squoffy says they intend, anyway.

Well, here's the minutes. Bit long. Will send them in two parts. Scanned. Sending now.

Kev receives…

<u>The National Action on Obesity Ministerial Advisory Group. To advise The Secretary of State. Richmond House. 15 October 2013. In the Chair, Sir Crank Lamparde. Minutes Secretary, Ms. Jessie Tompkins. Present, as in signed presence book.</u> Apology for absence: Lord Alascooke of Smugdominion.

Sir Crank: My Lords, Gentlemen, and ladies. May I extend a warm welcome on this very wet, cold, windy, inclement afternoon. We are very grateful for your advice. We have important work to complete. We have already dealt with the initiatives concerning The Airlines, the Entertainment Venues, and The Food Industry, as the previous minutes record. We can now promptly complete our advisory work, and submit our recommendations to The Secretary of State.

Professor Hampster: I have some points…One the one had…on the other…

Sir Crank: Yes. In due time, Professor.

Professor Hampster: Well, I *do* have some points….on the one hand…on the other….

Sir Crank: Please do not interrupt me when I am interrupting you! We need to get on.

As you all know, The Secretary of State is determined to tackle the National Obesity Crisis. And so I have been given the task of shaping the outline proposals, setting out principles and mechanisms, for national and local action. Urgently. Of course, I welcome your advice, which is why I invited you to join this Advisory Group. I am to organise the budget and the work programme. Here we have got to manage up as well as down. And to ensure transparency too. The work must be based on building local relationships. We will have a National pilot. Economics are seen as the central pivot to necessary change in individual life-styles. And we need to act before the NHS collapses under the weight of the Obesites, if I can use that dangerous phrase.

Lord Digger: Sir Crank, we should stress that politically this is heavyweight stuff. Relates to big ministerial guns. A key to the next election, too, perhaps. Appeal to the big grey vote. Representing the responsible consumer. Make very direct personal links between money and personal responsibility. Personal behaviour and NHS access to be made not merely an issue for debate, but a principle of change. BMI to be the magic phrase which everyone will know soon enough. Or else. Economic guns to heads. We business people know how the world really works…

Sir Crank: Yes, my Lord. Quite.

Sir Harry Verney: 'Bout time too. Jamie Oliver, Graeme Archer, and that Joanna Blythman in the *Telegraph* are all three right. If someone doesn't do something really serious the whole NHS will collapse. No good leafleting those who refuse to see or hear. GPs see what that produces, every day of the week. So do the A&E staffs. Under the weight of sugar and refined carbohydrates, saturated fats in processed meats, and the misuse of alcohol and drugs. So I'm very much encouraged that we are now to give something serious and new a real shot.

Dr. Jeff Neville: Sir Crank, may I just ask about this disturbing *Telegraph* headline, "Fast food-chains are good for us, says minister." Who is this Brendon Lewis, calling himself the high-street minister?

Sir Harry: High fat, high cholesterol, high obesity, low sense more like!

Sir Crank: Yes Harry. Mr. Lewis. Not to be taken seriously, you know. Don't mind him. Got his headline. But he hasn't got the saddle on the right way round, you know. Galloping in quite the wrong direction. Pay no regard…

Dr. Jeff Neville: Just seeking publicity and promotion, then?

Professor Hampster: Well, this is the time for my points…on the one hand…on the other….

Sir Crank: Well, I will not waste any more time today then. I will summarise the main proposals, in outline so far. We're also going to get a lot of action on the tax issues you've recently raised, Lord Carpetking.

The SofS is keen to animate everything. Very urgent. The Treasury is already signed on to the project.

And so here are the details of what we actually plan to implement, immediately…

NB. We will now ask the esteemed and informed reader to pass on to the further features of this jovial entertainment…

EPISODE 18

Enter Lord Ironsides. N£sd Musical Chairs. A New World, Perhaps? Part 2.

Dramatis personae:

Mr. Barney Wells BEM is Chief Executive of The Arthur Scargill Memorial NHS Trust Hospital, Chessingfield-on-Soke.

Kevin O'Grady is Chief Executive of the Coleraine St. Fortescue Hospital, N. Ireland.

Admiral Albert George Quincy Lascelles Vernon, Lord Ironsides, is a former head of the Fleet Air Arm, and now Chairman of The Arthur Scargill Memorial NHS Trust Hospital.

Brenda When is secretary/PA to Mr.Wells.

***

Kev: Hey Barney, it's me. What you listening too then?

Barney: Ah, the very great and special Dean Friedman. Hear it? The American bloke who made that great single *Ariel*, and then *Lucky Stars*. And a lot of other great stuff. I've got it on his CD, *Well Well Said the Rocking Chair*. Terrific stuff. Brilliant, original singer-song writer, and still going. Comes here every year. Still tours around. We go to a gig every year if we can. Saw him during the Edinburgh Festival. Do yourself a favour, look him up.

Kev. I'll have a listen. Remember him well. But today I want to talk to you about this Lord Ironsides. *Another* original, it seems. Gossip-in-chief, please! Keep hearing more about him.

You said he told you his job was to give leadership, and to be tough on the issues that matter. Well, saw him on the telly with Paxman last night. Never seen Paxman pasted about the place like that! At the end Paxman was just pleading for mercy! Leadership? Bloke's DYNAMITE!

Oh, zee docs vill luv IM!" Will all get trichotillomania. |

Barney: He may not be so keen on some of them either!

AND *actually he actually thinks he's here to actually run the place!*

ACTUALLY! Means to, actually, as well.

He even did a ward round today!!! Just like a senior consultant!

Kev: Unheard of…. Tell me the story, do!

Barney: 'Course, I don't ever go anywhere near the wards. Not if I can help it. Well, only if a Minister visits. But I had to go round with him. Nurse Deary Duffy guided me round with him. I tried to keep the peace. Ironsides was just like that James Robertson-Justice in the old Dirk Bogarde *Doctor* films! Dragged consultants round with him, too! Meek as mild, they seemed. In shock! Junior docs struck dumb. Couldn't believe what they were witnessing. Can't last, of course. The top docs will plot and caucus with the BMA in London on how to hit back hard. The Royal Academy of Vested Interests will surely be involved, too.

But it turns out that Ironside's really got the human touch! Amazing conversation with this young bloke in emergency ward, waiting for the anaesthetist!

Kev: 'Course, what did you expect? Bloke like that. Boss of Fleet Air Arm, doesn't take a job just to sit tight and collect the dosh, does he? Not interested in the old CBE-grab club. Means to do something real. Big change after Her Bugginsturnship though! Sounds the real thing. And if he's got top political backing, then, Barney, as dear old Simon Silverman used to say, *Now You're Tooting!* Ironside's there to get the job done. And he'll do it. Best to join in, Barney! Get into the lift, and rise with him. Jeremy Hunt keeps talking on about new leadership. Well, maybe here it is! *At long last.*

Barney: Well, Ironside's gone off like a rocket for sure. Seems a decent bloke, though. Everyone round here who knows him a bit says he's a warm, supportive, decent man. But very brisk and business-like. Evidently very good chums with Osborne, Hunt and Gove. Or as rumour has it. Wines and dines at Chequers too. Outranks me by about 365 levels!

Kev: Can't wait to see what he does to your hospital set up, then! HE won't be frightened of the docs, will he?!

Barney: Not very likely, is it? For starters, he did this ward round today!

Kev: Coo! Tell me!

Barney: Well, as we went along the world's longest, draughtiest, darkest N£S corridor he spoke in passing to that cocky A&E doc, you know, that Mr. Pierrot Carlossa Urugluee I've mentioned before. Arrogant so and so. The one with the OBE. Clown by name, clown by nature. And the blooming doc actually answered the Chairman back! In front of everyone, too! Can you *believe*? Chairman told him, "Hey, I pay your wages, you know! I *am* your employer!" Should have seen the look he got. Would have fried a Woolly Mammoth.

Kev: He's a very tough nut, the Admiral, then.

Barney: You can say so! And he actually interviewed four patients in their beds on his 'ward round.' Three drunks and a drug-dealer. Examined the patient's charts. Questioned nurses. I thought he was going to take their pulses! 'Course, the nurses love him. Big handsome powerful rich bloke and all that. The first bed he stopped at, there's this young bloke, just lying there in a bed. Can't be a day over 17.

Kev: Never heard the like!

Barney: Well, let me tell you.

"What are you here for?" asked the Admiral.

"Got bitten by a dog."

"Why did he bite you?"

"I was running away..

"Why were you doing that?"

"It was a police dog."

"Why was it chasing you?"

"Woz on my pitch, weren't I?"

"Ah. Doing what?"

"Selling me drugs, weren't I, eh?"

"Where was this then?"

"On Scooter's Hill. It's my regular pitch."

"So what happened then? How did you get here?"

"Cops out of window of squad car shouted at me: "Stop where you are!" So I ran. Scooted. Dog chased me. Caught me. Dog bit me leg. Ripped and broke muscle. Cops nabbed me. Called ambulance. Brought me here. Stuck into this bed. Cop at the door, watching me. Handcuffed me to bed. Now got to have an op. Fix me leg."

Admiral grimaced. "Good luck then, young man. And stay away from dogs!" Walked on…docs following in muted crocodile ranks.

Anyway, it gets better than fiction! That young man was successfully operated on that night. Stabilised. Recovering. But he had secreted three tiny smart telephones which the police hadn't discovered and removed. And the chap in the next bed heard him doing his drug deals from his bed once he'd come round!

Under the sheet in the dark: "Bonzoi, it's me, Stingo! Now, about the stuff…."

Kev: *Very* entrepreneurial! Admiral would have been impressed, if he'd heard him, perhaps.

Barney: P'raps. Anyway, fit again, the next morning the police re-arrested the bloke, took him away, and charged him. Usual list:

"Dealing…possession…concealment…evasion…breach of probation…lure and mistreatment of police dog…rode bike through wrong gate…the lot."

But what a GREAT COUNTRY this is! This young bloke gets bitten by police Alsatian. Injured. Gets nicked. Handcuffed. Cops put him into NHS ambulance. *Taxpayers Ahoy!*

Gets to us quickly. Tetanus jab. Examination. Gives history. Down to theatre. Fixed-up by the NHS. Discharged. Then arrested again! *Taxpayers Ahoy!* Again!

Kev: Well, that's just like that historical John Wilkes Booth business in America. Escapes from Ford's Theatre after shooting Abe Lincoln in Washington in 1865. Jumps onto stage. Breaks leg. Skeddaddles out somehow, down an alleyway. Gets onto a horse. Rides like the blazes into rural Virginia. Gets as far as a doctor's house in the country. Doc fixes him up, and is then arrested. Booth caught. Doc in hot water. Goes to jail. End of career.

Barney: Yes. But, as old Squoffy would say, *here's the lesson.* Just been reading about that Mudd bloke myself. I'm a fan of Lincoln. Reading him up after seeing that new Day Lewis film. The doc was that Samuel Alexander Mudd, a real MD.

Convicted and jailed for aiding and conspiring with the actor Booth in the assassination. Later pardoned by President Andrew Johnson and released. But never really acquitted. Despite repeated attempts by family members and others to have it expunged, his conviction was never overturned. S'how we got the expression "His name is mud!"

Kev: Just can't wait to hear what Ironsides does next, then! Sounds like the big shake-ups Hunt says he wants are really coming!

Brenda interjects: Yes, Chairman. And not before time, the big shake-ups. Can't come fast enough. But the lesson, please about the drugs chap! It's one of the entire lessons of the N£sd, the police, and the young drug-dealer with the dog bite. Just fix the leg in front of you! Don't stop to judge.

Kev: Quite so. The ever reliable N£sd! You don't pay your money. You takes your chances. And we makes your choices!

Barney: But cash with order now if you are from Bongoland.

Otherwise....*Taxpayers Ahoy!*

NB. The alert regular reader will expect to hear more of the sterling adventures of our reforming Admiral. Which we promise to deliver shortly...

EPISODE 19

Enter Lord Ironsides. N£sd Musical Chairs, and a New World, Perhaps? Part 3.

Dramatis personae:

Mr. Barney Wells BEM, is Chief Executive of The Arthur Scargill Memorial NHS Trust Hospital, Chessingfield-on-Soke.

The new Chair at Chessingfield-on-Soke is a local land-owner of aristocratic descent, Admiral Albert George Quincy Lascelles Vernon de St. Valery, Lord Ironsides, a former head of the Fleet Air Arm.

Kevin O'Grady is Chief Executive of the Coleraine St. Fortescue Veterinary Hospital, N. Ireland.

***

Kev: Busy day, here. So thought would just give you a quick ring. What's what up then now with the great Lord I?

Barney: Supposed to have been asked by another member at the Ath. "Is it true that you have a Renoir in your bathroom?" Said to have replied gruffly, "Certainly not. It's a Cezanne."

Kev: Aha! The Goths are always at the door. World as odd as ever. You following all the pre-election news?

Barney: I keep expecting The Millkibar Kid to announce his new election wheeze: the 'Get Out of Wonga Free' card. Course, all those borrowers were forced at machine-gun point to take the loans, weren't they? Stands to reason! "I just *had* to have that new laptop!" So used to living off the State, getting it all free, never read the small print, never had no job. "Wot, it's a *debt*, is it? Wot's that, eh? Will the Social pay it then?"

Taxpayers Ahoy!

Kev: Yes. FREE, the Kid's great touchstone words: it's all FREE!

Barney: Come and Vote For It Now! Roll up, roll up! Blinking Fairground Barker.

Kev: Where the prize Teddy Bears are glued to the counter!
Barney: And then we get the lot of them in A&E on Saturday night! Drink dopey. Drug wonky. Violent, bruised, foul-mouthed. Ah, paradise it is! GPs get them every day. Got to have sympathy for them. It's no wonder they skedaddle at weekends.

Kev: *Those* patients. Permanently, accidents waiting to happen.

Barney: But I'm still making time to tackle the *Guardian* 'backwards' cross-word. Need my coffee-breaks.

You know, the *Guardian* gives you the words and you have to make-up the clues. Then they print your clues another day, and someone else provides the words. And round it goes.

Kev: Sounds like our cataract booking clerks!

Barney: Well, you can't do your own words the next day, of course. Be cheating. Got two good ones today: antidisestablishmentarianism, and then honorificabilitudinitatibus.

Kev: Ah. Know that second one. It's the dative and ablative plural of the mediaeval Latin word. Can be translated as "the state of being able to achieve honours." It's in *Love's Labour's Lost*. A hapax legomenon in the Shakespeare canon. Second longest word in the English language. So, I win the Morphi…the Gin!

But you mustn't miss this chance, Barney. Ask your receptionists to change their names.

Could have a Welsh Ms. Antidisestablishmentarianism. And a Bulgarian Ms. Honorificabilitudinitatibus.

Barney: Keep the callers busy!

Barney: As to the real world…I see that The Wobbly Major, KG has joined Labour. Read in the *Independent*, too, that he's just been awarded an Honorary A Level GCE at the University of Grimsby. Seemed very smug about it in the photo.

Reminds me of the daft situation we had with him. And why we lost out on the necessary N£sd reforms that could have followed Mrs. T's GP fund-holding. Major, a dripping-wet Fabian Socialist, leading the Tories. Blair, a tough public-school Tory, leading Labour. No wonder it was all such a confused muddle. Major wrecked the Tory Party. Blair saved Labour, from itself. But where arte they both now? Blair head of the International Middle Eastern Bank of Blair. Major head of the website confusedaintI.com

Barney: Major – he'll be giving the Clem Attlee Up-With-Welfare Celebratory Memorial Lecture next. At the London School of Duffonomics. After Baccy Clarke, Sheepsavage Howe and The Lord Hezza. At least we missed some of *their* trains!

But their heritage? Not much kop for us, is it? We've got Camerounique, Cleggiquirk, and the Milliband Kid! And an N£sd that just stumbles along. None of the fundamentals being faced at all. Though Sir Mike is at least trying on cancer care. But that Colchester lot…be some court actions there, I'll bet.

Kev: Otherwise, in Whitehall, the usual Fabianised Marxigookery has no end. Osborne, Gove, and IDS seem the only ones with any time for meritocracy, effort, or achievement. All got to be On The Free otherwise, hasn't it? And we're landed with the consequences and the demand in the N£sd. No prices. So demand endless. Lot of it daft demand, too. Thanks very much, Sir Major!

ENTER LORD IRONSIDE. N£SD MUSICAL CHAIRS. A NEW WORLD, PERHAPS? PT 3

Barney: *KG!*

Kev: Well, my chum Bill P is right on all this. He says that the economy is up the spout, and it's hardly a surprise. Cheap money started it all of course. Europe obsessions too were no help. Then the neglect of asset inflation at home did huge harm. Help-to-buy thing is lunatic, too. But then there are election bribes to be distributed, alas. And we both know who will pay the bill, don't we? Not Lord Edth Balth, that's for sure.

Barney: But on the topic of Ironsides. I've been realising that it's all done with, the long-established policy of hush hush appointing of Chairs, as it was in our earlier days in the N£sd. New brooms! Favour-ocracy? Gone! Mate-ocracy? Banned! Local Labour-ocracy? Fini! Doco-ocracy?Not gone exactly, but gone a lot quieter! Out of order. For a bit, anyway. What we grew up with, 'tis no more.

Kev: Andy Cunningham, Reggie Maudling and John Paulson must all be turning in their multi-storey graves! Sir Sandy, too.

Barney: As we've learned from how we got the new chairman. No more tip-offs like the good old days from Region. You know, tell you what to do, and which back-pocket has the "extra" Emergency Funds in it when you've co-operated and done as you're told. So just take "The right bloke for the job. No need for ads or interviews. Here's your man." Worked like that for some Chief Exec appointments too. But ALL Gone! GONE FOR GOOD! And if you think about it, good thing too.

Kev: Well, Ironsides don't sound like The Late Sir-Socialistic-Sir-Nick-Sir-Expenses-Sir-Nicely-Pensioned-&-Will-Go-But-Not-Quite-Yet's choice, I'll be bound.

Barney: Nope. But Simon Stevens is surely a much better bet, despite his old obsession with targets.

Kev: Targets. Produced Colchesteritis. But Stevens, he's really a believer in competition shifting managers into action, isn't he? And in self-reliance, integrity and the self-responsibility of the individual?

Barney: Well, we'll soon see...

Kev: But someone up there must have waved a bigger stick, to get Ironsides in. And Stevens must have been consulted?

Barney:Bound to have been, I reckon. Those discussions about Sir Nickelodeon's job have been going on for ages. Involved the very top. Cameron, Osborne, Hunt, and Milburn perhaps. Of that I'm surer than my own chin. Said to have been several interviews with Stevens at No.10 with the PM. Flown in secretly from the States.

The story inside the story is, too, that the Admiral is rumoured to be very close mates with Osborne, Hunt and with that Michael Gove. Has had that knack all his career of making friends with powerful people. Special kind of networker. The right friends. All the Top Clubs. Had an extraordinary naval career, too. Not just swept along with the flow – made his own decisions, and got them right. Apparently, too, had a flaming row with Dimmo Patten about the handling of Hong Kong when he shipped in there. Doesn't think much of

Major, either. "Total duffer. Least educated man ever to be PM." Thinks neither of them were qualified for the jobs they had.

Kev: So, rings all the right bells! Sounds like the kind of Top Bloke we need in Chairs! No more of the Alderman Alfie Oldcocks, Labour Councillors-for-Life for Chesterfield Farest Eastest, eh?

Barney: *De nada.* But you know, the old expression, it feels like arriving in another century, but without your wallet? Like in that Michael Crichton film *Timeline.*

Kev: Well, Ironsides will surely go in where Mandarins Fear to Tread.

Barney: Yes. Fix the mergers, all that. Keen on consuymerism, too. Probably more so than Ministers. But enormous changes coming here. Duff the competition laws, aided by Them at The Centre. He's got class and status. Genuine aristocrat. He's emphasised to me already his belief in character, discipline and willpower together with rigorous training and clear decision-making.

Kev: Got that right, too, in actual war-time, of course.

Barney: Bloke who understands power and has enormous career achievements – which the Maharajah docs will respect. Got ideas, too. Which they won't like much. Great believer in initiative and in individualism. Worse still for the docs. And apparently knows Milburn. Worser and worser for the docs! And he's surely very much involved in more big changes to come in the NHS. So, expect mass apoplexy at the Royal Academy of Vested Interests!

Kev. But Milburn *surely* realises what wasn't done when he set up the first Foundation Trusts? Needs to push them to go further now. Competitive consumerist system is what we need. Milburn's close to Cameron. Simon Stevens one of his old mates, of course. Word is, too, that Osborne and Gove are really now driving the Tory policy saloon – lock, stock, boot, and barrel. And a key behind-the-screen bloke is said to be that clever Cambridge-grad. Kwasi Kwarteng. The MP for Spelthorne in Surrey? Wrote that book *Ghosts of Empire.* Very bright spark.

Barney: Serious stuff. Fast rising star. Best of the last intake.

Kev: So, a *proper* Conservative policy again then? Be a big surprise, wouldn't it? Unless they want to win the next election that is.

Barney: Jessie Tompkins at the DoH says so, anyway. Be much tougher policies now. And she usually knows.

Admiral Ironsides, a real Classic FM job he is, too. Talk about sound-around full-colour in-your-face IMAX! An Osbornista, too. Hot on economics and direct incentives. Apparently known him all his life. His Great-Aunt is married to Osborne's father-in-law Lord Howell's second cousin's sister-in-law's nurse's dog-walker's chef's cleaner in Guildford. Or summink.

And no flies on Ironsides, either. Starred Double-First in Philosophy at Trinity College, Cambridge. Ph. D from MIT in Naval Engineering. Ran Fleet Air Arm. Revved everything up. Falklands, of course. On the rostrum with Maggie. Then retired and made Chairman of some stiff-neck publishing companies. Common touch, too.

This new job not his epitaph, either. Means to do more, though has already done it all. Y'know. Submariner. Harrier pilot. Aircraft Carrier toff. Arctic explorer with that Sir Fiennes Whatnot. Distinguished career from day one at Dartmouth. Rolling in dosh, inherited money. And promoted up the greasy pole as fast as you can say to your Grandson "Gimme a fiver!"

Last nine or ten generations all big navy or army men. Viscounts, Earls, Baronets, and all that. Ancestors fought at Crecy and at Agincourt. On our side. Even though descended from Ralph de St. Valery, who came over with William the ["Lucky"] Bastard in 1066. Rich as sin.

Kev: Still, look at it this way. Take another perspective. The lift's going up. Jump in with him! *Now* you're tooting. Inside-track. Music from a different drummer. Tides of history. Top nob. Can see several moves ahead. There to get the job done. And he'll do it. So surf the waves with him! If he is indeed close mates with Hunt and Gove then it's best to join in! Go with the flow! Big smiles on camera! Swim with the sharks!

Sounds as if you'll finally got the real issues onto the table, too! Finish your career in a wave of glory! *Sir* Barney...

Barney: Well I've been doing my researches, to try to get on-side. Like Barkis, I'm willin'.

Kev: So, Be Prepared...

Barney: Well, I've got *Country Life*, from last May. Big feature on him. Five-page colour spread. Him, Her Ladyship, brats, gun-dogs and all. Lives in this vast great handsome sandstone pile, Keeble Hall, built for Ralph Ironsides in c.1580. Only 23 miles from my office. Even said to play Bridge with Gove. Wines and dines at Chequers. Outranks me by about 365 levels!

Kev: Bridge with Gove? Oh, now THAT is ominous! So he's the real gung-ho Admiral. As you've told me he *Shoots first. Aims next. Asks questions last!*

But, reflecting on it, he's exactly the kind of Chair we need appointed throughout the N£sd. If we are ever going to get anything real done about our problems...

Barney: And my most urgent first job is to get all the *individual* performance data on all our docs, and organise a fully lit-up, totally informative website for local people to see. Chairman very committed to that. With pictures, career histories, training and retraining info, death rates, recall rates, infection rates, and patient-group and individual patient comments and feedback. Feels like we'll be working with what my engineer cousin Harry calls "white-hot intensity."

Kev: Well, it's clear enough that your Chairman rose to the top because he was a very good manager, as well as being protected by family, cash, and politics.

Barney: So no more Three-Card Monte here!

Kev: Seems not. Big changes in the hissing snake-pit!

Barney: So bring on the dancing girls!

Kev: Aha. Be nice! But as a well brought-up Irish boy, I know my *Ecclesiasticus:* "There is a time to every purpose under heaven."

Barney: So bring on the fanfares for the Apocalypse? And if I'm unaccountably missing next Monday, call Perry Mason! Or Bill Murray!

Kev: Well, my advice is to be supportive, but be cautious too. P'raps we should both keep in mind the old Turkish proverb: "As the axe came into the forest the tree said the handle is one of us."

Barney: Yep Siree. I don't want to be the right man in the wrong place at the wrong time.

Do you?

NB. Lord Ironsides means to do much more, too, as the esteemed and attentive informed regular reader will shortly be advised…meanwhile, 'The System' prevails…

EPISODE 20

"The System." Little Dorrit and the Bradford Child, Little Hamzah Khan. Or, 'Nobody's Fault.'

Dramatis personae:

Sir Cyril Squoffington-Squogg, OBE, JP, is Chief Executive of The Tower of London NHS Hospital Trust, Tower Hamlets, London, EC.

Lady Bernice Squoffington-Squogg, his wife, is also Chair of The Wiltshire Artists Benevolent Fund.

***

Lady S-S: Cyril, you look very white and shaken-up? Whatever is wrong? You haven't been worrying about that nurse shortage again, have you? Not at all your fault you know. Sign of the times. And Peter Carter is dealing with it, you know. Good man, he is.

Sir S-S: No my love. It's not that. It's this dreadful business in Bradford. Has really shaken me up. Apparently it's all "Nobody's Fault"!

Lady S-S: Well, sit down here, and let's talk about it. I'll go out to the garden centre later for the new tulips.

Sir Squoffy: Well, I am in absolutely total shock. This official review into the death of that poor little starved and then mummified boy, Hamzah Khan. Killed by his Mother. And body only discovered two years later. How can such things happen in a so-called civilized society? *And just look at this official report!* Chillingly empty. And yet dreadfully revealing too. Tells you a lot about what social services were doing. Or, rather, just *not* doing. "Nobody's fault"!!!

Lady S-S: *Nobody's fault?* Can that really be right? Can that *really* be the case?

Sir S-S: No. But it's just the Paramountcy of Process. "The System." The boy was starved to death by his wicked Mother, Amanda Hutton. Jailed now. Should have been shot. That child lived a perfectly terrifying life. And no-one in "The System" ever properly noticed. No-one is to blame in "The System", according to this new report. That's "The System", too. Staggers me that does. Or if they did notice anything awry, no-one, it seems did enough to save the child, did they?

And then just look at how it's all being explained. Something laughably called the Bradford Safeguarding Children's Board – Independent, it claims to be – has just concluded that it's all the fault of "The System." It's concluded that no individual bodies or specific "professionals" *[sic]* could be blamed for failing to save the four-year-old.

Instead, he was let down by "The System"!

Lady S-S: So there's a very powerful message about individual accountability, isn't there? There *isn't* any individual accountability. Is there? Public employees get off scot-free, don't they? No accountability in the state system? No state-paid employee accountable?

Sir S-S: No. None. And "The System" is apparently more important than actually having an alert individual being personally and professionally responsible for actually knowing what is going on. And for an actual person taking actual individual action and actually being responsible to do something about it. It's *actually* totalitarian bureaucracy. *Actually* Marxist rather than democratic. As bad as that. Iniquitous. Ubiquitous, too.

And as to building real accountability, the situation is worsening. Look at what actually happens to any whistle-blowers. End of career that is. And all this is just gathering pace. No come-backs. No state-paid individual ever held responsible. Law unto themselves. It's all nobody's fault. Only "The System" at work. *Actually!*

Lady S-S: "The System?" Not some individual state employee? Who is being protected then? The vulnerable and powerless children? Or "The System"? And the paid individuals within it?

Sir S-S: Ah. You might well ask. As we must. No-one individual is being called to account. None. Anyway, none so far as I can see. No individual responsibility being taken. None.

Lady S-S: Looking after your own, it's called, isn't it? Usual social and medical attitude, isn't it? So will "The System" now be jailed for 12 years? Or will "The System" be placed on the Incompetent to Care for Children Register? Or will "The System" be called up by a House of Commons enquiry committee? Or will "The System" have all its professional badges and qualifications to practice withdrawn?

Sir S-S: What do you think? We both know, don't we? Of course, "The System" will still do all future assessments. "The System" will still see families [or not]. "The System" will still undertake future reviews. "The System" will still do the welfare visits. It was "The System" which attended the Magistrate's Court. It was "The System" which corresponded with health visitors, education officials, childhood services and social care. Dealing with other "Systems", no doubt. It was all the work of "The System."

Lady S-S: *And* "The System" was probably designed by a "System", too, wasn't it? Not by an individual?

Sir S-S: Well, it was "The System" which visited the child at his home. And what did "The System" see, and do? Ah. It was "The System" which missed many opportunities to intervene. Ah. It was "The System" which failed to act when one of the child's siblings spoke to the police about the Mother's violence in the home. Ah. *Thankfully, one very alert young police-woman, on her very first day in the job, insisted on going into the home.* Otherwise, would "The System" have slumbered on for another two years? Makes you wonder, doesn't it?

Lady S-S: Of course, "The System" can now lay all the blame on the Mother. Well, she *was* an appalling individual. And now she's well out of the way. For the time being, anyway. Probation Officers allowing. But who was supposed to be on the look-out for the interests of the child? Ah. That was not an individual. That was "The System." It was "The System" which saw his home, and his conditions. Where he died, poor love, in such appalling conditions.

Was it "The System" which now failed to explain glaring absences in the report itself, may I ask? Was it "The System" which was unassertive in its approach? Was it "The System" which failed to conduct a co-ordinated professional assessment of the child's situation – and those of some of his seven siblings who were each separately and severally variously in A&E, and in the local police court?

Sir S-S: Well, that's what it looks like, doesn't it? It was *only* two years after his death that his mummified body was discovered. And not by "The System", either. Meanwhile, another part of "The System" had been continuing to pay his Mother the state Child Benefits. Including for three children who had apparently disappeared from school entirely. Did "The System" even notice that? Seems not.

Lady S-S: So that Edward Timpson, the Children's Minister, is absolutely right to raise a big stink about it now. And I want names named. Otherwise, what are the messages to other care workers employed across the country? The Minister called the new report "useless." Very polite word to use, in my view.

Sir S-S: But NO SINGLE HUMAN INDIVIDUAL actually working in "THE SYSTEM", recruited and paid and pensioned in "The System", will it seems have any individual responsibility for what was done in and by "The System." Nor will there be any recourse against anyone in "The System. Not at all!

Lady S-S: So that's a big comfort to us all, isn't it?

Sir S-S: And will "The System" never be allowed again to design a "System"? How unlikely is that?

Bloody appalling business, the whole of it.

Lady S-S: Hmmm. By the by, I saw Lord Ironsides at the Royal Academy yesterday. Seems in fine form.

Sir S-S: Yes. Very keen on improving clinical practice, he says. Tackling some NHS "Systems"! Barney rang me about it. Asked my advice. Told him to be very careful. Very thin ice, that one. Warned Ironsides, too. But he's already asked the docs, "Where is what we do done best in the world? And how do we compare?" And he wants answers!

Lady S-S: So he's not going to be the first to blink. Not intimated by "The System", then?

Sir S-S: Not likely, not him. He's founding a special Clinical Performance Improvement Unit, too. Designed to pick up quickly on new research and to encourage much swifter clinical improvements. He even read out to Barney some stuff from the *New England Journal*. And he's asked Hunt to put him in charge of a Ministerial Working Party on doctor's contracts, employment practices, and outcomes.

Lady S-S: He needs to be careful there, my love. Watch his back. You remember what happened to the last bloke who tried that one, don't you? That Brighton bloke. He got a proper back-stabbing.

Sir S-S: Yes. I was still in the pensions department then, of course. Working my way up the long ladder. In 1994 I think it was? So, before my time that fuss. But Ironsides says his aunt at Worthing knew that chap's Uncle. Told her all the dreadful doings. Heard it from a local GP. The facts supposed to be very shocking, what the hospital docs did.

Apparently, those docs were encouraged or advised by the BMA in London. Very alarmed at any notion of a doctor's performance being linked to pay. They had some kind of a private meeting to make a decision to get rid of that Chairman, apparently. And many days in advance of the arranged discussion with the consultants to which they had already invited the Chairman. Collected proxy votes from docs in their own favour – and against the Chairman – even before the discussion was heard with him and before that Chairman chap had any chance to put his side of his case. Which he had the guts to do, before most of them – those that turned up on the night, anyway. Dirty business, it seems. Have to wait for that Chairman chap's memoirs to know it all, I s'pose. Being written though, as I hear it. "The System" yet again, of course.

Lady S-S: And yet here's John Major *[–KG. Ed.]* now so very upright and complaining – it seems to be his fortnightly grumble and grouse about …

Lady S-S: …about something which he could have done something about *at the time*…

Sir S-S: Which he could have done something about *at the time*, as you say…but never did.

Yet he says now that that people from the bottom ranks can't make it, and that's a scandal. Well, that Brighton chap's Granddad was born in the Workhouse, you know. Just like mine. Terrible part of East London then. Hoxton. Then his Granddad was killed in the Great War. Just as mine was. Both at Ypres. That gutsy Chairman chap came from a very poor family. His Mother was seriously disabled too. Working-class boy. Made his own way. And what did Major do then, when he needed support, eh? Turned his face to the wall!

Lady S-S: Takes some doing that, getting from where that Brighton chap started, as you know better than me. All those things true of you, too, of course. Came from the same place. Had a similar life. Same background.

Sir S-S: Yes. I understand all that very well. Never forgotten it, either

Lady S-S: And so when the legendary brown custard hit the fan what did Major actually do to protect that chap from the vested interests of the docs? What did he do to help him make the necessary management changes? To help patients. To change "The System"?

Sir S-S: Major? Did nothing, did he? Very brave now, of course. And Virginia Bottomley, too? But both *in absentia* then, weren't they?

Lady S-S: Did neither of them say that the docs don't appoint Chairmen, but they do?

"THE SYSTEM"

Sir S-S: Did they heck! Hid in the woodpile. Micely nicely quietly. But, it's "THE SYSTEM," my love!

Lady S-S: And did you see that Dave Bennett *[Chief Executive of Monitor – Ed.]* is again critical of how long the NHS still takes to copy positive clinical innovations?

Sir S-S: Yes. Good speech. Still a shocker, ignoring evidence as they still do. Can't be bothered to change! I'm struggling with all that every day at the Tower.

Lady S-S: And Dave's right, isn't he, when he says that the service will not introduce radical reforms unless under intense pressure from new competitors?

Sir S-S: Ah, yes. But "THE SYSTEM", my love!

Lady S-S: Well, we need these changes. It's not privatisation. It's just plain good sense. And patients don't care who the provider is, do they, anyway?

Sir S-S: No. Not at all. They just want the service. But their problem is that they have no certain way to command it. No enforceable rights. No influence over money, which is what gives the individual some control. You know, "Money talks and preference walks." Again, it's "The System." Most ordinary, powerless people are out in the margins.

Lady S-S: Well, without direct real and open individual accountability, no-one will budge, will they? Without individual financial empowerment, too. Otherwise, it's just "As you were!" isn't it? No individual is to be to blame, or take real creative initiatives, or take personal responsibilities, or be alert to troubles?

Sir S-S: Ah. No. None of that. To be sure. But it's "THE SYSTEM", my love!

Lady S-S: It's the standard Social Care *[sic]*, Child Care *[sic]*, and NHS *[sic]* co-ordinated Four Point Plan, isn't it?

Sir S-S: Yes. It is. Let me put it in **Big Bold Arial Black letters! The Four Point Plan:**

1. No-one is to blame. Deny it all. It's "THE SYSTEM."

2. Hide the guilty. And it's nobody's fault. *It's "The System."*

3. Promote the Guilty. Pay them more. Find them new prestigious jobs. Within the present set-up. Costs plenty. *But it's "The System."*

4. Pay off all possible whistle-blowers, to keep silent, if they will. A lot of that NHS cash has been about...

Lady S-S: Yes. But gone now! Was a new wrinkle of "The System", though.

Sir S-S: Yes. It's *"The System."*

Lady S-S: Beats me, too!

NB. In our next episode, Sir Squoffy will offer his own wise guidance on the newly announced (but unworkable) policy concerning the law, and prosecutions for the wilful neglect of patients ... and what is needed instead...as the alert regular reader will expect...

EPISODE 21

Who's for Wilful Medical Neglect or Negligence then?

Wilful, indeed?

Neglect, or Negligent?

And so to The High Court, 5-years in the Clink, or Transportation?

We Ask Away!

Dramatis Personae:

Sir Cyril Squoffington-Squogg, OBE, JP, is Chief Executive of The Tower of London NHS Hospital Trust, Tower Hamlets, London, EC.

Sir Harry Verney, CBE, is a retired GP, the founder in 1960 of the now large general practice at Tinsdale Weir, Suffolk.

Dr. William Pickering, trained at King's College Hospital in London, and worked in hospitals, as a GP, and as an expert witness. [He was a real friend of the author and of patients, but very sadly he died on 5 February 2015].

As previously promised, we (the readers) meet at the Charing Cross Hotel in London to overhear Sir Squoffy and Sir Harry get together over coffee, to discuss medical [and political!] errors, and in advance of the National Anti-Obesity Advisory Group meeting, which shortly continues at Richmond House......

As Robert Smith Surtees says in his novel 'Ask Mamma', "We will just run the reader through the lot, with the aid of truth for an accompaniment."

Sir Squoffy: Harry, I want a word about Cameron's new initiative to charge doctors – and others, too, if due – with "wilful neglect", is it? *"Wilful"?* Seems a bit strong. *"Neglect"?* Seems too weak. Isn't it *negligence* which is the real issue?

Travelled down on the train with my very good and wise chum, Dr. Bill Pickering. If anyone knows this field, he does. Now works as an expert witness. Knows his stuff backwards and sideways. Knows his Dickens, too!

Sir Harry: What does he think of it then? And what about you?

Sir Squoffy: Well, Bill is surely right on all this. Been thinking and writing about it for years. He thinks it's just another sop to the voter. PM to show he's "doing something" about Mid. Staffs, Salford, Morecambe Bay, all those unnecessary deaths. All that negligent medical practice….

Sir Harry: Yes. And Cameron is beside the point as usual. Hunt, too, on this one. Bill says that they're using the wrong terms, about the wrong issues, and so the real wrongs in poor medical practice will continue on.

Sir Squoffy: Yes. Read his stuff on the *BMJ* online site. His older IEA essay, too. His ideas ought to have been taken up years ago. A lot of people unnecessarily dead would now still be living and breathing. So help me God.

Sir Harry: And, anyway, Cameron and Hunt have got the language all wrong…As per usual….

Sir Squoffy: As per usual.

Sir Harry: Anyway, Bill always says we should be talking about *medical negligence*, not "wilful neglect" – which were Cameron's words. *Negligence* is what we're really concerned about. Failures in what should be ordinary day-to-day practices.

Let me say a bit more on this. It's a crucial distinction, between "wilful neglect" (which, as I remind us, is what Cameron said) and "medical negligence."

In my book "neglect" is not bothering, when a doc knows better. "Negligence" is not doing the elementary things which one is professionally paid and trained to do. But "Wilful" here is the wrong word to use. I take issue with that word. It's Cameron's attempt to avoid tackling the slackers, the lazy, the incompetent. "Wilful" errors in medicine do not happen – any more than they do on the roads or in people's houses.

Sit Squoffy: Well, I'm sure Dr. Pickering is right. He is always very precise, amd measured. But a lot of people would say that plenty of the recent "incidents" in care-homes have involved *wilful* behaviour by staff, wouldn't they? There's been some deliberate harming of people there, hasn't there? Not just neglect, bad as that is. Wilful harming, as well as casual and systematic neglect. And incompetence.

Then there are the very serious criminals. Dr. Harold Shipman in Todmorden was surely a case of entirely wilful, carefully planned, if entirely abnormal wilful and criminal actions. And there have been a few murdering nurses, like that Beverley Allitt. People would say she was absolutely criminally wilful, wouldn't they?

Sir Harry: Yes. Shipman was a terrible man. Should have been found out much sooner, too. Munchhausen's syndrome in Allitt's case. Dreadful serial killer – the 'Angel of Death', as she thought. Convicted of murdering four children, attempting to murder three others, and causing grievous bodily harm to another six. Locked up forever now, at Rampton. Been some others like her, too, in the past. But thankfully very few. Both of them, Shipman and Allitt, were really guilty of *wilful criminality*.

Sir Squoffy: That's so, I'm sure. Very unusual, too, thank goodness. Well, as far as we can tell, anyway.

Sir Harry: So what happens daily – and which Bill wants independently inspected, on a rigorous and systematic basis – are almost always elementary errors. Which *are* negligent, of course! When a doctor knows damn well (probably) what he or she should do, but just doesn't do it. Doesn't bother. Too lazy. Too busy. Too slack, rather than clinically incompetent. That's what we should be dealing with. But the PM doesn't want more tanks on his lawn. So, no go for an Independent Medical Inspectorate.

Sir S-S: More's the pity! It's much needed.

Sir Harry: The PM talks of "wilful neglect." It's the word "wilful" which is ridiculous. It's very unhelpful. "Neglect" is half-true. But "negligence" – as in "medical negligence" – is a better way to put it. However, you don't need this word "willful." It just muddles the picture, clouds the water, misplaces the discussion.

You, see "neglect", for doctors, is actually *a new word*. "Negligence" is what they understand. And elementary errors are often indeed "negligence", rather than neglect. But not "willful." We have to focus *on the errors themselves* – and their correction – not on some allegedly wicked motivations. We have to get this clear – all of us.

Sir Squoffy: So, d'you mean the problem is things like not referring the patient properly and promptly, or not looking at recent lab results properly, efficient analysis – *ordinary* day-to-day things like that?

Sir Harry: Absolutely so. Just so. Just that. For most medical errors are the result of failing to follow elementary practice. Things like failures to diagnose properly, so people are left untreated when they could be saved. That's negligence. That's bad practice. That needs to be caught early. That's what needs to be checked regularly. Daily practice. When it's wrong, inept, out-of-date, we *must* catch it before it kills people. Retrain the medics, stop the errors, increase alertness. Punish them when appropriate.

'Course, we are all of us on a human continuum, aren't we? We're not necessarily all good or all bad. Not at any one time. And good people do bad things. Not always fully aware. They need our check-ups. It would help them, and us.

Sir Harry: Yes. Right. Bill's argument is that the only way any improvements to practice will work – and the only way the guys and girls making elementary medical errors and errors in practice will get noticed early on, or even notice errors for themselves – is if every NHS district has its own Inspector/s. Every cluster of GP practices. And so on, too. And the Inspectors must actually be properly *clinically trained* people. Need them everywhere. Not just one national whizzo like Sir Mike. Daft to think it can be done by one man, or even a small cluster around him. Catch them doing things right, and where wrong, that too. Then correct practice, double pronto. Will take a decent sized staff, in every region.

Sir Squoffy: Well, Dr. Pickering must be right when he says that if inspections were carried out *by trained doctors*, doctors working as inspectors *and outside the NHS*...

Sir Harry: Be plenty of volunteers! Escape the grind, but do another proper job! Would do it myself if I was young again!

Sir Squoffy: Yes. Quite so. But it's got to be done by *doctors working outside the NHS.*

No croneyism! Properly independent, but properly clinically informed too. Got to know what it is they are looking at, what they are seeing, and what they are seeing actually means.

And then if such doctors were doing the inspection work, they'd catch things like Mid-Staffs in a moment. Failing clinical practices will stand out a mile high. Every Hospital and every cluster of GP practices, and so on, all being inspected by medical professionals. *By medical professionals*, not just by managers. And not by the kinds of ex-local government inspectors that that Care Quality outfit employs. That started terribly badly with the initial National Care Standards Commission, of course. Way back in 2001, was it? How I hears it, anyway. Terrible beginnings. Left it far too late to adopt unexpected inspections.

Sir Harry: 'Course, there are lots of errors in other parts of society, too. But it's usually neglect of proper practice, not necessarily *wilful* neglect. I think that's a fair qualification, not just word-play. Don't stop at a red light? Well, that's neglect. Be prosecuted for it. Don't need that other word. 'wilful.' But still need to stop failing medical practice *at* that red light.

Sir Squoffy: Yes. And think about it, getting the docs or nurses into court? Be much better to catch people's inadequate practice *before* it gets any further. Before a lot more people suffer, or die from it.

If you go to court, the costs will be huge. And can you really see judges convicting many doctors? Not very likely is it? In my experience they lean on the side of the medical professionals. If they possibly can. Negligence very hard to prove in court, too. Much better to check medical practice all the time. And to improve it. All the time. You know, they do do the wrong hernia. Wrong legs have been amputated. It happens. Unnecessary addictive drugs prescribed, all the time. By the millions. Instruments left inside patients. A lot of that. And the NHS compensation budget has gone up vastly – up by 20%, in a year, I think.

Sir Harry: Well, the stats *are* fearful. Paid out claims, at £19 billion annually, will soon be half of the NHS budget! Loads of big law firms are kept afloat by it. By that alone, so busy they are.

Look at Maternity services. It costs £700 per birth to cover possible negligence claims – and that alone in Maternity cost the NHS £482 million last year on cover. Meanwhile, have you seen the usual self-serving BMA responses? Usual outrage! Won't face the facts. Won't touch the solutions. Please just go away, will you!

Sir Squoffy: *Fancy that!*

Sir Harry: Ta dah! Yes. The usual down-the-escalator chitter chatter. Spend more on patients, not on witch-hunts. Leave us well alone. Ta dah! All that eloquent posho-voice gubbins. Meanwhile, leave us good chaps to check on our own good chaps. At school together, you know. Good chaps. Mid-Staffs some kind of fluke. Not representative. All that. Ta dah!

Sir Squoffy: *Witch hunts!* Lordy! Could have done with some of them! Salford. Morecambe Bay. Dr. Harold Shipman. Dr. Bodkin Adams all those years ago, killing off dozens of rich and vulnerable widows in Eastbourne, come to that. And what is happening right now in the lovely, friendly, uninspected, queue-you-up-for yours, St.Hilda's on the Hill, eh?

Sir Harry: Don't ask. Nobody knows. Nobody wants to know. Morbidity data? Whistle for it! Medical practises? "We know best." Inspections? Might see a national inspector every other year, perhaps, now. Meanwhile, please don't ask. Best not. We know best. That's the message. That's "The System."

Sir Squoffy: Some will say "Oh, here comes Sir Mike! Well, he'll be gone again soon!" Meanwhile, let's have the marchers and the banners and the car-stickers. "Protect OUR BELOVED St. Hilda's!" Hands Off!

Sir Harry: And so Cameron is now using the Big Words "Wilful Neglect" as a political negligee, eh?

Sir Squoffy: *General election Ahoy!*

Sir Harry: Yes. And all the time that the government is the boss, running the NHS politically, they'll never be too critical will they? Always claim it's better than it is. And in reverse when in opposition. Just like Millkiband is doing now. If the government would let go, and let proper competing providers and purchasers in – either with new facilities, or as bidders to manage what we've got – then it would and could and should all change. Otherwise, it just won't, will it?

Sir Harry: Nope. Won't. Which reminds me to ask you. What did you do about that doc you were so worried about? That old fuffer duffer. What was his name? Mr. Geoffrey Circuitous Fumbletum? Famed top-knob at the Royal Academy of Vested Interests. Big committee man. With all that alphabet of initials after his name.

Sir Squoffy: Yes. Him. Paediatrician. Bridge partner of old "Jurassic." Apparently has been a danger and a menace for years. Left alone by managers, fearful of the docs. And the BMA. Left alone by the docs – "One of us." Am trying to get an early retirement there now. But very hard to do. How dare I interfere, etc. And he's not the only one either. They all cover for one another, don't they? You know. "There but for the Grace of God...." Think they can't learn from others, either.

Sir Harry: Yep. Know the attitude: "Chessingfield's All The World." Don't want to know what they do anywhere else. Not invented here. All that. And anyway, as to checking on day-to-day clinical practice, just you try it!

Sir Squoffy: Well, GPs too, Harry! Not all shining stars on the Christmas tree, are they?

Sir Harry: Quite so, sad to say. But I hear that old Ironsides up at Chessingfield is shaking up the local GPS. Has Barney enquiring into referral patterns. And looking at timeliness.

Before it's too late to save the patient. Wants GPs in A&E, too. Wants to spread the wings and integrate health and social care as well. And do much more on preventive care, too.

Sir Squoffy: Good for Ironsides. He cited JFK to me, too. For a society "where the strong are just, and the weak are preserved." Kennedy's Inauguration Speech. 1960. Ironsides is going for the real issues. Much more real than the fluffy Cameroonesk puffery about "wilful neglect."

Sir Harry: Quite so. But they won't like Ironsides at The Lodge!

Sir Squoffy: No. He'll hear the usual Latin from the top docs, won't he? *Nihil declaro!*

Sir Harry: "I have nothing to declare."

Sir Squoffy: Well, we'd best be off. Sir Crank will be expecting us…

Sir Harry: Ah, yes. *Sic Friatur Crustum Dulce!*

Sir Squoffy: "That's the way the cookie crumbles!"

Sir Harry: Alas, it's still so…But *Subucula tua apparet!*

Sir Squoffy: "Your slip is showing!"

Aha! *My* neglect! But not my *wilful*, criminal negligence!

EPISODE 22

Obesity-Class in the NHS. The National Anti-Obesity Campaign....Part 4.

The charming [?] winter tale of Mrs. Gobble, and her three young plumpy but not very jumpy children, Goblitup, Goblthelot, and Gobblygook.

Dramatis Personae:

Sir Crank Lamparde, Permanent Secretary at the Department of Health.

Various business-people and some of the usual NHS suspects on the new National Action on Obesity Advisory Group...as previously listed. Apology for absence: Lord Alascooke of Smugdominion.

The National Anti-Obesity Advisory Group [Top Secret] meeting continues at Richmond House...

Sir Crank: So, as King Lear says, "We are come to this great stage of fools." Which is where we are with the OBESITES.

You all know we are on a very sticky wicket. We can beg, we can borrow, we can plead, we can advise, we can publicise. But the OBESITES grow in number, in size, and in costs to the N£sd. Every bite that they take. Every day and night. *We* are exercised! But *they* are not! And so we have got to get the guns really firing. Which means Economics! Tax incentives! Docking benefits! Shake 'em up in the wallets! Your money or your life! Or the whole system will go bust. No other way – even for a crusty old civil servant like me! AND I've lived through it all – Major, Blair, Brown, Balth [at the Treasury then] – the lot. Not a decent decision between them. Not a camel's breath of policy that didn't go tummy-up. Or WMD down. So now let's hope for better, my Lords, Ladies and Gentlemen.

As Mr. Walsh up at Coggeshall-on-Soke might say, *Obesites Ahoy!*

Sir Squoffy: Quite so. And a lot of the benefits they squander is *our* money, of course. And if Mothers are to get £200 Free shopping vouchers to encourage them to breast-feed, why can't we take money away from benefits if people won't exercise or diet sensibly?

If this government genuinely believes in economic incentives – which, if they don't, isn't this breast-feed idea just publicity wonk stuff? – why not make them *really* work? Tackle the big issues. *Obesites Ahoy*, indeed!

Sir Crank: Just so. As I've been advising JH. And as I've told him, first, we are here to find the problem, and then to fix the problem.

The NHS can no longer suffer quietly. We have to find *instrumental* ways to change the lamentable to the best.

We have already agreed on the reality that the NHS is in fact effectively divided into four classes:

First (for doctors). Business (for the middle-classes). Coach (for the working-classes). And Obesite, for The Obesites. With promotion from class 4 to class 3 if the Health Savings Account and the private insurance cover and co-payment is well managed by the Obesite individual. And if their BMI is improved and measured.

Dr. Jeff Neville: Bloody BIG ifs!!!

But, before we go on, can I just re-tell the story I told you over coffee earlier today, sir? About what I saw in the cinema! This awful and rough, already obese, family group of four. Let's call them Mrs. Gobble [17 stone if an ounce?], and her three young children – another 39 stone between them, but no more than 25 years, adding up their ages totally. Call them Goblitup, Goblthelot, and Gobblygook.

Sir Crank: Please do so. It captures the big points. And it sums up how we must pivot Anti-Obesity policy. We just have to *Blitz the Burger Bodies*. If I may descend into the colloquial. *And especially their Parents*. But before you tell us, Dr. Neville, let me say that this kind of group must be absolutely obliged to do daily exercise IF they are to get any State Benefits at all, let alone N£sd services.

Dr. Neville: Very serious points. Time for the tanks on their lawns. So here is the story of what I saw on Saturday when I took my eight-year-old grandson to see that new film *Turbo*, about the snail who races.

Sir Crank: Please go on, Dr. Neville. You are, after all, a GP and a chief executive.

Dr. Neville: Right. Well, my Grandson absolutely loved the film. Brilliant computer design. Good music, too. But I spent much of the time observing the audience around us. And in shocked fascination. I'm now absolutely sure that the only way we can tackle this Obesity issue is through the pivot of compulsory and additional personal insurance. And by compulsory annual check-ups by GPs of every person covered by the N£sd – taxpayers or not. And by the GP setting agreed targets on exercise, weight, and diet for each person. I'm sure that only if we use individual economic incentives will we get anyway here at all. Including docking benefits, and also rewarding better behaviours.

The story. In the cinema, sitting near us, I saw these three children who were being damaged by their own parent, despite all the public health information. It's the parents – as well as the commercial pressures – which are THE problem.

This was only 11.15 in the morning! But the Mother was already just stuffing them with popcorn, chocolate, crisps, coke and lemonade full of sugar. It's *the parents* who are the danger. The Mother probably thought she was being good to them, too. Which is part of the sadness.

Another point: the hypochondriac anti-poverty pressure groups say that such families are too poor to eat well. Well, that's gobble-twaddle *par excellence*, isn't it? A child's ticket cost £6.80 to that film, so for the three that's £20.40. An adult ticket cost £9.10. So that's £29.50. They must have had at least £20 worth of junk food between them. They were munching constantly for an hour and a half. So that's £49.50. Plus transport costs, say £5? We're up to £54.50. Plus their lunch spend in the burger café. Say another £3 each? Burger, chips, fizzy drink – only costs £2.99. Junk.

Sir Crank: Nothing in it, s'why it's cheap.

Dr. Neville: So the Mother's spend that morning must have exceeded £66! OK, they may have had some kind of special offer. Or be regulars – which makes the junk-eating picture worse! Even if they had a discount or a special early-booking deal, their spend must surely have been over £50!

Sir Crank: Desperately shocking. And in your folder today is evidence that one in four Britons fails to take even half an hour of exercise a month – not a week, *a month*. This shortens many lives, and by several years. Sir Squoffy wants to come in here, I believe.

Sir Squoffy: Yes, I have read the paper, Sir Crank. But in a liberal, open democracy, I do not see any way to enforce change, to require exercise. Even if we required people to attend exercise clubs, the cost of enforcement would be vast. We could offer tax incentives, but even that will cost us in government time and staffing. And a lot of them pay no taxes anyway. Could dock benefits, I suppose? The cost of failures to exercise is projected at £50 billion by 2050. So there is some considerable room for tax incentives or of docking benefits, isn't there?

Sir Crank: Yes, certainly. Could do both. And, as Fred Turok, Chairman of UK Active, has just said, "Poor fitness doesn't discriminate. It kills both thin people and fat people alike." We need to think all this through, before we report.

Sir Harry: And we've got to regulate the food and the drinks firms. 'Course we have. Look at this week's report on how just two sugary drinks a day can cause kidney damage. And kids like those in the cinema are almost 'chain-cokeing.' If I can say it that way. Somehow we've got to get these parents to change. And that's going to take real economic incentives which have bite. At the moment, they ignore all our guidance, all our advice.

Sir Crank: Just not interested. And they are not suffering from "poverty," are they? On the contrary, it is the opposite which has caused the problem.

Dr. Neville: Well, poverty of mind in the parents, it is, alas. And we have seen that leafleting them doesn't do it. Public health information doesn't, either. And even TV programmes like that one recently, *"Too Fat To Fly"* – well they just turn it off. And then they just turn up at the health centre and tell us "You're the bloody doctor. You fix it." So we cannot rely on what Francis Bacon wrote. He said "Let the injuries men do be their schoolmasters." Not now they aren't.

Sir Crank: Quite so.

Dr. Neville: The Mother and kids were decently dressed, too. And it costs real money…

Sir Harry: Or free benefits!

Dr. Neville: Or free benefits… to take three kids to the pictures. It's no longer just sixpence on a Saturday morning to see *Hopalong Cassidy* and *Flash Gordon*…

Sir Crank: And *Look-at-Life*, number 704!

Sir Squoffy: As it was when we were nippers.

Dr. Neville: Then the four of them left, chucking all the plastic packaging, the cans, the bottles, and leaving a lot of spilled popcorn trampled under foot on the floor as well. So they weren't trained at all to eat sensibly, or to clean up after themselves. Then Mrs. Goble Mum and one of the kids, the fattest one – call him Gobblitup – went straight into the adjacent open-plan burger-bodies café there. "I'm Bloody Starvin', Mum!" I went to the loo with my Grandson. Two of the kids – call them Goblthelot, and Gobblygook – followed us in. Both f-ing and blinding. Both left without washing their hands. Both "Bloody Starvin', ain't I, eh?"

Hardly a charming Saturday weekend tale of Peter Rabbit and the lettuces, is it? Hardly an advertisement for the enfranchised and voting proletariat, is it?

So I asked the young man at the ticket office why they didn't sell popcorn in smaller boxes, if sell it they must. "Consumer demand, innit? And that's where we makes our money, on the refreshments, like, see. Big boxes do best. The leasing costs of the films only leave us a small margin otherwise, see what I mean?"

So – as a GP whose colleagues take the brunt of all this every day of the week – I want to insist again that the pivot of all our policies must be direct and sharp individual economic incentives. The Obesites ignore everything else.

And so if they had all to see a GP or a nurse once a year, and have a target set of behaviours to follow, then if they did nothing their higher insurance costs would click-in. And they'd go to the back of the NHS queue, too. Those who just say that they don't care as the Social will pay, they will have to have their benefits cut. And those who then go burgling will just have to go to jail. Keys down the well. If it only worked 50/50 we'd all be a lot better off, wouldn't we? The costs saved would be many millions in a year. And the health of millions.

Jessica Pottlegun-Wedgwood-Benn-Tyza: *Never!* Never agreed to any of that! All bloody fascism! I came here to discuss the people's take-over of the leading 100 capitalist monopolies…The 'Sussex' plan….with Alan Woods just back from Venezuela…Oh. Oh. Will ring Shami…

Sir Crank: Thank you. So very helpful. Noted.

Jessica Pottlegun-Wedgwood-Benn-Tyza *splutters…and nearly chokes….stands up, sits down, stands up, sits down…covers her face with current copy of 'The Observer'….Moans…"Must ring Shami"…*

Sir Crank: So now, there's effectively to be a new national Obesity-Class for Obese

Patients Only, with their Tax incentives and, where relevant, their State Benefits, both directly tied to exercise and diet....

Dr. Neville: Like on the railways in the old days. Tickets and classes. A roof or not. Going back to 1830! Or a policy like what W.S. Gilbert called foreign regimes? "Despotisms tempered by Dynamite"? If so, that's the ticket!

Jessica Pottlegun-Wedgwood-Benn-Tyza *turns flesh-colour, with fury...* MUST ring Shami..."

Sir Crank: Well, economics and incentives – they must indeed be our pivot. Most certainly. You decide for yourself. Obese or not. Up to you. Buy your own ticket, as it were. Pay your own bills. And we will check your annual review document and measure your BMI when you want N£sd services. Or social care. Entirely the patient's life-style choice. Then you go to the service suited to you. Grossly Fat or Slimmer and Sensible? It comes down to individual choice. And accepting personal responsibility for the results of your own behaviour. And the costs.

Sir Snuffle Kettledrum *jumps up, like a startled grouse: Do they?* Since when? Not in my day they didn't! How long has this been going on?

Sir Crank: Thank you, Sir Snuffle. But I will continue. Nothing like any limits on choice in the minutes, so far as I can see. In fact, we want to augment a good deal more there.

Sir Snuffle Kettledrum: We in the Woyal College of Surgeons will expect to be paid more then, of course...The Woyal Academy of Vested Interests report says, er, hmm...got it here somewhere...*Closes eyes, and sleeps.*

Professor Hampster: I have some points...on the one hand...on the other....

Nursie Nursie Dixbungler: Where ARE the biscuits? Why am I always the last to know anything?

Sir Crank: HERUMPH! Please focus.

Those with an unacceptable BMI – like the people too fat to fly in last week's TV programme; like the 25% of men in Rochford, Essex, just judged obese or overweight – all those will have much more limited access to N£sd services. So we shall thus introduce direct encouragement and incentives for the individual to do something about their exercising and their obesity.

Sir Vinnie Earns: *Or else!*

Mr. McCeltic: Quite so! They got it one bite at a time. So stop the bites. Change the diet. Change the life-style. Change the exercise regime. Or else. Daft recent discussion by those heart-bleeding poverty-mob wobble-wonks on whether it's the parents' duty to tell their kids they are fat! Or not! Course it's their responsibility. Who do they think made them fat, for gobble-Turkey's sake?

Jessica Pottlegun-Wedgwood-Benn-Tyza *splutters*...'New Militant Today' says in its editorial this week that the leading 100 capitalist monopolies...

And Shami says…"

Sir Crank: HERUMPH! Please focus. *Please.*

Dr. Neville: Economics is the only thing that will bite.

Sir Crank: And so on the linkage to Tax Incentives and to State Benefits, to direct economic incentives for personal responsibility, to enforced daily exercise itself…and to the publicity event which JH will declare open, the new compulsory OBESITES-ONLY Gateshead Boxing Day 10-mile National Steeplechase Race…let's get serious about this at last…

NB. This LARGE topic is to be continued for one more episode….

PS. Is that Sir Krank related to that ex-Chelsea footballer? Often wondered.

EPISODE 23

The Richmond House Revels. Scene 3: Part 1.

How Unknown N£sd Doctors Practice. Or Courting Disasters. What you are not allowed to know.

Dramatis personae.

Sir Cyril Squoffington-Squogg, OBE, JP, is Chief Executive of The Tower of London NHS Hospital Trust, Tower Hamlets, London, EC. He is aged 67.

Lady Bernice Squoffington-Squogg, his wife, is also Chair of The Wiltshire Artists Benevolent Fund. She is aged 39.

Some medical "professionals," as named below.

***

It is a Sunday evening. Sir Squoffy and Lady S are settled in front of a roaring log fire at their house in Wiltshire, catching up on the newspapers.

In the flickering light, sipping Old Port, Sir Squoffy suddenly bursts out: *How long* have we had an NHS? *How can* all this possibly be? I know that the poets tells us that it's time which tries all things…but, oh, oh, *unbelievable this is!*

Lady S-S: What is it my love? Whatever now?

Sir S-S: Oh! oh! My corpuscles are aflame! Just *look* at this story in the 'paper today: "Hundreds of convicted doctors still practising"! Whatever next!

It's just got to be my next subject for the Richmond House Revels! Well, far from funny it is. But I must do what I can to draw more attention to this. It's totally shocking. Which says something for the N£sd, the system of shockers itself.

Lady S-S: Let me see that report…..

Sir S-S: In the *Daily Telegraph.* 25 November.

Lady S-S: Give me the gist of it.

Sir S-S: News because of the Freedom of Information Act. Otherwise we'd still all be in the very dark. Amazing figures and facts just been released. Astonishing stuff.

Here, the key points:

- That 761 GPs, surgeons and other doctors have kept their jobs despite being found guilty of serious offences, including taking indecent images of children, child cruelty, drug trafficking, personal violence including GBH, fraud – and the rest.

- All these docs were still practising in October this year.

- "Medical chiefs said that they cannot automatically ban convicted doctors because it may breach their human rights."

Lady S-S: *That old one again!!!*

Sir S-S continues…:

- Included one doctor who took indecent photos of a child, 2 with convictions for possessing child porn, 2 for trafficking in drugs, 3 for GBH. There were 31 offences of assault, 7 for soliciting prostitutes, 12 for domestic violence and 2 for child cruelty or neglect.

- Then there were 184 convictions for dangerous driving, 330 for drink-driving and 4 for driving under the influence of drugs.

- *And then more!* Other convictions for perjury, fraud, forgery, including threats to kill and violent disorder. Including rioting – would you believe!

Lady S-S: Golly! It's a catalogue of apallingness which would be the subject of a huge fuss if it happened out in Hackney, wouldn't it? You know, the headline: "Shoreditch Scum Threaten British Way of Life."!

Sir S-S: Yes. And here it is reported on page 8 only!

Lady S-S: If that was some kids in Shoreditch or Edmonton or Lambeth, there'd be a terrific ruckus from the Royal Academy of Vested Interests, wouldn't there? Calls for GPs to be protected from dangerous social loonies. Demands by the surgeons for special compensation, and extra insurance. Attacks on politicians, as usual.

So what did the Great British Whitewash Company PLC say and do about it all?

Sir S-S: Ah, there's the rub. We don't know. Can't be told. They won't say.

Lady S-S: *Won't say?* What do you mean Cyril? *Won't say?* How can that be?

Sir S-S: Seems that doctors have to appear before something called a "fitness to practice" hearing once they get a serious court conviction. But in many of these cases the doc just gets a warning or a temporary suspension. And then they're left to go on practising.

THE RICHMOND HOUSE REVELS. SCENE 3. PART 1

Lady S-S: So how many have been covered up then?

Sir S-S: More than 200 convictions have never been made public. Hearings held in secret. It's claimed some involved doc's own health conditions – depression, etc.

Lady S-S: Surely even with that they should be stopped from practising till cured? And isn't there an online register which any patient can consult?

Sir S-S: Yes. Includes some restrictions noted about individual docs – not allowed to practice with under 18s, etc. Big warning that. Keep your hands off my kids! But we still don't have all the names. And none of the detailed facts.

They *say* that they want to be able to ban docs automatically if convicted of serious crimes, like sex offences, without a hearing. *They say*.

Lady S-S: So what happens if a doc gets a custodial conviction? Can't practice from the cell, can they?

Sir S-S: No. But the GBWWCo says that doesn't mean that the doc is automatically unfit to practice. Most are removed or suspended for a time. *They say* the doc can only go back to work under strict conditions. And for serious convictions they will almost always – *almos*t always! – be removed from the register. *They say*.

Lady S-S: But we still don't have the names of more than 200 of them?

Sir S-S: No. We don't. *So they don't say.*

Lady S-S: Well, in your hospital at The Tower Hamlets, if a nurse or a doctor is a problem you know they've got to be carefully supervised. Supported, inspected, helped. And if a danger, stopped. All human beings, of course. But the security of the patient comes first at all times. Doesn't it? It's not only a management problem. It's a patient's problem. And if the GBWWCo and the politicians can't protect us from those they know are no good, what kind of a service are they offering us anyway?

Sir S-S: Well, HERE'S THE LESSON, as I'm always saying to Barney up at Scargills. Well, two. Well, three lessons actually.

Firstly, why isn't the Great Bruteish [sorry, British] Whitewash Company telling us who *all* the doctors are, what they've done – or not done – and what is being done about it? To protect us, is it? Or them? And the politicians? Are the docs, the politicians, and the civil servants all in it together? Makes you ask, doesn't it?

Lady S-S: It's surely no good at all that the docs and the politicians and Whitehall won't let us know who is no good.

Sir S-S: Right. Makes you ask if they really care what these doctors have been doing to patients – and to themselves, some of them, with drugs. You'd think that if they really cared, wouldn't the docs AND the politicians, and Whitehall [and let alone "Medical authorities"!] be checking up on doctors properly all the time? Unexpected visits, all that. Especially now we now that they know that a lot of doctors do illegal drugs, do frauds, are dreadfully violent, have been convicted in the courts, some a very serious danger to children – AND yet are still practising.

Lady S-S: Whose human rights are being protected? I ask you.

Sir S-S: And secondly, if this was a private business, no one would go anywhere near it, would they? But State Monopolies Is As State Monopolies Does. And this government has done its dandiest to avoid ever giving any individual patient any power over money. So they cannot ever become a consumer with some clout, can they? So they can't be demanding can they? Genuine choice? Can't go elsewhere with their NHS money can they?

Patient empowerment? Co-payments? Knowledge about all medical practitioners? Not b***** likely, say the ToryLibDemys. Lucky to get what you get, aren't you? Best in the world, isn't it? So wait in line quietly, please, if you will. And, oh, don't forget to Vote ToryLibDemys next time!

Lady S-S: Or LabLibDemys!

Sir S-S: Or LabLibDemys, yes. Makes no difference. But mustn't go near that nasty Nigel Farage, must we? Can't have that, can we? He means what he says, after all. Might get some real changes. Actually *thinks!* And speak in *clear language* that engages the public! Can't have that, can we? Goodness forbid!

Lady S-S: And all the docs are "Good Chaps" after all, aren't they? Good Chaps all.

Sir S-S: Ha! And the third lesson is that until and unless we get a proper Conservative government, with real leadership, which is prepared to give its full support to free enterprise, to make the case for it, to put in years in vibrant campaigning for that vision of a free, meritocratic, consumerist society – to enable us all to understand why things are the way that they are, and how they could be changed – we'll continue to slip and slide downwards into ninnyism, bureaucracy, corporate fiddle-faddle, and corporatist custard.

Lady S-S: And a worsening service, every day?

Sir S-S: Alas, that too.

Lady S-S: And more secret the-public-can't-be-told enquiries but-we-know-best-good-chaps-all. No doubt. For our own good, of course. And for the Good Chaps. Meanwhile, "How can I help? I'm a convicted doctor." But you can't be told that, can you?

Sir S-S: Ha. Quite so.

Lady S-S: Must be right, as you say, my love, those three lessons. And it's so very hard to believe that this ToryLibDemys government really based the celebratory, tell-the-world about Britain, the Olympic Opening ceremony, on the NHS. As the best of British. It's just fantasy. Cloud-Cuckootosh. Ritual but not romance.

Sir S-S: Staggers the willies!

THE RICHMOND HOUSE REVELS. SCENE 3. PART 1

Lady S-S: And so, with this sort of thing going on wholesale, will you write a scene for the Richmond House Revels?

Sir S-S: Yes, my love. Christmas is coming. So I'll ask Father Christmas why is it that so many doctors are so hopeless but secretly protected.

I'll deal with that headline: "Hundreds of convicted doctors still practicing." Follow up from the current fuss about medical neglect – by which they should really mean negligence – too. A lot of that about.

And express my concern that not enough is being done to remove doctors from practice when they ought not to be doctoring at all. And urge that we tell the public what's actually going on.

Lady S-S: Can you get the awful new OECD analysis in too, if there's space? Britain at the bottom of most of the league tables, or close. Dreadful cancer results. All that. Regular as the grass growing.

Sir S-S: Yes. Absolutely. Want to die early of otherwise treatable disease? Be born here! Be an 'ordinary' NHS patient! Best of British! As to the next general election, ToryLibDemys if you do, LabLibDemys if you don't!

Here it is, my draft, anyway. See what you think….

This enlightening scene will now go into rehearsal – unless banned from the stage by the Cameroons in ToryLibDemys secret session in the Downing Street garden. And so it can only be released to regular readers next week, when we promise to provide the material in public for a proper enquiry to consider….

No secrets here!

NB. Apology for absence: Lord Oakeshott [*who he? Ed.*].

EPISODE 24

The Richmond House Revels. Scene 3, Part 2.

How Unknown N£sd Doctors Practice.

Or Courting Disasters. And Patients requiring tickets for prompt emigration to Uzbekistan? Apply here.

The dramatic text…as promised.

Dramatis personae.

Sir Cyril Squoffington-Squogg, OBE, JP, is Chief Executive of The Tower of London NHS Hospital Trust, Tower Hamlets, London, EC.

Lady Bernice Squoffington-Squogg, his wife, is also Chair of The Wiltshire Artists Benevolent Fund.

Some medical "professionals", as named below.

THE SCENE: Ham & High Magistrate's Court, N. London. Wednesday 27 November 2013.

Sitting Magistrates: Councillor Orioglu Maintenanchance JP [in the Chair], and two 'wingers', Ms. Actressii Rosie Bruford, MP, JP, and Mr. T.U.C. BobCrowcouncilhouser, MBE, JP.

Clerk to the Court: Mr. Merfyn Merffyne Jones-Jones.

Clerk: Mr. Jones-Jones, please call Case No. 1. Call Dr. Sir Peter Cooke-Praster.

Sir Peter Cooke-Praster walks into the dock.

Clerk: Please give your full name and address to the court.

Dr. Sir P: Must I?

Clerk: It is a requirement, sir, yes. You must.

Dr. Sir P: Oh. May I write it down for you?

Clerk: No. You must speak up, please, sir.

Dr. Sir P: Very well. I am Grandmaster The Worshipful Sir Peter…sorry…I am… my name is Sir Peter Coquille Albert Perceive Aloysius Gravities Cooke-Praster, CBE. Of 'The Heronry', Harold Wilson Avenue, Hampstead Garden Suburb. I am a Doctor.

Chairman: Read the charges, please, Mr. Jones-Jones.

Clerk: That on numerous and various dates between 1 January 2005 and 12 October 2013, the accused did download sundry pornography concerning violent images of children, likely to deprave.

That on 27 September 2013, the accused was stopped in Green Lanes, Harringay, N.4 in charge of a vehicle, a Rolls Royce Silver Shadow II, and was found to be four times over the alcohol limit then in force.

That violent images, comprising 43 photographs of child rape were found in a locked box in the boot of the said Rolls Royce vehicle on the said date, as stated herewith.

That on 18 August 2013 the defendant was found in the said motor vehicle in Epping Forest with two young boys, who cannot be named, but who were aged 9 and 13. Both were from Kray Memorial Avenue, Bethnal Green. He was, it is alleged, trading in illegal Class A drugs.

That on 12 November 2013 the accused violently resisted arrest, causing ABH to P.C. Wilfred Nigel Walters of the Harrow-on-the-Hill Police, the accused having failed to answer bail at Camden Magistrate's Court on 17 October.

Chair: These are very serious charges. Are you represented here today, Doctor?

Dr. Sir P: Yes, sir. By Mr. Mansfodler Mansfodler QC.

Chair: Mr. Mansfodler, is there a plea in this – in these – cases?

Mr. M: Yes, sir. Not Guilty to all charges. We reserve our defence. We ask for a 28 day referral in which to prepare our case. I was only called in yesterday, when I was appearing in Kinnockles vs. The Treasury at the High Court.

Chair: Meanwhile, is your client continuing to practice?

Mr. M: He is, your worship. Yes. Well, on most days.

Chair: I see. Well, we will hear the evidence in chief, before we decide on whether or not we will send this case to Quarter sessions. On the face of it, that seems very likely. If, of course, we find that there is a case to answer, on any of these charges.

Mr. M: And we would prefer trial by jury, if you please, sir, if you decide that there is a case…which is, of course, most unlikely…

Chair: Ms. Poloddo Barnstormick, you appear for the CPS today? Is the CPS ready to proceed?

THE RICHMOND HOUSE REVELS. SCENE 3. PART 2

Ms. PB: Yes, your worship. I should advise the bench that the defendant, when interviewed at Hampstead Police HQ on the 13th ultimo of October last, said that he will deny all charges.

At his interview with the police at Harrow the defendant also vigorously denied that he was soliciting a male prostitute outside the Co-operative Bank in Barking, Essex, on 9 October this year. That was a case of mistaken identity, he claims. It was another surgeon entirely. He has also asserted that for the record he has never been convicted of fraud. That again was another doctor entirely. Perhaps two. I know that the recent convictions of 200 doctors have not been made public, and so....

Chair: *Excuse me.* Convictions of doctors not been made public? What do you mean? How so? And why ever not made public, pray?

Ms. PB: The medical case reviews were heard in secret I understand, your worship.

Chair: What, by the great British Whitewash Company PLC?

Ms. PB: I am not informed of that, your worship.

Chair: Well, astonishing. Beats me. I hope that none of those hundreds of doctor cases are at all like any of the charges we have before us today. Surely they cannot be? But proceed. Although this is all very unsatisfactory.

Ms. PB: The CPS case is as follows [she then gives unpleasant detailed evidence, not suitable for reproduction here]....

Mr. M: On behalf of my client, we deny all these charges, particularly in the context of recent reports that more than 750 GPs, surgeons and other doctors have kept their job despite being found Guilty of offences including taking indecent images of children, drug trafficking, and fraud.

Clerk: Your worship, I understand that under the Freedom of Information, The Help to Syria Act, and The Guardian Publication of Government Secrets Act there were recently shown to be 761 doctors practising in October this year in the UK despite accumulating 856 convictions between them.

Chair: Seven hundred-odd doctors? More than 800 convictions? Is this some bad joke? Surely it cannot be true? Is this so, Mr. Jones-Jones? How can that be? Do you know about this, Mr. Mansfodler?

Mr. M: Yes, your worship. I do. As I understand it, this is so. But my client is not one of those doctors, your worship. And, indeed, we regard the very idea of these charges as a breach of my client's Human Rights, as laid down under the European Convention on the Human Rights of the Guilty, of Terrorists, and of Illegal Immigrants, as amended, reference Euro-Bruzellerswodge L/9'/v/c/2179*, section 823, ii, 2012.

Chair: Oh. Do you indeed? Very well. We will retire to consider.
The bench withdraws.

In the retiring room – quite illegally – the Chair asks the Clerk, in a whisper, "Seems a very bad business altogether. Anything known?" Reply: "Oh, loads. This man has a long record. Amazing that he has never been to prison. Very High Mason, of course. Very big noise at the Royal Academy of Vested Interests. GBWWCo *has* hit him with a very heavy feather a few times. Served 10 minutes community service in an Oxfam shop in Lincoln in 2010. Unhappily, suspected of raiding the till there then. That sentence was for possession of child pornography – and for selling it on the net.

Did have a suspended 3 month prison sentence in 1999, for attempting to seduce a child of 6 during a piano lesson. Last time in court he was warned about his future actions. That case was dealt with alongside the charge of being three times over the limit, and being found with two young boys in his car, parked in Islington in a side-street opposite the Co-op. at 11.00 p.m. at night.

Chair: What did the Great British Whitewash Company PLC say? What did they do?

Clerk: Nothing in public, your honour. Said to have been very shirty in private. But I have no information which might help the bench today.

Chair: But he is still practising, is he?

Clerk: Yes, your honour. Well, on most weekdays.

The Bench return to Court.

Chair: Do you wish to call any character witnesses, Mr. M?

Mr. M. Yes, your worship, but the gentleman wishes to remain anonymous.

Chair: Very unusual, again. Very. But if this will allow us to proceed, so be it. However, he must write his name and address down and give this to the Clerk of the Court now.

Which he does…

Mr. Anon: My friend here today is a Good Chap. I say this in mitigation. But even so, we medical authorities have very strong views indeed on such cases. Your honour, we would ask for a large and exemplary total fine of £10, with court costs too, of course. This IS a very serious case. If it should recur another 27 times then we will wish the doctor to be struck from the Register. That's quite certain.

This kind of thing MUST stop. In his interests. And in ours.

Chair, *loses patience*: Tell me, then, Good Chap, eh? First what about all these reports of GP's ineptitude? Father with bowel cancer, fobbed off by doctors? Why aren't doctors like this doing their jobs properly? Why aren't they awake at work? Why are they so negligent? Why aren't they subject to unexpected inspections by medically-informed and competent, independent examiners? Why do taxpayers pay to train these doctors and then have to put up with this kind of thing – and in such numbers too? Tell the Court, if you will please. It's your job to regulate and discipline them, to protect the public, isn't it? And to identify them in

THE RICHMOND HOUSE REVELS. SCENE 3. PART 2

public, too? Guide us please. We most assuredly need enlightenment! As do the public!

Mr. Anon: May I respond in Latin please? *Scilicet scio quid sit hodiernus dies! Modo ei non possum meminisse verbum Anglicum.*

Clerk STANDS: Your worship, that sounds like a really vintage piece of Bunglerism, to me! But I could translate that for you, your worship, if you wish.

Chair: Please do.

Clerk: Well, your worship, I read it to mean that "Of course I know what day today is! I just can't remember the English word for it!"

Chair: Quite! We will retire again ….

The Court rises. For the Court's decision to send the defendant for trial at Middlesex Quarter Sessions see the Ham & High Millkiband Weekly FREESHEET, 6 December 2013.

***

Lady S-S: Not so funny, is it? *Nor a revel, is it?* But very big points, Cyril. And look at these other stories in the 'paper on 27 November, too. Worse and worse!

Just give you the headlines: I'll give you back the other file of cuttings.

I'll read mine out: "After mid Staffs scandal, NHS is still failing to treat patients with respect", says the Care Quality Commission. And, other stories from the same day: One in five nursing homes fail to meet basic safety standards. Beds cut crisis. Dementia patients more likely to die in hospital than other patients. Longer wait to see GP looms, says Dr. Maureen Baker of the practitioners' college…

Sir S-S: And look at this new study by the OECD: Britain's survival rates for cancer only on a par with some of *Eastern* Europe. Now, that's an achievement that is! And despite government promises to improve care.

Lady S-S: Tell *that* to Dr. Hogblinkered!

Sir S-S: And on a lot of critical conditions we do half as well as the USA – despite them always been reviled by the Left. But the Klingfilm Fund says differently, doesn't it? British people love the NHS, all that. Turn Left at all times, if you please.

Lady S-S: Now *there's* a surprise! *"Taxpayers Ahoy!"* As Barney says.

Sir S-S: Tell *that* to Professor Hampster!

And the OECD report I read said that N£sd spending is down in real terms in 2 years. Waiting lists longer. Patients with breast, cervical and bowel cancer fare worse in Britain than in the vast majority of all industrialised nations.

Lady S-S: Tell *that* to Dr. Hogblinkered!

Sir S-S: And there's a lot of stupid GP practice, too. And stupid demands by patients. Anti-depressant use doubled in a decade. We have the 7th highest proscribing rate for Prozac in Europe. On it goes. On and on. Statemuckitupopoly, in course.

Lady S-S: Tell *that* to Professor Hampster!

Sir S-S: That OECD report is called *Health at a Glance.* For us, it should read *Health, What Chance?*

Very quick read shows how tragic our situation is now in the NHS.

The leading cancer expert Professor Karol Sikora is reported as saying that if we just met the average of the rest of Europe we'd save 10,000 lives a year! *The average!* Not the best! And even the average – nowhere near it are we?

Lady S-S: Tell *that* to Dr. Hogblinkered!

Sir S-S: Yes indeed! And it shows that the NHS has far fewer scanners to detect cancers and other illnesses, compared with the majority of industrialised nations.

On strokes, we're 24th of 31 countries. Almost 160,000 die of cancer in Britain every year, more than 50,000 from a stroke.

Lady S-S: Tell *that* to Dr. Hogblinkered!

Sir S-S: What a bloody awful picture it is!

Lady S-S: Can *we* please emigrate to Uzbekistan as soon as possible?!

Sir S-S: *Can't* be any worse there, can it?

[NB. See Facey's Holiday Postcards, No.13, below – Ed.]

EPISODE 25

Our Wonderful NHS. A Seasonal Ode to Hopes.

We are honoured to be able to print below this distinguished contributor's much favoured and leading entry to The Annual NHS National Christmas Poetry Competition, founded in 2003 by Mr. Taxitt Spendyerwaytosecurity, MP, Special Adviser and PPS to Ms. Nevermindthemanagementfeelthedosh, MP, both long-term acolytes of Mr. G. Brown, the alleged PM.

The handsome sponsored prizes [courtesy of All Good Chaps Medical Care Inc.] to be given at The Royal Albert Hall in London on 2 January 2014.

Distinguished Prize-giving by the world-leading distinguished Very Hon. cardiology surgeon His Very Distinguished Grand Eminenceship The Lord High Grandmaster, The Worshipful Sir Pweeter G.G. Knatchbull-Bullknash, CBE, The Very Hon. & Very Distinguished Surgeon and Very Life President of The Royal College of Vested Interests [see full curriculum vitae and contact numbers at www.bringyourcashtoharleystreet.co.uk].

Supported by Nursie Nursie Dixbungle, Chief Executive of The Great British Whitewash Company PLC [who, however, admits he is unable to scan], and The Very Dr. W. Hogblinkered, GCE, last years clear winner with his sonnet "It's Nothing To Do With Me Chum!", as sponsored by The Klingfilm Fund of London.

Last year's rather distant runners-up will open the Ceremonies. They being Professor A. Hampster, who will read his Ode "Now I have some points...." and Lord Oakeshott, with his traditional unrhymed refrain in iambic couplets entitled "Who he? – Ed. [Who he?-Ed].

First prize, An Hon. & Very Distinguished Fortnight Caravan holiday in The Very Distinguished Hon. Cardiological Venue at Canvey Island, as sponsored by the Very Hon. Harley Street Harlequins Assurance Co. Inc.

Second prize, An Hon. & Also Very Distinguished "Work" Experience Month assisting THE Very HON. Nursie Nursie Dixbungle at THE GBWWCo. PLC, as sponsored by Spexravers of Nicaragua.

***

My Ode. Wonder if....it's really A Wonderful World?
By Facey Romford, Jr.

Wonder if the GP will see me.
Wonder if I'll last till then.

Wonder if it will be a locum.
Wonder if doc will speak the English.
Wonder if I see him this time,
Wonder if will ever see him again?

Wonder if they're open, on most days or only some.
Wonder how much advance notice have to give.
Wonder if 'phone answered, and after only 30 rings.
Wonder if there'll be any parking.
Wonder if I'll have the long walk there.
Wonder if I'll live till then?

Wonder if Nurse Jilly will see me instead.
Wonder if they're closed for Inspection.
Wonder if happens sometimes, now and then.
Wonder if I'll get the anti-whatnots.
Wonder if they'll be pink and strong again.
Wonder if I'll remember to take them then?

Wonder if pills will now stop working.
Wonder if to do what then.
Wonder if will get my flu jab.
Wonder if can wait in line so long.
Wonder if I'm gone down with somethink.
Wonder if will ever see same doc again?

Wonder if will need an op.
Wonder if insurance will stretch to it.
Wonder who does op when I'm gassed under?
Wonder what their record is?
Wonder if the rural bus will come along.
Wonder if I'll live till then?

Wonder if can pay as enter.
Wonder if get up the steps.
Wonder if copper coins will do.
Wonder if can pass that duff pound coin on.
Wonder where I got that, too.
Wonder if it will be alright if not?

Wonder if can afford hospital bed-side TV.
Wonder if these fancy Statins work on toenails too.
Wonder if NHS as wonderful as it always says it is.
Wonder if French doc'd be better.
Wonder if true that Swiss care best of all.
Wonder if could get there myself on trains.
Wonder if I'll live till then?

Wonder if could go Eurostar.
Wonder if collapse outside a Hospital,

OUR WONDERFUL NHS. A SEASONAL ODE TO HOPES

Wonder will they take me in?
Wonder if get free cuckoo-clock.And Toblerone?
Wonder, wonder, wonder… might.
Wonder might live some extra then?

Wonder if get cheap Essexjet flight, be there and back before 6 nights.
Wonder if might otherwise see my GP here by then?
Wonder why Frenchies have no wait-lists.
Wonder if Froggies have corridors with trolley-beds.
Wonder if know records of docs in advance.
Wonder if I'll live till learn?

Wonder why so many NHS complaints.
Wonder what happens then?
Wonder what this OECD thing can be.
Wonder why NHS bottom of league tables then.
Wonder what Millkiband gives out FREE today.
Wonder what this Health Savings Account would do instead?

Wonder if my GP is up in court again.
Wonder if on druggies, porn, prostitutes, violence, or mayhem?
Wonder if they'll take 'my history.'
Wonder if they'll weigh me too.
Wonder then if check me proper.
Wonder if I'll live till then?

Wonder if doc reads my tests.
Wonder if studies lab results.
Wonder if then refers me on fast.
Wonder if there's that neglecting.
Wonder if can complain – if so, to whom?
Wonder might live some extra then?

Wonder if will be in mixed-ward.
Wonder if be clean jammies *every* week
Wonder if I'll live till then?
Wonder if Nursie [B.Sc.] reads me socio-ological bedtime story.
Wonder if be tale of the three bear-faced PCTs again.
Wonder if will sleep easier then?

Wonder if sent to care home & die of thirsting.
Wonder if be starved instead.
Wonder if be care-home blood-poison-deaded.
Wonder if be pneumoniaed there, as it's said.
Wonder if get food as ordered, or the grub other bloke ordered 5 days ago.
Wonder if nurse will feed me, with my wonky hand just so?

Wonder if I'll get my Guinness.
Wonder might live some extra then.
Wonder if nurse be kind or gruff, & stuff.

Wonder if they'll bed-sore me.
Wonder if me urinary tract'll remain intact.
Wonder what this wonky CQC is all about?

Wonder if they'll let me take my Teddy.
Wonder which half of folks no need to be here at all.
Wonder what's this updated Liverpool Pathway, eh?
Wonder where I put my glasses?
Wonder will definitely vote UKIP this time.
Wonder if Farage be PM?

DO HOPE I'll live till then!

Wonder, wonder, wonder.
Wonder might just go home to bed.

Wonder, wonder, WONDERFUL WORLD.

EPISODE 26

The impending Bugginsturn North By-Election. The Nation Reveals All. A forthcoming and seasonal New Year's Entertainment.

Dramatis personae.

Mr. Barney Wells BEM is Chief Executive of The Arthur Scargill Memorial NHS Trust Hospital, Chessingfield-on-Soke. His Trade Unionist wife Rita is Labour's candidate in the pending Bugginsturn North by-election, and was formerly Chair of his NHS Trust.

Kevin O'Grady is Chief Executive of the Coleraine St. Fortescue Hospital, N. Ireland.

***

Unusually for this regular N£sd enquiry, we offer a POLITICAL SECTION. Demoskrokossy at work...

Kev: I see that the Bugginsturn North By-election has been declared then.

Barney: Yes, polling on last Thursday in January. Forecast to be a day of heavy snow, icy winds from Siberia, sleety and as cold as Northern Greenland. Probably only be a 9% poll.

Kev: Oh. And who are the candidates?

Barney: Lots, as usual. Usual by-election bunch. Protesters. Self-publicists. Nutty religious types. Wannabe pop-stars. Animal rights. And the usual can't tell'em apart politicos.

And the Con/Lab/LibDemsy Party are running *two* candidates. ToryLibDemsy and LabLibDemsy. Just in case!

Nigel Farage is running a good candidate. The bookies say he is 1-10 on to win. Already an MEP, of course. Be a big turn-up though. UKIP had no candidate last time out. But a lot of people like Farage.

Talks a lot of sense. Faces the issues. No fudges. Setting the agenda. Knows where he stands and why. *Thinks.* Looks like the revival of the old Thatcher Tory Party. Being told they'll let in Millkiband, of course. Well, he'd do a lot of damage, but then he'd be out on his ear after one Parliament. So we could even put up with him short-term if it meant we get the Cameroons out. Might be worth the short-term suffering. Four years of the Kid. Then a real Tory government for the next 20 years. Might go for that. Only way we'll ever get a decent health service in this country. My view, anyway. I find the muddle, the frustrations, the pervasive clangour of empty vessels so....the good intentions but the sad expediencies...

Kev: Serves the Tories right. No sympathy for them. None at all. Where is the argument for a free market liberal economy? Whyever didn't they just extend the already successful social care personal budgets system? That was the way to get to N£sd individual patient fund-holding into the set-up, and then to annual medicals, personal insurance, excess to pay if you didn't take any care of yourself, top-ups, and some sense of personal responsibility for your own behaviour. Didn't need a big fuss. Just extend it. But Hapless Lansley and Hopeless Cameron, our "experts" on the N£sd…

Barney: BMA stooges, those two were. What a pair! And the docs don't respect them for it. Never do. You know, "Be another one along in a minute…"

Kev: Will, too!

Barney: Yes. And Farage looks like a new kind of politician. Will get my vote, between you and me. But not a whisper to her indoors!

Kev: What about her indoors then? Will she win? Been a "safe" Labour seat for decades, hasn't it? Be a huge shock if the UKIP bloke walks it, won't it?

Barney: Yes. Labour since 1920s. Even under Ramsay Mac when he went National. But, whisper is that she's not being very well received so far. The People's Socialist State of Chessingfield changing fast. Her being proposed by 62 Unite branches has been no help. Influx of many Polish workers changing local employment, and for the better from service point of view. Not her sort at all.

Kev: Lots of new Hong Kong folks with good businesses moved in there too, didn't they? None of them go onto welfare, do they?

Barney: Nope. Start businesses and create jobs. And many of the Old Labour lot are moving north to Scotland, where everything is FREE. Well, for the time being anyway. If I got a vote I'd say Go Independent You Scots Lot. And take Brown and Co. with you. But leave the extra taxes we pay behind too, if you please. And move the missile base to Pompey.

At any rate, her indoors is not proving to be a shoo-in. Falkirk effect and all that. Millkiband flooding the area with leading Labour people. Edth Balth slated to visit three times. That woman MP, the one you call 'Sleeping-No-Beauty,' is speaking here, too. But not doing any good, the connections with Balth and Brown. *The Bugginsturn Chronicle* warns of THE GHOST OF GORDON BROWN. So might be in for a big shock.

It's Farage Ahoy! The UKIP bloke is drawing big crowds, on the streets and at his Monster Meetings. Like Gladstone all over again! He's giving out printed joke pound notes 3 metres square. And balloons with it printed on, for self-inflation. And offering to lend people vintage wheelbarrows, imported from Germany. Says that's what will be needed if Old Labour gets back in.

Oh, and lottery tickets for NHS queues, numbered from 1 million upwards. Each one embossed 'Waiting Time Until Result Declared, 3 years.' Keen to do something about too much immigration, too. Farage was here and said that anyone coming in should be on a work permit. And be required to show has health insurance. No benefits, no free this and that until been here and employed consistently for five years.

THE IMPENDING BUGGINSTURN NORTH BY-ELECTIIONS

Kev: He's concerned about crime, too, isn't he? Heard him on the radio. Said that there have been 27,000 Rumanian arrests for crimes in the past 5 years. A lot of ATM crime, apparently. Well, got to take this seriously, haven't we?

Barney: Yes, but look at a lot of the Poles. Hotels and restaurants would collapse without them. They take the dirty jobs our welfare-addicted £30,000 p.a. lot aren't prepared to do, too. The Poles come and clean cars at the supermarket, study English, and then move on to better things. Don't look to live on benefits forever, like our lot. As to bringing in welfare-claimants, malingering no-work blokes, obesities who pay no taxes, we breed the worst in the world for ourselves already, thank you very much.

Kev: Coo! Populist stuff then. Must dial up to my bookie, online, and put a fiver on him! And who are the other declared Candidates?

Barney: Well, 15 in all so far. And still some weeks to go to the deadline:

Mrs. Rita Wells MBE (Very Old Labour).

Ms. Virago Carmen (Selfie Party).

Ms. Alioops Parksahstan (Conservative But Not Unionist Party).

Ms. Gee Itsfreeall (New One-Nation-Re-Lab-elled Party).

Ms. Jennifer Samesever (ConsLibDemsy).

Ms. Jacqueline Extrahs (LabLibDemsy).

Mr. U. Knowitmakessense, MEP (UKIP).

Mr. A. Johnson (Boris-in-Waiting Party).

Mr. Alex Trouter (Independence for Rutland Party).

Mr. Alex McSalmon McFishcake (Independence for Goring-on-Sea Party).

Mrs. Glitterboob Fameforme (Simon Love Me Party).

Mr. Jeff Green-Barbedwirecutter (Animal Rights Party).

Ms. Jessie Nilfracker (Green Party).

Nursie Nursie Dixbungle (GBWWCo PLC).

Sir J. Major KG (Monster Raving Loonie Party). [*withdrew hurt*].

Kev: Cameron *has* put up a candidate then, although the Tory only got 89 votes there last time, didn't he?

Barney: Yes. Lost his deposit. Laughing stock. In the Lords now of course. Lord

Cameronmatey of Notting Hill. Assistant to Lord 'Owzat at Healthcare. *"Can't think why,"* as that Gilbert & Sullivan song had it.

Kev: Aha! Lolly for the boys. Nice expenses. Posh warm ermine gown. City board appointments. Central London parking space, free, too.

Barney: Nice work if you can get it. But got to go to the right school, in course. No good being at the Sam Weller Comprehensive in Southwark, eh?

Kev: Noper. Nor at my place, The Blessed Nuns-of-Glory Boy's Convent of Sligo.

Anyway, what are Cameron's by-election NHS policies then?

Barney: *Policies?* What do you mean? We are talking about Cameron, aren't we?

Kev. Yes. Point taken! But what do you think will happen?

Barney: Well, I hope and pray that *she* gets in! Be in London most of the time then. Stay with her Aunt Gladys in Whetstone. Some peace for me at last. And I can play my Elvis CDs uninterrupted by old Trot anthems.

Kev: Betcha! Seen any manifestoes?

Barney: Well, ToryLibDemys have just published theirs. Only one I've seen. Has Pears soap adverts and item on Beecham's Powders inserted. Paid advert. Proposing that maternity leave be given to Father's on an every-other-day basis, for two years. A major contribution to company profitability, efficiency, management and continuity, DC thinks.

Kev: *"Can't think why."* Big help to employment prospects for the over 45's, though.

Barney: Very progressive on the NHS, too!

Kev: Oh? What does it say about the NHS then?

Barney: Well, spend more, in course! None of that IEA and Adam Smith ideological stuff about free markets, control of costs, comparative performances, management controls, competition, improvement by emulation, power to patients, more information on morbidity rates, doctors to be inspected properly. None of that nonsense, as ToryLibDemys describe it privately. "Thatcherism? Oh, that was just a career opportunity!" as one senior minister described it to me. *[True story! – Ed.]*.

Kev: Seems to me that what Squoffy was saying is right on the button. Cameron just doesn't get it, does he? Don't want to. Don't intend to. Won't do to.

Barney: Nope. This is the government with the least ideas, the least thinking at the top, since Major. Whch *is* saying something. No overall explanations of society and its realities. Duffo-wonky on what human nature is really like. And poor old Major *[KG – Ed.]* was bad enough, heavens knows.

Cameron can't see, can he, that if this was a private business, no one would go anywhere near it, would they? Run a mile. He's done nothing to open it all up, has he? With the individual as a financially empowered consumer, controlling an individual heath savings account. We can gang on about it until we are blue in the face – IF that's the right colour! But hear us he do not.

Kev: Ah, so, Mein Herr. If I had my way I'd make it so you couldn't become an MP unless you've had a proper job for at least 10 years. Run a business. Made a profit. Served customers. Taken commercial risks. Got them right. Not all these political adviser-wonks who think they can run the world. Look at it, Cameron, a PR-smoothie. Never had a proper job of any kind. A PR-wonk, negotiating about *business* with the Chinese. Makes you laugh.

Barney: Or cry.

Kev: Or both together!

And until and unless we get a proper Conservative government, with real leadership, prepared to give its full support to free enterprise – and to put in years in serious, lively and well-said campaigning for a vision of a free society – we'll continue to go downwards.

You know, it's markets which breed prosperity, not Whitehall.

Barney: Can quite see why the UKIP candidate here has got the support of 5 out of 7 former local Tory constituency officers. His Chairman is Shackleton – related to the explorer – who once ran the local Tory shop. Happening everywhere, of course. People see Farage as helping to rebuild the proper Tory Party. Just you wait and see our result here, and then the Euros in the Spring. Be a UKIP walkover. This UKIP bloke here will be the first of their many Westminster MPs, mark my wordsies.

Kev: And until then, unless Osborne, Gove and Johnson can somehow takeover, then we'll go on suffering what Macmillan did – that Middle Way.

Barney: Muddle Way, more like. MacCamerooonism. Mod version of the Edwardian actor.

Kev: Yes. Quite. The PM just won't let the market work, will he? Interfering all the time. Won't make the argument for free markets and liberty, innovation and new wealth and prosperity. Adaptable trial-and-error. Learning and changing. Was ever so. Learn and go forward. But not on the DC Campaign Bus.

Barney: So the chief ToryLibDemsy headlines are just like the LabLibDemsys: "We will spend more on the best NHS in the world. We will send DVDs of our successes to every other OECD nation. We will offer advice to others who are higher on the OECD league tables than we are – which must be quite accidental, and the figures misleading. We will increase pay of all clinicians. We will triple sociology degree places for Nurses."

And "We'll build new huts for patients to wait in, on Bugginsturn Seafront."

Kev: Well, that's alright then, if you agree with that sort of thing. But seems a cert loser to me. So why be completely wrong *and* lose? Major [KG] all over again.

Barney: Yes. And the LibDemsy rumour is that Cleggy will issue a manifesto of one sentence: "I agree with Nick." But David Lorsst is said to be preparing his own boy-friend rebel printed 16 page manifesto. Eight pages, reading from the front, printed one way up; eight pages printed, reading from the back, the other way up. Depends if you are ToryLibDemsy or LabLibdemsy. Take your choice.

Kev: And Millkiband to demand a FREE vote? Betcha.

Barney: Yes, and Squoffy has sent me two application forms for Emigration to Uzbekistan. Like one of them?

Kev: Aha! Post it, just in case! And keep the car fuelled with petrol!

Barney: Even Bulgaria might do. Looked good on the tele today. All this fuss about possible immigrants from there. Surely only come here once Germany, France, Spain, Portugal, Italy and Mugabeland are full-up?

And talk about healthcare tourism – why would anyone come here for that?

Meanwhile, canvassing continues faithfully on the moorlands in the sleet and North Easterly snow of Bugginsturn North, as the nation holds its chilly breath...the result to be reported shortly by your faithful observer FR, Jr.

***

This informative episode and this Epic Ode closes to the Traditional NHS Aria, "So mought it be....", sung by The Very Distinguished and Honourable Presidential Luton Good Chaps and Boys Medical and Masonic Choral Very Silent Nighters [PLC], accompanied by The Hon. & Very Distinguished The Dixbungler Buglers and The GBWWCo Snowmen & The All Greatly Whitewashed Tambouriners [PLC]. [See You Tube shortly]. A James Stewart film flickers in the background, as at Every Christmas Past, Present, and Is To Be. Meanwhile, see the papers for today's latest new Care Home Scandal....

Apologies for absences: Lord Alascooke of Smugdominion, and Lord Oakeshott [*who he? Ed.*].

EPISODE 27

A Job Application [or two?].
We see into the N£sd future, and reflect.
Is it bye-bye Cameroon and Cluggy, hello the FREE Kid? The Hunted Fox satirically reveals some of all…

Dramatis personae:

Mr. Barney Wells BEM is Chief Executive of The Arthur Scargill Memorial NHS Trust Hospital, Chessingfield-on-Soke.

Kevin O'Grady is Chief Executive of the Coleraine St. Fortescue Hospital, N. Ireland.

***

Barney: Hey, look at this!

One of the first consequences of the forthcoming Bugginsturn North by-election. *Daily Snail* today says:

CLUGGY TO GO NOW!

Con/Lab/Lib/Demsy 'Leadership' Race Wide Open!

Collapse of poll-ratings force change. The UKIP-effect!

Kev: Looks like it anyway. Even if the Bugginsturn North by-election itself only happens in late January?

Barney: Well, just *look* at latest 'Guvdemo' poll. UKIP bloke in the far clear. More than half say they will vote for him. And they say – most of them – that they are determined to vote. Big issues are the economy, immigration, and health and social care. A&E. GP's hours. Houses. Jobs. Rumanians and Bulgarians. The lot. A goodly number of old people's homes here, too. So that QCC [*Quality Care Commission – Ed.*] gets a drubbing every time it's mentioned.

Kev: Now *that's* a shock!

Barney: Yers. And only 8% say they might vote Con/Lib/Demsy, and 6% Lab/Lib/Demsy. Even Mrs. Glitterboob Fameforme (Simon Love Me Party) gets 10%.....

Kev: Probably Four 10's!

Barney: Aha. *Strictly* speaking, yes!

Kev: So Cameroon and Cluggy both in all sorts of trouble?

Barney: Seems very so. No surprise really, is it? Had their chance. Blown it. Could have been ahead with the changes they could have made to the N£sd. Could have said that they were really on the side of the patients, not "The System." And shown it working too. Instead, you know what's next don't you?

Kev: Gawd! The Millkiband Kid then! FREE everything.

Barney: *Higher Rate Middle-Class Taxpayers Ahoy!*

Kev: Aren't any others, are there?

Barney: Not unless miracles can still happen.

Kev: Well, from what I've seen the usual bidding to spend more on the N£sd has begun, with the general election on the horizon.

Barney: Yep. Money no object. Just print more of the stuff. Plenty more where the last lot came from. Or just import it from Canada. Quantitative easing. Bundles of it, in old German wheelbarrows. So staring at the boom & bust lark all over again, then. Recession? What recession? Jim Callaghan lives again! Learned no lessons, have they? Actually had the chance to tell the public the truth about the NHS, its endemic problems, and to explain the genuine and workable alternatives to a state monopoly. Funked it, haven't they? IF they ever understood it.

Kev: *IF!*

Barney: Maggie listened to the IEA and to the Adam Smith Institute, didn't she?

Kev: But even she didn't tackle the demand-side. That's a generation ago, though. Got a lot worse since then.

Barney: Yep. And how can they ever think they can ever fund the NHS as is, and never control demand by price and by changed behaviour?

Kev: Free markets? "Not likely, we're *Cameroon* Conservatives!"

Barney: Control of costs? "Whatever do you mean? We are Cameroon *Conservatives.* We spend more."

Kev: Management controls? "Local issue, that."

Barney: Competition? "What, The Big C? *We* are Cameroon Conservatives."

Kev: Improvement by emulation? "Inoculated against that, aren't we?"

A JOB APPLICATION [OR TWO?]

Barney: Power to patients? "Have you a high temperature, sir?"

Kev: Publish information on morbidity rates? "Well, might do a bit on that."

Barney: But don't want to scare the horses!

Kev: Doctors to be inspected properly? "Aha. All done, that one!"

Barney: "Thatcherism? Oh, that was just a career opportunity!" as one senior minister described it to me. *[True story! – Ed.]*.

Kev: No wonder Cameroon and Cluggy are for the OUT! The FREE Kid in. The devil with the forked tongue.

Barney: AND the inflationary touch, too, remember.

Kev: But it seems to me that what your mate Squoffy says is right on the button. Cameron just doesn't get it, does he? Don't want to. Don't intend to. Won't do to. Wasted every chance. Won't change now, will it?

Barney: Nope. No overall explanations of society and its realities. Just PR sufficient to the day thereof. Duffo-wonky on what human nature is really like. Done nothing to open it all up, debates about the nature of the NHS. No offers of the individual as an empowered consumer, controlling an individual heath savings account. No idea of how to affect personal responsibility at all.

Kev: So what do all those policy wonks in No.10 *do* all day long, you have to ask?

Barney: Can't *all* be High Speed Rail, can it?

Kev: Well, that one is a loser, too, isn't it? Maybe Simon Stevens – the Lord Stevens of Bexhill-on-Sea to be – will get to it, NHS reform. But what hope has he, with a general election coming?

Barney: Snowball in Hell.

Kev: Hampster swimming in a pool of starving crocodiles.

Barney: Anyway, the local revived underground paper here, *The Hunted Fox,* has printed a satirical piece on what Cleggy will do when he's out of office. Apparently word for word as heard on the Durham miners march. Can't vouch for it. Probably just malicious gossip. But made me laugh!

Sending the text to your e-mail now:

The Hunted Fox. **Our political 'Insider's Report'.**

By Our Chief Political Correspondent, [Lord] Fogelstumped, at Westminster.

The scene: a very rainy day at Sheffield Hallam City Job Centre:

Mr. N. Clugg: Just came in to sign on.

Mr. A. Gorbachuff [interviewer]: Yes. Sit. Previous employment?

Mr. Clugg: Prime Minister. LibDem MP. National Treasure.

Mr. Gorbachuff: Full name?

Mr. Clugg: Nicholas No-No Clugg. Also sometimes known as Nick Clogg. "Fluffo" to best-friends.

Mr. Gorbachuff: No longer employed?

Mr. Clugg: No. Sacked. Very sudden. Without compensation. Voters…colleagues…no loyalty.

Mr. Gorbachuff: I see. No compensation at all? None? Any income then?

Mr. Clugg: Well no, not really. Well. A bit. Private. And Life Peerage, with its perks. Might even be an Earldom. And separation allowance for MPs. Not sure how much. Say, £35,000. Tax-free. Parliamentary Pension. Six figures, I think. With tax-free lump sum. Security personnel too. Oh, and government free-chauffeur and free-car for life. Rule made by Harold Wilson 2 weeks before he resigned. Applied to all PMs ever since. Major [*KG*] has a chauffeur-driven Bentley I believe. Blair a Jag. Brown a Nissan Convertible. Parked most of the time I believe as he's on all those big-free speaker's tours abroad. Lucky blighter. Chauffeur who used to drive him regularly to see his favourite Solihull Project kicking his heels, but still being paid as per usual. So that's all OK.

Probably I'll take several board appointments. BBC Trust. Might get the vacant Chair there. After Lord Hong Kong is sacked. I've also been offered some advisory roles by overseas governments…. and an International Quango Chair or two. EEC, etc. Speak fluent Dutch. And American lecture tour. Some decent US dollar fees. Paid into Tobago Bank of Offshore Islands. So tax free. Then advice to Chinese government on democracy and on free speech for dissidents. And to Soviets on Mansion Taxes for former oil industry bosses. You know, the anti-Putin crew. Other possibilities for me still being arranged. After-dinner speaking. Fees. Job-loss was all very sudden. So, will be a bit short…need the benefits due…

Mr. Gorbachuff: I see. We'll put all that down as "Initial compensation noted. Further information requested from Applicant." Well, we will see what we can do for you. No cutlery-making experience I suppose? We *are* in Sheffield.

Mr. Clugg: No. Well, have used a few knives at work….

Mr. Gorbachuff: I see. Skills?

Mr. Clugg: Well, can usually do a bit of fixing…good with glue…

Mr. Gorbachuff: Is that it? That all?

Mr. Clugg: Well, can tie a bow-tie. Quite well, actually. Says so myself.

A JOB APPLICATION [OR TWO?]

Mr. Gorbachuff: I see. Well, we will need your c.v. And a note on your career achievements.

Mr. Clugg. Oh…

Mr. Gorbachuff: References?

Mr. Clugg: Yes indeed! From Lord Oakeshott. *[who he? Ed]*.

Mr. Gorbachuff: Won't count, I'm afraid. Don't call us. We will call you….

Disconsolate, Mr. Clugg leaves quietly, unobserved by journalists and photographers, stage Centre-Left. In the corridor outside he is heard to whisper to Deputy PM, D. Cameroon, waiting on line for job-seeker interview, *"Wouldn't go in there if I was you…."*

NB. *The Daily Telegraph* reported on 24 July 2015, p.2, under the heading "Clegg charges £35,000 as after-dinner speaker", as follows: "Nick Clegg is touting his services as an after-dinner speaker, charging up to £35,000 for his oratory skills. The former deputy prime minister and Lib Dem leader has engaged events firm Leading Authorities who now list him alongside several other leading luminaries. His entry boasts that he can speak five languages and 'occupied the second highest office' in the land during his time at the helm of the coalition government. It also claims he oversaw the nation's recovery from recession after the 2008 banking crisis. Mr Clegg resigned as leader after the general election in which his party lost 48 of its 56 MPs."

The www gives this: www.leadingauthorities.com/ "Leading Authorities is America's trusted speakers bureau for keynote speakers, events and video production. Contact our DC office at 1-800-SPEAKER.

Organisers of the University of the Fourth Age, save your pennies!

EPISODE 28

The Richmond House Revels, Scene 4.

A mistaken but "expert" voice on a mysterious N£sd telephone call.

A Christmas Pantomime Jollification.

Dramatis personae:

Sir Cyril Squoffington-Squogg, OBE, JP, is Chief Executive of The Tower of London NHS Hospital Trust, Tower Hamlets, London, EC.

Lady Bernice Squoffington-Squogg, his wife, is also Chair of The Wiltshire Artists Benevolent Fund.

Mr. Barney Wells BEM is Chief Executive of The Arthur Scargill Memorial NHS Trust Hospital, Chessingfield-on-Soke.

Brenda When is PA/Secretary to Mr. Wells.

Kevin O'Grady is Chief Executive of the Coleraine St. Fortescue Hospital, N. Ireland.

***

Lady S-S: Cyril, it's two-thirty in the morning! What *are* you doing up? And is that Brandy I can smell?

Sir S-S: Just a small snifter, my love. Medicinal! Am just finishing Scene 4 for the Richmond House Revels. Just in time for the Christmas Panto season too. Here it is. Take it away and read yourself to sleep!

Lady S-S does so...

***

The scene: The Arthur Scargill Memorial NHS Trust Hospital

A Very Posh Voice: Hello, may I speak to Mr. Barney Wells, please?

Brenda: Who is this, please.

Louder *[but not entirely audible]* Voice: Lord Oakeshrotty. The very important Liberal Democratic peer. Seen me on television a lot, I expect? Unique!

Brenda: I will connect you…

Fuzzy Voice: Cogently, quickly, as fast as, please! I am a very important Liberal Democratic peer! Expert on the NHS, GPs, A&E, Consultant's new contracts, golf clubs, bedroom scales, tele-communications, children's hobbies, bathroom flannels, muffins, councils, tax, overseas investment, by-election defences, majority governments, student fees, leadership, defence, economy, education, pensions. AND the Loch Ness Monster. And etc etc etc. AND the NHS!

Brenda: I will connect you…

Muffled Voice: *Immediately, please.* I am a very important Liberal Democratic peer, and…

Brenda: I will connect you to the Chief Executive. One moment, please.

Brenda to Barney: Sir. Man on the' phone says he is Lord Somebody or other. Sounded like Pokeogot. Or Oakegot. Possibly Grottygone. Shall I put him through? Sounds rather a nutter, sir.

Barney: Didn't get his name?

Brenda: No. Sorry. Not clearly Very bad line. Might be Avershott. Or Oakergotte. Or Oakeshottt. Not sure. Says he is very important. *Modest* sort of chap.

Barney: OK. Put 'im through. Let's see what this is about.

Strident Voice: Hello. Is that Mr. Wells? Chief Executive?

Barney: It is. Who is this, please.

Aristo Voice: Lord Oakegrotty, I am a very important…

Barney: Eh? What? *[pause]* Oh, come off it Nursie Nursie! It's you, isn't it Dixbungle! Why are you putting on that funny Kenneth Williams voice? And wasting my time. It's not April Fool's Day, you know! Haven't you got any work to do? No biscuits to chew? Alright for you over at that Great British Whitewash outfit. Can't be running out of cover-ups, surely? But we've got work to do here.

Confused Voice: No. *No.* **No!** I do not know to whom you make such oblique ultimo sufflicating illiberal undie-culturally BBC references, sir. But it is I. It is me. It is Lord Oakegrotty. I am a very important….

Barney: Oh, *it is you*, isn't it Kev! Well, as the saying is "*Stop messing about!*"

Bewildered bureaucratic Voice: I beg your pardon. I am telephoning about the ConsLibDemys new policy on Tripling Toll-houses on all Roundabouts near NHS hospitals. And on closing unnecessary NHS booking-clerk offices. Policy with reference to The Millkiband Kid in next coalition, when I will be Chancellor and Secretary of State for Health and Road Transport…..assisted by Mr. Kable and Mrs. Willettizers.

THE RICHMOND HOUSE REVELS, SCENE 4

Barney: Oh, Kev. Enough! Stuff all that. I've got work to do. Very humorous, no doubt. But…now just hop it, will you…

Continuing but Bewildered Voice: You will be pleased to know that we will raise the tax free level to £45,000 – but ONLY if on benefits – and triple all taxes on incomes over £17,500, but ONLY if the person is actually working. This will pay for our FREES etc etc etc. Mr. Millkiband is compiling the full list. On page 37 at the moment.

Oh, I know that Osborne is doing it too now. Giving away millions, wasted on rich kids who don't need school meals free. WE will waste the money on those who don't work. Much more progressive.

As to the N£sd…

GP surgeries will now open reliably on alternate days, dentists be re-situated on motorway café sites, exhausted nurses retired at 29 [30, if Smokers], consultants be put into work-directed programme for ConsLibDemy access. For benefit claimants, free buses, train tickets to Moscow hospitals, internal UK flights to healthclubs, 24-hour schools, hospital food by Muggleburgers, etc etc etc – but only IF on benefits.

Barney: *Won't work, any of it, Kev!* Nice try though! Good larfs! Got ideas from early opening of Xmas Crackers, eh? Who's a Bad Boyo then?!

Intruding, Anxious Aristo Voice: What, you are *working*? Well, that's your lookout!

Barney: Oh, come on Kev! Good for a laugh, I know Kev. But look, Kev. It's too early in the day for this. So, 'op it! This is NO JOKE! Got to go!
Puts down telephone.

An hour later, Brenda again:

Brenda: Sir, it's Kevin. Putting him through.

Barney: What, *twice* in one morning Kev! What now?

Kevin: Don't know what you mean. I've just got back from the Outpatients' Business Meeting. Found that consultant has spent the money twice: once by his business manager, then him separately. Calls it "organisation"! Wanted a word…

Barney: Eh? But you rang me an hour ago…

Kev: Not me, mate. Some mistake. Now, about those surplus A&E trolleys from North Korea…

Barney: Oh, dear, not you then? Thought it was Dixbungle at first. Then thought it was you pulling my leg. Funny squeaky voice. P'raps *was* someone else. Can't think who, though. Called himself Lord Oakehotty, or summink. Oxford accent. Very put on. No idea who he is. Totally mad set of policies he's got, though. Very full of himself. Know who he is, do you?

Kev: Nope. Never heard of him. Some nutter, I s'pose. We get them too. But usually in

A&E. Lot of it about. Now, about those surplus trolleys…

Barney: Yep. Bought them in bulk, along with the used ward-drip kits, the re-coated ward-chairs and the extra second-hand ambulances, from North Korea. Had them 5 years in off-site storeage. Over in Bludgeon Buildings. Job lot. Sir Nickelodeon's idea. "Builds socialism", and all that.

Can let you have a few, on the cheap. How many d'you want?

His other telephone line sounds….

Barney: Hello…I'm on the other line. Is this urgent? Call you back?

Stupefied voice: This is Lordy Oakegrotty again. Now, about your son's University fees. I am a very important LibDem peer…and so…

Barney: Help, Kev. *Here's here again.* On the other line. What to do?

Kev: Send for the straight-jacket! Quick!

Barney *[to mysterious caller]*: If you will just come to reception in G-Block, and ask for Security…

EPISODE 29

Collector's Corner.
The Age of the NHS Postcard.

Dramatis personae:

Mr. Youknowwho, Senior Surgeon, The Bit Parts of England NHS Trust, West Midlands.

Mr. Youguesswho, Chief Executive, of the same.

Mr. Ian Clownlives, Medical Director, of the above.

***

"Detection is, or ought to be, an exact science, and should be treated in the same cold and unemotional manner." – Sherlock Holmes.

"I am the great. I am the one who knows. I am the one to decide. It is I. Conventum consuetum est." – Top Contemporary Surgeon.

***

Mr.Youknowwho: Sending you a postcard from Cape Town, Mark. Latest big stop on my world tour. Luxury stuff! Sorry to disturb. Know you are busy Pension Potting. But just to say on this idea of not operating proper, I'm as innocent as the Battlefields of Borodino. Happy days! Sun shining! Lovely vino! As ever, Yippee-I, IP.

Mr.Youguesswho: IP, am texting this e-mail to your mobile. Thanks for card. Looks superb! Just to advise that that busybody Sir IK is on the case. But isn't yet asking the right questions. So all kosher. Say hello to dusky ladies for me. Toodle-oo! As ever, MG. PS: Pension Potting every ball on the table! Clean break!

Mr. Youknowwho: Hello again MG. Trust pension potting proceeds I hopes. Keep up with the boys! Sending you a sepia postcard of an ancient Boer Shack. Bit of a mud-heap. But historic. 'Breaker' Morant slept here! Explored the part of district said to be King Solomon's Mines. All that Rider Haggard stuff. *She*, too, supposed to have been in a cave nearby. All Rider's imagination, in course. Books written above gateway at Rye. Hope not wasting our valuable money there recalling women for quite unnecessary further treatments. Keep up the long-term pension potting! As ever, IP.

Mr.Youguesswho: Making haste slowly. Am also keeping the statistics under wraps. Usual successful policy, "secrecy and containment." Clownlives is on side. Hope you are enjoying the Veldt. No need to hurry home. Take a really deserved break. As ever. MG.

Youknowwho: Hope you like this postcard of Suede Afrique diamonds and gold Krugerands. Quite a few of them in your pension potting I expect! Have pocketed a few for real, for myself. Aha! Recommend it. Spending some of my well-earned Merit Awards. Shot a Hartebeest too and had some of it for lunch. But meat spoiled. Hit it in the breast by mistake. Not enough breathing space or spared cleavage. Must try harder! As ever, IP.

Mr.Youguesswho: Sending usual e-mail. Medical Director against recalling patients. So may not have so to do. Send me some S. African grapes by courier, please. O/wise all quiet here. As ever, MG.

Youknowwho: Herebe a postcard from Jo'Burg. Messy place. Lots of shacks, and cars robbed at gunpoint at traffic lights. Keeping my doors locked. Was mistaken for Lord Lucan today, but let go when they realised I am not a danger to life, limb, soul or breast. Hope pension potting now above the 2 milkies mark. Afford a few choc bars, eh? Must run to catch post. Tootle-pip! Best to all, espec. all at the Royal Academy of Vested Interests. IP.

Mr.Youguesswho: You must be back on the *MV Breathwaster* by now? All those rich widows, and dances! Saw photos in *DT* colour supp. Big ship. On your way to Fiji now. Lucky blighter! You docs get all the best. Sir Ian here again today. But one of his chaps arrived having left his files on train. So *nil desperandum, null progressitchy*, all Q. on the W. front. Send me a postcard of dancing girls. And less of the "pension potting." That's a private matter! Yrs. MG.

Youknowwho: Here is a postcard of Fiji sunset. Seems a bit bloody, but then they were still cannibals here until the early 1940s. Nasty burghers. Need yr advice, a bit, while I sip this crème-de-menthe. Have had a frantic e-mail from Clownlives. Panicking? Says rumour is that some 4,000 women may be re-called for IK's enquiry. Thought he was busy with MP's salaries? Can't you sort this quietly? As to p. potting, I'm ahead of you by a few noughts! Yrs. IP.

Mr.Youguesswho: Doing my best re said rumours. On the QT. And Clownlives is cooperating. Everyone agrees that you are Prince Charming. Described as "charismatic and charming"! Bloke who played rugby with you at Cantab said were always The Rupert Brooke of the Party. Got lots of riverside crumpet, too! A breast man, they say! Dirty blighter! As ever, MG.

Youknowwho: Got yours. Nice card here of Porpoises leaping. Ref Cantab, all cobblers. Was too busy deciding on my new procedures with which to STONISH THE WORLD! Hope you are letting my waiting-list pile up. Will need the money after this Big Spendup. If my list gets big enough, plenty will want to come to The Drive with their £4,000, for quicker fixes. So you won't have to cope with all the pressure you know. Only trying to help, of course. Trust pension potting proceeds as per normal. Mine safely in the stratosphere, am glad to say. As ever. IP.

Mr.Youguesswho: Thank you for new card. PP up to £2.7m. So, with tax-free sum, indexed pension, decent investment in central London flats, should just about get by now. Might even get another job when get fed up with this place. Quite fancy Isle of Wight, actually. But not that Royal Bournemouth Hospital in Dorset. Die like flies there. Anyway, made a few bob myself this week. Put those lovely postcards from you onto e-bay. All sold too!

COLLECTOR'S CORNER. THE AGE OF THE NHS POSTCARD

[Increasingly frantic e-mails follow…]

Youknowwho: **What???** *You did what?* Oh gawd! What date for bidding-to-end did you put? Go and grab them back this minute. Take them off again pdq. *Do it now!*

Mr.Youguesswho: Can't do that. All sold. Efficient site that. All gone. The lot.

Youknowwho: What? Golly. Bloody idiot MG!

Mr.Youguesswho: Yep. Gone. Got the cash already, too, via Paypal. Bloke used the 'Buy it Now' option, within first hour. Got a tenner for each of them. £110 in total. Plus postage. Charged another fiver for that. So I owe you a drink!

Youknowwho: What?!!! Gawd for Murgatroyd. *Who was the buyer?* Do you know?

Mr.Youguesswho: Some bloke called Nick Timplekins. Works on *FT*. Chess correspondent? Evidently collects postcards. Very quick payer. V. g. record on feedback page. Sent me a very friendly acknowledgement. He seemed pleased to know my full name & address. For future sales I s'pose. I'd used my usual e-bay address, BMARFloppsybunny97% to start with. Hope you land happily at Wellington. Lovely harbour. Was a jazz festival when we were there. Send me a colourful card. MG.

Youknowwho: No bloody picture card today. This note please read & burn. Send me fullest info on rumoured enquiries there. V. Urgent. IP.

Mr.Youguesswho: IP. Long e-mail. Do not accidentally forward to anyone! Here are alleged! "facts." It's being said that more than 4,000 women may have been left with an increased risk of breast cancer – "weak" management being blamed for allegedly covering up your failings. Can't be so, can it? Going to be a full enquiry. Be expensive nuisance. But you will have to fly home from Wellington. Going to be examination of your 15 years practice here. Already recalling more than 600 women in case need more treatment. Sir IK says your death rates 5 times as high as those from conventional surgery. Never so, surely.

Anyway, allegedly hundreds have died since surgery, but not necessarily result thereof. Lot of fuss about your "cleavage sparing." Said to leave dangerous breast tissue in the body, which against nat. guidelines. I'm copping it, too. So are some other docs. Alleged that your practice said to be known as unsafe as long ago as 2003. Others knew but said nothing. So you were still operating until 2011.

Apparently we should have recalled more than just the 12 patients we saw again in 2009, too. Me and Clownlives made that decision. Anyway, it's getting a bit hot and chilly here. I may have to take myself off, even, and stop earning my £230,000 p.a. Seems a bit rich! But the GBWWCo PLC probably will suspend you. So *must* be serious! Trust will prob cop big compensation bills. Said to be 1 million at least. Taxpayers money, of course. But I am trying to settle cases in secret. On the QT. So far 10 women have taken the dosh. Most we've had to pay so far was £150,000. But we're being compared with Solihull and Sutton Coldfield – can you believe??? So, come home! From Your best chum in the world, MG.

Mr.Youguesswho, Chief Executive, then calls into his office the Trust's Medical Director, Dr. Clownlives.

Need to ask you some questions, IC.

Don't you have peer reviews of surgeons' operations?

IC: Eh?

Mr.Youguesswho...on results, death rates, comparisons, outcomes, patient's complaints, all that?

IC: Eh?

Mr.Youguesswho: Don't you listen to whistle-blowers, and take warnings seriously? *Even from concerned colleagues?*

IC: Eh?

Mr. Youguesswho: When you discover something *seriously* amiss, don't you study the situation and counsel the surgeon, halt operations, and ensure adherence to national guidelines?

IC: Eh?

Mr. Youguesswho: What am I to say to Sir Ian's enquiry?

IC: Eh?

Mr. Youguesswho: Are you going to remain in post as Medical Director?

IC: Eh? *What?* Are *you* going to remain in post as Chief Executive?

Mr. Youguesswho: Are *you* going to have a meeting of all consultants to consider what we should do next? NOW? *I need a good story...*

IC: Ay, up! *Trust me!*

***

As the great essayist and playwright poet said, "Read not to contradict and confute, nor to believe and take for granted...but to weigh and consider." – Francis Bacon.

***

SPECIAL: NOTICE TO THE READER: See Solihull Hospital Kennedy Breast Care Review. Review of the Response of Heart of England NHS Foundation Trust to Concerns about Mr Ian Paterson's Surgical Practice; Lessons to be Learned; and Recommendations, by Professor Sir Ian Kennedy:

"This is a tragic story. It is not a story about the whole of the NHS. It is about something that happened in one corner of one hospital Trust in one part of the NHS [sic]. But, it has lessons for the whole of the NHS.

COLLECTOR'S CORNER. THE AGE OF THE NHS POSTCARD

It is a story of women faced with a life threatening disease who have been harmed. It is a story of clinicians at their wits' ends trying for years to get the Trust to address what was going on. It is a story of clinicians going along with what they knew to be poor performance. It is a story of weak and indecisive leadership from senior managers. It is a story of secrecy and containment. It is a story of a Board which did not carry out its responsibilities. It is a story of a surgeon who chose on occasions to operate on women in a way unrecognised by his peers and thereby exposed them to harm. 19 December 2013; also, Laura Donnelly and Patrick Sawer, 'Bosses covered up cancer surgeon's errors', Daily Telegraph, *20 December 2013, p.10 – Ed.*

*NB. Facey Romford Jr comments. "**None** of this is actually funny, is it? "Board not carrying out its responsibilities"? Indeed, it could not be More Serious. Might have been better, too, if politicians Major and Bottomley and Cumberlege had backed that Brighton bloke when he raised national issues about the national standards of cancer care, in 1992-94, don't you think?"*

EPISODE 30

Snakes and Ladders. Or how the N£sd so carefully guards scarce taxpayers money.

And, Redundancies Ahoy!

Dramatis personae:

Sir Cyril Squoffington-Squogg, OBE, JP, is Chief Executive of The Tower of London NHS Hospital Trust, Tower Hamlets, London, EC.

Lady Bernice Squoffington-Squogg, his wife, is also Chair of The Wiltshire Artists Benevolent Fund.

Mr. Valentine Vox CBE is Head of the NHS Re-Settlement branch, Recompense House, Elephant & Castle, London, SE.

Mr. Alfie Peach, a recently [but regularly] redundant senior NHS manager, is a new applicant for welfare-support and NHS re-settlement.

***

The Scene: A small cottage with a seaview in West Wales, at Newgale Beach in Pembrokeshire, to which our Squoffington friends have retreated for a few days of peace after the Christmas celebrations.

Lady S-S: **Cyril!** Are you having a heart-attack? You've gone purple! Have you been eating those walnuts again? Got one stuck in your throat? Quick, let me slap you on the back.

Sir S-S: *[Coughing]* No. No. No need my love. Not doing the dying today. But catching up on my papers. Have you SEEN this House of Commons Health Committee report? Reveals that more than 19,000 thousand – NINETEEN THOUSAND!!! – NHS staff were given redundancy payments under Lansley's re-organisation of the NHS.

And almost ONE IN FIVE have since been rehired!!!

Great paying caper, too. For the staff that is. Not so for those Barney Wells calls *Taxpayers Ahoy!* And this is for England alone. Goodness knows what's been going on here in Wales. And as for 'It's All Free' Scotland…

Lady S-S: Let me see that… *[reads]*. Oh, it says here that at least 2,300 managers received six-figure redundancy payments. The highest sum was £605,000. Went to a female NHS executive whose husband also received a payoff of £345,000 in March. Nearly a million between them! AND then BOTH were rehired elsewhere in the health service!!!

Sir S-S: Yes. Beggars belief. 'Specially when you can't get to see a GP, or get seen in A&E. Or staff nursing properly.

Lady S-S: It says here that 3,261 were paid-off handsomely and then have since been rehired by the NHS…

Sir S-S: Yes. The great majority in the past 12 months.

Lady S-S: And that includes 403 who were back working for the NHS within four weeks – FOUR WEEKS! – of taking redundancy.

Sir S-S: Yes. Unbelievable! Probably took a sunshine Caribbean winter-break, and then back to the same desks.

Lady S-S: As ever – the NHS truth's are much stranger than fiction!

But at least that Labour MP Barbara Keeley pursued it.

Sir S-S: Well, I'm going to spend a couple of hours on this today. Could be the first scene in my new theatre project: THE WHITSUN WANGLES OF THE N£sd. Needs continuing attention.

And so…

THE WHITSUN WANGLES OF THE N£sd.

Scene One: The NHS Re-Settlement branch, Recompense House, Elephant & Castle, London, SE – a grim, soon-to-be redundant, early 1960s T. Dann Smith/Paulson/Maudling white tower-block at the Elephant roundabout. [Scheduled for demolition. And for prompt rebuilding as is].

[knock on door]

Mr. Valentine Vox: Come!

Mr. Alfie Peach: Right place? Re-settlement offices? Need help. Redundant. Again.
VV: Sit. Pull up *two* chairs. Sit.

Your story please.

AP: Here's my complete NHS employment-mobile-file. All the papers. Just been made redundant. Again. This time by the Up-e-Spout NHS Hospitals NHS Trust, Whipswhichup-on-Sea. Only been there a little while.

VV: Ah, Yes. Whicker's old place. Lots of redundancies there. Very regularly. See you chaps all the time. Always re-locate you. Sure can help you this time too. Not seen you before though, have I?

AP: No. Last few times I was dealt with in Leeds. BUT now, I'm here in two capacities. As a recently redundant NHS manager. And then as the founder today of my new consultancy. My first day in that job.

VV: Ah, yes. I see. Get to that in a moment. Quite usual. I see that you have been made redundant three times in 12 years. Total redundancy payments received... let me see... ah yes, received £96,000 in 2001; £123,000 in 2006; and lastly £260,000 in 2012. And your wife, too, she's just had £149,000 herself. Oh, and before that at Clactonk, £214,000. Only twice in her case, redundant?

AP: Yes. She's the unlucky one. But we are both still pensioned, of course. I *keep* being made redundant. Can you help me?

VV: You're rather like one of the yo-yo clubs. Say, West Brom. Up one year, big financial bonus. Down next year, parachute payment of £30m. Up again, another big bonus, and so on. No need to win anything ever, eh?!

Well, on the scale here it says that after your total of 17 years of NHS service you would be due only £190,000 this time. Won't affect your CBE, I see. That's going through as normal. Keep your car, too.

AP: Thank you sir. I can accept that. I will accept the £190,000. Tax free. Can I now move from the first chair I'm sitting in, the well-worn one marked *NHS Employee Redundant*, to the other one.

VV: Yes. Do so now. It's marked *New Consultancy Owner*. Brand new furniture, actually.

AP jumps up. Re-sits in the second chair.

VV: Now we can properly proceed. First, here is your cheque for £190,000.

AP pockets this, very promptly.

VV: Now tell me about your new consultancy. Called 2-to-Quango, is it?

AP: New firm. Just started. Today. Already have three clients. Me, and my wife Annie. And Curtis Walters at Progressive NHS, Walltiled, Cheshire. He's just been made redundant, too. Got only £176,500. Fairly new bloke. Came in from British Leyland. White-van line manager.

VV: Well, as a new consultant how can you help me, then?

AP: Here's what my new consultancy can now offer the NHS. To help you. I will go to Curtis's old job. Salary, £225,000 p.a. He will come into my old job, at the same rate. My wife will come into these offices here as a Senior Adviser on Re-settlements. Probably manage on £120,000. All to have proper redundancy agreements, of course, just in case. Can't be too careful nowadays, can you?

VV: Well, that's all settled then. Alice will send out the usual letters to you all today. Come by courier so no time is wasted. Now, let's have some fresh coffee. And a look at today's paper! Start with the front-page, at the back, on the Premier League. But you're a Spurs fan, aren't you? Well, poor old AVB. Who'd be a football manager? Keep getting sacked. Course, they get these big-pay-offs. Disgraceful. Terrible waste of money. Scandalous and sinful. That's hard-earned money paid in at the turnstiles by the fans. And just look at that Sven. New job every year. Never wins anything. In and out of jobs…big pay-offs galore. Always being re-hired too. Should be stopped. But what can you expect in such a piratical free-market?

AP: Yers. Sven in and out of jobs. And beds!

VV: …And beds. Always gets a couple of millions in compensation. Moringo too. He'll get another big wallop from Chelski. Same for Mousey at The Moaners. Still, we're lucky. In genuine public service. We can't actually get sacked. Much better than retiring to the bottle, too!

AP: Just so. And the NHS is still keen not to lose valuable employees. My consultancy will do all it can to help you.

VV: Quite so. S'why I'm here. With my 247 staff. And the Leeds people too, for dealing north of Watford. Another 600-odd there. Just on redundancy-making and re-hire services. Did our best even for that Mark Goldman. But he already had his pension pot of £2.7million, so he didn't need any further help from me. Usually I can get people back on the payroll within weeks of them taking redundancy. And, 'course, with new excellent re-organisations due under The Millkiband Kid, we'll have to increase our own staff. Be a lot more redundancies and then re-hiring to do. Could use your new firm, with its good record, as advisers. If you have time.

AP: Can quite see that. Be fees, of course. As a consultant, of course. And as an old, and as a new, past and future NHS manager. Hard to keep up with who's who and what's what, actually. NHS. NHS Monitor. NHS England. NHS Upwards, Forwards, Sideways, and Backwards. NHS Great Train Robbery PLC. All got their own staff and C/E's, too. AND very busy HR directors, making new redundancies…

VV: And re-hirings!

AP: Every day!

VV: Makes the world go round!

AP: And makes it come round again nicely, too!

VV: Yes. But we are VERY economical in our workings, you know. Under Sir Pensioned-Orff Nickelodeon – the newly re-hired Viscount of Midstaffs himself – we had a projected annual budget for redundancy payments of £1.5 billion p.a. But we've only spent between £600 and £700 million this year. Try as we might. And that even with advice from the BBC Trust on pay-offs and sweeteners in severance packages. Still, it gives you chills, doesn't it, when you think of what we *are* achieving?

AP: Got to do better this coming year though, sir! Otherwise, The Treasury just snatches back any unspent budget. I'll help you, of course. Will get plenty of new clients, I'm sure of that.

VV: Yes. Quite right. That Treasury snatch'll never do! But we've got a plan to sort it…come and see me again next May 1st. We can see about your next redundancy payment and your new job then…Course, the rules have changed a bit lately. Caused by that fuss. Can't be re-hired now in your actual old job for a year. Will work something out between us though. We need your specialist skills. As ever.

AP: Putting the date into my diary right now, sir!

VV: Right. Now send in the next chap. The one out there in the red outfit, says he was Father Christmas. And then the three old blokes in gold cloaks and floppy hats. Say they be The Three Kings of Orient Are….

NB. Facey notes concerning that for a redundancy budget of £1.5 billion it would take you 32 years to count to a billion alone, starting now.

EPISODE 31

Facey's Frightfuls. As noted in My N£sd Diary.

Extracts, to be read on train when Oscar Wilde Diary is finished. Part 1.

1 December: Where'd the year GO?

Time passing…a lot of sand in the glass. Years all ticking on. Finding grey in me hair. What there is of it. Still here, though. Alive, *and* kicking! AND have kept my diary going all this year. So, a reward for me: a big box of Thornton's chocs, for display when watching football…Come on The Arsenal!

Today I decided to start my new listings: FACEY'S FRIGHTFULS. First 10 herewith.

This is my new record of N£sd Worsers & Worsers. Bungles in the Jungles. Vested Interests at Play. And in charge. And other adjacent parallel events in education, social care & other distinctly British state monopoly bureaucratised fully socialistickered dee-zarsters!

If I can find enough note-books….

2 December: FACEY'S FRIGHTFULS, 1: Have been thinking about our beloved political leaders, who are in charge of the N£sd. And what it is which so disqualifies them from any such a role.

So I have set this GCE A* Exam.

Question 1: List all original ideas of products or services imagined/created by DC, NC, and The Millkiband Kid, and then successfully brought to market.

Question 2: List businesses established and run profitably by each, serving willing customers who had a choice of providers.

Question 3: List all previous non-political jobs held by DC, NC, & The Millkiband Kid.

Time allowed by examiners: 1 minute.

Alternative question [for very advanced students, usually from Asia]: Name which of these "leaders" proclaim themselves on the side of the individual, of open-ness to the new, of the imaginative and innovative spirit, of economic and social dynamism, of entrepreneurship and of improved services through competition?

Time allowed by examiners: 2 seconds.

3-13 December: Very busy preparing my New Year Edmund Burke Memorial lecture. Still polishing it.

14 December: FACEY'S FRIGHTFULS, 2: See that 8 VeryTopDocs have signed a letter to the *Daily Telegraph* complaining about poor weekend care in hospitals, and lack of proper consultant cover. Have they only just noticed??? Ah, but it's happened to one of "Our Gang." As a patient... Well, then that's different, innit?

Didn't they notice the report earlier this year which said that of 4 million patients who had surgery on a Friday 44% or more were more likely to die [and a lot of them did!] than those operated on on a Monday? That's a heck of a lot of Mums and Dads, Grandmas and Grandpas, as well as Little Johnnies and little Jillies. *Telegraph* can't have published their letter then, eh? Must have been lost in the post.

BUT this time it's been a problem of apparent weekend neglect for a retired surgeon. Ah. Then that's different, isn't it? Time to Yell Blue Murder!!!

Why are docs writing to the 'papers protesting? It's THEM, isn't it who are the cause of poor weekend care? They won't do the hours. But you've got to give it them: for self-focussed propaganda they've got North Korea beat hollow. The care they give is not so hot on week-day evenings, either, is it? Where are the experienced docs then? Aghast? Or at home, sipping the brandy? Of course, it's alright, isn't it? For 'process' is in place then – if not them.

Well, it was the very same when I was a student. No change in all these years. Although it has actually got worse and worse. Salaries up. Quality down. Pensions up, hours down. Status up, burials more numerous. AND still the 'process' does not require anyone to take *personal responsibility*. And the high salaries, perks, indexed pensions, and honours remain unchanged. So mought it be. *[See also previous Episode 22 – Ed.].*

15 December: FACEY'S FRIGHTFULS, 3: Yesterday a bad day all round. Some Father killed his 16 week old daughter after becoming "agitated" when he ran out of cannabis. Shook her to death. He with IQ of 52, and unable to read. How can such a man be considered suitable to be a father at all?

16 December: FACEY'S FRIGHTFULS, 4: Tuned in to BBC Breakfast programme. Astonishing! They have a woman "business editor" called Steph. Here she was, meeting a bright & happy postal worker, 28 years in service, doing his job. Supposed to be showing us how Christmas sorting was going. First thing she said to him: "You've just been privatised? Aren't you worried?"! NOT, "Exciting times. Sharer now. Company doing well, new investments and growth. Parcels business booming. Happy customers. Future looks good, yes?"

BUT THE ASSUMED AND UNCHALLENGED BBC BIAS is so prevalent and deep-seated, the anti-business soft-leftie assumptions they make just tumble out, unquestioned, invisible to the management [under Lord Hong Kong himself]. This woman evidently anti-business, anti-entrepreneurship, anti-growth. Whatever is she doing in that job? And look how they report on any alternatives or reforms for the NHS, too. Biased? You can guess! Sent in my complaint. Await response.

17 December: Good job there is something to laugh about. Heard about that C/E

FACEY'S FRIGHTFULS. AS NOTED IN MY N£SD DIARY

Stewed Bludgeon in trouble again. ["I will not resign!"] Apparently 'Emergency Planning & Instant Action' at Richmond House *[Surely not? – Ed.]* called him up. One of those tests they like to do. "The biggest local road bridge has blown away! Action!" Bludgeon's reply: "Oh, gawd! I've not got me bike. How am I to get home?" The caller was actually Sir Nickelodeon himself. He asked Bludgeon: "Do you *know* who I am?" Bludgeon: "No." Then Bludgeon asked the caller: "Do you know *who* I am?" Sir N: "No." Bludgeon: "Thank gawd!" And Bludgeon slammed down the phone. 'Course, His Royal Ever-Alert Midstaffs Knightly CPGB Thought Police tracked Bludgeon down. Double-quick. Crime Against Majesty. Verbals. Dereliction of Required Subservience. Unkowtowing.

The said sad Bludgeon last seen as an incommunicado in-patient at the Rotting-Junk-on-Thames Trust at Gullingdodge on the Medway in North Kent. Electrolysis? Electro-convulsive therapy? Counselling? Sparks! Ah, eh, eee, ow! That Bludgeon. An accountant of sorts wasn't he? Never thought him up to much, anyway. Won't do any good for him. Much too late in the day. Big sponsor of old Sitting Bull sweeties, of course.

18 December: FACEY'S FRIGHTFULS, 5: And then there's Gove. Shock, too, this. Even he is reflecting the soft-leftie socialism which is in charge of the NHS and of education too. Failed to support parent request for Grammar School expansion in Sevenoaks. How can that be? Apparently it was "against bureaucratic rules", and those rules made by Brown & Millkiband of all people. Well, isn't Gove now the SofS, and so there to make the rules??? Oh, why didn't we just say to Uncle Joe in 1945, "Come on in Joe, and make our lovely country just like yours. Help yourself!"

What hope for a better NHS, let alone education, in such an ant-heaped socialistically entwined rule-embraced candle-snuffed bureaucratised imbroglio? Go to Betfair. You'll get very rotten odds on that one.

19 December: Reading absolutely brilliant, sensitive, reflective, kindly new novel on the quandaries of the frail, the elderly, Alzheimer's and life in all its aspects by that Melvyn Bragg. Called *Grace and Mary*. Really moving work. Made me think of a lot of the fundamentals concerning the NHS and social/long-term care. How individuals have to take actual personal responsibility. Every day. Not rely on 'process' or on 'the system.' Will get copies to give as Xmas gifts. Have missed posting dates to OZ & NZ – so send by courier? Must check. Need to get copies for my nephews in Sydney, and to Soapey Sponge's GGGrandsons in Melbourne. Trying to find copies of Bragg's other books, too. New one an amazing work.

Bet it won't win the Booker, though. You have to be the half-Scottish, half-Lithuanian multi-sexual nephew of a dusty-carty worker person from Twiggleystan via Middlesbrough who has lived on benefits all his/her life, then hitch-hiked to Katmandu carrying a fridge. AND be related to at least 7 BBC employees earning over £750,000. *[Plus pension and kick-out allowance – Ed.]*. Best if a Trot-skier, too. Usually preferred.

20 November: Started to do my Christmas cards. Nice print this year. Me on a brisk hunter, a-leaping the blackthorns. Up, Away! *Tally Ho!* But can't find me last year's list. My desk covered in all these NHS reports. Urgent. Shock. Horror. Scandal. Outrage. Running out of words. Need a bigger *Thesaurus*.

23 November: FACEY'S FRIGHTFULS, 6: See that hospital death rates are up 16% on Sundays. Now there's a surprise. Consultants "on call"? To be called in? You a Junior Doc? Want a reference? Want a career in medicine? Want *my* support, your senior doc? *Just you try it.* Dean Royles [Chief Executive, NHS Employers] stressed the need for proper GP and consultant cover again in talks with BMA. Stress away! As Mark Porter [Chairman of the BMA Council] is still piffling, waffling, driffling: "On the one hand, yet on the other hand." Just means "Hands out for more dosh!" As per usual. Just you wait. Desperately cash-starved government *will* find the money. Votes in it, after all. *[Taxpayers Ahoy! – Ed.].*

24 November: Saw Sir Nicko at DoH meeting. V. glum. Applied for C/E role at Dog's Rescue Home in Montevideo. Only long-listed. Simon Stevens named as successor. Lord Bexhill to be, no doubt. Apparently the PM found it hard to interest anyone, but he's a good choice. I hopes. 'Course, Brian Edwards should have succeeded Duncan as NHS chief executive in the 1990s. Bloody stupid waste not giving him that job. Or Chris West from Pompey. Either could still be there, doing the job well. Usual bureaucratic bungledom, could have been avoided. Lot of odd souls appointed instead. Followed by usual rations of CBEs and Knighthoods. One – forget his name – was even kicked upstairs by Milburn. Now Lord Coughdrop, or some such. Soaking up the daily fees, no doubt. And on some private co boards too? VERY public spirited all that, I have no doubts whatsoever. If others have doubts they just be naughty cynics.

25 November: Said hello to Barney Wells at Waterloo. On the escalator. He going up, me going down. He just called out *"Taxpayers Ahoy!"* Have to love him for it.

26 November: FACEY'S FRIGHTFULS, 7: Squoffy says that new Chairman Lord Ironsides at Barney's hospital has discovered that a consultant who was supposed to be in the op. theatre one recent Wednesday was actually elsewhere doing private work. But when Ironsides and Barney went back to the theatre to look at the record book next day the consultant's signature *as in attendance* had mysteriously appeared in the record. Evidently had heard of their earlier visit. Mysterious signature – happens a lot, I suspect.

27 November: FACEY'S FRIGHTFULS, 8: See ever-more dreadful care-home scandals. That National Care Standards Commission spent £200m of public money over three or four years from 2001. *To achieve what?* The fundamental issues still seem to be unresolved? *Who* was it who chaired that quango?

28 November: Saw Harry Verney at the Ath. yesterday. Now a retired GP. Good old sort, that Harry. But in a minority in Whitehall. Had chat over good bottle of old port. Talked about all these fashionable think-tanks. He uses another, similar word. Bit ruder. Says it's a pity we get little help from some of them. A lot of so-called policy "thought", like at that socialisticised Klingfilm Fund, is thin soil over thick concrete. My opinion, too. And I'm not alone in that rocky field.

Lot of this policy wonkery about. But just can't understand how it's possible for anyone to be a leading policy wonk and make a career staying just half a rain-drop ahead of the wave and just describing the new weather. But apparently it is. Some have it off to a fine art. Call it Klingfilmery meself.

28 November: FACEY'S FRIGHTFULS, 9: Chat on telephone with Squoffy. Thinks that this Patient's Association isn't much help either. Their spokes just saying "Oh dear" when a bad news issue comes up. Not much theoretical understanding there. Critical analysis? Hah. "Politics there the art of the impossible." Right as rain!

Constantly just get from the lot of them the old unthinking soft leftie stuff which have seen not to work, suffered from wholesale, and rejected. A lot of bridges gone under the water since the unlamented Brown. But we've still got these duffle-coated wonks in place. Could easily give the NHS a harder time over the endemic structural problems. And offer positive alternatives. Analysis of why things must always be as they are under the present set-up. But don't, can't, or won't.

30 November: FACEY'S FRIGHTFULS, 10: Bumped into an old antiquarian bookseller chum in Burlington Arcade. Old Dr. "Foxed" Magazzie. Top man in his field. Brilliant bloke. Great raconteur. Went to tea with him at Fortnum's. Told me food & politics story. Relevant, too. *True story.* Said he can vouch for it absolutely.

Seems that when his Father was Managing Director of a big City Finance outfit with dozens of branches he had to deal with Trade Unions. Had an official meeting with Jack Jones & Hugh Scanlon, the big Trade Union bully-boy figures in the early 1970s. He decided to take them to the best (& most expensive) restaurant in Jermyn Street, off of Piccadilly in London. Thought it be a real treat. Jolly them up. So, took them to this splash-up, posh-up, top-toffs place. Lovely linen. Best cutlery and china. Cut-glasses with the wine. Waiters everywhere. *Cordon bleu* food. Fine wines. Service fabulous.

But he was surprised that Jones and Scanlon seemed to know all the staff. And when paying the bill (which he remembers being about £120, and this was in about 1971!) my chum's Dad asked the head waiter if he knew these gents. "Oh yes", was the reply, "They eat here every day when they are in London"! Socialism, eh? "What's yours is mine, and what's mine's me own!"

1 December: To lunch at the Traveller's today with Sir Humpy. Discussed New Year list people make. And usual new Sirs. Duffer lotta than everer. Noted too that Sir Bruce puts "7-day NHS" as Top of His List. H & I agreed. Noted on napkin that that's *just as important* as No.2, Self-responsibility by individuals; 3. Obesity challenges & economic incentives; 4. More money – top ups, co-payments, more personal insurance, and health savings accounts; 5. Prices for many services to deter daft demands. *Or don't we want any sort of NHS by 2020?*

We had our usual quiz-game, to name the Oxymoron of The Year. Humphy won. As he always does. "The Klingfilm Fund has a Director of Leadership, no less." Whatever next? Humpy's comment: "As Seneca says, 'Light griefs are loquacious, but the great are dumb." He paid the bill, too. Or the Treasury or DoH, I s'pose…And all the staff at The Ath. know *him* very well indeed. So, make mine another large brandy, please, Humpy!

PS: Nearly forgot, 5 November: Bonfire Night again! *No Popery!*

NB. My old pocket diary bound in Blue 'Croomalin' is now an archival heritage item. *To be continued in my New Year Diary, with the John Leech engravings…*

EPISODE 32

Facey's Frightfuls. As Noted in My N£sd Diary.

Extracts, to be read on train when Oscar Wilde Diary is finished. Part 2.

26 December 2013: Christmas as far away as ever!

Still collecting FACEY'S FRIGHTFULS. My new record of N£sd Worsers & Worsers. Bungles in the Jungles. Vested Interests at play. And in charge. And other adjacent parallel events in education, social care & other distinctly British state monopoly bureaucratised fully socialistickered dee-zarsters! Using huge new notebooks.

My New Year series, No.1....

Now this one is VERY SERIOUS. So Listen Up, please dear regular Facey-ites.

It's Medical Errors and Negligence, again. And this news about GPs and alleged inspections. The government *pretending* to fix poor practice. General election in view. So trying to give impression of doing something about medical negligence. So that we are all comforted and all shut up about it. Well, my message to them, to the BMA, to The Royal Academy of Vested Interests, and to the GBWWCo, is – *We Won't!*

Remember that the Gov named half a dozen "inadequate" GPs? And reported that ONLY a third of GPs are inadequate at their jobs. Ah, that's a great comfort then, isn't it? Well, maybe. But it doesn't address the problem at all. *Not at all.*

Here's why.

As per usual, this particular bit of fuss about GP practice is beside the point. The politicians and the BMA/GBWWCo PLC want to make the public think that they are doing something about medical errors. BUT the great bulk of those have nothing to do with a few docs in Manchester being caught with out-of-date tablets in the cupboard. Or re-using newly scalded needles, awful as that is.

As Dr. Bill Pickering – the "expert witness" – reminded me the other day, the government's new "policy" won't do at all. Because most medical errors are actually made by reasonably good and conscientious doctors. It's reasonable doctors who often make mistakes. Often by not following the basics. You know. Didn't get tests done. Didn't study them if had them. Didn't diagnose properly. Didn't refer on in time. 'Course – in the absence of an Independent Medical Inspectorate, as advocated by Bill for some years – the GPs have no fear of a ban, unlike dangerous and dodgy drivers. Or of a fine. Or of being caught 'on camera.' So what will change? Tiddlypops.

I'll make this *serious* point again. *Dr. Pickering is right on the button on this.* The key here is that medical errors are NOT the domain of thick and feral doctors. Some are. Most are not. The BMA/GBWWCo claim that there is a race of separate, sheer bad docs who can be wiped out and then the problem is solved – that's all self-serving tosh. This is NOT the way to fix the problems.

As Dr. P tells me, it will hardly touch them. Most errors arise from doctors not following absolutely basic, traditional ground rules. Many, indeed, *know* what to do but just can't be bothered. After all, no-one's looking are they? Doesn't affect their income, does it? Or pension? No fines, are there? And the NHS doesn't even make proper and systematic use of patient's complaints, does it? Which should be the first base from which all enquiries and corrections/punishments should start. What does the BMA, GBWWCo and Royal College of Vested interests say and do about this? You can put their actions into a thimble. Tip it up. It's empty.

[The late Dr. William Graham Pickering, who died on 5 February 20125, trained at King's College Hospital. He was later a hospital doctor, then a GP, and a noted expert-witness in legal cases concerning the NHS. A real friend to better care. Independent advocate of a National Medical Inspectorate. See William G. Pickering, 'Systematic clinical accountability is required', BMJ, November 2003, 327: 1109; Pickering, 'An independent medical inspectorate', in D. Gladstone (ed.), Regulating doctors (London: Institute for the Study of Civil Society, 2000), and Pickering, 'Clinical accountability: check it out', http://bmj.com/cgi/eletters/338/jan15_3/b157#207651, 25 January 2009)].

AND these errors are happening every day of the week. They all need to be checked properly, not on a needle-in-a-haystack system. So, again, the message is that we need a proper Independent Medical Inspectorate working in every district, staffed by medically trained staff who know what to look for and why. Bill said so years ago. Was right then. Is right now. Time to listen and act! Then you'd see some changes! But from the present smoke and mirrors? Forget it.

Want an example? Look at that 16 year old girl from Worthing. GP told her that head pains were due to stress. Saw her, was it, four times? Then she dies of an undiagnosed brain tumour. *These kinds of errors are happening every day up and down the UK.* What is being done that actually works so as to prevent it? You can write the answers on the back of half of a 1d. postage stamp. This kind of thing is at the heart of the daily disasters of the NHS. So this is a FACEY'S FRIGHTFUL to which we will return. *[See also previous Episode 22 – Ed.].*

2 January: FACEY'S FRIGHTFULS, 2: What hope in this New Year for real NHS reforms? Snowball in Ecuador? Christians versus Lions? England more likely to beat Brazil 9-0? Wallop Germany on penalties? Tory Party making no progress. Well, so-called "Tory Party." Tory Pastry more like. Can't be an elected majority government next time. Couldn't even beat Brown last time out. So more Lib.Dem fudges to come. With or without The Kid. All that ConLibDemsy/ConLabDemsy stuff. Which one is the margarine? No can tell. And if CameronClegg can't "get" something real done about the NHS – changes in finances, in access, in quality, in costs, in coordination – then the Tory 1922 Committee will have to have "The Conversation" with PM. So Bye-bye Mr. D. C., Sir. Sleep tight, Your Dukelship of Notting Hill and Chipping Thompson.

FACEY'S FRIGHTFULS. AS NOTED IN MY N£SD DIARY

3 January: See that DoH stuff is still being leaked to that Roy Lilley site. Best source of info we've all got! But mis-prints in DoH announcements as bad as ever. See that they say emergency admissions must be given a thorough clinical assessment as soon as poss. and at least within 14 hours of arrival. Don't they *mean* 14 minutes? *Surely* not 14 hours? Or *days*? Just checking!

4 January: FACEY'S FRIGHTFULS, 3. Good lunch with Old Humpy. Always has good stories. Apparently that Ferguson allegedly ran into that alleged Rooney in an alleged motorway café. Over two alleged health-food breakfasts of six sausages, large helpings of baked-beans, four big mushrooms, three servings of black pudding, six slices of bacon, French-fries, mushy-peas, several eggs, two large chunks of fried bread, several pork-chops, kidneys, white-bread toast and jam, two mega-sized buns [each], big mugs of coffee, couple of lagers, etc. Munching away, each of them.

Ferguson asks, mid-munch: "Have you read my new autobiography?"

Rooney replies: "No. *Have you?*"

Love it! Never thought he'd got it in him! Two planks, and all that. Not chums, though, are they? See old ["Roy Keane Off!"] Keano is giving it back to the Retired Hairdryer, too. Deservedly, in my Very Biased Opinion!

5 January: FACEY'S FRIGHTFULS, 4. Got a funny letter today. Must keep in my files:

From Amalfi Holiday Caravan Park, Amalfi, Italy. 27 September 2013.

Sir,

I have been a very important person in the NHS for many, many years. Why have I never been mentioned in your stories, Mr. Romford?

Yours faithfully,

Ms. Lynda Lamentable.

***

Reply from me:

Dear Ms. Lamentable,

Unmentionable.

Yours, etc.

Dr. FR, Jr.

6 January: Re-reading Shelley. *The Masque of Anarchy.* Masterly. Born in Horsham – can you believe? Also, reading Milton. See Dante's Nine Circles of Hell in the Inferno in John Martin's illustration of the Bridge Over Chaos in *Paradise Lost*. Apparitions ghostly and weird in ever-receding lines behind them. The Sufferers of NHS Policies Past, Present, & Future?

7 January: FACEY'S FRIGHTFULS, 5. Heard some BMA top doc [BMAtD] on radio. Clearly had too much of the plonk. Did he *really* say that doctors are not motivated by money? *Heck-as-like*, as my old cousin's dance partner Alfie Willoughby used to say in the Blackburn Roxy when the judges got the Samba marks all wrong. Gave the doc none out of 10.

8 January: FACEY'S FRIGHTFULS, 6. Evasion projects galore in NHS I see. Evaso-flourishing as never afore. "Evasion" too often the name of the game. Just look at all the evasions about A&E. Docs demand comprehensive new policies, but never mention their own contracts which forced people into A&E wrongly in the first place! More care in the community? More social provision? More family care? More staff? Yes. All that. But *they* aren't doing it! Too busy catching the wriggling worms as their bait for their afternoons off GP fishing, p'raps.

9 January: FACEY'S FRIGHTFULS, 7. New Year. Well, still New Year-ish. Time I think of those gone before us. One of my own best friends, GP, trained with me, Gerry D – dead now, alas, sudden heart-attack – had told his wife very sternly that if he was ever seriously ill she was to drive him as fast and as far away as possible in any direction away from the Royal Sussex County Hospital in Brighton. Well, if patients had any control of the money then the best feedback would be where they ask to be seen… and from where they asked to escape! Who'd go *there* voluntarily?

Wouldn't need all this nonsense about filling in feedback forms about nurses then, would we? Have to compete for willing revenues then, though, hospitals like that Brighton one, eh? Not like now, where the local folks just have to go there. Sent like parcels – with usual delays in the post.

10 January: GPs always a worry. But if your GP practice is very good, alert, and serves the whole range of people – the elderly, the young Mothers to be, the family groups – you'd get the financial support from the patients holding these personal, tax-based lifelong healthcare accounts. Be properly inspected, of course. System tax-based of course. But with financial top-ups encouraged, and with extra insurance possible. Like in Oz, as Soapey tells me. The PGCAs would be democratic membership organisations, owned and controlled by its voluntary subscribers. And the tax-based fund would not be an extra benefit. It would be a core fund for us all. Extension of social care personal budgets. Makes sense.

11 January: And if there were these health care savings accounts for individuals – tax-based, of course – there could also be mobile, digital, record cards. They could carry them with their credit cards or their Tesco Club card. Be very valuable if they were picked up by an ambulance, or went to A&E themselves. Or were ill on holiday. Just scan the data. Stop the scandal of people in A&E with no notes, no history. No way to tell us their ailments or allergies otherwise. And if the ambulance had a scanner, they could send the data on to the hospital, and take the patient to the most appropriate facility, too. Patients should own their own records, their own data, anyway.

12 January: FACEY'S FRIGHTFULS, 8. Got on No.24 bus to Camden. Old BMA hofficer-type Dr. Spanner Unworksit got on at Tottenham Court Road. IMMEDIATELY

FACEY'S FRIGHTFULS. AS NOTED IN MY N£SD DIARY

opened up with topic we last discussed 4 years ago at Harrogate! "Choice! *That again!* I thought we'd got that sorted and limited already? Already too much of it about. And people don't want it. Bewildered by it. Read the Webbs. Went to the USSR. *Saw everything*. A New Civilisation, as they said! *They knew!* So why bring that up again, that choice thing? Millkiband won't have it, either…" He got off at the old Black Cat factory in Newington Green. Off to buy some antique silver pots. He said. But saw some of those cards from 'phone boxes in his top pocket. Must be for making medical notes.

15 January: FACEY'S FRIGHTFULS, 9. Today must go to the Klingfilm Fund to hear speech by Great British Whitewash PLC boss-guv Nursie Nursie Dixungler on 'Transparency in Public office.' No, but seriously…am taking several linen hankies, as may need to stuff my mouth to stop laughing out loud. Mustn't embarrass myself. Holy place, after all.

16 January: FACEY'S FRIGHTFULS, 10. Saw The Very Rev. Dr. Bishop Hogbin GCSE on ITV. Surprised he deigns to appear *there! Money!* Amidst commercials! The very idea. Docs adjacent to £sd. Too saintly, surely? He was talking about his new set of Thomas the Tank Engine. *A-mazing!!!* H-bin, he's everywhere when talking head wanted, it seems. BMA favourite sun. On the BBC and ITN list of medico-religio-"experts" to call. I actually had a chat about Thomas & Tank Engine only the other day with him at the vast BMA Palace in Euston. Religious nutter, y'know. Theo-illogical adviser to some NHS Hospital Trusts. Talks a funny mix of Trotsky, "Libertarian" Theological, and BMA-Medico-lingo. Doubly qualified. Trained as an orang-utan heart expert and then at Lenin College of Advanced Theology, Chesterfield. [Prop: A.W-Benn].

Said to me – made a note of it at the time, as best I could! Classic stuff! Have to larf!

Said to me, "Thomas The Tank Engine is a defibrillating commodity icon in the apre-degenerating late postal-capitalist pre-culture of early 21st century late-capitalist Britain and contra-sub Europa. Just like NHS local management itself. That itself is a clear argument against a free society of centralised politburo decision-making. In post-structuralist de-speculating And de-commodifying nanno-modernist commentaries on the condition of divisive sub-Bukharinite ex-Gorkyist post-modernity and the ubra-underfunded-NHS itself. As it is. But TtheTE is a key transitive representative if a semi-contradictory and partly-alienated semi-conducting symbol and archi-signifier when sub-compared with the Glorious Necessary Proletarian Vanguard. All hail to Our Advancing Millkiband IT'S ALL FREE PARTY which is taking us Forward to State Progress and to Our Worker's Paradise in Our glorious Socialist Future…As Gramsci told us…

H-bin then added: "So, to increase taxation & wealth distribution from non-benefit-receiving citizens I propose…" Last seen wandering beneath the pier at Brighton.

Sounds like that Polly Toynbee…But said it all, *he really did!* Might have even been a direct quote from *The Guardian*? What an argument against care in the community those two are!

18 January: Troubles at Dublin IRA Infirmary, it seems. Big fuss in media. Bloke launching fund-raising midnight walks: "Ghost Trails in the Irish Hospitals." Phantom Physios, Spooky Septicaemia, Lost Soulless Complaints. Spectral Secs of State of the Past…The Headless PM…. V.g. On You-Tube.

Oh, blow it. Me pencil's broke...BUT a Very Happy & Healthy New Year to all my readers! And do keep sending me the racing tips...

NB. Further extracts from Facey's Diary will appear occasionally, we hope, as he notes recording real events & for entirely historical purposes. However, his request to the Klingfilm Fund for sponsorship has thus far not been answered....We wonder why?

EPISODE 33

Britain to Teach the World How to Improve its Cancer Care. Part 1.

Major new PM international initiative.

NHS to lead radical cancer care changes in ex-Soviet Republic of Muckitupkistan.

Dramatis personae:

Lord Puggy Pointsdarn, the former left-wing ex-mariner, is a noted "expert" on this, that, and the other. Sometimes. Usually. When telephoned. However, he has no known previous interest in the NHS but he is the non-executive Chairman of Co-op Theatres and Circuses PLC, the leisure division of The Woyal Bank of Overlegs, Little Fiddlestown, Essex.

Ms. Serpentine O'Privilege is a long-time "associate" of his. She was formerly a horse-jumper at trials. She is known to Lord P as "Popsie." She is a comfort in his distresses.

Bernice Camden, formerly a leading amateur wrestler, is Chief Executive of the Hoop-la and Hula-Hoop Women's NHS Hospital Trust, Wiggers-on-Acveon, Soomersetshire. She is a key adviser to the Institute of One Idea at Monologue House, London, and to the IT'S ALL FREE Party.

***

Lord PP: We've got an urgent new challenge! CANCER.

We have to EXPORT the wonderful NHS successes with Cancer Care!

The PM is calling this the WMW-NHSCC4u.

The World's Most Wonderful NHS Cancer Charter For You.

To use the PM's new striking-language phrase: "WMW-NHSCC4u." He *does* get vibrant language right, doesn't he?

I'm to be in charge. Which means you, too, Popsie.

Ms. Serpentine O'Privilege: Coo!

Bernice Camden: PM trying to be populist like Nev? You know, the Call Centre Chorister in Swansea. His catch-word: SWSWSWN! Some Will, Some Won't, So What, Next! But he hasn't got Nev's touch, has he? PM that is.

Lord P: Trying, though! I spent New Year's Day at Chuckers. With the PM and his Notting Hill and Oxford chums. Well, those not in that High Court case that is. He was on tip-top form. Great weekend.

Bernice Camden: Yes, Puggsy. He was really hot on this. Very insistent that it's our next task to bring the whole world up to our standards of cancer care. Well, it's our bounden duty, isn't it? After all, when you see how far ahead of everyone else that we are…poor devils abroad….

Lord PP: Right. Right. Right. And the PM is so very pleased with the OECD scorings on our Wonderful NHS Cancer Care. Our very own *System!* Leads the world! PM very excited – now that we've again finished clearly and absolutely at the top of all of the performance tables for every clinical condition, once again. Especially on cancer care. In that OECD analysis.

Best diagnosis. Quickest and most appropriate referrals. Best 5-year survival rates. Best possible outcomes. Lowest costs, too. Hurrahs all round!

BC: Right! We're Globally tops! THE best! Bestest. Fourth year running too. And given five-stars in particular all round for our startling performance on Cancer Care.

WMW-NHSCC4u, indeed!

Ms. Serpentine O'Privilege: Coo!

Lord P: Well, we'll start by getting much better cancer care for the old USSR – the former Soviet Republic, now calling itself – temporarily – Free Muckitupkistan. In Central Asia. Where they elected a market-liberal social-democratic government 5 years ago. Disaster! It's been very hard sailing since. No WMW-NHSCC4u for them.

BC: Au contraire.

Lord P: I've already got a hit list of what they do so badly over there.

- Worst cancer care outcomes in the world.
- Huge numbers dying too early.
- Survival rates rock-bottom.
- Too late, too crude diagnosis by GPs.
- Slow referrals.
- Incompetent oncologists.
- Lack of diagnostic tools.
- Consultants only working short weeks. Many absent weekday evenings too. Junior docs too frightened to call them out.

FACEY'S FRIGHTFULS. AS NOTED IN MY N£SD DIARY

Now, if only they had a centralised health care State set-up, like us.

BC: Instead of what that democrat boss gang-leader Umanuvote Smith set up. When he got rid of old Mikhail Grimmotrot Keenknockoff. All that free choice! Terrible results.

Lord P: As you'd expect.

SO'P: Coo!

Lord P: And they've still got all the old names for cities, too. I ask you – Leeds-yer-astrayski. What a name for a capital city!

And because of this West-leaning revolution they've now got a strict non-class system there. All these potty innovations, too. Half of hospitals with hot water. And MRI's everywhere. Modern hugely expensive cancer drugs. Controls over management, doctors, costs – all by markets. But terrible cancer results. Terrible. Not like our wonderful outcomes at all. We don't waste that kind of money on that kind of kit, thank goodness indeed.

BC: Right! So now they are in a great fix on cancer care. They've got to be especially vigilant on breast cancer, bowel and cervical cancers. 'Cos they haven't got the great results which we have. From the centralised monopoly they could have had if they'd made the right decisions.

Lord P: BUT they made all the most basic mistakes – unlike our wonderful centralised state monopoly! Free markets indeed! Deezaster!

SO'P: Coo!

BC: Just look at what they did. Made every possible basic error.

I put together a list on the way here, on the back of the tri-weekly *Guardian* 64-page local government jobs supplement.

Errors, Mistakes, and Contrasts with our own monopoly State set-up:

Look at what they instituted – all based on quite hopeless political bias:

- Free individual choice.

- Massive public information programmes.

- Advice centres in supermarkets.

- Hot-line telephones.

- Financial empowerment of all individuals through tax transfers or tax incentives.

- Full use of direct electronic contacts & diagnosis via the net.

- Tackled smoking, drinking, lack of exercise, & bad diets by direct economic incentives.

- Health savings accounts.

- Local management freedoms.

- Increased salaries and shorter hours for all medical staff.

- Competing providers.

- Independent Medical Inspectorate in every district.

- Co-operative, mutual purchasing organisations owned by their members.

- Publication of the individual records of all doctors.

- Morbidity data on every facility.

- End of necessary postcode lotteries.

AND:

- Constant interference with GPs by re-training them.

- Billions wasted pushing hi-tech diagnostic kits into their hands.

- Tax income squandered by incentives to encourage exercise, dietary change, reduction of smoking and drinking. All those issues are a matter of "rights", not for state interference.

AND SO what did they expect in terms of much worse results! Entirely predictable, wasn't it?

Lord P: Unavoidable. And in one vast Asiatic region, Central Gorbichoffi, urgent referral rates fell to 7% – all working-class miners and such of course. But yet in another nearby region, East Kahmerinoff, the rate was 35%. We can guess who lived there! What sort of news-of-the-world is that then?

SO'P: Coo!

Lord P: So the PM is going to get it all dealt with. By us, on their behalf. WMW-NHSCC4u!

Then there's every chance of a Nobel NHS Prize. Catch up with Obama. Because of our wonderful cancer care results, too. Best in the world. As PM puts it so clearly, "WMW-NHSCC4u"!

SO'P: Coo!

BC: 'Course. We have the best health service in the world. So what would you expect? No-one has done it better. Copied everywhere. Only in the Isle of Crusoe did they make that personal, self-responsible insurance mistake…

FACEY'S FRIGHTFULS. AS NOTED IN MY N£SD DIARY

NB. More such truthful accounts and details of the great contrast between the WWNHS4u and the actualite *elsewhere in those barren foreign parts follow in part 2...watch this MRI space!*

EPISODE 34

Britain to Teach the World How to Improve its Cancer Care.

Major new PM international initiative.

NHS to lead radical change cancer care change in ex-Soviet Republic of Muckitupkistan.

Part 2.

Dramatis personae:

Lord Puggy Pointsdarn, the former left-wing ex-mariner, is a noted "expert" on this, that, and the other.

Ms. Serpentine O'Privilege is a long-time "associate" of his.

She is known to Lord P as "Popsie."

Bernice Camden, formerly a leading amateur wrestler, is Chief Executive of the Hoop-la and Hula-Hoop Women's NHS Hospital Trust, Wiggers-on-Acveon, Soomersetshire.

***

Lord PP: Just to remind you…We've got this urgent new challenge! CANCER.

We have to EXPORT the wonderful NHS successes with Cancer Care!

The PM is calling this the WMW-NHSCC4u. His vibrant language! PM says it's our responsibility to help others not so fortunate. I'm to lead an Urgent UN/NHS Joint Health Care Improvement Parliamentary Delegation. To Muckitupkistan.

SO'P: Coo!

Lord P: We'll correct the worst of everything. And even now, if they do change the government back to proper central controls and healthcare monopoly, it'll still take decades and decades to correct the awful results from those free markets.

BC: You can see that the return of State monopoly services is being demanded by The People. All these street riots. Barricades. Tear-gas in the streets. Busted beer cans on every corner. Litter everywhere. And look at here in London too. Sympathetic actions by students. "WE Want State Monopoly." Kids from the Burkitt University Student Riots Centre in Gower Street screaming blue – sorry, I mean, red – murder.

SO'P: Coo!

Lord P: Over in Muckitupkistan they've thousands of students protesting against the Western-leaning government, too. Want a return to old-style Communist life. Want central direction. Know then where you are. Know what you can and can't get. Proposing to put up what they call 'Sympathy Statues' to The Millkiband kid, and to JM *[KG – Ed.]*.

SO'P: Coo!

Lord P: Just look at these really sensible People's Demands. No confusion about all these TV channels. Have just the one. No need of all these competing newspapers. Their tabloid daily 'NHS Truth' can do the job well. So we do need to help them close down the so-called Freedom of Information Act. And to re-subscribe to the Strassbourg-Knows-Everything-Best-Project. No need of all these ghastly digital interferers with democracy. I-pads, personal computers, tweets and bleats, all these personal choices. Confused everyone. Bewildering. Unnecessary. Anti-social. Thankfully, the students there are leading the way backwards. Anti-commodification. Pro-fees. Anti-free speech ["so-called"]. Anti-privatisations. Bring back Bevanist-Brownite-Kinnockianism!

SO'P: Coo!

Lord P: So, to get their cancer results up to our great levels we're to help them:

- Re-nationalize their health services again.

- Make a bookplate copy of our NHS so that they too can have the best outcomes in the world.

BC: …and at the lowest costs!

Lord P: Quite so. And…

- Ensure that they can copy our example and be top of all the cancer-diagnosis and cancer-cure tables. That'll show the OECD! *And* those Ozzies!

WMW-NHSCC4u!

They know they have got to go back to centralised controls. And fast. Go back to state monopoly. Centrally decide on budget levels nationally. Prevent all these freedoms and all this adaptability in markets. All these adaptive surprises. All these local variations. Call a halt to all the risks they have undergone since the fall of Madame Eddie 'One Nation' Milkki-Blavatski, the Great Leninist Bevanite-Brownite-Kinnockian leader. Will put up a lot of new statues of her, too. And to the Brillig trio. All Socialist Heroes of Old Labour.

BC: So they are now turning round to face the wall to go backwards forwards again.

SO'P: Coo!

Lord P: My bag's packed! First stop will be to the capital city. To Leeds-yer-astray-ski.

Already arranged to have private meetings, unreported in the media, with the likely new KGB boss, the next PM, Mr. Samsonia Simonski. He was, of course, formerly the policy-wonkite-in-chief under old Millpond when he was People's Commissar for those failed Bestest Newest Trustseeskis.

SO'P: Coo!

Lord P: Anyway, we've done some good prelim work. Getting them ready for good advice, in advance. First, on doctors. Already told them that they must make sure that the MMA – the Muckitupkistanski Medical Association – will take full and proper control of everything that matters. How many doctors to train, where're they'll work, what they're paid and their pensions, and especially to whom they'll report. Usually to one another, of course.

And to make sure that, like us, all their GPs are fully trained, speak the local language, and get early diagnosis and referrals right, as ours do so well. They must set up a new People's Academy of Vested Interests, too, to get All Good Chaps properly organised again. Will all need new ceremonial robes, of course. New Lodges, &c. Unison to open up Lodges – I mean, branches – in every City too. Essential step, of course.

SO'P: Coo!

Lord P: We're already making some decent progress.

- Shutting down the information centres which gave all that outcomes-data which so worried and confused the public.

- Eliminating that dangerous website muckitHEALTHmanagement.com – been shut down.

- Those two loons Willey and Wonky, both in the clink. Not be seen again.

- Stopping all that waste of money and effort collecting individual performance records for GPs and consultants.

- That Independent Medical Inspectorate bloke, Dr. Pickers, been sent to be Ambassador to Scotland.

- The FREE budget tripled, too. Advice on this from the Millkiband Kid invaluable.

- Re-introducing helpful post-code rationing.

- Personal Searchlights and torches made illegal. So no more so-called Dark Corner Enquiries. All that ideologically-unsound Edwardsism. Stopped.

So now they have every hope of getting Muckitupistanski cancer diagnose and cure records up to *our* standard.

SO'P: Coo!

Lord P: *They* need WMW-NHSCC4u!

But just look at the list of disasters in policy there. It's beyond belief. How could any country *ever* get itself into such a state? S'what comes from not having a proper reliable State monopoly. S'what comes from markets and giving people empowered choices. S'what comes from local initiatives interfering with central management. S'what comes from all that confusing public info. Morbidity Data. Individual leverage. With some subversive outfit called Dr. Worster's checking up on everybody. Constant interference. Stands to reason…Can't possibly get best Cancer care that way, can you?

SO'P: Coo!

Lord P: What's been allowed to happen out there is indeed a national disgrace. All those years of free markets. So, total collapse of previously essential monopoly services. Terrible cancer results then came. Bound to have happened. Totally unlike here.

See some examples. Just pick a few areas of the Muckitupistanski country.
Just look at:

- their late diagnosis,

- their variations in accessing radiotherapy and drugs.

- shortage of MRIs.

- disparities everywhere.

How can such a thing have been allowed to happen? All this comes from those 5 years of free and individually empowered choice! Markets, indeed…

BC: So what do you expect? See their figures. Premature mortality rates are twice as high in working-class Hackersney-on-ice as in middle-class Gorki-ville-on-caviar. Not like that here. Not ever. Affluence does not buy better care here. No. Not at all. Not ever.

And just look at what the OECD and the recent report by their own Muckitupistanski MPs shows. That a lot of patients who died early *never even knew that they had cancer* until the bell had gone and the lights were virtually out for them. Can't happen here.

Lord P: Well, just one immediacies job for you then, Popsie. Ring up old Dr. "Jurassic" Johnson and Dr. Hogblinkered, GCSE. They'll lead us in the proper direction.

Then the Russkis can have every hope of very rapidly having our levels of cancer diagnosis, treatments and outcomes.

Be just like ours.

WMW-NHSCC4u!

SO'P: Coo!

BRITAIN TO TEACH THE WORLD HOW TO IMPROVE ITS CANCER CARE

Lord P: *Sir!*

***

<u>Official Complaint:</u> "Why am I not included in that delegation to Leeds-yer-astrayski? I am a VERY IMPORTANT…" Lord Oakeshott *[Who he? Ed.]*.

EPISODE 35

Where there ain't a will, there's definitely a way! Or waiting list? What waiting list? Part 1.

Dramatis Personae:

Sir Cyril Squoffington-Squogg, OBE, JP, Chief Executive of The Tower of London NHS Hospital Trust, Traitor's Gate House, Tower Hamlets, London, EC.

Mike Stickit, MA, is Chief Executive of The Two Counties and Twin Piers Seaside and Downs NHS University Hospital Trust, Squivington-by-the-Thames, Sheppley, Kent.

Syd Bishop-McHancox, JP, is Chief Executive of The Square Peg National Exceptions Hospital Trust at Bicknoller in the Quantickle Hills.

***

Mike: Syd, I rang to catch up with you on these new waiting-list pressures from His Highness Jeremydom. You said you needed guidance?

Glad to give it. Was once my speciality as you know. But listen up! Before we got onto that, here's something else new. I'm an old fish, but still you do get surprises. Guess what?

Syd: *What?* Tell me!

Mike: I was walking down Piccadilly on the way to meet you on Friday and ran into that Squoffy. Not really my cup of tea. But he was on his way to deliver a lecture at the RA on Walt Whitman. Now, him I like – Whitman that is! So I went with Squoffy. Stood you up – sorry! But he is an amazing bloke in his way, that Squoffy. Said some really interesting things about poetry, and the NHS. Connections I'd not made before. *All very cultural.*

Syd: Hm. Well you were *supposed* to meet me to talk about waiting lists. I need ideas on how to fix mine. But I gave up after an hour waiting. Went to the Walthamstow dog track instead. Won a bit on Conker-boy at 5-1.

Mike: Well, we'll get to waiting lists next. But I wish you could have come with me! That Squoffy has the knack of finding the telling anecdote, the illuminating incident, and putting it into a broader context. Told me a lot about dilemmas and contradictions in the NHS. How we got where we are now. And how to get out of the hole we're in. Very reflective, too. He's deeply engaged with the NHS. But says it's no longer modern. It's no longer logical. It defies logic. Hurts patients, and hurts our staff too. It's a very conservative system. Got to liberate both staff and patients from a busted flush....

Syd: ...and which no other country in the world has ever copied.

Mike: Yes. That, too. Squoffy favours patients getting direct access to a consultant. No more GPs in the way. And much greater integration of hospital and social care. Proper co-ordination, which we none of us have got now.

Syd: Hmm. Really interesting observations, even to an old cynic like me.

Mike: Well, he had a close reading of particulars. And a clear expression of principles. Says he wants people working for us energised, and released. In a system with a sense of shape and unity. But not all monumentalist. Lots of necessary parts, but freed of the ideological biases of the 1940s. A new ensemble. The whole better than its parts. Not *retardaire* – that was his word.

Syd: That's what my Chair says, too. That if we changed we could actually be a powerful source of inspiration in society.

Mike: Well, Squoffy said a lot of stuff about the sources of "authority", including different kinds of "knowledge." Patient experiences, mostly. And how "democracy" should really work. Asked whose vision is in charge, and why? Asked which incentives drove which kinds of actions. Wants to nourish the spirit of invention, and the world of intellect. But put together with compassion and empathy. To enable patient's own intuitions more space in choices. And to enable professionals to do what they thought they were training to do in the first place.

Syd: Aha. Sounds like Squoffy all right! All about national purpose and civic virtue. Democratic ends. Politics of culture. Issues about institutional power. Heady stuff!

Mike: Anyway, he definitely wants to fuel innovation and reform. Remove persistent institutional rigidities. Better access. Better outcomes. Proper inspections. Improve millions of lives. Really enable patients to represent themselves.

BUT – he kept saying – our NHS people are all trapped in this broken, out-of-date, system. Free them then, improve care, and liberate patients.

Syd: Revolutionary stuff!

Mike: Had a drink with him afterwards. He stressed that these issues underlie the real lessons of waiting-list management. Did make me think, anyway!

And apparently, he's not the nob you might think, either. Comes from quite humble origins himself, it seems. Grammar School boy, not Eton. His Grandad was in the Hoxton Workhouse and killed in 1915 at Ypres. Mother scrubbed school and pub floors, left with four young children and no husband. Got where he is by hard work. The K came with the civil service rations.

Syd: I'd heard that. And the name? Apparently an adaptation from Jewish pogrom immigration way back.

Mike: Anyway, he's very committed to better health services, and for all. But he ended his talk by contending that the NHS has to take a new and constantly self-adjusting attitude. Not one with YET ANOTHER Grand Master Plan. But, instead, to work and change adaptively in response to the everyday demands of millions of ordinary people.

WHERE THERE AIN'T A WILL, THERE'S DEFINITELY A WAY! OR WAITING LIST?

Syd: Can't escape prices, though, can we? Otherwise demand never be controlled?

Mike: Agreed. But there was a surprising amount of support for his ideas. I think we're seeing a generational change.

Syd: Can still be a bit of a mouthful though, eh?

Mike: Well, the pivot of his talk was actually the poet Walt Whitman. D'you know, he was born in Brooklyn. Wrote his best poem, 'Crossing Brooklyn Ferry' there. Not all about ponds. Not all about living in a lonely shed. A self-fashioned man, like Squoffy.

I was particularly interested in what he called "self-fashioning." You see, Whitman was self-fashioned, and always welcomed change. Whitman was a carpenter, then a journalist, then a poet. But look what he made of himself. So, like him, embrace change Mike!

Squoffy said that neither Whitman, nor his poems – and so, neither the NHS – could ever be complete.

Nor could or should it be. That was Whitman's human strength, too. His artistic genius, his creative message. Keen on dynamic human change. Poetry – and society – always growing, changing, responding, coping with contradictions. Poet of the intentionally unfinished art. Never finished *Leaves of Grass*, you know. Started in 1855. Never stopped adding to it, and revising it. Continuous copy. Continuous revision. Great cultural implications for NHS in this adaptive change.

The NHS, too, should be essentially and continually in the making. Never completed, or fully resolved. Dynamic motion, excitement, diversity, permanent amendment. Just like Whitman's works. Just like James Joyce's *Ulysses*. Just like the NHS as it should be. Whitman's works an ever-re-shaped collection of feelings, people, ideas, things. Morally compelling images, too. We should copy!

And everyone in the NHS has just got to take this new map on board, in their minds and hearts. Cognitive and emotional! Unified and practical! Generalised and particular! Personally, to genuinely believe in changes which empower patients. And to make it happen in their daily work. Otherwise, we're sunk!

Sure, regulated by a participatory political process, you say. That's OK by me. But driven by investment opportunity as well, to serve patients – and staff – and directed by individual, financially-empowered demand.

Syd: So, he's started great bees buzzing? But what about my Waiting List Management which we are supposed to be discussing?

Mike: *Wake up, Syd! Just bloody told you!* As to waiting-lists: we've got to stop fiddling about using the old juggling and deceptive wheezes. Same points as I've already just made. Got to liberate the best energies of our people. Very different from the old days, summed up in that old 1990s document I promised to give you. Well, I'll send it over. But that's just for nostalgia now. A bit ashamed of it now, in fact, as I look back on it.

Meanwhile, it's time we really made an effort to explain ourselves to ourselves, and to be more aware of what we are doing and not doing! Open up ways of thinking about larger patterns and meanings. Different ways of doing things. Learning from other changes in society around us.

Syd: Hm. Well, all I know is that every time they tell me to cut waiting-lists I don't think Whitehall knows snuff. I've got a big hospital. The biggest hospitals inevitably have the bigger waiting-lists. Big population. More specialists here. Demand! GPs refer to us. So, waiting list. And if the list gets shorter, GPs just refer all those they've been holding back as the wait was so long. So, back to square one. Fiddledeedee!

Mike: Yes. 'Course that Lord Ralph Harris at the IEA used to say, "If it's free, I'll take two!" Unpriced services, and all that. Never stops.

Syd: And the real issue, of course, isn't can you get the job done quickly, but does it work? Outcomes. "Did they die in the car-park on the way home? No? Phew!" And as to speedier treatments, you don't want to be more quickly into the hands of Dr. Deadwood, do you?

Mike: I don't, anyway! I'll wait for Dr. Up-to-date. And best to be focussed on the numbers you can deal with, the results, and not the wait times. Can't ever end the list. Gets shorter, so GPs jump up and make it longer again. New drugs, new treatments, third new hip at 95. Constantly rising expectations. In marginal seats, MPs yell! And GPs still send us loads of things they should be dealing with themselves. *There's* where we need big changes!

Syd: We know what we should be doing, of course. Open theatres day and night. Overtime. Better planning. Consultants on the job. Out-patients clinics open 7 days, day and night. And a lot less EEC-dom.

Mike: But it's hard to deliver unless you can attract willing revenues, and from competing for that in a market. That's Squoffy's theory anyway.

Syd: Yep. Definitely. But I do want that waiting-list document from you. I do want a serious word, Mike. My Medical Director is up in arms over the waiting list. That old grinder! But you did that special document, '20 points To Help Manage Waiting-lists.' Showed it to me at Torquay. A while back, I know. Still got it?

Mike: Yes. But SO out-of-date in this New World. Archival only. Triple-locked. Coded covers. Wax-sealed. Dynamite. Dangerous in these times. We did it all in the 1990s. But it's got a lot hotter since. Watching over us! Still, I can send you an anonymised copy by Secure Courier, if you pay the gubbins. Read just for fun. What we used to do.

Syd: Done! All agreed. Thanks mate! Just between us. "So mought it be." Just a little handshake, eh? Onzie Square. Solomon's Rules. S'Ok, too. All's secure. Phones not bugged. Don't think so, anyway. But you never know with His Sir Mid-Staffsship.

Mike: *Live the life!*

NB. Part 2 – the *real truth* of how the NHS do manage its precious work bank [aka as waiting lists] – follows.

EPISODE 36

Where there ain't a will, there's definitely a way! Or waiting list? What waiting list? Part 2.

Dramatis Personae:

Mike Stickit, MA, is Chief Executive of The Two Counties and Twin Piers NHS University Seaside and Downs Hospital Trust, Squivington-by-the-Thames, Sheppley, Kent.

Syd Bishop-McHancox, JP, is Chief Executive of The Square Peg National Exceptions Hospital Trust at Bicknoller in the Quantickle Hills

***

Syd *[to himself]*: Right. Mike says this exchange of info is just an example of NHS 'meritocracy.' Maybe. But I'll just settle down and have a good look-see at his old waiting list plan.

Must still be some good stuff I can use, no matter what he says about being a bit out-of-date. Cultural change and all that gubbins. Cobblers to that! And anyway that good old dyed-in-the-wool socialist Sir Nicko has done his best to stop Lansley's daft reform plans working out. So must still be some room for maneouvre for me…

Let's read what Mike wrote. Will use it if I possibly can.

CONFIDENTIAL.

The Two Counties and Twin Piers NHS University Seaside and Downs Hospital Trust.

20 Point Waiting List Plan. June 1994.

1. *Off, off!* Keeping folk OFF the list is the first essential strategic move. The red-card gambit! Here you will need consultant's co-operation – but always tricky! Remind them of the morale-boosting new sofas and coffee-machines you supplied recently for junior docs lounges. And improved Dial-a-Whisky slot-machines in Senior Consultants lounge. And your own new Spexicgrazers Looking-the-other-way Glasses worn on Private Work Days. See if your docs can get booking clerks to write back to GPs querying the necessity of any referrals. Always the first step. Gains time.

2. *Pre-admission advisers.* Introduce these to 'help' patients gain some understanding of what is required before they are admitted. Deters patients. This will help 'catch' the overweight, the heavy drinker, the heavy smoker, and offers constructive advice about

"capacity to benefit." Some will tell you to "f*** off." Other will self-refer back to waiting list. Staff to undertake this role? A few jaded out-patient nurses perhaps?

3. *Self-responsibility tests.* Each patient must complete life-style form J/bumpf/NHS/J.Cumberbund/pee2. If they are heavy smokers, tell them that must give up smoking. Then omit from active list and refer back to GP for smoke-stop support. If they must lose a LOT of weight – omit from active list and refer back to GP for gym work and diet changes. Mention Weight Watchers voucher scheme.

4. *Risk-management.* Ensure that you inform prospective patients that both surgery and anaesthesia are *very* risky. Hospital bed a dangerous place to be. You can only give generalised statistics. Cannot say if the individual concerned is at the wrong end of the curve or not. "Only time will tell!." Good ammo: surgical wards are risky places – super-bugs etc. Provide your own alarming data on local infection rates, and otucomes (if you dare!). Have to gather it first, of course. This info deters many patients. *[Deters me! – Ed.].*

5. *Options support.* Advise patient to carefully consider the options. "There is no pressure or hurry. Take a while." Settle them down comfortably in the queue to see your Patient's Advocate [Whisperer]. Omit them from your 'active' list and refer them back to GP.

6. *Enhanced choice.* Tell them that you strongly endorse greater patient choice. But they should really consider whether this is the right hospital for them. Choice is a good thing! Empowering, etc. So advise them to travel the country for a few months visiting other hospitals and talk to satisfied customers there (survivors!) – while they consider their options. Suggest they can stay cheaply in Youth Hostels. Start their tour in Birmingham. They can use their free travel passes. Ask DoH or NAHAT if they can arrange trial overnight-accommodation in any local NHS facilities. Deters many. Can omit from 'active' list and refer them back to GP.

7. *Administration of referral letters.* Enormous scope for chaos here, to delay additions to outpatient appointments & subsequently to the list! But beware, there are 'standards' for how soon appointments must be offered and letters responded to. Those tricky buggers in Richmond House keep shifting the start lines. When sending out letters, use First Class stamps. Not a false economy as are always delivered late. The referral letters from GPs will have to be date-stamped as received on the day they are opened. So.... avoid opening them if the number looks bigger than the number of patients who are likely to be removed in the current month.

Try employing some poor soul who needs a job to wheel these incoming letters around the hospital on a trolley for a few days before they are opened. Inevitably they will have to be dealt with in the end. But you can manipulate the timing a bit to avoid crisis periods – ie when the monthly waiting list count is reported!

8. *Triple-booking essential.* To give everyone nice, early appointment times you should triple-book the outpatient clinics. Book a patient every two minutes, and they each MUST have a unique appointment time! You can't let everyone turn up, of course. So, a week before the clinic, call and re-book two thirds of them to later dates (consultant's holiday is a normal reason given/very credible excuse). You'll still have hit the target of their first appointment as having been offered a date within 'x' weeks of referral date!

WHERE THERE AIN'T A WILL, THERE'S DEFINITELY A WAY! OR WAITING LIST?

9. *Language matters.* Beware clarity! Re-read the useful material printed on the back of any bus-ticket, or in any British Rail Guide. Adopt language, qualifications, refer across to other guidance, which refers back to same guidance, which cross-refers, whereof, wherefor, &c., etc. Ask solicitor to add some other whys and whatnits. Patients: Go back to Old Kent Road. Do not pass "Go." Do not collect your op.

[Hand-written addition, 4 Sept.2013: If the patient is under 25, use old-style BBC language. Thus: "We are pleased to send you this formal and official invitation..." They will not understand what on earth you are saying. If they're over 25, send a letter in new-style BBC language, which begins "Hi! See, like, know what I mean, kinda thing, like, see ya, ya? like, op. Wed. 11th Aug, like...OK? See what I mean, kinda thing, like...." They will not know what this means, and thus will conscientiously re-cycle the letter in their compost heap and among their Butterfly-friendly flowers. But you will have done your duty. In the clear with the DoH. The medium you use matters, too. Do not use Twitter, Facebook, or other social media. Responses too prompt].

10. *The Summer Holidays Rush.* Send out all invitations to an operation in mid-July. Post the letters on the first day of the school holidays. Watch State-school term dates carefully. The private lot go to The Drive anyway. And many of the others will be away with their buckets and spades too. No reply in 7 days? Back to the end of the queue.

11. *The Christmas Gambit.* Pray for very heavy snow-falls and very icy roads, cancelled buses and trains, burst domestic and office water-pipes, power-cuts, etc. Also, call those who have been waiting the longest two days before Xmas and offer admission – but avoid the very aged & single! The old and lonely will accept! If they refuse saying they'd rather wait for the New Year – remove from list etc. (But, a timely warning – *if* they accept you may have to operate on some of them!).

12. *The Lord Tony Traffblogg of The Wrekin [or Sicilian] Gambit.* A variation on 11, above. Write to patients a few days before Xmas offering short-notice admissions – is it your fault the post office can't deliver it before their proposed admission date? If they DNA – remove from list etc. Best to give your Complaints Officer prior notice on these to get responses drafted in advance. You can bulk-buy those A4 pre-printed forms with 17 optional boxes to tick or not, from the NHS Anti-Congestion Unit, Elizabeth House, Elephant & Castle, London, SE. Very good value! This waxed paper is quite hard to write on, though, and does not take biro ink.

13. *The Birthday Wheeze.* Send invitations for their ops to be scheduled on their actual birthday. Many will have family commitments. Result: back to the end of the queue...as above.

14. *The Bonfire Night Caper.* Good day to fix for children's ops. A lot won't turn up. Result...as above.

15. *Consultant's pride verification.* Be very careful here! Many senior consultants have more letters after their name than in their name. Check carefully incoming letters on the referrals from GPs. If they have any of these letters-after-the-name wrong, send the letter back as "Consultant Unidentified. Refer elsewhere." Gains time.

16. *Immigration friendly forms.* To ensure that you encourage good race relations, you

must ask for an *original* birth certificate from every potential patient – but only after you get the GP referral letter – to authenticate that the individual was born here and is entitled to service. Or they must provide a copy of their Home Office Form, Pink One, fifth version, in triplicate.

[Hand-written addition, 4 Sept. 2013: as recently revised and re-authenticated under the Burnham Birdnumb Act, reference section 67 [b], viii, Appendix 7, HMSO, London, 1998. This is the form now listed by the DoH as W/L Requirement Immig/EEC/Afrique/Asiatica/ Polski/SovRuss/NZ/Oz/Can/Yankee 607b [ex-Jackie Smith; iv, 7k, plnhsdohw/l, 9].

This will authenticate their permission to be here. It will, alas, inevitably result in long delays.

17. *Join an exclusive local Golf Club*. Well worth the annual sub! For you will need some GP friends. You need them to tell patients "You'll need to have this done eventually, but we don't need to refer you yet…" Remember the GPs at Christmas. Bottles preferred.

HOWEVER…

If they **somehow** do manage to get ON the list – and quite a few still do…so here's what's to do next…

18. *Didn't accept date given*. The 'portmanteau' easy one. If anyone is offered a date to come in and doesn't accept for any reason (didn't get letter in time; family weddings, funerals, holidays etc. – none of this good enough excuses to interrupt the efficient operation of a busy hospital!) – remove from list and refer them back to GP. Plead 'Not Guilty' to DoH if questioned.

19. *Still amongst the living?* Write a few times a year to check that they are still alive, at the same address and still want op. Best time to write is a day or so before monthly count for waiting-list report. Then you can consider everyone you've written to as temporarily suspended from the active list pending confirmation until they reply (i.e. after the count is reported!!). If no reply received – remove from list and refer them back to GP.

You could also do this by phone – preferably when they are likely to be out. Use 'computer-voice' marketing-style tone. There is here a job opportunity for many newly arrived people seeking political asylum. Calais has regular supply. They can practice their English on this job. Train staff properly so that they leave as reasonably an unintelligible message as possible. Leave only the very busy main switchboard number. NEVER leave an extension number for the waiting list office and NEVER a ddi or a named individual! *[Added by hand, July 2013: Do NOT leave an e-mail address on any papers]*. If the prospective patient doesn't reply within 48 hours – which is pretty likely given the chaos of hospital switchboards and the fact that the waiting list clerk will be on the phone full-time calling others on the list – remove from list etc.

20. *OR…You could actually operate a bit!* But never forget, although actually operating on patients can sometimes reduce waiting lists, staff in theatres and equipment/drugs cost money. And these costs inevitably rise if you use operating theatres on more than 4 days a week. Or if you use them all on any one day. Remember, too, likely absenteeism of docs for private work. You will, in any case need to get the docs to keep re-admission rates low

or there's more stress on those busy theatres & wards.

BUT BEWARE! *Unforecast A&E admissions* will also take a big chunk of your bed capacity. This is a sneaky way for patients actually to get round your moated systems, over your electrical wire fences, past your portcullis, and actually into a BED! (of which you have too few/too many?)

So....necessary extra strategy...Drastically reduce A&E car-parking. Reduce use of oil on swing doors. Reduce budget for access-slope repairs. Try to get bus stops moved. Do not repair jammed pay-for-parking meters. Shroud these in black 'Out of Order: You will be towed if you park here' signs. Encourage staff to park closest to main doors. Remove information boards and site-maps for essential "refurbishment." Increase Study Days for A&E staff. Second night nursing stuff after twinning with Islamabad Institution for the Study of International Institutional Institutions. Increase 'fire alarm practice days.' Multiply Board-level Committee meetings requiring Emergency Doc attendances. Treble 'Nurse Study Away-days' to Isle of Man. Recommend your Business Managers for local JP service. Improve A&E staff "understanding" of pressure on beds, and necessity of retaining spare capacity for "booked admissions" [on which see above, *passim*].

[Hand-written note added by Mike this week: Syd, **If** *none of the above works then I'm stumped, clean bowled, lbw-ed, caught in the slips, run-out, and off to a hot bath! But if it does work for you, make me one promise. Give me NONE of the credit!*

This stuff is ALL in the foggy and scandalous past, of course.].

Syd: Well...seems to me....

EPISODE 37

Old rope for money? The British Doctor proposes innovative ways to fund The N£sd.

Dramatis Personae:

Sir Extrasmuchsatisfied Perceval Nowtdunne, CBE, President, Woyal BMA.

Nursie Nursie Dixbungle, Chief Executive, The Great British Whitewash Company PLC.

Mr. Damien McBridge, Consultant Orthopaedic Surgeon at The G. Neville NHS Hospital Trust, Burton-on-kickemharder-at-Tweed.

Mr. "Jurassic" Johnson, the famed consultant and Woyal BMA negotiator.

Nearly 60 first-class consultants & other away-day professionals in the meeting.

***

THE SCENE: The 5-star Connaught Hotel, Central London.

A joint Woyal BMA, Great British Whitewash Company PLC, & Woyal Academy of Vested Interests special meeting. [Op. Theatres closed, pro tem.].

Sir Extrasmuchsatisfied Perceval Nowtdunne, CBE, President, Woyal BMA *[in the chair]*:

Gentleman, and Lady. Mr. Damien McBridge has taken this opportunity and occasion to ask for discussion of NHS funding. He has many radical ideas, which we would like to see go forward.

First of all:

- All doctors and especially consultants to be individually sponsored by pharmaceutical and other companies – could include Airlines? – with company logos on their gowns.

With full-image, high-resolution cameras in strategic places in all operating theatres and consulting rooms so that they have the fullest marketing exposure on the internet and throughout the hospital too. All agreed?

Unanimous voices of assent.

- Four-an-hour commercial breaks to be instituted during all clinical operations, with live individual operations and advertisements all viewable on bedside televisions, as they happen. Also, several different channels – from different operating theatres – to be provided, simultaneously. All broadcast in the hospitals on bedside TVs, so patients have a choice of viewing: Cardiac, Orthopaedic, Brain operations, etc. Also, contract with YouTube. All agreed?

Loud delight expressed.

- Splash Advertising in these commercial breaks, to be sold to commercial enterprises for viewing on hospital, care home and hospice bedside TVs. 24-hours, 7-days a week – as JH insists! All agreed?

Unanimous cries of pleasure, and applause.

- Flavoured anaesthetics, by major sports-drinks providers, to be introduced. Lots of attractive choices – mint, raspberry, coffee flavour, you name it! Also, music sponsored in recovery facilities. Virgingetsubetter, etc. With order forms by which to buy copies.

Yelps of assent from all present.

- Sponsorship of all e-mails, written invitations to GPs and patients, and with company logos on all surgical instruments etc, etc. All agreed?

Me-too voices of assent.

- Then there are the ambulances. We need to properly badge these. Many likely applicants for this – as they are so visible racing through towns, blue lights blinking, sirens blaring, advertising flickering in full colour. We can charge well here. Inside and out.

- *Gleeful applause and hurrahs.*

SirP: And there should also be a national radio station – N£sd Radionet – broadcasting national and local advertisements into every ambulance and other N£sd facilities, too.

- *Many hear, hears!*

DMcB: Laundries to be included also. Large company logos on all pillows, sheets, towels, baby-clothes, and bed-covers. And those electronic, constantly-changing, advertising boards on every corridor and in every waiting room, as in football grounds.

Mr. "Jurassic" Johnson: We should also have a look at who is treated first. And last. Lots of opportunities here. Why not have the old railways class system back? Charge differently for those who want express treatment? The beautiful simplicity of a single class system is nowhere near achievement, so why not introduce proper supplementary fares? Just as they once had for high-speed trains, or for superior accommodation or meals service on Pullman cars. Just as they once had especial Excursion trains, carrying people ready to pay for it. So have services of a different kind, at charges fixed for that?

DMcB: Yes. Let's adopt that, too.

SirP: It's common ground that the N£sd's finances are collapsing. Will continue to collapse. And needs major new approaches, new funding sources, new attitudes. We might ask ourselves, what is being done now by Westminster and Whitehall which will make it all better in the next five years?

DMcB: And answer came there none! This ConLibDemsy government is ignoring the issues. Lord Howzat only the other day said that "We are so wonderful, and all the world knows" – all that gubbins. *None* of us are Tories, of course. And we are none of us motivated by money, either, are we? We are all full-time NHS, too, aren't we? So we do want the N£sd to have enough to go on. As it is. But better funded.

Of course, we are not stupid. I know that the radical right say that if patients controlled the money, they would use the internet to choose where to be treated. But as a Trade Union we do not favour Health Savings Accounts or that kind of economic stuff. Do we? Indeed, information technology is a menace. And we want no foolish movement on cash top-ups. Squeezes the poor.

We need no action on individual patient economic incentives. Squalid notion. Demotivates doctors. Need no consideration of Health Savings Accounts. Wasteful bureaucracy. No more complications with additional private insurance, either. We do well enough with that already, in The Drive. No need for incentives for taxpayers to provide more for themselves. Not British.

SirP: *Taxpayers Ahoy!*

DMcB: I say, too, "No thank you" to any mutual, purchasing co-operatives and member-owned purchasing organisations. *We* are the experts.

SirP: AND don't dare mention the eye-care market! Or individual social care budgets, for that matter.

DMcB: No fear! None of that! And we don't want to fiddle about with paperwork, either, charging foreigners or even Brits for GP visits. Would only reveal the financial issues which cannot be resolved in ways that suit us. We don't want to be like the French and the Germans, with all their funny mix of monies from here, there and who knows what where. More doctors than jobs, too. *And just look at their OECD ratings!* WE ARE THE ENVY OF THE WORLD! Justly so. And so we want The State to provide for us – oh, and for patients, of course. Basic 1948 principles apply.

SirP: Quiter so. Quiter so. As to Prices? Not a problem for us, is it? NHS deals with it. Costs? Not our department. Have Ministers for that. Discourage wasteful demand? Ah, but what counts as that? Who decides? And why should we involve ourselves? We are here to HELP. But we are not Nannies.

DMcB: Yes, sir! But the Money *is*, however, running out. Longer lives, increased demands, higher expectations, ever more opportunities, new cancer drugs which N£sd won't or can't afford like that effective break-through lung-cancer drug Nivolumab. Now, that's a very serious mixture! And demand *is* outrunning the money. It's a dismal situation. If decisive action is not taken soon it will be harder and harder to resolve the crisis. Lord Howzat notwithstanding.

Total financial meltdown is on the horizon. And the resulting collapse of the social order as we know it in Britain. Clearly, nothing is going to happen on new funding nationally. The PM makes no moves. Rough sailors make bad seas. And even the Millkiband Kid will not be able to raise much more from taxes, even if VAT goes to 25% and capital gains tax to 60%. Evasion – and Inflation! – will run riot again. And so we doctors have got to act locally, for ourselves – so to speak. Got to have our own Apps.

DMcB: As to the extent of possible fund-raising, I estimate that in the first year we can raise £4billion with our new ideas. At least that. And then, exponentially, thereafter, much more. It will take some of our clinical time, of course. And so our local consultant commissions on these new funds – we do the negotiating with Acme PLC etc, of course – will only be 20%. We must be modest.

As to PR, we must get the message right. But Mr. Dixbungle has already offered the GBWWCo PLC PR department to help here. I will also, privately, in conversations later, suggest some clear sanctions which we can enforce, if necessary, to "encourage" the politicians and the slower local managers like that notorious and much-criticised Mr. Stewed ["I will not resign!"] Bludgeon. To ensure prompt local facilitations.

Remember – as that old-Labour PR guru whose name is very like mine says in his book *Power Trip* – "As Al Capone once said, 'You can get more with a kind word and a gun, than you can with just a kind word."

SirP: Yes. As the great Dr. Thomas Arnold of Rugby said, "But, of course, deeds must second words when needful, or words will soon be laughed at." And that we NOT want!

SirP: Well, we are all agreed that this is the basis for our new N£sd campaign then, to be launched at the Woyal Albert Hall in Kensington on 1 April? Excellent! I will send out All-Party invitations – JH himself, Mr. Birdnumb, Mr. Farage, etc.

DMcB: So we agree to face the situation as it really is. We need a clear and coherent strategy, which the ConLibDemsys are not providing. Otherwise, we won't be fully funded. We also need a clear media strategy, to sell our proposals. Get public on our side. Enunciate broad objectives, and clear specifics. Fund St. Hilda's properly. Defend *our* heritage. March with us! Then, get rigorous local management processes. Proper management by us. As to PR, our anti-botch programme is needed here. Dixbungling. And I have set out a clear 'grid' of issues, objectives, and actions with a timeline. This is in your pack today.

SirP: And, on other matters, Gentleman – and Lady – I hope and trust that your rooms at The Savoy and The Ritz are all to your satisfaction? Yes? Excellent! Those of us at the Connaught are pleased to welcome you here. You should all have found your Opera tickets in the bedside draw. Your sponsored invitation to the Specsmightwurk New Drugs Conference in Barbados will be handed to you today over dinner. Your carnets of whisky and gin vouchers are current until 31 December 2014. In order to accommodate you all in First Class several aeroplanes for Barbados have been chartered. So please make a careful note of your own flight times. I will take the normal Presidential route, via the Orient

OLD ROPE FOR MONEY?

Express to Venice, and fly on from there.

DMcB: Thank you, Chairman. Can I just reiterate a key message for the new campaign? It is this. We have always been, as an organisation, *much* in favour of the NHS. Pioneers, actually. We were so long before Nye Bevan thought of it at all. Long before William Beveridge's report, too. Always enthusiastic. However, it must be said that we cannot possibly support new funding ideas which do not help attract new doctors, pay them properly, reward them appropriately, ensure living standards continue to rise. All that. But you know it without being told by me.

We have to present our case well, of course. Can't just be accused of serving ourselves. Perish that thought!

SirP: We are preparing for this carefully. We really need a Gettysburg speech! Short, sharp, memorable, philosophical, and focussed. And one that makes the nation tingle. We need a Jenni Murray or a Paul Lewis to speak in those tones, too. Be listened to. Be trusted. And using language that carries over the barricades. The English language is eternally subtle. So may I turn to Mr. "Jurassic" Johnson to organise these essentials. JJ?

Mr.JJ: Well, Chair, let me say this: *Sedilia haec, nonne praestant.*

SirP: In English, if you please.

MrJJ: Ah. Yes. In English. "These are great seats, aren't they?"

Sudden noisy interruption: Lord Klinnockles of Brevity enters the room unexpectedly.

"Is this the Personal Finance Enhancement Meeting? No? It isn't? You sure? Is, isn't it? Heard the talking. Money, money, money! Very odd if it's not the Personal Finance Enhancement Meeting I want? Should be. Sorry to interrupt, if not. But was sure it was here. This place is an absolute maze. And all these entirely empty suites. Got directions from an Italian lady. Nice enough. But she was lost herself. Looking for Gladyss. Here somewhere…here somewhere…*here somewhere*…. Was…Is…Should be…Needs the £sd….Nicely, extras…here somewhere surely?"

"You know what that Nixon film said? "Follow the money!" So here I am. But, oh, you're all doctors are you? Well, no good for this then, eh?"

Leaves noisily. But pops back in: hands out business cards. "Still, my mateys and Comrades, here's Gladyss's card for you all: can recommend a trip to her place in Turks & Caicos Islands. Taking bookings now….."

See www.incomeaugmentation.co.uk.

Unless you all Go Free anyway, with The Big Pharma Gangs, that is?

Episode plays out to music from "Cabaret*", Money, money, money….*

EPISODE 38

Just Call 999 – if your Budgie is sick!

Culture, Effort, & The Great Educated British Public after 65 years of the NHS. Or a quiet evening on 999 – and in A&E, too.

Dramatis Personae:

Sir Cyril Squoffington-Squogg, OBE, JP, is Chief Executive of The Tower of London NHS Hospital Trust, Tower Hamlets, London, EC.

Lady Bernice Squoffington-Squogg, his wife, is also Chair of The Wiltshire Artists Benevolent Fund.

Mrs. Lesley Crooper is an extremely unpleasant, semi-literate, impatient patient.

Ms. Maisie Spry is a 999 operator at Broxbinge, Herts.

Ms. Janice Waldegrave is an A&E reception nurse at Broxbinge NHS Hospitals Trust.

Mr. Jeff Thomas is another nurse, more senior.

Also, a Man with a Fierce Dog; a Hoity-Toity Woman; Ms. Ahoy Yew, a drunk patient; an unidentified, bewildered, immigrant patient; and a fearsome & ignorant woman patient.

Sir S-S: Just look at this in the *Sun*! This week's NHS diversion! Might we or might we not charge £10 to those who waste everyone's time in A&E! Ha! Old Dr. Foxie is quite right. But we won't get it. Voters will scare the ConLibDemsy politicos.

Lady S-S: But it's a perfect topic for your new *Whitsun Wangles of the NHS* Series, for the summer show at Richmond House, Cyril!

Sir S-S: Yes, my love. Here's my first shot at a draft text. See what you think….my usual approach.

First, The Problem. Then, The Lesson.

Or, as Barney would say, *Taxpayers Ahoy!*

The Whitsun Wangles of the NHS. Scene 2.

THE FACEY ROMFORD PAPERS

Telephone rings in Emergencies Centre at Broxbinge, Herts.

Miss JW, 999 operator: Hello. Emergency Services. Fire, police or ambulance?

Caller: It's Mrs. Crooper. Mrs. Lesley Crooper. It's me Budgie. Little Roberto. 'E's got 'iccups!

999 operator: Madame, you need a vet. This is the *emergency* line.

Mrs. C: It *is* a emergency. E's 'ad iccups for an hour.

999 operator: Madame, please. We are very busy…floods, fires, violent crimes, elderly falling down stairs…trees crushing people in cars, other people just found wandering…pub fights…*please clear the line…*

Mrs. C: Oh, wot? Oh, sod you then! I'll take 'im to the A&E. Bloody show yer!

Mrs. Crooper slams down telephone. She then takes no.73 bus to Broxbinge NHS Hospitals Trust A&E, carrying bird-cage. Stumbles into A&E and goes to Triage desk.

Mrs. C to Nurse receptionist: E's in 'is cage 'ere. E's got -iccups. Want 'im treated. Quick. Urgent!

Nurse Janice: Madame, this is an A&E department. We do not treat animals. I am so sorry…

Mrs. C: Well, I ask you…bloody cheek! What's this place for, then? *Emergencies*, ain't it?

Nurse Janice: Mainly for injured people, actually, Madame. Serious. But, as you prefer. I will call an Anaesthetist now….

Mrs. Crooper: No you bloody don't! Not bloody likely. I'm not 'aving 'im gassed. I'll go down to the Farmersee. You see if I don't.

Nurse Janice: Thank you Madame. Next, please.

Mrs. Crooper stomps out, effing and blinding, throwing crisps packet onto floor as she leaves.

Man with VERY big dog: 'Ello. Don't mind Rufus. E' Don't bite. Quiet as a babe. But I come 'ere two hours ago. About me garden-mower. Won't bloody start. Want it mended. Why am I still bloody well waiting?

Nurse: You need the Exopostulate Roses & Garden Centre. Just down the hill….you can't miss the big gateway covered in ivy…

Man with dog: Wot? Ain't this the blasted Garden Centre then? Why don't you have some proper effing signs 'ere then, eh? Been 'ere bloody ages, I 'ave. The big blue notice said

JUST CALL 999 – IF YOUR BUDGIE IS SICK!

Oncology or summink – ain't that a posh dog-food then? I 'ad to pay two quid to park 'ere, too!

Nurse Janice: No, Sir. Need the Garden Centre. Sir, the porter will show you where to go. Just down the hill, on the left.

Man with dog: Oh, *$!$^*fuggle it all!

Nurse Janice: Next, please…

Ms. Ahoy Yew, a very drunk teenage girl: This the sex-clinic? I woz cooking with this banana. And it slipped. Can't sit down. Can't pee. 'Urts like 'ell. Want to see some nurse 'bout it. And quick 'bout it, too….

Nurse Janice: Madame, please wait at the end of row 17. You can stand there. Lean against the pillar. We will see you as soon as possible.

Ms. AY: Frigging liberty! Been 'ere an hour. Bloody 'urts too. Oo runs this place?

Nurse Janice: Madame, there are people here with very serious burns, broken limbs, suspected brain tumours, and so on. We will do what we can for you. But you will have to wait your turn.

Ms. AY: Frizzing liberty!

New patient [name not supplied]: Here, me, next, please. Me got broke bone. From pub fight. Look. Cuts. Blood. Help! Me qualify for docs.

Nurse Janice: Right, sir. Let me just register you. Name & address please. And do you have a GP? And how will you pay the usual £10 – refundable if your doctor says so. We take most credit cards, or Paypal, cheque, or cash.

Patient: Eh? Not understandin'. Come 'gin?

Nurse Janice: Ah. You are a foreign gent? Well, in England now there is a small charge at A&E. Helps us help those who really need it. Sends the others home to see a GP. Easy to pay, too. Millions now use electronic money, shop on Amazon, e-bay, etc. So we take it here now too. Just pass me a credit card. Or a Benefit Registration Identity Card, for exemption in our records. Or we take A&E stamps. People buy them, stick on a card. Any pharmacy…

Patient: Me got none of it. Me dunno it. Just arrive lask weeks. Me from Solamikandia. Lorry from Sangate. Very long trip. Up boat on Danube. Then lorries. Cost all my monies. No food. No drink. In back, under bundles of blankets and rice. Me in black economics. Me heekernomicks meegrater. Me work though. Dish-wash. Me live under pier.

Nurse Janice: I see. Wait here, please. *Pushes button connecting front desk to Almoner's office.*

Meanwhile, at the 999 centre: telephone rings.

Hoity-toity female voice: That emergencies? I've run out of onions for my stew. Can you send me some now?

999 operator: Madame, this is the *emergency* line. We are very busy…floods, fires, violent crimes…

Hoity-toity female voice: *But all the shops are shut…*

999 operator: I suggest a taxi to Tesco's, Madame.

Hoity-toity: Ah! Right! Can you call me one, please?

999 operator: No, Madame. I cannot. I have other urgent calls coming in…

Another call comes in:

Fearsome Woman: I've run out of them clamponges fings. For yer time. You know. Can you get me some? I'm at Flat 69, Block H, Birdnumb Mansions, Battersea…

The 999 operator, Maisie Thomas, then says to the next person in the call-centre, "Elke, I'm going to take my break now. Can you take this one?"

Maisie leaves her post.

In the staff-cafeteria Maisie sits down with a cup of tea, next to Jeff Thomas, another more senior 999 operator. "Unbelievable! The calls we get", Maisie remarks. "But I 'spose if you spend half a century constructing a welfarist, dependent, uneducated society where everything is Free, where no-one takes any notice of costs…"

Jeff: "…and where no one expects to be self-responsible, actually earn incomes or make informed and responsible choices about what anything costs…

Maisie: "…then this is what you get?"

Jeff: "Yes. Amen. But be VERY careful, Maisie. This is pirate talk. They'll shoot you if they hear you. Walls have ears, and shoes have tongues. That O'Brien isn't just in *1984*, you know. He's real here!"

Maisie sighs, and dreams of her holidays in Pembrokeshire…

CURTAIN falls, to tune of 'We don't want no education….'

***

Lady S-S: Cyril. I see. This is all actually about character then? About individual character. And the character of a free society?

Sir S-S: Yes. What all this represents is a fundamental cultural and doctrinal struggle. As ever was. A choice between – on the one hand – the freedoms of individual self-responsibility, self-culture, self-discipline, self-control, personal *effort*, and reflective self-analysis. And – on the other hand – a state-directed, bureaucratised, central system where politicians make the choices for you.

Lady S-S: Ah. As to the claims made for the NHS by the politicians, wasn't it Carlyle who said that actions and results must prove a doctrine? And that no doctrine is ever proved merely and just by its declaration? For this, see the NHS?

Sir S-S: Indeed so. And Samuel Smiles's *Self-Help, with Illustrations of Conduct and Perseverance* [which the IEA republished recently] tells it all. Came out as long ago as 1859. But still fundamental and current. As he said, "The spirit of self-help is the root of all genuine growth in the individual; and, exhibited in the lives of many, it constitutes the true source of national vigour and strength."

Lady S-S: So, the A&E problems – overwhelmed by daft demands – and the absurd calls on 999, are all a *cultural* snag?

Sir S-S: Yes. They derive directly from the enfeeblement of our society by welfarist, "progressive" education and social structures. Like the NHS itself. We'll only get out of this deep hole when, like Smiles, we understand how to marshal the strength and cultural growth in the individual and for the good of all. We need the moral core of all this. Which is Character. By the by, Smiles was originally trained as a doctor!

Lady S-S: So, people will only change how they behave if their personal culture changes? But the "progressive" and welfarist society provides no cultural incentives for individuals to do better, does it?

Sir S-S: No. None. Education has collapsed. Personal culture, civilised attitudes, the work-ethic. All enfeebled. People no longer value duty, self-responsibility, or indeed civilisation itself.

Lady S-S: Yet these are the people who have the political future of us all in their hands?

Sir S-S: Yes, the mob of voters. The results of "progressive" education. And from education, from welfarist government, from the dogmas of centralised services which have encouraged individual indolence. We've all suffered a succession of terrible blows. So what can you expect in A&E, and all the irresponsible demands? Or on 999 calls? By our own actions or by our apathy we've all constructed these shadows over our own lives. We've done it. It's us who have to undo it. If we can.

Look at the key virtues we've put into the margins. Disinterested endeavour. Duty. Conscience. We can charge a bit to sort out demand in A&E, and we should. But critically we've now got to end intellectual apathy and reliance on the Bigger State. And at long last dismiss the pernicious superstitions about the NHS being the best we can have. Hard job, though, to wean an entire nation from Nanny. Still, as Tennyson said, *"There lives more faith in honest doubt, believe me, than in half the creeds."*

Lady S-S: And Matthew Arnold, too:

"...we are here on a darkling plain

Swept with confused alarms of struggle and flight, Where ignorant armies clash by night."

Sir S-S: Aha. And we should expect more sense from a Tory PM, in course. But it's not there, is it?

Lady S-S: Cameron is a *nice* man...

Sir S-S: ... but with *no* philosophy.

Lady S-S: *Honest* man...

Sir S-S: ...but with *no* structured understandings of society.

Lady S-S: *Decent* and compassionate fellow....

Sir S-S: ... but *with no clue what to do* to give incentives for individual and collective improvements.

No real appreciation of the truths of human nature, and how to motivate the human spirit in personal self-awareness, self-responsibility, individual sovereignty and decent behaviour towards one's own self and to others. It's a great pity, as he has *real* gifts. But he hasn't yet used them to open out the real debate, and to lead it too. He hasn't even, yet, begun to help people to see the intermediate steps which need to be taken to get to a very different whole. So he goes on with the NHS Fairy Story.

Lady S-S: As do his colleagues, Lord 'Owzat, & co...

Sir S-S: Yes. So no moves to require everyone to insure for A&E cover, which would release billions into other services where the money can be effective. No moves to introduce Health Savings Accounts with an insurance excess, to deter abuse.

We are entitled to a national leader with the courage and originality of mind to challenge received but worn out socialistic ideas and their very visible results. And then to offer decent alternatives with clarity and purpose. We've got to campaign and insist ourselves. The ConsLibDemys won't. So for a better structure it is we who each individually have to lay these foundations, on which to rebuild for all. *W*e have to challenge deep-rooted prejudices and convictions.

The time is ripe. But *where* is the leader?

***

Meanwhile, Telephone rings in Emergencies Centre at Broxbinge, Herts.

Miss JW, 999 operator: Hello. Emergency Services. Fire, police or ambulance?

Mrs. C: *It's me again.* It's about me newts. They won't eat the new food...

***

Facey's Relevant Reading List Recommendations. To escape all this – and to appreciate how these dee-zasters fell upon us – see Simon Heffer, *High Minds. The Victorians and the Birth of Modern Britain* (London, Random House, 2013), which I gratefully received at Christmas, and on which I have drawn. Also, I urge readers to study a book only seen by me nearly two years after all these Episodes were completed: Edmund Phelps [Nobel Prize-winner in Economics], *Mass Flourishing. How Grassroots Innovation Created jobs, Challenge, and Change* (Princeton and Oxford, Princeton University Press, 2013). Pure gold for managers – so probably not *one* copy is to be found anywhere in the N£sd. Wot a surprise, eh?

EPISODE 39

Cameron launches NHS Inter-Galactica. "World's Best Service" – Now to Serve Space.

Astonishing N£sd Venture.

Dramatis Personae:

Barney Wells BEM is Chief Executive of the Arthur Scargill Memorial Trust Hospital at Chessingfield-on-Soke.

Kevin O'Grady is Chief Executive of the Coleraine St. Fortescue Hospital, N. Ireland.

***

Barney: Hi Kev. Quick call. I'm just back from RAF Bombasods in Norfolk. Was a special guest at Cameron's launch of NHS Inter-Galactica. We're all to journey into space, for our high-level NHS services! You'll see! To help us, and any Moonbeams or Marzipans out there in deep space!

Sat next to that Bob Geldorf. And, alas, near that total Moaners Moron Smalling. He of the ant-intelligence, if that – to understate the case! He of the pretend exploding terrorist party vest. *He's* definitely going on the first flight to Neptune. Moaners fans have also nominated Moysey to go.

None of this Intergalacticawoffle is surreal, y'know. Actually to happen! NHS Space Health Tourism! Well ahead of the Russians this time. And the Yankee-doodles too! Lord Oakeshottup to be an early pilot. *[Who he? Ed]*.

Kev: Bet they haven't given that Smalling a return ticket! Or Lord Oakeshottup either. *[Who he? Ed]*.

Barney: Nope. But he'll have to have help from several nurses even to find the door! Not sure how he finds his mouth in the morning!

Kev: Well, me old mate, you get all the luck. Invited to that Big Beano. Tell me the inside-story then.

Barney: Amazing speech by PM anyway. NHS Inter-Galactica! Who'd-a-thought-it?

Kev: Yes. Read it in *The Sun*. They claim to have suggested it, of course. "It was *The Sun* Wot Bunged It!"

Barney: Lord 'Owzat there, too. His usual speech: "The NHS The Envy of The Known Universe."

Kev: And beyond...

Barney: Anyways, after the Big Speech they showed us the training place. Put us all in shiny new simulators. I had to lie down, kitted up in a special plastic and aluminium suit. Lay on the floor. Floor fell away. Was weightless. Floated about a bit. Then landed on an NHS trolley. Sucked a ballistic biscuit. Was able to wheel myself up the corridor. Very cold and dark. All needed a paint job. Even though new. On my knees. Got to a chair. But then had to wait for my name and number to be announced.

They called it Triage Ticketing. Seemed to have been there a long while. Very crowded. Thought I'd been forgotten. Then heard the traditional friendly NHS porter's call, "Oi! You!" So knew all was OK. In familiar territory after all. Then taken for blood tests, ECG, and all that. Had to wait there, too. All staff out to lunch. But never mind, eh. Lucky to get it. All in a converted cargo plane. I was lighter than air. Practice in weightless conditions. Went over the weightless-curve...no resistance...

Kev: Anti-obese too then, eh?

Barney: Just so. But had to eat powdered sprouts though, so not so great!

Kev: Be a Health & Safety enquiry about that then!

Barney: Then the PM told the assembled The Goods & Greats – you know, usual reality TV people; pop stars; BBC news-readers; the Aston Villa goalie; and his hairdresser, MBE – that as the NHS is THE outstanding global customer-service in THE WHOLE WIDE WORLD it was time to introduce it to Inter-Galactic Space. Martians lucky! Help The Others too. Show them how we do it. Everyone in the Milky – not The Millkiband! – Way. To replicate our GP, A&E, and outpatients clinics. The NHS to colonise space. Wonderful Jubbly! Buck Rogers has nothing on Mid-Staffs, he said. Dan Dare? Eat your heart out.

Kev: So the idea is that instead of waiting five hours in A&E they can inject you into space, and you can be treated at a Satellite NHS Trust, up above? Coo! Be there & back before they notice you are even there at Coggeshall-on-Soke, eh? NHS Starships. NHS takeoff. NHS on Saturn.

Barney: Best not to see that George Clooney space film first, though? Still all to be achieved by these new super-propulsion engines. Whamazamazoo, as Bransonic Himself might say. And if they can fly you to Oz that way in just four hours, why not to the Major KG Satellite instead? PM says it is a major new British business opportunity. Consultants as cosmonauts. Jet fuelled, of course.

Kev: As per usual!

Barney: Yep. Concorde just a kid's toy. PM says it is to be His Greatest Achievement. NHS Inter-Galactica.

PM said that this is not just kid's stuff. The dream of interstellar space travel has long been a goal and a catalyst for both incremental and revolutionary advance.

CAMERON LAUNCHES NHS INTER-GALACTICA

As Mrs. Whizzlers MP of Universities likes to say in Kable's Department, *Ad astra incrementis* – "To the stars in ever-increasing steps." The unknowns are out there, the goberlins, gremerlins, gruffer-aloes, and viruses too, all just waiting for the NHS to start real life for them. Just you watch. *Intergalactic Taxpayers Ahoy!*

The PM is also to offer a new BBC Service with the lovely Carol – Weather in Other Worlds! To combine technology, ambitions, nano-tech, and the World's Best NHS. How could it fail?, PM said.

Kev: How, indeed.

Barney: He added that we already have in place all of the key components of "The System" – the BMA, The Royal College of Vested Interests, Unite, and The Great British Whitewash Co PLC. And all the key processes. Waiting lists too. And we are busily printing new money, too, to be imported from Ontario. To pay the bills.

Kev: So all will be swiftly and fully integrated and in flight. Bransonic Biffaboom! This pre-launch presages the supersonic rapid expansion of the NHS's Inter-Galactic responsibilities then, eh?

Barney: Yep. The Best Service in The Whole Inner & Outer World. And in what Sir Richard Branson himself has called "a powered flight envelope." Health History in the making. If this isn't Time Travel itself, then at least it's a big cut in waiting lists! Come in Starship Trooper, and collect the new hips!

Kev: Beam me up, Potty!

Barney: Apparently, it's a joint project with Yabbadabadoo Yogi B Investments PLC. It's said that there's a loophole in Einstein's general theory of relativity that could allow an NHS spaceship to traverse vast distances in less time than it would take light. The trick? It's not the starship that's moving — it's the space around it.

Kev: Sounds very Nursie Nursie Dixbungle, that.

Barney: And Cameron says that the first NHS Space-station A&E will be called Alpha Centauri, after our nearest star which has planets. Only a short hop…

Kev: Sounds Very Millkiband Kidding, to me!

Barney: Well, *in de factio*, the scientists at NASA are right now working on the first practical field test toward proving the possibility of warp drives and faster-than-light travel. Or so my geeky neighbour Alfredo D'Fuser tells me, anyway. You know, the retired Nursing boss at old Stewed Bludgeon's old place in Sussex. ["I will not resign!"] And some bloke called Tsiolkovski apparently said that "Earth is the cradle of humanity, but it is impossible to live forever in the cradle." And wasn't it Carl Sagan who, when asked what's out there, replied "Billions!"

Kev: Aha, NHS loot, eh? *Intergalactic Taxpayers Ahoy!*

Barney: Aha – my line! And patients on earth always ask "What's out there?" But they mean in the long NHS corridors where they think some service might exist for them, one day!

Kev: So now we'll have NHS A&E Inter-Galactica as some sort of Ecto-Moon, circling a star then? But knowing DC the whole thing will vanish into some inter-space wormhole – isn't that what they're called? Or a black hole. Or it'll be whacked by passing meteorites. *[Called "David Davises" in the trade. Ed.].* Virtually speaking, that is.

Barney: Like Sir Nickelodeon's expenses! Meanwhile, down on the earth beneath our feet....an uninhabitable system, which we know only too well...NHS processes valued, not people; no-one taking any individual responsibility; chaos in hardly-funded Care Homes; major hospital blunders including 40 patients given surgery on wrong limb, revealed recently by official statistics.

Kev: Yes. Almost 150 patients suffered from major errors which are so simple and serious that they are categorised as "never events." But happened, of course. And then Dixbungles galore...

Barney: As per usual. We know all about Zero Propulsion, don't we? In our very own Cosmic N£sd Backyard! *The Old Frontier!* Our very own much beloved Lord Howzatified Bevanite and Brownite Ed Balthic Space Debris. *Virtually speaking*, in course.

And now we might even live long enough to see the state-monopoly N£sd vanish into outer spooks, eh? And be extinct on earth then? As we should if we are to reform British healthcare properly. Get proper funding; insurances; health savings accounts; self-responsible patients. All those space dusty things.

Kev: But as the traditional English schoolboy might say, "Some 'opes!"

Barney: Yep. And as Lord Ironsides himself says, the PM *should* have started 4 years ago to pull abandoned junk and redundant objects out of the skies.

Kev: But the PM now says he's got a new NHS Inter-Galactic Manifesto, eh?

Barney: Uyerp.

To find the NHS space-pioneers and support them to make progress. Sending them off to NHS Satellite Hospitals. Up, and beyond.

Applying the scientific method. Be best in the Whole Outer World. INTERGALACTIC UNIVERSAL NHS!

Using science fiction to depict possible futures, and inspire the best choices.

Break the NHS habit of waiting until the last minute to start solving all problems. Export them by rocket instead.

Eliminate non-essential distractions. Like patient complaints So the NHS Passenger will follow a ballistic trajectory into A&E!

Kev: PM to be The Man In The Moon, eh? Well, he was always thus. Moon or Moonshine? Might meet The Mekon, too! Or that nasty bloke in *Flash Gordon*. Well-cast. As *Star Trek* told us, "To explore strange new worlds, to seek out new life and new civilizations." But meanwhile, back on Earth in the N£sd... Winter Realities Beckon...

Barney: *Intergalactic Taxpayers Ahoy!*

EPISODE 40

How To Be Top. "Total Management" – The Bergkamp and The Arsenal Way.

Dramatis Personae:

Barney Wells BEM is Chief Executive of the Arthur Scargill Memorial Trust Hospital at Chessingfield-on-Soke.

Kevin O'Grady is Chief Executive of the Coleraine St. Fortescue Hospital, N. Ireland.

***

Barney: I've just sent you a book. Lord Ironsides gave it to me. Amazing stuff. Best book on inspirational management I've read for years and years.

Kev: Tell me!

Barney: It's by that genius Dennis Bergkamp.

Kev: The Arsenal footballer? The brilliant Dutchman? Best player they ever had! A shoo-in for a World Team of All Time! Up there with Pele, Eusebio, Henry....

Barney: Yes. THE man. One of The Invincibles. Book's called *Stillness and Speed*. His memoirs. Full of wisdom. Reflective, and extremely relevant to us. Directly so. *"Total Football" as applied to management.* THE Guide to How to Be Top! Brilliant stuff!

Kev: Well, we *do* need something special...a Magic Potion, a Universal Pill, Leadership out of all our NHS fixes...Tell me about it!

Barney: First, let's start with 10 Bergkamp points:

1. Balance. Pluck the ball out of the air, with instant control. Need a reliable and a perfect touch.

2. Actions. "It's not thinking. It's *doing*."

3. The message. "With every pass, there needs to be a message or thought behind it."

4. Creativity. Do something that others don't do ...not following, but creating your own thing.

5. Striving. Strive for perfection. Take small steps all the time, improving, moving on.

6. Development. Develop yourself. Don't wait for others to do it for you.

7. Opportunities. Ask how do I get the best out of this situation?

8. Be special. Try to be creative and unique, giving something extra, instead of just copying what's been done in the past. Find this uniqueness in yourself.

9. Ambition. Know what you want to achieve. See what you can do about it – now.

10. Confidence. Do what you are good at.

Kev: Can quite see why The Arsenal are one of the best teams in the world!

Barney: The Centre of World Football!

Kev: ...and what a subtle and inspired player he was. What a *thinker,* too!

Barney: Well, any amount of NHS managers could benefit from his words. And actions. The DoH should issue 950,000 copies, as hand-outs with wage packets. Worth the weight in gold!

Kev: And goals!

Barney: Bergkamp always said that adversity stimulates learning. In a relentless demand for improvement and excellence.

Kev: So...Total Football, Total Management!

Barney: You can't just be fiddling about – you have to see the whole picture before you make that pass with that ball. You play football with your head as well as your feet. If you don't think, your feet won't be sufficient by themselves. So, the message to management? Pay attention to the whole picture. Be in the right position. See the possibilities. Choose the right position – and the right pass.

Kev: So you can be the one man advantage?

Barney: *Exactiment!*

Kev: So notice everything, pay attention to everything...

Barney: ...and get the ball into the net! While you're at it, too, get out of your comfort zone. Adapt. Meet new challenges. Respond as circumstances change. Then you can be well organised, crisp and creative, move astutely between the lines, be quick and daring, learn to turn in limited space, be precise in your finishing – and give the goalie "the eye"! Be THE main man! And show the Vested Interests what you are made of too!

Kev: Well...structure...clarity... ambition...ever-greater energy...could be innovative, ambitious, and even attractive to watch....

Barney: Like every team that Bergkamp graced! You could almost see him thinking creatively, critically and swiftly about every aspect of the game – *and while he played*, with and without the ball. Course, he had to train meticulously, too. Improve everything. Make no assumptions. Consider, practice, learn, emulate every good move. Always aware of everything around him. Watch for opportunities. And then be decisive at the key moments!

HOW TO BE TOP

Kev: No bad menu for NHS managers, that!

Barney: Lot of it is instinct, of course. You are or you aren't made of the right stuff. You either do or don't want to be the best player on the field. It's instinct plus skills. To be an exceptional player, because they are the ones who decide matches. And they work hard for their money, in all weathers. Just like us!

Kev: You need a season ticket, too. No cop-outs on wet Fridays! No duff-ups away to Sunderland in the February mud!

Barney: Nope. And it's your job to manage like this, to make outcomes best, and not merely better processes! Collaborate effectively with team-mates, too. All to be talented players, but as an effective unit.

Kev: Big part is creativity. Quite see that. Not the bolt-the-door, boot it to heaven Morino Arroganita Chelski 1-0 style. Not The Moaners We-Want-More-Time attitude, either.

Barney: No. The best approach is pass and move, pass and move. Best ever teams are all like that. Vision. Quality. Technically-high skills. Instincts. Incredibly gifted players. *The* Arsenal. Barcelona. Real Madrid. The old Ajax. Herbert Chapman's title-winning and cup-winning teams. The Push-and-Run Spurs teams of the late 1950s. Then Matthews on the wing at Blackpool. Wilf Mannion at Middlesbro. Robert Pires alongside Henry at The Arsenal. And other Greats. Garincha, Puskas and Hidekuti, Pele, Di Stefano, Cruyff, Van Basten, Peter Ward, Messi, Xavi, Iniesta, Ronaldo – THE men. And new managers now, like Laudrup at Swansea, Rodgers at Liverpool – they show the way, too. All the greats were like Bergkamp. But he was one of the very best of them all. As was Arsene THE magician, too, of course.

Kev: Well, we can all learn a heck of a lot from that book.

Barnety: And, to NHS Managers, it effectively says don't be shy – be The Leader! *Act on* your philosophy, let it be your input, *be there!*

Go and buy a copy! I'm re-reading mine for the third time! My project is push and run, push and run, press and play, an attacking game. And in a structure which brings out the best human qualities of all around us. This is what Lord Ironsides says he wants. Must be why he gave me the book.

Kev: Course, in football, you have to face and embrace change, evolve, create new things. Be the best. Always want to improve. Just like Dennis B.

Barney: Yes. As Dennis himself said and did in front of goal – Boom, boom boom! Make the ball talk. Make the ball tick. All attitude, natural class, and elegance. Be the manager who affects people, who makes changes who makes others better players or better people – and who then pass this on to patients. It's not done for the cameras. It's done because it's right. Be a manager of intense awareness, like DB on the field of play.

We're considering here the real difference between the top level, being the very best, and either the merely outstanding or the too commonly met apathetic. How the *whole team* functions, too. Get the best out of every player. Focus on learning, and on experiences and their lessons. Work or play with passion, focus and precision. Push one another. Put in the hours. Do the training. Control the difficult balls. Play with a smile.

And then Mesmerise! Be THE No.10! Be better than yesterday! Interact. Influence the culture. Confront the resistance to change, and deal with it. Take and manage risks. Imagination from you. Imagination from everyone around you. Welcome and inspire it. Look for new possibilities, new opportunities, satisfy the punters, satisfy your own instinct and self-respect, and keep Arsene onside too! Everything, a 100%.

Show the drive to be the best in the world – the Bergkamp way! No fear of failure, if you please. Think like a winner, and be one. Solve the problems in your organisation, starting at the very bottom, with all the first points of contact with patients. And then on up. And then you can make your life mean something! Indeed, think about the meaning of meaning…and control the game. Set yourself different standards. Total football, total management, build from the back, forwards. Strive for perfection. Hit every ball right.

As Lord Ironsides says to me, "Strive for the maximum results. Push the boundaries. Make your life an adventure. See the bigger picture. Transform the situation. Be a leader, not a follower. And yet free your staff to be creative too. Above all, always see the space, see where you can create new space, and where the right ball can make the biggest difference."

And so, let's get to it!

Up The Arsenal!

G-o-o-o-a-l!

NB. Mr. Birdnumb and Prof. Hampster contribute the following joint policy note: "When we return to permanent Socialistical Government we will blow off-side and side-step those NASTY words – entrepreneurship; being directed by financially-empowered patient vouchers; making full use of irresponsible patient complaints; enabling customer decision-making to guide investment; considering outrageous measures of well-being and of human and national progress; and financially empowering the individual service-user in a market. Instead, Vote N£sd!"

EPISODE 41

Shock Horror Tory & Labour Disasters At Bugginsturn North By-Election.

UKIP Sweep in with record majority.

PRIME MINISTER GOES INTO SHOCK THERAPY CLINIC AT ESHER. THE MILLKIBAND KID "CONSIDERING HIS POSITION." CLEGGY "IN RETREAT." FARAGE "IN PUB."

Triple Leadership Challenges Launched.

Very Old Labour candidate demands recounts, fraud enquiry, voter registration examination, coroner's inquest...

IEA report urges market solutions for continuing NHS crisis.

A Special Report from Bugginsturn Junction.

***

Dramatis personae.

Barney Wells BEM, is Chief Executive of The Arthur Scargill Memorial NHS Trust, Coggeshall-on-Soke.

Mrs. Rita Wells MBE, was formerly Chair of his Trust, and then became Labour's Parliamentary candidate for the seat of Bugginsturn North, in the by-election.

Kevin O'Grady is Chief Executive of the Coleraine St. Fortescue Hospital, N. Ireland.

Mr. Nick Robinhoode is an unusual, independent-minded BBC reporter.

Sir C. Squoffington-Squogg is Chief Executive of The Tower Hamlets NHS Hospital Trust, London.

***

Kev: Hi Barney. Bit surprised to find you at work today, actually. Golly – the result at Bugginsturn! Should be called Bugginsburn! *What a turn-up!*

Barney: Her indoors is appoplexitised! Not sure what she'll do next. Was dead set on being MP. Thought she was there already. But properly stuffed! Local Old Labour gang nearly in riots! And Rita's already talking of going to the EuroCourt of By-Election Fixies. Me? I hid under the pillows until she'd slammed out this morning. She's off to see Galloway. Might join the Arobe Party. Very Old Labour down the drain. Blamed everyone but herself, in course. What shocks to come nationally, too, you'd have to say.

Kev: Yes. But usual very low poll. Yet just think about why. Makes an important point. It's not *voting* which can secure you any individual, personal services – like health or education. Everyone knows that it's open markets which give you choice and any individual power. Then you can get what you want, and reject what you don't want. Can't do that in politics any more. They are genuinely, deliberately and really ALL THE SAME. Well, 'cept for that UKIP lot anyway.

Barney: Sounds so. Yes. S'why they don't usually turn out to vote.

Kev: Just saw that Nick Robinhoode interview the PM on the BBC just now. PM looked very groggy. Made note of the interview....

Nick Robinhoode: Prime Minister, the NHS was a major issue at Bugginsturn. Especially shortages of funds. So what are you doing to bring in more funds for the NHS – and not just from more taxes?

PM: Well, you see, it's like this. In 1948...

NR: Yes, yes, Prime Minister. We know the history. But what is to happen NOW? Why is there no wider use of co-payments, for example, or more personal insurance, and so forth?

PM: Well, you see, it's a difficult task to discharge, with so many factors...

NR: And what are you doing to increase personal responsibility, so that the individual takes responsibility for their own behaviour? And then bears more of the costs? What, too, are you doing to reduce demand, while also – by the by – using economic incentives to tackle obesity?

PM: Well, I'm giving more power to the doctors and nurses....

NR: Like at Mid-Staffs, you mean? And at Alder Hey?

PM: Well, with more money from Whitehall...and as the BMA says...

NR: You'll just get more waste, less productivity, and more consultants and GPs vanishing, too? Won't you? Just as happened under Gordon Brown...

PM: Well, there will be more and better central and local management....

NR: Like at Morecambe, you mean? Or like the scandals of people redundant one minute and re-hired the next, with big compensation payments? Or like all the entirely avoidable deaths at weekends....

PM: Well, you see Nick, The Royal College of Vested Interests urges that...

SHOCK HORROR TORY & LABOUR DISASTERS AT BUGGINSTURN BY-ELECTION

NR: And are you going to require everyone to take up extra insurance to cover A&E services, releasing billions for critically underfunded community care?

PM: Well, thank you Nick. Always good to talk with you. I must get back to work.

NR: And so – to sum up – the ever-present NHS crisis has caused a new sensation at Bugginsturn North! But we are no nearer real change, it seems. This is Nick Robinhoode reporting from 10 Downing Street.

Kev: Aha. No PM's vision there then? And no enthusiasm to push a new vision through? The PM's certainly not *le roi soleil*! No wonder there's lots of speculation on what's next – all over the 'papers and tele today!

Barney: Yep. Saw Dixbungle whiffling and waffling, covering-up as well. As per usual. With Edth Balth demanding new old spendalotta policies. And with Birdnumb reading from his old NHS prompt-cards...

Kev: And those two Profs – Applecore and Hampster – saying their usual Klingfilm stuff. Don't know how they keep a straight face!

Barney: Yes. But Squoffy has a piece in the *Telegraph*. In later editions anyway.

Usual LESSONS.

He's bang on the button, as ever.

Squoffy's main point is that without a philosophical analysis of society the PM has no chance of coping. It's all just 'process.' And so it's squealing chickens inevitably all coming home to roost.

Cameron and Osborne are running the government which is historically the least interested in ideas, or philosophy since The Grand Duke Himself. And with no understanding of human nature and of how society works. Worse than Major. Even. *Can you believe?* The Millkiband Kid offering everything FREE, too. But voters not as dim as he thinks.

Kev: And the whole self-appointed political elite has turned its face against the market economy – all of them. Well, with a few exceptions like Foxie and Davis. Both nugatories now, alas, they are.

Barney: Yep. We've gone all the way back to Heath, or worser. Just look at it. No attempt at all to explain why the NHS can no longer work as it did in the 1940s. And, in the wider economy, wee're now getting Cameroon's price controls, government interfering in industry, no respect for property rights. Acceptance of higher inflation and low interest rates. Bribes on housing to voters. Coalition fiscal budgets all against enterprise solutions and entrepreneurship. Big government. Lots of it. Cuts? Maybe? Urgent! But only from 2025!

Kev: You're right. And Cameron has made no attempt to argue for free enterprise solutions, both to economic and to social problems. Could and should have set out basic philosophy and then referred every action and every event to that. Instead, he offers thin varnish over thick concrete. Every NHS event explained as just another muddled bungle – but quite by accident, not seen as part of a collapsing whole.

Barney: Yep. And we managers have to take the heat. But as it is he has no explanations, 'cept spend more money. He's made no effort to encourage genuine understandings. And some so-called Thatcherites – Mrs. Whizzlers MP, for instance in Cable's department – sit on their hands…

Kev:…and in their government-issue cars.

Barney: And leave us all just paying the price now – as we all are, too. But the PM will probably just go on giving us more paternalism, not practical change. Heaven help the NHS then. Nobody else will. Without co-payments, personal insurance, price to discipline demands, excesses to pay, we are well and truly Turkeyed for Christmas!

Kev: Meanwhile, no markets freely at work in key areas – literally the Big State We're In. No political leadership. No vision.

Barney: And so no votes! The Bugginsturn Effect!

Kev: You were at the count, Barney, weren't you? I saw it on Sky. The Mayor, Mr. Sid Hoglebin, OBE declaring the result at 12.07 a.m. "…and I declare that Mr. U. Knowitmakesense has been duly elected to serve as Member of Parliament for the said constituency of Bugginsturn North."

Official result was:

Mr. U. Knowitmakessense, MEP (UKIP), 19,607.

Mr. A. Johnson (Boris-in-Waiting Party), 4,904.

Mrs. Rita Wells, MBE (Very Old Labour), 4,030.

Mrs. Glitterboob Fameforme (Simon Loves Me Party), 2,900.

Mr. Alex Trouter (Independence for Rutland), 1,704.

Mr. Jeff Green-Barbedwirecutter (Animal Rights), 403.

Mr. Alex Salmon Fishcake (Independence for Goring-on-Sea), 399.

Ms. Jessie Nilfracker (Green Party), 117.

Ms. Alioops Parksahstan (Conservative But Not Unionist Party), 115.

Ms. Jacqueline Extrahs (LabLibDemsy Party), 113.

Ms. Jennifer Sameserver (ConsLibDemsy Party), 112.

Ms. Gee Itsfreeall (New One-Nation Re-Labelled Party), 19.

SHOCK HORROR TORY & LABOUR DISASTERS AT BUGGINSTURN BY-ELECTION

Nursie Nursie Dixbungle (Great British Whitewash Co PLC), 4.

Ms. Carmen Virago (Selfie Party), 2.

Sir John Major KG (Monster Raving Loony Party), *withdrew hurt.*

Barney: Corker! All but the first four lost their deposits! Now we know what it must have felt like at that Orpington by-election in the early 1960s. Tory seat lost to unknown Liberal. When that Eric Lubbock got in. Or when The Moaners lost 6-1 to Cockles-and-Whelks FC from Whitsea in the third round of the FA Cup. Or how the Chief Postmaster felt after the Great Train Robbery!

Kev: And at this rate there'll be no Tory MPs north of Sidcup. Bye-bye His Hon. PR-ship, and the Cluggytriffid, too. No one agrees with Nick now!

Barney: Runner-up, too, was Boris's bloke. Big warning, that! All his supporters wearing blonde wigs! He a weather-cock, of course. Opportunist, as ever. Rumour is that Cameron has asked to be made Governor of Coventry Island. Lot of declared Leadership runners already: 2-1 Gove; 3-1, Boris Himself [if can quickly get a seat – probably promise Mr. Alfie Smith, safe-seater, a Peerage?]; 6-1 Hunt; 9-1, Hammond; 10-1 Ms. Goody Two-Shoes; 11-1 Osborne; 12-1, Dr. Fox; 333-1; 600-1, Davis; 33,000-1 Haig; and Lord Oakeshott, disclaiming peerage temporarily. *[Who he? Ed].*

Kev: Some nice thoughts out of it all, though. But any new leader will still mean no change. We have to get markets working, and get rid of the Big Stateites.

Barney: Ah. Best to move to Mongolia then. And take with you the lovely Mrs. Glitterboob Fameforme, too! Reminds me of that Mrs. Du Maurier Weaknees!

Kev: Stay with the issues, Barney, please! I see that the UKIP bloke got 19,607 votes. Very clear message. Now proposes we leave EEC, leave Euro Court of "Human Rights", leave European Cup, leave Euro-exchange markets, leave Danish Butter – heave-ho the lot! And what will happen to all those losing candidates then?

Barney: Well, most of them will go back to the day job. Special Advisers. Special Bag-carriers. Special Bottom-Wipers. Look for new seats to fight. Some go directly to The Lords. Collect the £200. Even though haven't passed "Go." They will pay no price for losing, will they? Well, lost deposits for their Party, of course. But most will go back to benefits, free housing, the lot, as per usual. Aha! *Benefits Ahoy!*

Kev: Not like these Pole and Rumanians, eh? They tackle the jobs our lot aren't prepared to do. They come and clean cars at the supermarket, study English, and then move on to better things. Don't look to live on benefits forever, like our lot.

Barney: Nope. Be really interesting, though if Cluggy loses most of his seats, the people truly rumble The Millkiband Kid, UKIP get a t'riffic lot more Tory votes, and whoever takes over from The PR Ghost has to form a new coalition with Farage! Need to know now what his N£sd policy would be.

Kev: Lead on Macduff!

EPISODE 42

Lord 'Owzat's Corner of NHS Wonders.

Lord 'Owzat said that "The NHS is the Envy of The World."

Facey Romford Jr. says: "That's as maybe. But what of actual daily NHS realities?

AND:

"If you artificially lower or eliminate prices (as does the NHS) you will both increase demand and reduce supply. If you eliminate competition, you will reduce quality. If you do not have market disciplines, you will have no disciplines that are non-political. If management is not challenged, it remains condescending and protected. If there is a culture of ignoring the individual and of producer-interests dominant we will continue marginalising basic human compassion. We suffer delay, denial, and unnecessary deaths as the inevitable results. Chaos necessarily ensues. And enormous numbers of avoidable deaths"

"As to a society which does nothing to encourage self-responsibility, there is little wonder that GPs are overwhelmed, let alone Accident & Exit departments. We can see why no other nation has ever copied the NHS. And we can see from the following examples from only a few months of press reports which very clearly show what the true situation is. Morale is low. Professional mistakes are rife, and too often ignored or covered up and thus never rooted out. Transparency? Accountability for practice? I should coker! And what would a year's worth of incidents show us? But what do I know when compared with a Government Minister? IF he still believes what he has said, "That the NHS is the envy of the world." – FR, Jr.

HOWEVER, here is some **evidence** to consider.

Charles Moore recently and very wisely wrote in his *Daily Telegraph* column that "Most egregious of all, the National Health Service continued under the appalling ex-Communist Sir David Nicholson (funny how these people can swallow their principles when titles come their way). Sir David had done nothing about the practices which meant that hundreds of patients in mid-Staffordshire died unnecessarily, but he was allowed to keep the whole thing in thrall to the producer interest. Compassion was as rare in the NHS as drought in Muchelney."

As to Sir D - The Silent Knight!!!- Stafford Crown Court heard in February 2004 that just one senior nurse was in charge of 84 beds at Mid-Staffordshire hospital, and that there was "no effective oversight" at the NHS Trust. A major public enquiry has already said that this may have needlessly caused the deaths of 1,200 patients between 2005 and 2009 – due to appalling failings in care.

HOWSOME-EVER...

No managers, *no* doctors, and *no* nurses have been prosecuted. Only two nurses have been held to account. David Nicholson, later knighted and appointed Chief Executive of the NHS, was head of West Midlands Strategic Health Authority between 2005 and 2006. This was the body "supervising Mid-Staffordshire." Its managers failed to pick up the horrific standards of care at the heart of the scandal. *Who was in charge?*

Meanwhile, while Nicholson goes off to enjoy his vast pension pot – and while Ministerial cars await their occupants – some small gathering *of* recent press reports which say that:

- HUNDREDS of urgent NHS operations were cancelled in December 2013 and in January 2014 as hospitals ran out of intensive care beds, forcing ill patients to travel hundreds of miles to other units. Others who needed life and limb-saving procedures had to endure risky delays.

- Some cancer surgery was suspended at Maidstone Hospital in Kent, and incidents were referred to the General Medical Council, after five patients died due to unexpected surgical complications. Dr. Paul Sigston, the medical director, apologised that "some patients did not receive the level of care and treatment that they should have."

- Thousands of women recovering from breast cancer are being left at risk because doctors fail to provide information about signs that the disease has returned, said a new report by the Breast Cancer Campaign. Only one woman in five was given a care plan of this kind, amongst 14, 000 patients studied. Health-care professionals are doing "virtually nothing" to ensure standards are met, and imply "paying lip service" to the needs of their patients. NHS bodies which are supposed to monitor quality of care have made no attempt to check on the standards. In some NHS Trusts fewer than 8% of patients were given a care plan. And trust are supposed to be the elite hospitals!

- One in five consultant posts in A&E departments remain unfilled. But the NHS has no clear strategy to deal with this issue.

- Blood-spattered walls and patients waiting for hours on trolleys at A&E at Medway Maritime NHS Trust – which has been told once again to clean up its act. In Special Measures, too.

But **Lord 'Owzat said that "The NHS is the envy of the world."**

YET:

- Scores of premature babies could be dying needlessly because of inadequate maternity wards, a new study has reported.

- Patients are to have "more say", but no control over funds.

LORD 'OWZAT'S CORNER OF NHS WONDERS

- The number of patients suffering blunders deemed so serious that they should NEVER occur has almost doubled in a year, according to figures disclosed in answer to a parliamentary question. Many due to standard procedures not being followed. A BBC investigation showed that over a four-year period 762 patients suffered such errors. Including 320 patients who had medical instruments left inside them after surgery, and 214 patients who underwent surgery on the wrong part of the body.

- A leading children's hospital [Alder Hey Children's NHS Foundation at Liverpool] has taken shortcuts in its operating theatres, creating "high risk activity." It is potentially unsafe, according to the Care Quality Commission, due to shortages of staff and equipment in operating theatres. The Trust failed four out of five national standards on quality and safety. The emergency call alarm system was faulty, while safety incidents went unreported. There was also poor training.

- A pledge by the PM that all cancer patients would receive the necessary advanced radiotherapy has been broken. According to the report, *Vision for Radiotherapy*, this aim has been abandoned. An NHS circular said that "rates of radiotherapy in England are lower than would be expected of a modern service." More than half of the 269 NHS radiotherapy machines are outdated. Or near to the end of their useful life. The aim of delivering a minimum of 24% [only!!!] of all treatments with an advanced technique called inverse-planned intensity modulated radiotherapy by April 2012-13 has not been met. Another advanced treatment, stereotactic ablative radiotherapy, is not properly funded or available.

- Treatments which are Gold Standard in other countries are thus not available. About 52% of cancer patients are thought to benefit from some form of radiotherapy, but only 38% of NHS patients are getting it even in the most basic form. This has contributed to lower cancer survival rates in Britain, where our results are worse than the European average – some of our survival rates are worse than in Poland and Slovenia, otherwise unfortunate countries long dominated by Communist shortages of everything. Sir David Nicholson claims that results elsewhere are worse. But *The Lancet* reported 5-year cancer survival rates for lung cancer: France 14%, Germany 16%, Slovenia 11%, Poland 14%, Britain, 9%. We are below almost everyone else in 5-year survival rates for breast cancer and kidney cancer, too.

<u>But Lord 'Owzat said that "The NHS is the Envy of the World."</u>

HOWEVER:

- A patient who had part of his lung removed as treatment for lung cancer at Derriford Hospital in Plymouth, Devon was placed in quarantine for TB, then told he had HIV, before being informed that he had none of these conditions.

- Every year 14,000 people over 75 die of cancer who would have lived if UK survival rates matched those in the USA, according to Macmillan Cancer Care. People over 80 with cancer have seen mortality rates worsen in the last 40 years, said Age UK, as older people are not routinely offered the drugs or surgery given to young patients.

- Only one in ten GPs routinely raises the subject of prostate cancer with high-risk men, according to new research. And thousands of men with the disease now face being denied life-extending treatment following policy changes by NICE, the NHS rationing body.

- NHS Trusts have faced financial penalties of £390 million during the past three years over patients who were readmitted because of alleged failures in their initial care, according to NHS England (which withheld payments).

- A single doctor was left alone to care for 130 patients at Basildon Hospital, and the Essex Coroner called for a ban on junior doctors working unsupervised at night.

- The new model of General Practice and out-of-hours service has not been a success, and the old concept of the family doctor is now a fond memory.

BUT Lord 'Owzat said: "The NHS is the Envy of The World."

HOWEVER:

- The Chairman of NICE, Professor David Haslam, said that too many patients are not being offered effective and clinically appropriate medications that *have* been approved by NICE.

- We are well behind the USA in the use we make of computers and medical software to diagnose some medical conditions and to save many patients from unnecessary invasive procedures. Compare, for example, the work here of The Mayo Clinic in America and your local District General Hospital.

- Mortality rates rise among emergency admissions by an average of 6% when new trainees start work on the first Wednesday in August, when other junior doctors swap specialties. For patients suffering heart attacks and strokes there is an 8% increase in deaths. August is known by doctors as "the killing season." No joke. Where is the supervision by senior staff?

- Nurses, doctors and hospital managers could be prosecuted for "reckless or wilful" neglect or mistreatment of patients, Professor Don Berwick advised the NHS. Staffing levels caused particular concern. NHS bodies also withhold information, and a Duty of candour is now being demanded to overcome the standard bureaucratic obstructions by official organisations. A new "learning culture" is vital, Professor Berwick says.

- A former mental health patient called for better safeguards for the vulnerable in hospitals after claiming she had been raped up to 60 times in a year by a senior member of staff. She received £100,000 in compensation from Kent & Medway NHS Trust following her ordeal. The care worker was *eventually* charged. He pleaded guilty to one act of unlawful sexual intercourse and was given a 12-month *suspended* sentence.

- Officials at the NHS drugs body NICE, in charge of rationing, ran up a

£115,000 spend on perks on taxpayer-funded credit cards over the past two and a half years. Of this, £3,346 was spent at Searcy's – a chain of champagne bars in London. So less money was available for life-saving treatments, scans and medicines. NHS hospitals faced having to cut staff and services in the worst financial outlook for almost a decade, with almost half forecasting ending the financial year in debt, amid a £30m NHS 'black hole.' This news from Monitor, the regulator for foundation trusts.

YET LORD 'OWZAT SAID: "THE NHS IS THE ENVY OF THE WORLD."

BUT CONSIDER:

- Two of Britain's most eminent heart surgeons were among five doctors under investigation by the General Medical Council over alleged poor care for a patient with a rare life-threatening condition. Unacceptable delays and poor conditions at the Royal Brompton Hospital in London – a leading UK specialist unit for heart disease – were alleged at the hospital in 2010. Dr. Sheila, the DoH's former deputy chief medical officer, was concerned that the hospital had failed to investigate the patient's complaints properly. It was alleged that the shortcomings had the potential to endanger hundreds of other lives.

- An NHS Trust gagged a senior hospital official who quit after warning that the taxpayer was being ripped off by patients she judged to be health tourists, and who were not charged for treatment as non-UK residents – though they should have been paying. A number of NHS Hospital managements did not discharge their statutory duty, and instead fiddled the figures on health tourists by wrongly claiming millions of pounds in public funds for their care. Free NHS care provided for ineligible non-UK residents is estimated to cost the taxpayer more than £400m a year.

- Reports of abuse and neglect of the elderly and vulnerable have risen by 20%, official figures by the Health and Social Care Information Centre disclosed.

- NHS watch-dog the Health Service Ombudsman admitted it fully investigated fewer than 400 of 16,000 patient complaints in 2012/13. Of 178 complaints made over 5 years against the University Hospital of Morecambe Bay – the NHS facility at the heart of recent NHS scandals in which up to 16 babies died unnecessarily – just 15 were fully investigated by the Ombudsman. Patients have faced extraordinary battles to get results.

- In 2013 NICE turned down 16 out of 17 new cancer treatments, even though several had been shown to extend patients' lives for weeks if not months.

- However, cancer cases in the UK are up by a third since the 1970s, new figures from Cancer Research showed. In 2011 there were almost a third of a million people in the UK diagnosed with some form of cancer – due in part to longevity, and also in part to poor life-style factors.

- Survival rates are improving, but are still not at European levels.

BUT Lord 'Owzat said: "The NHS is the Envy of The World."

- Sir Muir Gray, Co-Chairman of the Executive Council of the government's own Information Standard (which promotes evidence-based health-care information) said that much money is wasted by NHS on biased and misleading leaflets. An Oxford academic researcher said "the NHS still fails to take this seriously."

- GP practices are letting receptionists with no clinical training decide who gets seen and who needs urgent treatment, said a survey by Campden Health, a clinical research and publishing company.

- The doctors' Trade union, the BMA, offered its staff private medical insurance, while opposing government reforms to create a more competitive market in health-care.

- One in five A&E units has a shortage of senior doctors, with a national shortfall of more than 300 consultants. Staffing levels are at crisis point. In 2013 two-thirds of A&E departments failed to treat patients within 4 hours of arrival; almost 4,000 waited up to 12 hours in the autumn of 2013.

- Almost four in ten patients in England would not recommend their local A&E to friends and family, according to the government's own 'Friends and Family' report.

- NHS Chief Executives earn up to £280,000 a year, with average pay around £160,000 p.a. But they work in organisations where there is no market competition, and where politicians will not allow failing organisations to go bust. GP salaries have quadrupled in a decade, with most paid six-figure sums, including more than 600 on more than £200,000 p.a. While the number of patients per GP has fallen by 11% in 10 years, due to more GPs now working. Weekend services have, however, significantly worsened.

BUT Lord 'Owzat said: "The NHS is the Envy of The World." Did he not?

- However, The General Medical Council fails to take action against many doctors convicted of serious crimes. They are allowed to continue to practice, even when patients – and children among them – are put at risk.

- Nearly 10,000 claims for medical negligence were made against the NHS, in latest figures from the NHS Litigation Authority for the year 2011-12. In addition, there were 4,618 non-clinical negligence claims. A&E departments are the worst hit sector. This is a pay-out time-bomb for the NHS. And it reflects devastating effects on patients, according to a leading firm of solicitors.

- Patients admitted to hospital as medical emergencies on public holidays are 48% more likely to die within 7 days than "normal", said a new study in the *Emergency Medicine Journal*.

- Seven-day surgeries will require an extra 20,000 NHS staff, and cost an extra

LORD 'OWZAT'S CORNER OF NHS WONDERS

£1 billion of taxpayer's money for GPs to recruit and train staff, says the Royal College of GPs.

- Luke Jenkins died age seven at the Bristol Royal Hospital for Children on Good Friday last when his heart stopped a week after he underwent surgery – and an inquiry heard that a cardiac surgeon had to be called from home to resuscitate him.

- Doctors at Hillingdon Hospital in Uxbridge and at Chelsea and Westminster Hospital in central London missed a tumour on a two-year old toddler's CAT brain scan, and the child died, Westminster Coroner's Court was told.

BUT Lord 'Owzat said: "The NHS is the Envy of The World."

- Revalidation checks aimed at identifying poor-performing doctors will do nothing to help find or stop them, according to a poll of more than 5,600 colleagues by doctors.net.uk.

- Many people are still dying needlessly from bowel cancer as they are not screened early enough. Less than half of 60-year-olds have endoscopic screening.

- Fears for the elderly under new NHS drugs policy arose when NICE changed its criteria, to the disadvantage of the vulnerable elderly. Everyone is "equal", but some are more equal than others?

- NICE continues to refuse to fund new cancer drugs. One, which can sharply increase survival rates for patients with advanced pancreatic cancer, has been licensed for use in the UK but will only be available on private prescription. Survival rates for those with the disease have remained very poor and are little changed in the UK since the 1970s.

- Age discrimination & post-code lottery still abounds in the NHS, with some elderly people routinely denied potentially life-saving treatment simply because of where they live, said Paul Burstow MP. He showed dramatic variations between the availability of surgery for those over 75 in different parts of England. Huge care gaps in colorectal excision, breast excision, hip replacement, knee replacement, Inquinal hernia repair, Cholecystectomy, &c.

BUT LORD 'OWZAT SAID: "THE NHS IS THE ENVY OF THE WORLD."

- Surgeons warned that the largest hospital in Wales – the University Hospital of Wales in Cardiff – is "dangerous," with patients regularly dying because of increased waiting lists. Almost 100 relations of patients treated at the Princess of Wales Hospital at Bridgend in S. Wales have complained of poor care, with many suggesting problems akin to those in Mid-Staffordshire. Police have arrested three nurses there on suspicion of falsifying records.

- A police investigation has begun into the deaths of patients treated by a cancer surgeon, Mr. Sudip Sarker, who worked in the West Midlands and London, allegedly for falsifying his CV and whose fatality rates were found to be twice the average. He had, however, been allowed to continue working at Worcestershire Acute Hospitals Trust during an investigation into his practice and patients were not informed of concerns about his performance. He was *only suspended* after a study by the Royal College of Surgeons, *but its investigation remained unpublished for a year.*

- Cancer patients experienced life-threatening delays in diagnosis and treatment at West Hertfordshire Trust over at least three years, with over 120 patients affected. The Trust's Chief Executive, earning £282,000 p.a., resigned, with a pension pot of £3 million, but declined to comment. Local MP and government minister Mike Penning called for a national investigation on whether cancer patients are being denied care in this way.

- The proportion of outpatients waiting more than 18 weeks for NHS treatment has risen to its highest for 5 years.

- One in five NHS hospitals will face a funding deficit by the end of the 2013/14 financial year.

- Hospital Trusts are fiddling figures on NHS 'tourists' to protect their budgets, claiming public funds for overseas visitors who they know are not entitled to free care. Estimated annual cost to taxpayers is £400 million.

But Lord Owzat said: "The NHS is the Envy of The World."

- Mistakes are made in more than one in five of disciplinary cases against doctors that are dropped without a full investigation, a national audit discovered. More than 9,000 cases are referred to the General Medical Council each year but only about 200 reach a full tribunal hearing. This suggests that more than 2,000 medical staff each year may be allowed to continue to work even though allegations against them have not been investigated properly.

- NICE criticised the variable type and quality of care for people with autism in England, and set new standards to reduce the variability of care.

- NHS staff were given big pay-offs to keep quiet in a series of shocking NHS cover-ups, the Public Accounts Committee revealed. The Treasury had signed more than 1,000 severance payments linked to a compromise agreement for departing staff since March 2010. More than £28.4million was paid out.

- The number of elderly people taken to A&E units has doubled in 5 years as people have lost faith in care outside hospitals – and even though a hospital bed is itself a dangerous place to be. Figures from the Health and Social Care Information Centre.

- The NHS is scrapping key services for the elderly, especially concerning mental health, loneliness, bereavement and other problems, according to the Royal College of Psychiatrists and others.

- The Care Quality Commission's inspections were reported as "superficial" and produced reports that "bore little relation to reality" – this after years of its existence, in succession to the unlamented National Care Standards Commission, &c. [Chief Executive later knighted; Chairman gonged, too].

BUT Lord Owzat said: The NHS is the Envy of The World."

- Hospitals are wasting up to £63 billion a year by over-paying staff in pay-office blunders, with poor record-keeping and inept auditing.

- The NHS wasted more than £12 billion – a conservative estimate – on its failed central database IT project.

- The West London Coroner called for a female doctor to be suspended after she failed to recognise that a dying four-year-old girl was suffering from fatal septic shock and then laughed at a junior who questioned her diagnosis. The coroner ruled that the doctor's failures directly contributed to the girl's death.

- Thousands of patients are denied effective drugs – or never even told that they exist – when suffering from cancer and other serious illnesses, a report from the government's own Health and Social Care Information Centre said in January 2014. Professor David Haslam, Chairman of the National Institute of Health and Care Excellence (NICE) said patients should become more pushy to get medications which NICE has approved but which are still not offered by doctors or funded locally. Deference produces unnecessary deaths. NICE draft guidance, for example, said that a drug hailed as a potential cure for skin cancer will not be available to NHS patients as a first-line treatment.

- More than 10,000 cancer patients are dying needlessly every year because of 'blatant ageism' among doctors, Macmillan Cancer support said in January 2014.

- Thousands of men with prostate cancer may be denied life-extending treatment as NICE has limited access to new drugs.

BUT LORD 'OWZAT SAID: "THE NHS IS THE ENVY OF THE WORLD.

- Every year 14,000 people over 75 die of cancer in the UK who would have lived if UK survival rates matched those of the USA, according to a Macmillan Cancer report.

- Lung cancer survival rates in the UK are 9% worse than the European average for people under 45, but 44% worse for the over-75s – a pattern of ageist service-denial repeated for the common cancers – including those of the breast, stomach, ovaries, kidney and lymphatic system.

- Appalling standards have been revealed at 'killer' hospitals – Mid Staffs scandal, Morecambe Bay, &c., wich were then put on 'special measures.' An NHS culture prevailed where debate about failings in services and risks to patients was not tolerated.

- GPs were secretly charging care homes for basic treatment of elderly patients that should be provided free on the NHS, according to leading charities.

- Some NHS trusts are charging taxpayers for hundreds of private patients who have already paid for their own treatment, an NHS whistle-blower revealed in February 2014. Cover-ups by management, destruction of revealing documents, regulators looking the other way, lack of individual accountability and individual responsibility and an obsession with the dominance of process and 'the System.'

BUT Lord 'Owzat said: "The NHS is the Envy of The World."

- The National Audit Commission found that figures regularly published on hospital performance may bear no relation to the reality for thousands of patients, with waiting list times being falsely under-reported.

- The media regularly reports that a continuing crisis in nurse staffing numbers; fall in training posts available; and standards on the wards compromised. But there remains an NHS nursing focus on academic qualifications, with many "too posh to wash" the elderly.

- More than 60 years after the foundation of the NHS the Secretary of State for Health felt it necessary to tell doctors to stop thinking of patients just as "bodies harbouring a pathology" and instead recognise them as people.

- As late as January 2014 the care quality Commission made "continuity of care" one of its key 'indicators' in its assessments.

- A Poll revealed that 80 per cent of hospital medics would not want their friends and family to be treated by their colleagues.

- NHS England has made a dreadful and hugely costly boondoggle over the issue of the database of patients' medical records.

BUT Lord 'Owzat said: "The NHS is the Envy of The World."

- Another Poll showed that among GPs 67 per cent believed that there are doctors in the NHS not fit to practice. In fact, all doctors make elementary errors. But no elementary errors are uncovered by the profession, or remarked upon. As Dr. Bil Pickeirng has stressed, it is very dangerous indeed to allocate doctors into good performers and bad performers. All make errors. All need inspecting. But his proposal for an Independent Medical Inspectorate has been ignored.

- Meanwhile, there is *systematic* under-reporting of NHS mistakes which have damaged patients. And no appropriate checks on the performance of doctors.

- The Princess of Wales Hospital at Bridgend in South Wales was at the centre of a police investigation and an independent review ordered by the Welsh government, concerning standards of care, and alleged neglect which "amounted to torture" – according to a complaining family. A former nurse said that five years ago she raised serious concerns several times about patient care, but was ignored.

- Jeremy Hunt has sought to make his reputation by attacking inadequate NHS care. Rightly so. But...cf his colleague, Lord 'Owzat.

- Rural communities faced losing access to a local GP doctors' leaders warned, due to funding changes. Long waits for heart surgery in Wales were causing unnecessary deaths, and doctors expressed "grave concerns." Six hospitals had persistently high mortality rates.

BUT Lord 'Owzat said: "The NHS is the Envy of The World." Didn't he?

- Nursing cut-backs were linked to higher patient death rates in hospitals, as researchers argued that a nurse's work-load was crucial to post-op survival. Hospital patients were also more likely to die after surgery if they were treated by nurses who did not have a bachelor's degree. Nurses with a degree make up only 28% of Britain's nursing staff.

- A survey by NHS England found that a third of nurses, doctors and staff would not be happy to recommend their hospital to a friend or relation.

- Thousands of GPs were paid bonuses of up to £14,000 p.a. simply for staying in their jobs, (and irrespective of performance) official statistics revealed.

- Jeremy Hunt has now demanded a revolution in dementia care. And he revealed that by March 2015 dementia patients should receive a diagnosis within six weeks – *rather than the six months currently the case in parts of the country!*

BUT Lord 'Owzat said that "The NHS is the Envy of The World."

He DID, y'know!

- <u>All this information is from recent press reports. In addition, since this column was written on "facts" given out in 2013-14 I have collected an enormous file of new reports and cuttings on these and many other very seriously worrying NHS failures.</u>

Well then...

EITHER "We *are* the envy of the world", as Lord 'Owzat said. And so, please sign here on a £100 note & post it to me if you believe that, I say. I will send it on to a Swiss hospital, where the OECD – clearly quite wrongly – says the best care is to be found, and reliably so too. *They must need the money.*

"OR the entirely independent OECD in its global comparisons correctly shows the UK to be indeed miles behind the best in its services. In which case, it's time to yell for root-and-branch changes and a full, honest mature public debate about the alternatives!!!"

As they say in the Consultants' Masonic Lodges, "So mought it be!"

BUT Lord 'Owzat said: "The NHS is the Envy of The World."
Does he STILL say so??? A-mazing!!!

***

There is, of course, much very good NHS care – IF you can get it. But it remains a very mixed picture, as Roy Lilley's invaluable eletter nhsManagers.net shows regularly.

For example, as we go to press, the *Daily Telegraph* reported (31 July, 2015) the wonder of a golf-ball sized artificial heart implanted for the first time, by a surgeon, Professor Stephen Schueler, at the Freeman Hospital, Newcastle-on-Tyne.

BUT it also reported that "Cancer patients only sent for tests after three visits to doctor."A quarter of cancer patients were dissatisfied with their care, and were losing faith in their doctor, said scientists from University College, London and the University of Cambridge. They studied data from 70,000 patients, and found that of the 60,000 people who were diagnosed by their GP, nearly 13,300 had been seen two or three times before they were referred for cancer tests. More than one in 10 felt that information had been deliberately withheld from during their treatment.

Britain is eighth from bottom in league table comparisons of cancer survival in 35 Western countries, latest research shows. We are on a par with Poland and Estonia. Almost half of cancers in the UK are diagnosed at an advanced stage, when treatment is less likely to work.

So, Lord 'Owzat and others...as Joel Chandler Harris wrote, in *Proverbs of Uncle Remus*, "Youk'n hide de fier, but w'at you gwine do wid de smoke?"

EPISODE 43

The PM & The N£sd 'Reforms.' An Early Extract From His Memoirs, Part 1.

Obtained Exclusively for nhsManagers.net by Facey Romford, Jr.

I Stood In Time. My Prime Ministerial Memoirs [HarperEconomica; New York; Pentecost Publishers, London; The Humanity Press, Sydney, 2018].

By The Duke of Notting Hill and Chipping Thompson, KG, OM, FRSPR.

Chapter 19. Why were we never The Party of The Consumer? Our lost NHS opportunities & my mistakes herewith.

We ambushed the British people on the NHS.

We then took our peerages, our pensions, our gongs, our lecture fees, our company directorships, our retirement long-service pay-offs – and skedaddled to the sun. Incidentally leaving the fastest growing economy in Europe – even if with one of the biggest deficits in the Western world. That last inherited from the socialist trio of Mr. Gordon Brown, Mr. Ed Balls, and Mr. Ed Milliband!

I am a practical, pragmatic man – and self-confessedly not particularly political or ideological. But, it is indeed confession time. And on the NHS, my conscience pricks me still. I was guilty of wishful thinking. I was guilty of a lack of understanding of political philosophy. I concentrated on the sizzle, and not the sausage. And so we seriously misled the nation about the alternatives to a centrally-rationed state-monopoly health service. This, too, significantly because of our quasi-religious idolatry of a failed system. We played it "safe," instead of tackling the problems. As I will now seek to review.

We have thus gone on endorsing an illusory reality. We have declined our opportunities to use our political talents both to conciliate and to consistently insist on necessary change, directly confronting vested-interests. Macaulay was right to say that "agitation is inseparable from popular government," and we should have argued our case colloquially and directly. With energy. With knowledge. With passion and commitment. With veracity. In demonstrative language. At pace. And with all the commanding qualities of the best of us. This is what our expensive education is for, after all.

But, instead, a few thousand arrogant medical and trade union leaders have successfully opposed every measure which could have prevented many disasters, preventing us achieving a care system like the best in Europe. Knowledge has been borne down by self-interest.

It was *our job* to be interested in the feelings, wishes, and preferences of the 70 million instead. Yet a spirit of caste and of pernicious oligarchical domination has been allowed to prevail. We could not have changed the hearts and minds of a nation in a day. But with energy, focus, careful reasoning and citing the many daily examples of why things are as they are (and how they could change) with integrity and with humanity we could have made progress. And we could and should have cited the nature of the opposition to justify our changes, too!

But we have still not reconciled our knowledge and our opportunities. We have remained passive despite very visible wrongs. We have gone on telling private individuals that we know their business better than they know it for themselves. With condescending paternalism, too, we have sustained a two-tier system which reserves the best care for a small number, and whose cases differ from the rest only by their monetary value. And with our marginal reforms, too, we have made ourselves unpopular for nothing. We have not been alert to a keen sense of the absurd, although the revelations of NHS realities should have rung alarm bells far sooner. Our key mistake – mine, I admit – was failing to set out clear arguments for a free and competitive society and a pragmatic, trial-and-error structure of constant learning and innovation.

As Facey Romford, Jr. has shown in his columns, and as Gove was always telling me, I should have created educated public support for change, and then participated as a leader by directly implementing it.

Instead, we have gone on accepting that power must be exercised by educated "experts," a small elite acting in the interests of the people. This idea has been maintained despite universal suffrage. But it has produced neither self-responsibility in the individual, nor acceptable NHS services. The right to vote, too, should be inseparable from a level of education that would ensure it is exercised responsibly, too.

It was the great Macaulay who wrote "There is only one cure for the evils which newly acquired freedom produces, and that cure is freedom…many politicians of our time are in the habit of laying it down as a self-evident proposition, that no people ought to be free till they are fit to use their freedom. The maxim is worthy of the fool in the old story, who resolved not to go into the water till he had learnt to swim. If men are to wait for liberty till they become wise and good in slavery, they may indeed wait for ever."

Critically, I should have insisted that *we* were the Party of the consumer – and that we would give everyone control over individual funds. I ask myself now, when will any politicians realise that the only real power for the individual is when they control a budget, and when there is a proper competitive market??? Give them the money! Then stand back and watch huge change! Give individuals real controls. Abandon the protection of the so-called 'public- service' Trade unions and the medical vested-interests. Give up central controls. Trust the individual.

At the same time I would now remind the nation that it is people and businesses that create wealth, not governments or bureaucrats. Indeed, that it is diligence, energy, judgement and thrift which builds investment. This is led by entrepreneurs not by bureaucrats. It works best, too, in a world of law-based liberty and of fair-dealing, as Edmund Burke has it.

In my first days as leader of the opposition I should have broached with the nation this issue about the true basis for a really fine health service. For real reform has many elements. It takes authority. It takes time. It takes cooperation. It takes leadership. It requires a vibrant use of language. And in a tight electoral cycle it cannot be done unless

THE PM & THE N£SD 'REFORMS.' AN EARLY EXTRACT FROM HIS MEMOIRS, PT 1

you make the right start from the first day. I should have broached these issues on day one. And then built up understanding in the public mind, day by day, until we came into government. We could then have gone forward creatively once we were elected. We did not do so. I did not do so. The Party did not do so.

And so....by sabotaging our own imaginations, by refusing to consider creative changes, by side-lining the real solutions, we produced neither new arts nor effective services.

We should have founded all that we did with the NHS and other public-services in free-market economics, self-reliance and individual responsibility. Certainly, with market regulation. Certainly, with much better education so that people understood the choices before us. And at the heart of the matter we should have pursued bold political thinking and radical supply-side and demand-side reforms. Instead, the NHS remains a national disaster.

I appreciate now – and with startling clarity – that if you are going to change anything big, you have to do it right at the start of your government. Tony Blair says the same in his memoirs. Professor Milton Friedman made this key point decades ago. For very soon the vested interests and their licensed pressure groups – which are very well financed and with strong media profiles – take over the debate. They frighten the public. They are very well organised. They are relentless. And they influence the polls against you. You have to move swiftly, and with determination. Indeed, Tony Blair's own memoirs make the same points. Indeed, we now have the very same regrets.

In the year 2,000 *we* should have been much better prepared to be the government which constantly emphasised that the best services and the best businesses are those which prosper because they serve the wants of others in a competitive market. One where individual service-users have a genuine choice of providers. One where they can take their tax-based money to a preferred alternative purchaser and to an alternative competitive provider if they wish. The best purchasers and the effective providers profit because they serve real needs well. This is not a crime, although by not making the case for the good we made it seem so. The NHS should offer a timely, uniquely personal, intimate and effective service. The record, is, however, very significantly short of target.

All these errors on my own part reflected a great emotional and psychological conflict within myself. I am a liberal conservative, not a Thatcherite. I wanted the State to be right. I wanted the existing NHS to work. I believed in what you might call its plot, its structure, its narrative. My family life-history was a big influence, too. I thought the problems were merely technical. And that they could be relatively easily resolved.

In addition, self-deception has played a major part. We have been blinded by our own assumptions. This has worked at an institutional level, too. And we have refused to see truths because we would have been obliged to deal with their implications. There are things – like the disasters every day in the NHS – which no politician has wanted to discover or admit. If we had told the full truth we would have faced immense public criticism, ridicule, loss of confidence, loss of credibility, stature – and parliamentary seats. So at the institutional level our motives were fairly clear, even if on a personal level they were less so.

Nevertheless, we created a myth and then buried the truth. The human penchant for self-deception is immense. Our minds unconsciously screen out the unpleasant and filter in the pleasant. However, for decades we have not distinguished true from false, right from wrong. And when the false is cast in the image of the world's desire and the true in something the world will neither face nor fathom or wants to do, then serious damage prevails.

Once we committed ourselves to the erroneous position of the NHS as a state monopoly public service, we reacted to contrary evidence from other systems by refusing to admit it. A poet – I forget who now – wrote that "Faith, fanatic Faith, once wedded fast/To some dear falsehood, hugs it to the last." A rosy glow of wishful thinking has marginalised scepticism. Bureaucratic structures let responsibility fall between many stools. And we all gave way to social pressures rather than trust in our own judgements or powers.

This is the classic conflict between mind and heart, thought and emotion. Our assumptions lead us, unconsciously, towards accepting what others say is reasonable, and which favour our own self-interest too. I say to my successors now that we have ignored the warnings that experience has offered, and led ourselves away from conclusions which cause us bother, or which threaten us politically. And it is easier, too, to repeat at the ward level what the higher-ups say than to think for oneself. And those who have tried to do so in the NHS – like the whistle-blowers or the dissident Chairmen – have paid a dreadful personal price when questioning the general framework set by the top people.

The defence of budgets, too, has been a major actor. For the budget, power and prestige of NHS leaders has encouraged them to repel any suggestion that it has erred, duped itself, misled or manipulated the public. To them any cure has seemed more damaging than the organisational disease. Dissenters and other theorists have faced a wall of disbelief and disinterest, and the media – until very recently – have reinforced the illusions.

Too late perhaps, I have learned in my "journey" that I was wrong. We needed to be truly bold. This is the time to say so, if we are to recover the situation now. It is no good remaining mundane, and only talking about things which the vested interests and the trade unions permit. If you like, this is a conflict between art – or the ways in which innovations come about – and existing mediocrity which quite suits the producer interests but which does much harm to the users of services.

We needed to take some risks – without putting patients *at* risk. We needed to be intrepid, in a new context which we could and should have created over many years by educating the public. But we avoided making the vitally necessary cultural and educational arguments, and thus evaded the necessary economic reforms of the NHS which we should have undertaken. We suppressed the necessary, innovative trial-and-error originality, variety and creative novelty which the situation demanded. And we still paid the political price anyway for the much less fundamental tinkering that we did. Ask Lord Andrew Lansley!

We ought, instead, to have bitten the real bullet and gone for the real transformative actions. There were many good ideas presented to us – by the Institute of Economic Affairs, by the Adam Smith Institute, by the economists at George Mason University in Virginia, by UK commentators like Roy Lilley and Professor John Spiers, both of whom I knew. And by the late Arthur Seldon, who had blazed the trail with Lord Ralph Harris at the Institute of Economic Affairs. But we chose not to notice them.

What do I say to my successors now? It is this. To get to the root of the problems of the

NHS we needed to take a creative leap. To make the impossible possible. To go beyond what people said was required. To encourage new ways of seeing and feeling. Indeed, it is always those transformative changes which are initially forecast to be disruptive which actually make the great changes in cultures and in society.

Of course, I know that any real attempt to reform the NHS wholesale will be tumultuous. But here I wish to quote the novelist Hjnif Kureishi, who, in talking of the works of the imagination speaks of being "in useful trouble." We should be there! Kureishi says that "Being truly transgressive is one of the most difficult things there is." And that imagination, though hazardous, though apparently producing disorder, though often combustible, is actually the source of all our illumination. The world is risky, he says. And "So it should be."

Alas, I repressed, foreclosed, and ignored creativity. And so I allowed us to be comfortable within the existing impasse. However, we did not will away the issues. And so the same problems arise, repeatedly. Yet, in Emerson's words, "Growth comes by shocks." It is a key element in us reconceiving what we think we know.

As Kureishi makes clear, we need to stress again that we are the creators of our own situations, our own lives. It is up to each of us to help reshape "realities." What services we can have are what we make. It is the daily question for us all of how we want to be, to live, and within what kind of culture and structure. Or, as I would now put this, we are not merely the product of the forces of Milliband Marxigookery and Klingfilmerology. It is, instead, up to each of us to imagine, and to act.

Even at a much less philosophical level the NHS has still to learn the abc of economics. That the only way any service or business can fulfil itself and prosper is by providing goods and services that people want and will fund. Working out how to deploy assets effectively, and investing capital in demanded services. All of which, by the by, boosts economic growth, creates new wealth and jobs, and lifts all living standards. We need many more such businesses.

And we need incentives to encourage entrepreneurship here too – in business and in so-called 'public-services.'

It is only a society open to real new talent and ideas – one which encourages innovation (and social mobility) – which will give us a better health service. Meanwhile, we have allowed the NHS to be controlled by an economic and professional aristocracy – in effect – and by trade unions whose role is to serve themselves. It is they who rig markets, who get government to favour them, who erect barriers to new entrants, who restrict competition, and who use their political clout to embed their positions and their privileges. Instead of concentrating on adding value as determined by service users they defend their own interests, and then present these as the 'national interest.'

NHS organisations have long been safe, too, in the knowledge that we would not allow any of them to go bust, and so there has been no market discipline. Politics! We did make some small gains in allowing private firms to compete for contracts. But alas, as PM, I mainly allowed commercial relationships to be side-lined, and permitted politicised relationships to dominate NHS debates. And so we are still stuck with corporatism. With subsidies to the incompetent. With political push-and-shove. With restrictions on innovation and entrepreneurship. And with the dominance of entrenched and too often complacent and condescending professional power-structures.

It was Lord Macaulay who said that "the most efficient weapon with which men can encounter falsehood is truth." And so Iain Duncan Smith has thus reshaped welfare. Most importantly emphasising that work is the key to fulfilling your personal potential.

So, too, Michael Gove brought back the emphasis on excellence and higher standards in schools. I made a mistake in moving him. For he was recovering traditional teacher-led lessons, emphasising core knowledge, toughening grading, reforming the training of teachers, encouraging schools freed from LEA control, and closing down the progressive-haven that was Ofsted. All initiatives fiercely opposed by teacher unions, defending their entrenched power bases. But Iain and Michael stood up to the producer interests, which have for so long intimidated governments. Of course, the quite dreadful results from so-called progressive liberal education helped Michael in particular. But it still took guts to get it done. Treading softly could not have done it.

These two colleagues did much to reshape our political positioning, as I should have done with the NHS. They realised the importance of opportunity cost in society – that if you do one thing, you can't do something else with the same money. And that competitive pressures push performance up and costs down. Both have realised that it is necessary to change the situation so profoundly that no future government will be able change it all back. We can defend our actions intellectually *and* politically. They are achieving genuine long-term change which is both transformational and irreversible. This is what must now be done with the NHS too.

Both Iain and Michael have emphasised that the solution in society is to promote competition, encourage performance-related pay, remove barriers to entry, unleash informed and financially-empowered consumer choice, reduce subsidies and provide direct economic incentives for better performance. The key rubric has to be that you do not survive if you do not serve customers. And if you do not allocate your capital efficiently so to do.

Both Iain and Michael have the common-touch, with a colloquial style, and one which hits the targets too. They have each expressed the popular voice. They each had the necessary command over the matter, together with the language, the courage, the integrity, the humanity, the veracity, the suppleness and powers of reasoning, the energy, and the audience. The public admired their courage, and strongly approved the results. But on the NHS we were neither brave nor ambitious nor relevant to the real needs for change. We continued to quarter a failed health system on an unfortunate and misled nation. In many senses this was repressive.

Ian's and Michael's reforms proved to be widely endorsed – and this despite the howls of outrage on the left and especially from the BBC. And if we had consistently made the case – during our years in opposition and then in government – for a realignment of the NHS on market-principles and disciplines the British people would surely have supported us.

We could then have deliberately focussed on improving both the patient's experience, and specific outcomes for individuals. We could have reconstructed the NHS to achieve the results that everyone in continental Europe takes as the norm. Improving access,

THE PM & THE N£SD 'REFORMS.' AN EARLY EXTRACT FROM HIS MEMOIRS, PT 1

standards, funding, and liberating the service-users from the predominance of 'process' and bureaucratisation. But just following the rules, without any personal compassion, produces merely obedience and mediocrity. And so we see the actual disasters in treatments, and the hundreds of thousands of unnecessary and entirely avoidable personal tragedies. Yet on the key task of encouraging much essential self-responsibility and lifestyle changes we made the progress of nowt multiplied by zero, squared to the 55th.

I urge a future Conservative PM not to do what we did. When we came into government we faced moments of truth. But we distorted the future, and shut-out the genuine possibilities for great improvements in services, and in outcomes. The repercussions are with us, and the *next* generation, still. We wasted our chances to make patients feel better and get better, as well as raising morale by helping staff feel better about themselves. If outcomes had improved, if costs had fallen, if satisfactions had risen then staffs could have been proud of what they achieved. Good services require an exactness of execution, reliable access, consistent coordination and integrity over time, and high staff morale – all important to motivate attitudes, production, and cooperation.

It's a key truth that in the complex tasks of the NHS people have to know what they are doing, they have to want to learn and improve. People cannot be driven. They have to *want* to cooperate both with fellow workers and with the patients themselves. If they do this it is a formula for better workplace morale, consistency of execution, and better outcomes – including those defined by the individual patient's own values and preferences.

Reliability of services is essential. But the NHS is still very hit-and-miss. To make services reliable requires a conscientious commitment by all staffs, from janitor to top doc. And good team-work in a structure which has order, coherence and certainty in the supply chain. Most NHS employees are not doctors, of course. But the juniors and the top docs all have to follow proper procedures. Look at the difference that washing your hands makes when necessary. But they still don't do it! Or getting the right data onto the patient's chart and records. Or measuring lab results properly and acting on them promptly. Here, the requirement is extreme reliability and competence. And in a system with market-disciplines this is all surely more likely to happen than in the secret garden of the NHS?

But we hid the better ways to go forward, behind our treatment of the NHS as a national religion, behind our own fear, and in the dark shadows cast by the self-interested barricades erected by the vested interests. By doctors, by nurses, by managers, by trade unions, by all the producers who want the services to suit themselves first and foremost.

1. We failed to hold elites to account.

2. We accepted their own view of how they expected to be treated.

3. We also permitted professional influence to be wielded in secret.

4. We failed to individually empower the users of services with a specific personal tax-based fund which they could move to a preferred provider.

5. We failed to introduce Health Savings Accounts, with an 'excess' to discourage marginal demands.

6. We evaded the opportunities in a new digital world to measure procedures, values and outcomes, and to be more demanding of ourselves and of others.

7. We ignored the modern truth that all career paths are becoming more demanding, in a more complex, necessarily more coordinated, large-scale production process.

8. We failed to ask the question about public-services as to how many staff protected by government and trade unions do or do not actually produce as much value as their pay and on-costs. Certainly, many people in the labour force were under-employed, and given insufficient chances for personal improvement. Many others should not have been there at all. We need to raise the productivity of the entire workforce.

9. Crucially, we allowed personal aspiration to be a negative phrase.

Instead, we got the politics and the persuasions wrong from the start. We should have made it clear what we intended, come what may, and then gained public support and understanding over time, as well as negotiating a necessary and conciliatory flag of truce with the professionals.

However...

10. We allowed the predominance of process to get in the way of compassionate individual concerns.

11. We protected "professionals" from public displeasure.

12. We failed to make full use of public complaints, and the truths that these should have told us. Look at The NHS Ombudsman – seriously investigating only 3% of complaints!

13. We undermined individual self-responsibility, on the part both of potential patients and by those employed in the NHS and in social and elderly care.

Indeed, we got the balance between freedom and control wrong in so many respects. An unlucky 13 indeed!

More...we failed to use new digital technologies to make step-by-step changes to regulation and accountability.

And we failed to remove many evils and anomalies which damaged both patients and the staff themselves.

Critically, we did not tackle the obesity problems with the necessary resolution. And we did not use economic incentives to encourage individual self-responsibility and changes in life-style. This remains a lethal combination.

With state paternalism we thus did enormous damage to hundreds of thousands – indeed, cumulatively, to millions – of lives.

And, indeed, when scandals did come to public light – I think here of Mid-Staffs. and Morecambe Bay, and of MPs expenses, in particular – this revelatory knowledge was not swiftly acted upon either. What was discovered was also not due to we politicians but to the brave internal NHS whistle-blowers (many of whose careers were thus wrecked) and to the media, especially to the *Daily Telegraph* and the *Daily Mail*. NHS managers and doctors hid disasters in hospitals, and protected one another, again to the great detriment of the public. *Perhaps they still do?*

We faced a historic challenge. We had to confront science and its innovations; longevity and its consequences; population increase and its intensification; the brilliant innovations of new drugs; the narrow reliance on tax-money, and its shortage; increased expectations and demands; falling productivity and enormous wastage, together with managerial bungling and a lack of transparency and accountability. All of which now combine to ensure the nemesis of the NHS as it is presently constructed.

The NHS was started 65 years ago. It is an obsolete object from Another Age. It is by now a creaking, an unsustainable, and a mythical relic of a long-gone period. But it remains – like the BBC – the default position of the left. However, both of them (allegedly the envy of the world) have in fact been left behind by modern realities and by consumer preferences which now remain to be properly and fully empowered.

We do all, of course, want to live in a fair and sensitively humane society. But… *Time has indeed revealed the hidden truth. State monopolies do **not** deliver.*

[to be continued]…

NB. Editorial note, 5 August 2015. When this and subsequent Episodes were written in 2013 it was widely assumed that Mr. Cameron would lose the forthcoming 2015 election, whereas he did win an overall working majority, leading to the resignations of Mr. Milliband and Mr. Clegg. However, the analysis offered remains very cogent. Even if there is now very little likelihood of Labour ever forming another majority government. The Great Escape, indeed! However, what will the Conservatives now do?

EPISODE 44

The PM & The N£sd 'Reforms.' An Early Extract From His Memoirs, Part 2.

I Stood In Time. My Prime Ministerial Memoirs, By The Duke of Notting Hill and Chipping Thompson, KG, OM, FRSPR.

[Continued from previous episode].

Now that I am out of the firing-line at long last, and serving as Governor of Coventry Island, I have carefully appraised what we did and did not do for and with the NHS. Well, it IS a grim story indeed. And more damaging, too, to millions as yet unborn.

It is time that we faced the real problems and truths of the British myths about the NHS. It is NOT the envy of the world. Far from it. No-one has ever copied it! It is time that we faced this, and ceased to prolong the agonies by deceiving ourselves.

As I have said, our key mistake – mine, I admit – was failing to set out clear arguments for a free and competitive society and a pragmatic, trial-and-error structure of constant learning and innovation. At the same time, to remind the nation that it is people and businesses that create wealth, not governments. And that diligence, energy, judgement and thrift builds investment, which is led by entrepreneurs not bureaucrats. In a world of law-based liberty and of fair-dealing, as Edmund Burke has it.

It well bears repetition that we should have founded all that we did with the NHS and other public services in free-market economics, self-reliance and individual responsibility. Certainly, with market regulation. Certainly, with much better education so that people understood the choices before us.

And at the heart of the matter we should have pursued bold political thinking and radical supply-side and demand-side reforms. Instead, the NHS is a national disaster.

It has been a grave error to insist upon passionate and undying love for the NHS, which is a man-made and not a God-given institution. And one which needs to be fundamentally re-made. However, our genuflection to this imagery has made a rational public debate about funding healthcare impossible. Even though in every other avenue of life people have seen that as financially-empowered individual consumers they can influence services, choices, quality and outcomes.

We have failed to build on this knowledge, and to argue persistently and consistently for what should have been the core values of open markets with reference to every incident in health care. We should have based all our vitally necessary changes to the culture of the NHS itself in these fundamental values. We should not have been timid about argument and agitation, either. For that is inseparable from popular government. We could not change the heart and mind of the nation in a day. We should have applied ourselves over time.

We should have broken away from the consensus on the NHS, and all its myths about its uniqueness, its fairness, and its clinical qualities. It is not the existence of markets which has denied people good services. It is their absence. And thus the loss of the vitally necessary appraisal of management and services where the need to attract willing individual revenues should be a condition of existence for any institution set up to offer individual services.

This failure in our thinking led us for many years to tolerate an NHS culture in which any debate about deficiencies in services and risks to patients was not tolerated. Look at what happened to that Chairman at Brighton. He told doctors that potential cancer patients were clearly anxious about waiting times, and would like their symptoms checked much sooner. This was regarded as outrageous, and the docs [a theodicy!] ganged up against him. Yet we have seen recently in a new report in the journal *Lancet Oncology* that almost 90% of such patients wanted further and faster investigation, even if their symptoms carried just a 1% risk of cancer. Which is surely a normal, human thought.

Yet any implied criticism of anyone – and especially a senior doctor! – has been entirely contrary to the prevailing NHS culture. It was a career-ending issue for that Brighton chap who suggested people should be seen by oncologists sooner. He depicted a very poor picture of Brighton in his book, *The Invisible Hospital and The Secret Garden, An Insider's Account of the NHS Reforms* [*See footnote with details – Ed.*]. And even now, 20 years later, there remain many deficits in fixed thresholds in the NHS giving times by which such patients must be seen, and for understandable psychological anxieties to be laid to rest. Although NICE guidelines *suggest* – but do not require – that patients whose symptoms indicate a 5% risk or higher need further tests to be done.

And just look again at the Mid Staffs scandal. At Morecambe Bay. And at the many other NHS Trusts in 'special measures.' 'Killer hospitals.' We have seen, too, that the many illusory substitutes for giving individual patients control over funds – 'community' consultation; Citizen's Juries; hospital ratings; socialisticised enquiries by the Klingfilm Fund – have still not made sufficient difference. If any.

Even Ofsted-style outfits like the often enfeebled Care Quality Commission have only scratched the surface. And even when a CQC inspection report is reliable (which it often is not) just being told about local services being good or poor does not help individual patients move elsewhere, nor enable them to command a necessarily individual, personal, timely service. Only money does that. Mobile money, in the hands of the individual. Tax-based funds, transferred to them for this purpose. For, to the provider, only the potential loss of revenues 'Speaks Truth to Power.' Only the removal of funding makes employees jump.

GP Fundholding had shown this. But we were too timid to put patient fund-holding in place, following the successful example of social care personal budgets. We missed that one. We should have extended those personal tax-based budgets into every nook and cranny of the NHS.

What a shock it would have been for the self-satisfied NHS provider and the complacent and condescending manager and doctor if every service-user could say "Thanks, but no thanks. I'll go round the corner to another provider." New providers would have bid for the work. Either with new facilities, or for a management contract to do better with what was there already. But we dropped the ball. We missed the opportunity to release the real power of direct economic incentives.

Instead, we remain with a two-tier NHS, in which the rich wisely enough go private – which no-one does in Europe, since all can get to good and reliable services. Here British patients, however, still differ in their monetary value to the medical professional. This is morally wrong. Indeed, the reasons for wide and market-led changes are rooted here, too, in fairness and in self-responsibility. Which is underlined by the nature of the vested interest opposition itself to such changes. Many professionals, managers, bureaucrats and trade union officials have no interest or feeling in common with the many millions who might well otherwise insist on being treated as individuals.

We opened the book on the wrong page on day one, alas. Lansley, as it turned out, was the wrong man, too. A bureaucrat. We could have done much to improve quality, to change attitudes, and to make a reality of choice by introducing patient fund-holding for all. It could have cut costs. It could have prompted new suppliers to come into the picture. It could have said to everyone in the NHS: "Make your moves now on change and improvement. There is no going back."

Especially if it had been linked to personal insurance, paid by taxation and topped-up if required by the individual. Here, money, choice, self-responsibility [with an insurance 'excess' to deter some daft demands] could have been closely inter-woven. And if those who were said to be unable to use personal social care budgets successfully – the elderly, the disabled, those with long-term conditions – but who have succeeded with them, why not everyone else?

The workings of the new social care budgets also produced greater staff satisfaction, higher morale, with both personal and customer fulfilment. It freed much of the "system" from mystification. It changed many lives in positive ways. And it put into the hands of every user personal controls over money, placing everyone on the same footing as the middle-classes.

But in the NHS itself what now is the situation for all those *compelled* by state diktat to be equally badly served, by Milliband's and Cable's collation of socialisticied muddle?

Let me here deal with one of the black doves which socialists like to have hovering above – that the individual cannot be trusted to make decisions for themselves. Recent experience – under Labour and Conservative governments – of social care budgets given to individuals for their personal decision-making proves otherwise. As well as raising morale amongst staffs. And the new generation around us have shown how skilled they are, too, at learning new and apparently complicated things.

In his recent book *Average is Over* (New York, Dutton, 2013), the Harvard economist Tyler Cowen has shown that the enormous global growth of digital games have produced important new evidence about cognition, entertainment, education and the ability of the individual (apparently otherwise unskilled, if we are to believe self-appointed NHS "experts"!) to process information rapidly and effectively As Cowen says, "These games are changing the way we interact with one another and how we spend our time. What they reach us will show up in our work lives, as indeed it already has."

AND: "Even those on the low end of the income scale can now afford astonishingly complex games that require computational muscle far beyond what was conceivable a decade ago."

In fact, people make complex decisions all the time, once they have the information. We should stop hiding it. Indeed, the internet is breaking down all these barriers to professional performance data and accountability. Everyone is getting very familiar with machine feed-back, and we must surely move swiftly now into enabling this in the NHS. By providing both the factual and the analytical material for individuals to consider, and by giving them individual financial leverage so that they can make use of the new knowledge.

People expect to use the internet now to help them negotiate opportunities, assess and manage risks, navigate complex situations, compare results and outcomes, and thus seek out entirely legitimate individual advantages in terms of personal healthcare. They are finding that they can indeed learn and develop talents and make choices long thought by "experts" to be out of their reach. They are getting used to expecting something more than ordinary or average, and they want to find out where they can get access to something special. Which, if you are diagnosed with the deadly cancer of the pancreas or of breast or lung cancer, for example, makes the most utterly perfect sense!!!

I'm not surprised to read in Cowen's work that the most consulted "doctor" in the USA today is Google. It gives users access to over three billion medical articles on the web – and by typing your symptoms into Google you can see the science, and advice and experiences from expert patient groups. You can then decide to see your doctor or not, to go to A&E as an emergency, or either take more medication or stop taking it completely. There is growing evidence that intelligent machines are already very good at evaluating human performance, and the day is very near when they will measure the quality of doctors. They will replace the 'magic' by the facts.

We are surely not so far away from this – despite the Moose-like yells of the docs and the public-service unions. We will soon reach the situation when everyone in the UK has such access to individual doctor performance. Who they are, where they were trained, what are their specialisms, what do expert patient groups say about them, what are their outcomes, their rates of unexpected recall, infection rates, necessary repairs, and do other doctors send their daughters to them?

Some doctors will refuse to take part. This may not be supportable for long if they want to go on having patients and being paid. After all, it was public money which paid for their training. Those doctors rated in the lower quarter will have to retrain and improve. Average or below-par performance will not be tolerated, or be enabled to be hidden by doctors, who today cover-up for one another. The poor and the less-well served will do better in terms of services, too. Access to information will be equalised. Today, the poor and culturally/socially powerless do least well, while the informed middle-classes know how to find out about the best professionals. Today, mateocracy rules. And it reinforces the protected situation of accreditors, of tenure, of slackness in medicine. A new world is only just round the corner, however.

THE PM & THE N£SD 'REFORMS.' AN EARLY EXTRACT FROM HIS MEMOIRS, PT 2

This digital revolution – and the consequent rise in competitiveness – will be the greatest incentive to improved individual performance that I can envisage. It will probably be the end of condescending doctors, sanctimonious Royal Colleges and powerful professional vested-interests, arrogance in white coats, and the awe in which they expect to be received. It will entirely change the protective role of accredited regulators and supervisors of public-services, who have been failing us all so seriously. Just look at the "performance" of the Care Quality Commission, and its predecessors. The lamentable National Care Standards Commission. Or the NHS Ombudsman. And the General Medical Council, The Royal Academy of Royal Colleges, the King's Fund, &c.

This new digital analysis and publication of data is only just over the horizon. Of course, the patients who benefit most will be those who live self-responsibility. Those who drink heavily, smoke, do not exercise, live on sausages, Fried Mars Bars and Big Macs, do not take medications properly, do not look out for changes in their bodies – all these will still do least well, whoever their doctor. Just as doctors will have to live with the reputation that their performance reveals, so too patients will have to live or die with their life-styles. Indeed, the incentives for both sets is to improve, to achieve better results, to be motivated for change.

Let me reiterate the point that people can indeed make their own choices, and be informed so to do. Let me quote again from Tyler Cowen:

"It's remarkable what a good job the games industry, especially in its online manifestations, has done educating us in playing the games. ...the educational accomplishment and intellectual advances are remarkable. Many of those role-playing, time-extended, multi-player games are forbiddingly hard or at least so it seems. They involve hundreds of virtual characters, not always human, spread across (virtual) geographic space and engaged in trade, battles, elections, and many other activities, all governed by complex rules within the game and governed by complex software at the level of player interface. And yet people learn those games nonetheless and often master them."

AND: "The many millions of people these games have educated include millions who would not otherwise be thought of as educational winners or job market winners. It is actually the most astonishing education success story of our time and it is driven by commercial incentives and the desire to make learning fun. Games-based interaction tends to be hands-on and step-by-step, moving up a ladder of complexity with rewards along the way to keep the game player interested."

Cowen stresses, too, and surely correctly, that machine-aided self-education by the iPad and many other computer-related devices and programmes encourage trial-and-error advances, and the assessment of possibilities by the individual.

And so...do you still want to insist that only self-appointed NHS "Experts" can make decisions about *your* personal values and preferred outcomes?

A big lesson, too, is that for government wanting to help improve healthcare, long-term strategy is paramount when compared with political tactics. A bias towards the familiar is probably the quickest way into the quicksand, too. To make the kinds of progress which we need, to have assets in place, to achieve the best structure of openness, we need an adaptive and a self-revising system. Or in chess-terms, we have to reach a superior position so that the structure "plays itself."

Pawn to King four! *Your* move!

[to be continued]...

EPISODE 45

The PM & The N£sd 'Reforms.' An Early Extract From His Memoirs, Part 3.

I Stood In Time. My Prime Ministerial Memoirs, By The Duke of Notting Hill and Chipping Thompson, KG, OM, FRSPR.

[Continued from previous episode].

As I sit here under the palm trees on Coventry Island I ask myself…

Did we plant the English Oak of freedom and success in the NHS more widely, under which service-users could safely shelter? No.

Did we even seed the acorn? Did we nurture it? Did we help change ways of thinking/feeling/living for millions? No. We did not. None of it.

Did we show people how they could do more, without being always directed by government? No. We did not.

Did we enhance self-responsibility and necessary changes in life style? And at that time, too, encourage much more acceptance of individual responsibility by those working in the service? No. Not that, either.

Did we do much to undermine centralised statist controls? Alas, not that.

Did we improve the NHS, or did it prove un-improvable? You know the answer as well as I do. More so probably as you are probably stuck with using the threadbare services.

As I look back now, all this failure to act seems incomprehensible. But, alas, again we listened to the Royal Academy of Vested Interests, to the great British Whitewash Co. PLC, to the doctor's trade union BMe-Me, and to the socialisticised Klingfilm Fund. There was an obvious answer to follow, and one we should have adopted without needing to start any new wars. The successful individual Social Care Budgets could have been extended into acute care. But again we failed to extend the gains of these new social care budgets to the entire NHS. Just as we evaded the need to price services.

This has produced the inevitable result that we were always overwhelmed by demands. And we did not have the broader range of funds – which I see working so well in nearby Australia – to provide the services which are common-or-garden on the European continent too.

And, as the neo-classical economists make clear – and which I have been reading, in retirement – if you artificially lower or eliminate prices (as does the NHS) you will *both* increase demand *and* reduce supply. Hence all our shortages in care. Hence a non-virtuous circle of misery. Hence the absence of economic incentives – both for new supply and for self-responsible demand.

Here I recall the actor Joan Allen, cast as the unfairly beleaguered Senator Laine Hanson in the film 'The Contender.' Where – as a nominee for the Vice-Presidency – she says that "Principles only mean something when they are inconvenient."

It *was* politically inconvenient for us to pursue root-and-branch radical market changes for the NHS. But we were wrong. Real market-change was an idea whose time had come. Yet we made serious misjudgements. We were deterred by private polls, by partisanship, by malevolence, by vested interests, by ignorance. We completely failed to educate the public. Indeed, as a political leadership we failed to educate ourselves! We failed to lead. We failed to deliver. We had a choice – to be faithful to our short-term Party interests, or to the necessary results of change. We were loyal to our Party, and to ourselves. But we played the traitor to the necessary outcomes. This I very much regret.

Dr. Liam Fox (a GP before he became an MP) was right to argue that ring-fencing NHS spending reinforced the idea that the NHS is sacred, and also that money would solve its problems. We spent much more. NHS budgets went up from £57b in 2002 to £111b in 2015-16. This year, 2017, they will go beyond £115b. And next year? But we see that the problems go on getting worse.

Outcomes remain behind those of the best nations in Europe. Look at our dreadful cancer results. Waste, inept management, too many dreadful individual patient experiences, domination of services in their own vested interests by the producers and their Trade Unions. And, critically, too, we refused to countenance the better mix of spending, and the over-lapping sources of funding which more successful health services have adopted for years past.

Annual expenditure on the NHS has almost doubled since 1999 – BUT we are still spending less than France or Germany (which have mixed funding systems in a combined public/private structure). And our results are MUCH worse than theirs. On cancer, on strokes, on other key killers.

AND if we want to be able to pay for future medicine – including the many innovations not yet thought of – and with a much larger and older population with co-morbidities too, we have to find new ways to fund this. And to do so with fewer taxpayers. So, price. Charges. Compulsory extra insurance. Co-payment. Fees to see GPs. It may seem odd coming from me, but it is obvious that there is no other way! And it is high time we set out the real facts, the real choices, and prompted a mature public debate.

It is, of course, harder to argue for more support for free enterprise, and to mobilise public opinion if you are half-hearted about it. Here, I confess, I got it badly wrong. The European funding examples were at our elbow. But we ignored them because we kept on with the myth about the NHS being the envy of the world. You might call this 'Owzatism!

Our key mistake was failing to set out clear arguments for a free and competitive society. In which a much improved health service would have been a natural extension.

THE PM & THE N£SD 'REFORMS.' AN EARLY EXTRACT FROM HIS MEMOIRS, PT 3

So, some health warnings to begin with – for my readers and for those who come into politics next.

Those who believe in Mr. Milliband's anti-capitalist view that we should all join hands and cross the finishing line joint-last together, read on for re-education! Or observe the events in France since the advent of Mr. Francois Hollande! Who Mr. Milliband so much admires!

Those who believe that we are not all the same, and that we should celebrate differences while doing all we can to encourage quality in services, read on and tell a friend!

Those who believe that a key to a better NHS is to actually listen to patients, tell your MP and your doctor!

Those who accept that doctors knowing best is not the same as listening best – surgeons please note! – buy several copies of this book as gifts to friends!

Those who believe that we should go on allowing process to rule and that this should be reinforced by left-wing populism, kindly leave the stage now!

Those who would endorse radical leadership and changes focussed on increasing self-responsibility, improving individual outcomes, inspiring necessary change, read on!

Personally, I have always believed that any politician – or any professional, such as a leading surgeon, for that matter – who claims to be right all the time and to know it all is a very dangerous individual. Several names come to mind! But I hope I have not been like that.

Indeed, I have done my level best to make our country a better place for everyone. Decent, caring, responsible. Human nature and politics is complex, of course. But we were not entirely idle, you know. We tackled the examination system. We helped create a million extra private-sector jobs. We froze council tax. We cut crime. We opened up the Europe debate – especially on human rights. George and I did all we could to rebuild the country's economy after the disastrous mad-spend-and-gone-bust inflationary years of Mr. Brown, Mr. Balls, and the two Mr. Millibands. Not one of whom, by the by, have *ever* worked in a real job where they have had to serve customers who have a choice of provider, where entrepreneurs have to take risks, where costs and investment are critical, and where you have to respond to demand or the customer moves elsewhere.

But, looking back at the NHS and on our reforms now, it is not possible to deny that all our hopes and efforts achieved very little. The whole set-up remains process-governed, not patient-focussed. Process and regulations are still everything. It is difficult to litigate against them, if you are an aggrieved patient. And so it is up to we politicians to encourage major cultural changes. To encourage innovative purchasers and providers normally and genuinely to offer a service which is timely, convenient, personal, and responsive to the individual.

However, we shall see no progress here under Mr. Milliband and his clique. There is no doubt that he does not believe in free markets or in capitalism itself. Or in the power of the individual consumer. He is riddled with statism. He grew up in a household of

Marxigookery. His is the party of the trade unions. Of the providers. Of the past. BUT we are the Party of free enterprise and of entrepreneurship. And so we should certainly have ensured that this applied to the NHS itself. Alas, as I consider – like a novelist or a film director or a painter – how to tell the story some large facts do stand out. Indelibly so. They really hurt! *[- and as to Corbyliner & the Redco gang... - Ed.].*

[to be continued...]

EPISODE 46

The PM & The N£sd 'Reforms.' An Early Extract From His Memoirs, Part 4.

I Stood In Time. My Prime Ministerial Memoirs, By The Duke of Notting Hill and Chipping Thompson, KG, OM, FRSPR.

[Continued from previous episode].

Here I type up my further notes on topics for my next chapters. And to conclude my thoughts on the NHS. Here I am on the beach at Coventry Island – reading Thackeray, sipping freshly-squeezed pineapple juice, and pondering the imponderables of that great and ghastly NHS.

As It WAS, IS, and seemingly EVER SHALL BE. [BMA Without End].

'Processes' and bureaucracies without end. But NOT with an amen from Me!

Because…

- We did not make the case for the enterprise culture, and so this has let in the dangerously left-wing and pessimistic anti-business, anti-jobs, anti-profit, socialistic, anti-capitalist, anti-free-market economy culture of Milliband and Kable. *[- and now in 2015-6, Corbynliner bids in multi-lunacies galore, too… - Ed.].*

- With devastating results to the dynamism of the economy, to jobs, and to living-standards – including the social benefits only ever able to be funded by wealth-creation. This duo are in the business of being hostile to business. As is "the Great Economist" Ed Balls – he, the latest shiny model in 'The Gordon Brown Series.' Each leads a Party favouring public-sector special-interest groups, which fund them.

As I have said…

- We allowed the producer trade unions to dominate everything that happened.

- We did not financially empower the individual, and so place the poorer on to the same platform of health-service purchasing as the middle-class. So they remain at the back of every queue.

- We did not use economic incentives to increase personal responsibility – by patients and by staff. So obesity is now bankrupting the services. And staff condescension is still at the front.

- We did nothing to build mutual, member-owned, local purchasing organisations.

So individual involvement in support for better local care was not encouraged.

- We did not challenge the mystical idea that the NHS is saintly, which disabled attempts to reform it. We have worshipped at the crumbling feet of a false god, and thus undermined any attempt to make major changes – for example, by studying how things are done so much better abroad. The OECD shows us clearly how much better care is in the Netherlands, in France, in Germany, in Scandinavia, in Switzerland – all, by the by, insurance-based models, and still mainly free at the point of use. Those nations each have a set-up where the patient is welcomed and respected. Do we?

- Charles Moore wrote in the *Daily Telegraph* on 20 July 2013 that "From its inception, the NHS has been a nationalised industry. All nationalised industries put those who run them first, their trade unions second, and their customers nowhere. They are by nature indifferent to human need and so their effect, whatever the intention, is cruel. Until this is acknowledged, nothing much will change." We should have reprinted this article and sent it to every voter in the land.

- We did not improve *reliable* access to what should necessarily be personal, intimate, timely – and certain – services.

- Nor did we successfully integrate hospital, social, and community services.

- We ignored price, which is the only way to curb ludicrous demands.

- We were too frightened to charge overseas visitors for A&E services, too, although we eventually did this. These visitors almost all have travel insurance. But we have been very feeble at actually collecting the monies. NHS staff remain very reluctant about it. We should have charged for GP visits, too. Here we have been unrealistic about the costs and demands on services, and how to fund them.

- Outcomes with the key modern diseases – notably, cancer, and Alzheimer's – have remained very poor.

- Our survival rates, our services and our outcomes are still much less successful than almost all of the countries covered by the regular and authoritative OECD surveys. This, even when death rates from cancer in Britain have fallen by more than a fifth since 1990. [Why were our results so much poorer until then, after 42 years of the NHS? And now?].

- The support we provide for survivors of treatment is also inadequate, not least in helping patients to develop the skills to manage their own condition and its side-effects after treatment.

- We failed to link salaries to performance. Nor did we encourage flexible local pay deals, within a much simplified national framework – a failing which we repeated in teaching, too. We could and should have ensured that professional staff expect appraisals and pay to reflect how well they do their job – and we should have fully utilised patients' complaints as an important aspect of this appraisal. Failing professionals would not be rewarded for failure, and very damaging mutual doctor-led cover-ups would be unearthed.

- We spent more, but got less. And – just as under Mr. Brown – productivity continued to fall.

- We failed to introduce mutual purchasing organisations, controlled by willing members, using taxed-money, with the buying done from doctors and by doctors who could have then asked the basic question, '"What are we getting for our money?"

If we were a football league club, we would have been relegated to a much lower league, long ago.

We didn't even get a single point for an away draw!

[to be continued...]

EPISODE 47

The PM & The N£sd 'Reforms.' An Early Extract From His Memoirs, Part 5.

I Stood In Time. My Prime Ministerial Memoirs, By The Duke of Notting Hill and Chipping Thompson, KG, OM, FRSPR.

[Continued from previous episode].

Regrets, like National Debts, are never paid orf.

Our key mistake – as I have said – was failing to set out clear arguments for a free and competitive society. When we should have been applying these principles to the NHS. And so we failed to take the NHS forward to become a quality service to match Switzerland, France, The Netherlands, Germany, and Australia.

We should have guided the politics and economics of the whole nation in the same way. But I got it badly wrong, and thus opened the door for the destructive socialistic nonsense of Mr. Milliband and Mr. Kable.

We did not make the argument for a free society, and so we let Milliband in by default. This is a terrible lesson for us all. What this deadly duo did can be studied in all its appalling detail in their weekly newspaper, *Free*, seemingly produced for them in North Korea.

We *were* and *are* supposed to be the Party of free enterprise and of entrepreneurship.

And *we* are supposed to be the party which improves the standard of living for everyone. As the economist Paul Krugman shows, a nations' ability to improve standards of living over time depends almost entirely on its ability to raise output per worker. We are not doing this yet. Innovation is how productivity growth happens, if we want growth and prosperity.

We should have ensured that all this applied to the NHS itself.

Alas…

- We did so in only the most limited respects, and we were much too often instead found interfering with existing markets, prices, and controls and in every aspect of the economy.

- We knew that the 6 big oligopolistic energy firms had to be made to compete, to improve customer service and price.

- We required the 5 big banks to compete, for the same reasons.

- But we ignored the *one* even bigger behemoth which is the NHS, at least in these terms. Yet if energy companies and banks had to be forced to compete, to serve individual customers and not themselves, why not the NHS?

- Indeed, the requirements for customer-focus were [and are] even more urgent here. Yet services for NHS users and quality of outcomes have never reached the levels commonly expected as normal in Europe itself.

The OECD reports here are *very* damning, and they are worse now than even 5 years ago.

So…

- This is not a country in which to contract a cancer, or many other serious conditions.

- This is not a country in which to grow old, unless you are rich.

- This is not a country where you want to require A&E service quickly.

- This is not a country where you want to need a GP at the weekends.

- This is not a country where you want to risk having an operation on Friday, Saturday or Sunday.

- This is not a country where you can expect to have access to the very latest and best drugs for cancer care.

- That is the bare truth.

It is a shameful situation, for which I accept my share of the blame. Until we stop all the mystique worship of the NHS – which no other country has ever copied, by the by! – *and* face realities, we will not make any real gains. Realities? Human nature. Cost-conscious choices. Economic incentives. Changes in personal life-styles and behaviour. How to fund, run, and use a modern service in a modern society. All that very obvious stuff.

As to the continued leftie worship of that old rogue Bevan, and the totally barmy clinging onto the time-warp of *1948?* Well, *the parents* of most of my readers were not even born then!!! So, as the independent radio boyos say, "Get Real, Britain!" [Well, *not* Mr. Salmon Fishcake's Not Very Independent Scotland….].

When we came into government poor old Andrew Lansley did his best to begin with, but ultimately he made a big muck of it. So, a bad start. Jeremy Hunt did his best to recover the situation for us, and to limit the electoral damage. He is an able, emollient, persistent, eye on the ball and a surprisingly tough figure, and he did well viz the docs. But this was never a winning wicket for any Conservative politician. Decades of public ignorance, and of faith in the mystique of the NHS, made it a very hard ball to play.

And when Milliband came into power he then had to face the NHS music, too. With all the trade unions in concert: The BMe-Me, The RCN, Unite, The GBWWCo PLC, The Royal Academy of Vested Interests, the GP College, the Klingfilm Fund – & so forth.

All the old tunes played ever more insistently. "More money; less politics; more power to us; leave 'processes' alone; protect our employment; give us new & cast-iron contracts; leave us to manage ourselves; costs? aha – not our problem; just provide even more money again, &c." Taxpayer's Ahoy! Lots of noise; but little advance. But all of these bodies, like the individual doctors, *even now* need to appreciate that their job is to focus on the patients – all of whom who matter – and not on themselves. Patients are more important than them. They are there to help patients, and to deliver preferred outcomes. They have to improve all the time too.

We Tories entirely failed to educate the public about the truths and the choices. We did not ever manage to tackle the fundamentals on behalf of the isolated, individual, unorganised service-user who is very properly not obsessed with politics, but who just wants a personal, intimate, kindly, effective, *reliably certain* and individual local service when necessary. And otherwise just wants to leave the NHS to get on with organising itself properly meanwhile.

But, William, it is in your capable hands now! I remember being told as a child that it is adversity which makes you stronger. And, as Sir Winston Churchill once said, "Kites rise highest against the wind, not with it."

Why have we forgotten this?

[to be continued].

EPISODE 48

The PM & The N£sd 'Reforms.' An Early Extract From His Memoirs, Part 6.

I Stood In Time. My Prime Ministerial Memoirs, By The Duke of Notting Hill and Chipping Thompson, KG, OM, FRSPR.

[continued from the previous episode....]

Just back from our short trip to Spain. Wonderful to see Granada and Seville. Learned a lot, too, about good health work when my chum Geoff slipped coming down marble steps to breakfast and cut his arm badly. In case of any infection, he went to a Spanish GP and had an x-ray and a blood test. He also had an injection for tetanus – just in case, as the welcoming nurse said. He got there before 10 in the morning. He was seen and treated within 15 minutes! By 5 p.m. the same day he'd been e-mailed the results! He also received a comprehensive and typed e-discharge letter, in English, and with a digital file giving what treatment he had received!

A real eye-opener! Geoff received excellent medical care – and in conversation with others he observed that there seemed to be continuity of care from the same doctors and nurses throughout the day.

Golly! A *real* focus on the customer experience!

When my dear cousin Cynthia had a similar experience in England last year she was told she'd have to wait for nine days to get an appointment with a nurse at her local surgery. Or she could come in, sit, and hope. So she went to A&E, and was seen within five hours. An hour after the target. Which is itself ridiculously long.

And she *still* had to wait several days before the results were sent to her GP. Worse, the letter the GP got was only partly legible, incomplete and delivered a month after the event. Not be e-mail, either, but by a hospital van! Amazing!

She was lucky, too. In that hospital a surgeon sewed up his watch into a patient during an op. Another patient had the wrong hernia done – he'd evidently forgotten to write "This side please doctor" on himself with a mauve pen. Another had his new-hip op. cancelled 7 times. And there were cases there of people being jabbed with the wrong medicines and in the wrong quantities, too. Two were rumoured to have had the wrong foot amputated.

People having their operation on the WRONG LIMB, can you believe?

There was also a junior doc with 140 patients over one weekend, and with no senior supervision. Too frightened to call the so-called 'on-call' consultant, in case his future job-reference was jeopardised, it seems. And this just in *one* so-called superior NHS Trust hospital!

THE FACEY ROMFORD PAPERS

We found that in Spain services are run and managed locally, to meet the specific needs of the people in each locality. There's a good mix of private and public services, clinics and labs. Same in France, The Netherlands, Germany, Switzerland and in Australia. Everyone insured. A mixed-funding set-up. No two-tier system. Top-ups, and direct economic incentives. Why not here?

We have obviously got it so badly wrong. Our NHS services remain shoddy, inadequate, and pompously self-praising – all at the same time! The Millkiband Kid and Mr. Birdnumb – as Sir Squoffy calls them – ignore all that. The usual religiosity about the best service in the world. Owzatism itself! *Taxpayers Ahoy!* Newly Labelled Old Labour are in a deep hole. And yet they are still busily digging.

We started in government fighting the wrong battles in the wrong way, too, and we paid the political price. But they have never even tried. So we have even more shortages, more imbalance in the system, more distortions, more frustrations. In government we might just as well have been much more courageous and ambitious in financially-empowering individuals, and then in requiring people to face the costs and consequences of their own behaviours.

We should have tackled the key dangers, most notably obesity and the abandonment of personal responsibility, together with the difficulties in attaining the affordability of long-term elderly care.

My biggest error of all was in failing to pursue public education on the systemic snags of the state-monopoly NHS. I should have made the Party the champion of the consumer. From my first day as Leader of The Opposition. Especially in healthcare, social and elderly care. But I listened too much to the 'wets', and then to the LibDems. And so we have remained the party of the producer, just like Labour and the LibDems. We paid the political price as usual for what proved to be entirely marginal reforms, which the TU's easily negated locally – after decrying them as disastrous. In all frankness, we could and should have instead achieved something worthwhile by tackling the real economic and personal behavioural issues at the start.

We were subject to a Tsunami of big waves, of course: the onset of a 50% rate of obesity; the constant innovations from the big pharma companies with new drugs, which worked but which could not be afforded; NICE being NASTY; rising expectations; the new longevity and elderly people presenting with multiple conditions; the care homes costs and the weakness of the local-government business model to fund such homes; the failures of every recent generation to save sufficiently; the deterrence to individual self-responsibility in a permissive welfarist society; the deficits in economic incentives for people to change their own behaviour. And the fundamental problem that it is the oicks in a mass democracy which decide all our fates. It has been a caustic mix.

But – repetition, I know! – my own biggest failure was in not educating the public about these issues. Here we ambushed ourselves. Mea definitely culpa! We ended playing blind man's bluff with the docs. But we could and should have begun this work in our opposition years, and then drawn upon a new public understanding when we came into government. This should have been our abcd.

The IEA and the Adam Smith Institute tried to tell us. We sent people to their policy lunches. But we didn't listen. Alas. Facey Romford, Jr also sent me regular papers. I read that Roy Lilley eletter assiduously – Foxie sent it to me as a print-out. Again, I passed these to the policy unit, where they seem to have vanished without trace. I should have been more alert myself. But I also had Zimbabwe, Egypt, China, India, Burma, Saudi Arabia, the Yemen, Iraq, Gibraltar, and the Murdoch media trials on my platter.

It is clear to me now, quite clear, that there is much still to be done to bring Britain up to the necessary competitive mark as to service and quality. We need a competitive workforce, a much less cumbersome tax system, much improved productivity, investment and growth. The left grizzle on about 'the cuts' and 'austerity.' But Government still spends far too much of our money. We need lower prices, better quality, and improved returns on investment. We need to curb government spending, to no more than 33% of national income – which is what the successful governments of Australia and Switzerland spend.

Those are good societies. And that level of spending has not produced disasters. Indeed, it has improved self-responsibility. Of course, many mind-sets have to change, not least among civil servants and so-called public-servants. A lot of things which have just drifted need our attention, too. For example, why is government funding charities – which were supposed to appeal to a giving community and to voluntarisms? There are some 75,000 charities which depend on government for three-quarters of their income. How has such a thing come about?

As to healthcare, and pensions, we need a mature and rational national discussion, and one not dominated by vested-interests. These services are going to continue to be more costly, and we do not know how to finance them. A correction here, too concerning the NHS: Sir David Nicholson, the recently retired Chief Executive the NHS, had the bare-faced gall to claim in the *Sunday Times* that most of the alternative system in other countries cost more and their outcomes are worse. This is *entirely false*, as the OECD reports regularly show. Where would he rather be treated for a serious condition? Here, or in Europe or Australia. No prizes for the answer!!!

I discussed all this with old *KG*, before he removed himself to New Zealand with Mrs. Curried. But he, too, never faced the key NHS issues. No real help at all. "The Doctors were far too powerful. Always will be. They do things which we cannot do for ourselves. We didn't dare tackle them. Tanks on my lawn and all that. Would get behind the arras if I was you!" But I now appreciate that only a long-term public education project to explain and reinforce the free market society could have had any impact at all on necessary NHS changes which are crucial still. Possibly not even then?

I am not and have never been a Thatcherite, of course. I am a pragmatic, liberal conservative. I have never intended to make the market my base. That was never my magnetic north. But we have tried everything else, and without success. So William is right to tackle it all from that base now. Good luck to him! He'll stick at it, I'm sure.

My own biggest strategic error was made at the very start, I confess. By refusing to go for the 'Harold Wilson gambit' – when I had quite unaccountably failed to deliver a majority Conservative government in defeating Gordon Brown and Edth Balth. I should never have agreed to the Coalition with Clegg. It has been a nightmare of policy vetoes by Clegg. What happened to the old ideas of shared Cabinet Responsibility? The opposition has been opposite us in the House. The enemy has been behind us! Two or three days every week I have had one of my own people on the *Today* programme arguing with a LibDem Cabinet

Minister about GOVERNMENT policies which were fully agreed in Cabinet!

The Deadly David D and galloper Dr. Foxie warned me. But the economic situation in 2010 frightened us all. Still, it need not have been like this. If instead we had said to the nation that we would govern as a minority administration for a few months, challenged Milliband and Clegg to defeat us, and then gone for a second election that autumn, we could and should have successfully got a majority government then. We could thus have avoided the many terrible years, including the Party divisions over Europe and the rise of that wretched nuisance Farage – all of which then ended with the very damaging and inflationary – but mercifully short-lived – LabDemsy coalition of 2015-17 of Milliband and Cable.

This outfit was anti-business, undermined civil society and did much to damage markets and thus freedoms. Deficiencies in the NHS, in teaching, in mind-sets, all worsened the infrastructure of the economy, and each service was even more politicised. Not least the worst consequences were that these services failed in that most basic task of ensuring that those from lower-paid households got the life chances to which they should have been entitled in a fairer society which can be created by markets alone.

The crucial necessities of long-term planning, a genuine dialogue with the private sector, and agreement across-party for meaningful and sustainable reforms were never achieved. We were never able to enjoy the advances in productivity which create their own demand, reduce prices, create more jobs, and again enhance demand and quality outcomes. And just as science and pharmaceutical innovations increased the potential supply of life-savings drugs demand fell back as funding was not made available.

The mind-set, both for equipping workers for the new technological world, training with the skills to succeed, and benefitting from health care was never set in place. It required radical reform, and a new consensus to support it. But left-ideology blocked the road.

You can quite see why Herbert Spencer wrote "Experience has long since dissipated my belief in men's rationality."

And then we come to the continuing attempt by doctors to limit our knowledge of what they do. Here, they will have to give way to the digital age. Here, everyone is now accustomed to dealing with on-line content, and to accessing it at home. This facility has exploded in volume, velocity, and variety. It has produced new ways of acquiring knowledge, and itself prompted higher rates of innovation in the wider society. We will very soon surely be able to call up on our electronic devices in our hands all the data on a doctor's training, history, and results – including reports by patients of their experiences. About time, too!

Doctors will not be able to hinder or limit this development, try as they might. Huge amounts of digital data are provided free already. Just look at Wikipedia, entirely created by users. And the demand for this clinical information will only grow, especially as more and more scandals are unveiled. Computers already diagnose diseases, listen and speak to us, and for patient choice we must now do much more to make technologies work for them.

For example Tyler Cowen, in his book *Average is Over. Powering America Beyond The Age of the Great Stagnation* (New York, Dutton, 2013) shows that the Mayo Clinic in America has used artificial neural networks – or ANN – to assess whether patients have endocarditis (a kind of heart infection) to achieve more accurate diagnoses and have thus saved some patients from unnecessary invasive procedures. General Electric and Artificial Intelligence in Medicine, Inc. are developing further software programmes for diagnosis. We are already accustomed to automated imaging systems for screen pap slides, which identify those images that a human expert needs to scrutinise carefully. It is evident that machine-man collaborations outperform humans working alone, both in terms of accuracy, speed and cost.

Yet misdiagnosis in many clinical specialities remains common, and also late. Here we need more technology to help us. Cowen shows, too, that the most consulted doctor in America is Google! For millions it is the first step, typing their symptoms and considering what to do next. In addition, research that Cowen reports shows that machines are able to evaluate human performance with extreme accuracy. It can pick up errors that are often repeated. We need such digital systems to help – and to evaluate and reward (or re-train) – doctors.

Cowen is surely right when he says that "Machines aren't just about producing goods and services at lower cost; they will also improve the quality of service in the professions. Sooner or later, most professionals, especially at the top end of the market, will be graded by teams of skilled workers cooperating with smart machines…Let's say it is a lawyer. Potential customers can ask their smart phones where the lawyer went to school, what her class rank was, and what kinds of promotions she has received. That information will be accompanied by an asterisk: 'This information explains only 27 per cent of lawyer performance.'" *For lawyers, read doctors!*

Every potential patient (and parent, in the schools) who is wise will consult the ratings, and check on line with expert patient groups and their reports on experiences. The better doctors (and teachers) will willingly publicise their records, to enable potential patients to evaluate their quality and expertise. We will see who is in the top 80th percentile of the peer group, and who trails behind. Sooner or later most professionals will have to submit to ratings, or bear the consequences of being without clients, save perhaps for those at the lower and less informed end of the queue. And politicians like me will then have to insist on their re-training or retirement.

However, Cowen argues that it is the poor – so ill-served by the NHS now! – who will do better. Because the informed middle-class who throw cultural clout already know how to find out where doctors would send their own daughters, which professionals are up to the best mark, which facilities do best. So a public ratings system, will put everyone on a par – and especially so if we then have individual health savings accounts and all patients have direct control over funds!

In terms of networking, the future is of countless blogs, websites, discussion forums and *local* sources of online information together with *international* comparisons. These will include many sites which are generated by users, and the political demand for information from the Royal Colleges will be unstoppable. As so it should be.

Computers – and robots – are going to continue to improve exponentially, and to do new and unprecedented things, not least the capture and exchange of information. Digital information is exponential, and combinatorial. Computers will be on the side of the consumer of services. This is the modern drumbeat to which doctors must listen.

The key building blocks are already in place. And processing speeds, storage capacity, download speed and the range of complex tasks easily discharged will add exponentially to our opportunities. Rapid and accelerating digitization will change everything. It will capture and create value. It will reveal and unfold new bounties and much more freedom of choice. All the digitised information will be sent over networks, compared and contrasted by consumers.

In all our lives digital technology makes available massive bodies of relevant information, and results from the NHS and from doctors cannot be excluded.

We are at what technologists call an 'inflection point.' Digitization increases knowledge, understanding, and action. And people anywhere can access data, consider it, take advice, consider the problems, and make a personal decision about their own preferred solution.

Doctors should welcome all this, too. For IBM estimates that it would now take a human doctor up to 160 hours a week reading the literature just to keep up with new material. Only computers can now cover all the new medical information in many clinical journals, report a summary which is relevant to a particular specialist – as well as help a doctor match a patient's symptoms, medical history and test results with current knowledge. Together they can then formulate both a good diagnosis and a modern and individualised treatment plan.

I have just read an interesting new book, *"Coming, Ready or Not!" The Realities, The Future and The Politics of the NHS*. This gives an introductory note on the impact of digitisation on health care. I summarise this here. Already, Erik Brynjolfsson and Andrew McAfee, in *The Second Machine Age. Work, Progress, and Prosperity in A Time of Brilliant Technologies* have shown that the number of digital pages and images on the Web exceeds one trillion. And children with smartphones today have access to more information in real time via the mobile web than the President of the USA had 20 years ago! This information is available today for free, together with over 1 million apps on smartphones.

Last year users collectively spent 20 million hours EACH day just on Facebook – much of the time creating content for other users to consume. As we are told by Brynjolfsson and McAfee, that's ten times as many person-hours as it took to build the entire Panama Canal.

There are apparently 43,200 hours of new YouTube videos created every day. Google fields 100 billion queries a month. There are 250 million new photos uploaded every day on Facebook. There are hordes of user reviews on Amazon, TripAdvisor and Yelp. Facebook reached a billion users in 2012. Electronic devices are deliberately designed so that users can add value for other users to access. They deliver huge amounts of data continuously. Why not about the results from doctors, adding this to our collective wealth? Will this not increase choice, and improve quality?

As Brynjolfsson and McAfee argue, *most of the digital gains are ahead of us!*

In the next 2 years the planet will add more computer power than it did in all previous history. Over the next 24 years, they say, the increase will likely be over a thousand-fold. They suggest that our generation is likely to experience two of the most amazing historical events: the creation of true machine intelligence, and the connection of all humans via a common digital network.

This will transform the planet's economics. And so the bounty of new technologies is spreading everywhere. How can – and why should – doctors hide their results? And limit global feedback? Or discourage and prevent information flows? It will surely be widely disseminated, newly focussed and precise, and the basis of individual decision-making about ourselves. This will be the best kind of unforced and artificial equality

Digital models of learning and teaching are an essential opportunity. Such innovations would surely improve standards, require re-training where quality was inadequate, and oblige managements to re-examine decision-making authority, governance systems, recruitment, incentive systems, information flows, hiring and training and many other aspects of organisational processes Quite right, too, for such changes can generate many productivity improvements and quality gains. And the second and third-best will have to get their acts together.

Digital oversight will ensure what we have not thus far been able to achieve with the NHS. It will reveal for all to see *relative* performance, and measured against *absolute* standards. This will impact on individual doctor and NHS Trust earnings. Standards will have a new and transparent importance. For patients will surely prefer to be treated by those with the best proven quality, even within the capacity constraints of the existing NHS.

The best performers, too, should be given the opportunity to expand their facilities – attracting willing individual revenues from Health Savings Accounts – while the less good performers will face harsh competition. And in a digital economy the poor performers, who kill people now, will no longer be able to hide behind consumer ignorance, geographical barriers, or incantatory professional obfuscations. Consumer ratings will chase them in public. Differences in quality, convenience, attitude and price will really matter, as they should.

With a few clicks, over 2 million books can now already be found and purchased on the net. But aren't your medical and clinical prospects as important? Why not information for free here about the results individual doctors and clinical teams achieve in the NHS? What if we had had this on Mid-Staffs? Or at Alder Hey? Or Morecombe Bay? Or St. Hilda's, near you? Dynamite indeed! Wikipedia, Facebook, YouTube, Twitter, Instagram, Pinainterest, Craigslist, Pandora, Hulu, Linked-in, Whatsapp, Google – no doctor can turn back this tide. No Royal College can step aside.

There *is* no way backwards. And consumers will rapidly learn, in mutual exchange, which questions to ask and what counts as a useful answer. As Brynjolfsson and McAfee say, digital technologies can replicate valuable ideas, insights and innovations at very low cost – and people will increasingly ask why the information they want remains hidden by the politicians, by the Royal Colleges, by the GMC, and by the NHS.

Digital information is good at disseminating how others have defined and measured value. Millions choose restaurants, hotels, airlines, cheaply, quickly, efficiently, using the net. Millions use structured comparison sites like FindTheBest.com and Gocompare.com. Why not on doctors? Consumers must be enabled to search for and compare doctors. This will definitely change sub-standard performances, too. The weaker will no longer be insulated by NHS bureaucracy, and by long waiting-lists or self-protective claques of doctors. The issue will be who can deliver the better service, and for less?

There must be better matches, greater timeliness, improved customer service and experience, and increased convenience for the service-user too. Then the incomes of NHS facilities can rise or fall *depending on how well they use the four key intangible assets: intellectual property and expertise, organisational processes and capital, user-generated information, and the human capital of their staffs and how work is organised more effectively.*

And so, in the NHS, the transformation that will be brought about by digital technology and personalised medicine is inevitable. And digital medicine can not only be profoundly beneficial to consumers. It can improve the lives of professionals, too. By doing a better job they can feel better about themselves, better about the world around them, better about their work. Managers, too, need it to co-ordinate increasingly complex processes in which specific, timely, intimate and individual patients are the real focus.

Digital information – and global health-trips, too, with people wishing to travel and to pay to go to better services overseas – will rapidly produce many new interactions. These will all change existing transactions and relationships. Including improving the personalisation of care, much more specific targeted drug treatments, a new precision of the execution of clinical tasks, adequate training, integrity and the much more consistent co-ordination of work, together with higher morale to motivate work and co-operation.

All this is a team process. And the sharing and networking of information helps people to know what and how they are doing, helps them to learn, encourages them to cooperate with fellow workers. It can lift morale, and the reliability and consistency of work too. Reliability and coherence and basic competence and conscientiousness in discharging routines – taking a history, studying test results, washing your hands! - are all essential. But too often lacking in the NHS – despite its grand promises.

A much fuller picture of what is going on here, and with networked comparisons, will help us all. It had better do so, as demands for healthcare continue to increase, and we do not have the resources to do it all well if we waste much of doing it badly, if many are under-employed, if a good number do not add value as defined by the customers.

Of course, doctors will try to 'game' the system, but we are already alert to that. In addition, some of the Godlike respect for doctors will ease. And this is no bad thing, even if faith in healing does have a beneficial effect. Doctors will certainly become less condescending, arrogant and sanctimonious. Again, no bad thing.

I expect we will find that there are a few really outstanding doctors, and many in the middle range. Of course, if patients join a mutual purchasing body – the proposed Patient Guaranteed Care Associations – then the managers there will know what the ratings mean, and be doing the purchasing on behalf of their financially-empowered members. They will also help patients to know and understand what they are doing. And try to ensure, too, that the problems which patients cause to themselves can be addressed with self-responsibility.

We will be told that people cannot handle the digital programmes and the machines. That old scare. Well, the new generations live by them. Children as young as two now use i-Pads, if parents are not watching! And the machines teach them, so that their skills grow. They are very soon very competent 'players.'

As the economist Tyler Cowen says, too, it is remarkable how the computer games industry, on line, has educated millions. The educational accomplishments and intellectual advances required are not trivial for game-players. As he says, "Many of those role-playing, time-extended, multiplayer games are forbiddingly hard or at least so it seems. They involve hundreds or thousands of people manipulating hundreds or thousands of virtual characters, not always human, spread across (virtual) geographic space and engaged in trade, battles, elections, and many other activities, all governed by complex rules within the game and governed by complex software at the level of player interface. And yet people learn those games nonetheless and often master them."

A prospective patient who wants to consult with an adviser? No problem. Easy-peasy. Genie, he/she already out of bottle.

We can expect that some appraisals of doctors will be brutally honest, and shake them up. New training, re-education, hard work, discipline, change will be enforced. Equally, doctors, no doubt, will rate patients too! And try to avoid the worst of them! We can also see that some doctors might decide to take on the worst patients, do what they can for them, and perhaps expect to be paid a premium for taking them on.

At all events, this I surely the end of the notorious Secret Garden of doctor's lives. The end of them preventing us from learning about their practices, and their mal-practises too. And any failures to disclose will be damning. We will expect to see a slow refinement of practices, improvement in outcomes, and generational changes in attitudes, all well-geared for improving our lives.

Digitisation will thus be absolutely at the centre of medical practice. And in this new digital world of transparency, individual accountability and appraisals we are looking at a gradual process of radical but incremental, trial-and-error evolution which will change almost everything we do. As we go forward new machines, new man-cyber partnerships, new evidence will create other programmes and capabilities.

We will at last clearly see how much value each player is contributing in goods and services. In partnership – men and machine, two blades of the scissors. I welcome this new era, which will be both different and better. It will take into the consumer's hands much that is currently held inappropriately in the hands of politicians like me. And Doctors *must* climb aboard.

More broadly, we know that we will have to deal with immense difficulties. Make your own list. There is intensifying cost-inflation in health care. The population is growing, retiring earlier, and living much longer. Older people, too, often suffer from more than one difficulty. For example, being diabetic and with dementia. Demand for greater spending on health care is growing. And those demanding it actually vote. Big cuts on care services for the elderly are thus not on the agenda. The total spend on health for the elderly will rise, in absolute and in per capita terms. To support this spending we are seeing governments taking 40% of GDP.

This is itself unsustainable. Politics will not, however, let us cut spending, nor much increase taxation.

We see delay, denial and dilution in the NHS and in inadequate and often chilling care homes. This itself is causing outrage. We might be able to get the richest 1% to pay more in taxes. There are more of them than there were, but they already pay plenty. They have many ways by which to evade us. They also have political clout, which will curb governments. And if we go too far they will just be driven abroad.

We are tinkering with entitlements – for example, curbing the access to services by health-tourists. We are squeezing welfare and waste, but this itself is proving very difficult. And as low-level jobs vanish forever due to digitisation, we will be stuck with providing some kind of living-wage for the weakest, least-skilled, uneducated, and for the whole of their lives. Those actually in work will be encouraged by tax incentives to make some more private provision, and for everyone else who does not do so access to services will very likely decline.

As we struggle with all this, unequal treatment, post-code lotteries, denial of new and clinically-effective cancer drugs will all continue to drive the debate. In all honesty, I do not see how we can make the numbers add up. Which is why we need the mature debate which, alas, I failed to initiate in government, much to my own regret now.

Meanwhile, we will inevitably increase taxes, notably on higher earners – not to advance, but just to stand still. We will increase waits, and dilute access, tighten eligibility requirements. We will try to shift costs onto non-governmental shoulders, and we will do all we can to cut wasteful management, ill-advised demand, and failures to be self-responsible. Rationing will certainly increase, however we label this. And when we get to the point, in 15 years time, when more than one in five is aged over 65, what will we do then? In America, Obama has tried to work this trick by passing the bills to businesses, mandating them to provide employee health insurance. This is not something which looks feasible here, in a very different culture.

It is difficult, too, to see how existing disparities in access to services, understanding of advice, and self-responsible living will do anything but get worse. All that we know about people tells us that those with higher education, more skills, more income, more savings, less debt, contribute more. They start and run businesses, and they invest and save. They look to the future, not to welfare. We know, too, that these middle-class people get health care when they need it, and keep up their productivity in the economy and their standards of living.

All these factors compound over time, for and against you. No amount of after-the-effect action by Whitehall can do much then to help those who have lived for the moment, failed to exercise, gorged on junk-food, drunk and smoked heavily, and exercised no self-control at all. The message here is that there is going to be much less access to healthcare for all, but in a more polarized society. And we need reminding that how you live contributes much *much* more to your state of being than medicine itself.

So, Be Aware!

As to the role of the politician, we are squeezed by circumstances. And, in this area at least, all adjustments look equally impossible. Even so, the by-rote demand for NHS services as they were, and the claim that ours is the best in the world and envied everywhere – well, how can *anyone* now say so? And tomorrow, worse?

Meanwhile, we must negotiate with a highly unionised work-force that deeply resents having its entrenched privileges – and incompetent members – questioned at all. Here, the digital revolution will reveal all!

[to be continued....]

EPISODE 49

The PM & The N£sd 'Reforms.' An Early Extract From His Memoirs, Part 7.

I Stood In Time. My Prime Ministerial Memoirs, By The Duke of Notting Hill and Chipping Thompson, KG, OM, FRSPR.

[Continued from the previous episode.]

Well, I did not pass the election victory onto my succesor, alas…

And you have now seen a Labour government in action again. What did you expect from Relabelled New Old Labour in power! Ha! Just look at its history!

The comic/tragic story is easily revealed in detail in the weekly newspaper, *Free*, and in the monthly socialist magazine, *Juggernaut*.

This 'popular coalition' swiftly almost bankrupted the nation. And we can still hear the echoes of the late Milliband Marxist Father. The hard-line Communist. The friend to Bolshevism. The dreamer of such a totally controlled society for us all.

Just imagine if the *older* Milliband Pere had become Prime Minister! What sort of Sovietised society we would have had.

Just imagine if another Labour leader had signed a so-called 'Friendship Agreement' with the USSR! We would have rapidly become another Cuba.

Just imagine if Milliband Junior had followed his Father's advice!

In fact, imagination is not necessary on voyage. Just look at the facts of post-1917 history!

If the older Milliband had had his way then this document would now only be circulated in illegal typescript, *samizdat*. I would be a *zek* in the Gulag. My passport stamped 'Exiled.' Or I would be in a psychiatric 'hospital,' being treated for psychopathic negativism and from suffering from anti-Soviet thought. Treated with sodium amytal and other drugs, taken down a long dark corridor to my fate, all the time struggling to retain my reason. In the *fiksatasiya*, the chemical straitjacket.

The older Milliband Father was the man who favoured the overthrow of all capitalist regimes and the international victory of Communism against all democratic societies. He denounced social democracy and left-wing pluralism, as did the arch-terrorist Lenin himself. He dreamt of the long-term goal of world-wide revolution, followed by a permanent international dictatorship of the proletariat. By which he meant THE PARTY. Something only ever imposed by brute military force anywhere in the world.

What must have been the bed-time stories told in *that* Hampstead house?

What values were stressed *there* over the cornflakes and toast? What 'natural order' preferred? What unrealistic falsifications were served with breakfast? Which other values over-turned? What life-line was given to the Milliband sons as the way to live, and to think?

Well, the rest of us know – as Robert Conquest showed us in his work *The Great Terror*. And as Richard Pipes has written – that the Soviet-created Comintern constituted a "declaration of war on all the existing governments." The Bolsheviks read Marx not as just some theory amongst many *but as scientific fact*. The entire world was projected to be run by Communist regimes. Sovietised. Fraternal. Comrade. *We* know this. *Do* the Millibandites?

Fortunately, as liberal capitalism has progressed throughout the world, people have ultimately preferred to try to be middle-class rather than class-less. And standards of living have risen and are rising wherever there is freedom and creative economic liberty.

But, indeed, during the black economic period of the recent but short-lived Milliband/Cable 'popular coalition' I always woke up each day and expected the *Today* programme to tell me that they had in fact renamed the 'One Nation' Re-Labelled New Old Labour Party as the British Workers' Social Democratic Party, with its new Free British Democratic Party Youth. All on 'Socialist Motherland' GDR lines and with annual People's Parades and hordes carrying flowing red banners. The dream of the older Milliband.

I see them all marching in sing-song unison, holding aloft giant and awe-inspiring pictures of the Great Stakhanovite Heroes of Labour – Marx, Engels, Lenin, Stalin, Attlee, Kinnock, Brown, Balls, Milliband, and Cable. Wearing their ribboned Red Orders of Labour, of Lenin, &c.

I still have *terrible dreams* – recurring nightmares – of having only just and miraculously escaped such a destiny. And of my escape from years in an 'Anti-Fascist' re-education camp. I would surely have been called 'an obstacle to democratic process.' With George as cell-mate. We know what the Bolsheviks did to people like me. Remember the USSR, the mass murders in the Gulag and the genocide of inconvenient 're-settled populations' which *every* Communist society has produced. The Stalinization, the Sovietization, the Totalitarianization, and the end result of mass misery, mass starvation, and mass murder. A land of chains and death.

I still do have these dreadful nightmares. Based on actual realities like those that were experienced by millions in Europe and the Soviet Union. We all know the details. But has Mr. Milliband ever read Anne Applebaum's study, *Iron Curtain. The Crushing of Eastern Europe* (London, Allen Lane, 2012; Penguin Books, 2013)? For example. Or her earlier work on *The Gulag*? Or the studies of the USSR by Robert Conquest or Richard Pipes. Or Solzhenitzyn's works. Or the novels of Donald James. He certainly should do so.

He needs to move away from general theories to actual practical detail, to hear individual stories, to grasp what was actually done to millions of real people. And then to re-build his understandings of how and why the institutions of civil society and of creative spontaneity were destroyed, undermined, deformed, manipulated. How a legal and civic system, a functioning economic system, a democratic political system, an independent educational system, independent organisations, advocacy groups, charities, churches, newspapers, literary and educational societies, retail and wholesale shops, stock markets, banks, sports clubs, colleges, all the richness of a diverse culture of voluntary organisations, private businesses and competing political parties was made impossible by THE PARTY.

And how so many millions of human spirits were crushed in the thuggish Bolshevik terror and purges in their drive for permanent and universal power and conformist control of *every* aspect of human life and society while grotesquely failing to deliver the promised prosperity and higher living standards allegedly guaranteed by 'scientific' Marxist-Leninism. Which still insisted on eliminating any kind of dissent. The Berlin Wall of 1961 was not constructed by Soviet boss Nikita Krushchev to prevent people from the West breaking *into* Eastern Germany!

As Boris Pasternak wrote in *Doctor Zhivago*, "And so it was necessary to teach people not to think and make judgements. To compel them to see the non-existent, and to argue the opposite of what was obvious to everyone...." Is this to be the touchstone of High Millibandism too?

Anne Applebaum's superb work tells you all about the terrible and arbitrary repressive cruelties – and the incessant and turgidly grotesque propaganda – suffered by many millions that uniquely arose from the *imposition* of Communism in post-war Europe alone. Professor Milliband's favoured system. The system based for its very existence on lies and fakery, with mendacity as the foundation stone and terror and cruelty the everyday consequence.

The Communists maintained two systems of government, two systems of reality – one real, one imaginary. The real one was sheer hell for billions. The dictatorship of the proletariat [whatever that could mean] was a mockery of resounding hollowness. The dictatorship of the Party bureaucracy was the hardest, bluntest, bloodiest fact in a structure of total central controls.

Might it have happened here? Could we have had to suffer what was imposed on East Germany, the Baltic States, Hungary, Czechoslovakia, Bulgaria, Romania, Cuba, Communist China, Poland, Yugoslavia, and the territories of old Russia?

'Gather ye rosebuds while ye may', the poet Herrick sang. For certainly it *could* have happened here, if the *far left* had had their way. George Orwell specifically warned us, in *1984* and in A*nimal Farm*. We might well have been brutally driven into a new society...which Mr. Ed Milliband no doubt would have abhorred? But once it was in place how would it have been dislodged? And what would have been the fate of social-democrats? No secret, that.

I imagine that society, with 24 thoughts:

1. With the special training-centres, with such euphemisms as the 'fight against banditism', with the leather-coated KGB knocking at the door at 3.45 a.m., with deportation to another 'operative centre' or a labour camp in the Gulag, and never being heard of again. With Chekist controls and ongoing political 'purification' everywhere.

2. With the Cabinet renamed The Politburo, and the governing tribal troika dubbed the Central Committee or the Committee for National Liberation.

3. With the House of Commons renamed the Provisional National Assembly, and the Home Office renamed the People's Commissariat for Internal Affairs, &c.

4. With the key organisation HQ in Ballsworth Pond Road, renamed BritPolRevCom – the British Political Revolutionary Committee.

5. With a rigid and peculiar culture of specific individuals from the clique named as responsible for Ideological Affairs, for Cadres, for Propaganda, and for Internal Security in its ginormous cream and green HQ on the banks of the New Volga [formerly, The Old Thames].

6. With the transformation of the police into The Red Guard.

7. With a new Leninist 'normality' enunciated in every detail by the official press agency and by BritRevCom TV and Radio, the sole permitted Brit owners of transmission equipment.

8. With every primary and secondary school required to teach Marxism, dialectical and historical materialism, and the history of the Communist Party of the USSR and the Comintern, from age 5. As no doubt the Milliband father had himself hoped.

9. With every significant business nationalised, and private property eliminated.

10. With mass printings of the works of Kinnock, Marx, Engels, Lenin, Plekhanov, and Stalin. Not forgetting Balls on Economics.

11. And the 'middle-class' speeches of His Venerated Leadership Himself?

12. With the LSE renamed the International Lenin School for Cadres. Incorporating the NKVD [National Klingfilm Veterans' Department].

13. With every youth required to study The Great Leader's Great Book, *The Tasks of The Times in the Democratic Reconstruction of the Peoples' Economy*.

14. With Socialist Heroes shown driving Tractors, projected digitally onto every public building.

15. With the TKGB [The Klingfilm Guards Britain] providing not even very secret assistance to the nascent new state, and leading the theoretical way against reactionary pluralist 'petit-bourgeois decadence' and un-socialist organisation.

16. With every trainee for anything required to join the New British equivalent of the *Volkssturm*, or People's Militia. For 6-nights-a-week 'voluntary' ideological training.

17. With The Peoples' League of Pioneering Working Youth unifying workers, peasants, and students under the universal non-partisan banners: "Those who are not with us are

against us. The rest are Fascists", and 'All Power to the Peoples' Passions, Talents, and Free Time for the Party.'

18. With the previously free media closed down, replaced by the official Party daily *BritComPolTruth*. All other media shut as being a source of 'anti-BritComSov propaganda'.

19. With all previous artistic and cultural groups of all kinds made illegal – replaced by the new *Kulturbund* to encourage proper 'self-understanding', 'self-criticism' and ideological purity.

20. With all personal computers, telephones, ipads, ipods, iwatches, kindles, and other electronic devices officially registered, and subject to individual inspection by the Red Guards.

21. With all churches closed down, but reopened as food rationing centres.

22. With BritSov-tweet, BritSov-net, BritSov-linked, BritSov-ipad, and BritSov-mugbook replacing all the net media of a democratic free society. No personal access to the worldwide web.

23. With the official censor *BritSovOmnipresent*, playing a key direct, operative and organisational role in the required BritSov-transformation of life in BritSov itself.

24. With BritComSovEduc socialising all children politically in all nurseries from age 3, and in elementary schools from age 5.

Thus, a comprehensive, people's Sovietised Britain, with a constant and brutal attack on all the organisations of disruptive civil society? With man to be forcibly 'perfected' on the Soviet model? *Homo Brownieticus? Homo Milkkibandius? Homokablerised? Homobirdnumbit.* In my nightmares that is. Oh, woe indeed!

We are a long way from all that, thank goodness. But when I consider what attitudes such possible anti-business political approaches seem to me to reflect I am uncomfortably reminded of Mussolini's words, "Everything within the state, nothing outside the state, nothing against the state."

Direction always matters. I feared where High Millkibandism might lead.

Somehow, we have avoided seeing all other political parties hostile to 'socialism' banned. Though some would have tried if they thought they could get away with it. Somehow, the economic and social chaos produced by the 'Popular Coalition' has been escaped. Somehow we have escaped the older Milliband's visions. Somehow, our often inadequate democratic institutions stood our own test of time.

To do otherwise would necessarily have required deep inroads to be made into the private economy, with the distortion of markets by central planning and by price controls, by the deterrence to enterprise, by the expropriation of financial institutions. With the deprivation of private capital as investment in the economy, with hyperinflation created by politicised industrial policies and the consequent shortages of basics. Including food, due to the kinds of Bolshevik nationalisation of wholesaling in Communist Europe after 1945, and of which we have such evidence.

The war against independent retailers, the failures of distribution, the central regulation of prices, the outlawing of functioning stock markets, the anti-business propaganda and high taxation – all backed up by criminal penalties for dissent. No need to look into the crystal ball. Look at history. Communism never been properly tried? Tell that to the Poles!

Lord Ironside's forthcoming new study will show how it all fell apart here. Indeed, the return of a new Conservative government led by William Hague was the triumph of democracy and of the sanity of the British people. But even now William is still struggling to put things right, and to rejuvenate the nation. George is very glum, however, and no help. Now in Washington at the World Bank, of course. But very cautious about any new loans to the UK. Can hardly blame him.

Well, set aside my nightmares. We can still see very clearly the sufficiently awful social-democratic results of this LabLibDemsy government – of which we are now so gladly rid. It's bad enough, without Communism! Look at the sector of small business, for example. The arch-terrorist Lenin himself realised that here was the driving force of much successful capitalist development, and so he crushed it. Here, recent UK economic growth was starved of investment capital by Milliband's policies. Business cut off from being intrinsically linked with the global community in emerging markets. Entrepreneurs driven away abroad by Balls's taxes and by the consequences of the pervasive Milliband/Cable ideological bias. And anything but very marginal profits made illegal, under the BNEP [Balls' New Economic Plan].

We know that investment fell sharply. No private business earned a yield. No economic incentives survived. Taxes rose and rose, but with no wealth created by which to pay them. 'Public services' collapsed, unfunded. Instead of business people being enabled to be in the right places at the right times to meet new partners for world markets and make new contracts a great hush fell over the economy. And so there was no agenda for enterprise and growth. Quite the reverse.

Worse, as global commodity prices rose, and as UK productivity fell, Relabelled New Old Labour put up VAT to 30% – and then to 40% – as well as raising the top rates of income tax to 80% – and then to 90%. Allegedly, to help the poor. 'Governmental Administered Prices' – like extra taxes on fuels, to fund higher benefits and many FREE services – made it all worse, too. Then the government allowed wages to rise quite unaffordably, entirely due to the capricious but unrelenting demands of its Union paymasters. Public services inevitably collapsed.

We know from Applebaum the old Hungarian tale: "The definition of socialism: an incessant struggle against difficulties which would not exist in any other system." We should all take our nightmares and dreams seriously. They are warnings as well as sign-posts!

In these memoirs I have focussed on the NHS itself, as a prism and perhaps a harbinger. It has reflected these wider errors and socialisticised mind-sets, over many years. Even now, it is still the last surviving post-war state Monopoly. I have looked at my own files on various specific NHS and social care issues, for my years in government and in opposition. The list which we should have tackled is lengthy. Funding, clearly. Personal insurance, co-payments, Health Savings Accounts. Management changes. Economic incentives. Obesity. Self-responsibility. And – crucially as ever – prices. For without them there is no way to curb demand. The introduction of co-payments and these other changes is even more essential now. More personal insurance, too, with the introduction of an 'excess', as in other insurances. This would help curb daft demands. We should have gone for a rapid extension of the social care personal budgets system into acute care, as well. And a separate compulsory individual insurance for A&E services. This would have released billions for other care budgets.

Is it all lost, even now? Surely not?

As T. S. Eliot says in *Four Quartets*,

"All time is unredeemable.
What might have been is an abstraction
Remaining a perpetual possibility
Only in a world of speculation."

But I still recognise what he calls

"The passage which we did not take
Towards the door we never opened."

Despite all the evasive bleating from The Klingfilm Fund and others, we still *can* concentrate on the individual empowerment of patients, with individual health savings accounts. That *must* be the future! That *must* be the door to the future! And so now I hope that William will indeed act on Health Savings Accounts and a broad mix of funding. Introduce Patient Guaranteed Care Associations, as voluntary, mutual, purchasing bodies – as purchasing bodies to genuinely empower individual patients. And tackle all the issues of power, and of self-responsibility.

It is time to stop evading the only thing that works. Which is money in the hands of the individual. We can then get all the necessary consequential and transformative changes.

It seems likely that managers and doctors will only then respond. When patients have individual financial power. When they can actually remove their individual tax-based funds – together with any extra personal insurance-funds they may provide from their own savings – and go round the corner to another and a preferred provider.

Makes even Lord 'Owzat seem innocuous!

And, as some Trust Chair or other said a while back now:

"Money talks, and preference walks".

[to be concluded....]

Note added by The Editor on 3 October, 2015. *Far fetched?* Maybe. But consider a possible proto-Marxist Corbyn/McDonnell government, printing inflation galore and forcibly creating *Homocorbyn*. Note, too, that in his acceptance speech as Labour leader Corbyn called Professor Milliband "great." 'Course Corbyn was elected democratically, by some 250,000 Labour activists and £3-riders, wasn't he? Which is more persuasive than the 34 million who decisively and deliberately voted against Labour in the May 2015 General Election, isn't it? Democracy at work and all that. So that's all right then?

EPISODE 50

The PM & The N£sd 'Reforms.' An Early Extract From His Memoirs, Part 8.

I Stood In Time. My Prime Ministerial Memoirs, By The Duke of Notting Hill and Chipping Thompson, KG, OM, FRSPR.

[the final extract].

Of the NHS it cannot be said that "The lenient hand of time did much for her by insensible gradations in the course of every day" – if I may cite *Northanger Abbey*....

But, as PM, I did have some entertaining times. Sending Eddie Izzard to the Lords did produce some illuminating dress-occasions. He being very gaily introduced to the Upper House by his sponsor, Lord Gordon-Brown. Alongside Baroness Grayson Perry, who was introduced by Baroness Sitting Bull of Emertonii. Both with new bouffant hairdos for the occasion. Gaily holding hands so nicey. So very touching. Lord Ironsides was a brilliant appointment at Chessingfield-on-Soke, too. Great mover and shaker. Need many more like him. If only could get them.

Sir Barney Wells continues to do well at the re-named Edmund Burke Memorial NHS Trust. Shining light in the North. Sending "Jurassic" Johnson on a 30-year contract to be Ambassador to Tristan da Cunha was a good move, of courseBusiness. And sponsoring that nuisance Dr. Hogelbin to conduct his inquiry into lethal Mosquitos on the Zambezi. Still has five years left before has to report back. No news lately.

As Thackeray told us, the sun shines every day on Coventry Island! And no doubt on the Zambesi, too! So I am able to read and re-read the great books on these beautiful and cloudless days. Currently, Thackeray's *Vanity Fair*. Which reminds me…send this note on economic policies to William, the new PM!

The key policy for us now must be for a genuinely low-tax, incentives economy, with a much smaller take by the state, and an expansion of the economy by entrepreneurs and by those who genuinely give service to consumers. Very notably, too, in education and in health. We should be aiming at a lower target of *at least* the 38.2% of GDP spent by the State which George Osborne has promised for 2018-19. State expenditure needs then to be on a further downward trend, with continued changes in supply and demand. Our economy *is* getting stronger when compared with the mad free-for-all under Brown and Balls. But productivity remains low relative to our major competitors, and, worryingly, the Office of National Statistics says that it is getting worse. Output per man hour in the UK is 21 percentage points below the G7 average.

So, when we hear the Labourite cries against "the cuts" we need to respond by deluging business with encouragement for much greater productivity. Not many cuts, actually – but we did slow down the increases. And we cannot allow ourselves to remain 30 percentage points less productive than Germany, France, and the USA. We *are* creating jobs. We *are* the fastest growing economy in Europe. *But* we have also become a low-wage, low-productivity, low-ambitions economy. This bodes ill for our future. We need to consume less and invest more, and to urge our companies to embrace the competitive disciplines of export markets too. We need efficient producers, efficient managers, and major supply-side changes. Without these changes, we are for the knacker's yard!

None of these cultural shifts will be easy – especially if we allow the so-called examples of the way public-services (so-called) are run to be held up to us for admiration. Similarly, the challenges of funding the pensions of an increasing number of elderly people will not go away. It is not possible to sustain borrowing nearly 40p in every £ that government spends.

Inevitably, too, if we can continue to lower all taxes then the better-off middle-classes can and should pay for more services directly.

This, too, will impact positively on management, producer, and quality. The working-classes would benefit, with their own money in their own pockets. We must ensure that they find themselves as genuine customers. They will then be *pursued* by private and public services who *want* their custom and not remain merely condescended to by public providers. It's time that we properly emphasised to the so-called 'public services' that there are competitive pressures to keep costs down and quality high; that running services is a competitive business; that with too much waste there will be unwelcome consequences for managements.

Milliband and Balls destroyed much of Britain competitive edge, and we can only now rely on the vivacity of the nation to recover from their depredations. The echoes of their lack of realism in most things actual will continue for years, however.

They pursued the wealthiest top 1%, and enforced much higher taxes. Marginal tax rates at 50% had results which Milliband and Balls did not expect. Some rich people fled abroad. Which it was obvious they would do. Some hid money in tax shelters. No surprise there. Lawyers and accountants were very busy. And those a bit lower down, middle-class earners without good lawyers at their beck and call, rebelled politically.

But Milliband completely missed the real economic point, which is that in a modern, digital economy the wealthy will actually grow in absolute numbers. This larger class of a richer higher middle-class – the economist Tyler Cowen projects that they will make-up 10% of the population – will be much more powerful politically. Indeed, those who actually produce the wealth seem certain to be the dominant economic, political and social influences. Services will then have to change. We know already that in the UK the top 1% earn nearly 14% of income but pay a record almost 30% of it in income tax. The income tax paid by the highest 300,000 earners – the wealth creators! – paid last year was 7.5% of all tax receipts.

The dramatic reduction in pension tax relief for high earners, the sharp jump in Old Labour corporation tax, the absurd and costly-to-collect annual wealth tax on homes worth more than £2m, extra super-taxes [so-called one-offs!] on financial institutions, price controls, more and more direct Whitehall interventions – all this a recipe for Francois Hollande-style disasters. Which were predictably achieved. Entrepreneurs, business managers, professionals of all kinds were all hit hard. And for why? To pursue an out-of-date Bob-Crow-like ideology Hardly any wonder that so much of our enormously important financial services have now gone – forever – to Frankfurt, New York, and Singapore.

As to state spending, it's certain that the biggest government budgets will remain health and social care, education and welfare. The elderly will increase in numbers, and in their demands. They vote, too. Medicine and care, one way and another, will take upwards of a fifth of the economic output. Indefinitely. We will all be a lot older, and there will be many more of us. We will be more conservative, too, but not less demanding. We can shift some of these inevitable health and elderly care costs, and we can each plan for ourselves now, if we are still young enough to afford it. But these costs cannot vanish. Indeed, they will go on rising both in absolute and in per capita terms.

And so if we are to pay for all this we need to help *businesses* to create wealth constantly. We need to ensure much more for the buck, too. Difficult choices will have to be made as well. We have to face either dilution of services, or enormous fiscal changes, or changes in eligibility, and much greater self-responsibility and life-style changes too. Probably all of these. Certainly, as a nation we need to waste less on poor services and on hugely wasteful unearned welfare, too. Those who have little or no income, little or no education and training, who have saved nothing, started no businesses, lived in debt, invested nothing, demanded all from the state, failed to get up in the morning or turn up for medical appointments – these will continue to burden public services.

It is neither possible nor wise to try to create a false and politically imposed equality. This is a political ideology which entirely falsifies realities. And the so-called 'deep State' has dug terrible pits into which we have all fallen.

But we are in a terrible fix here. And, frankly, I do not know what society can do now about these people at the lowest levels. More rationing, more delays, and less waste in consumption seems inevitable. Much more personal effort to be healthy is essential – and it is exercise, diet, self-care, self-motivation and conscientious attitudes – as well as demographic status and genetic inheritance – which makes the most difference anyway. These factors are the determinants of the greatest health outcomes. So much of poor health status is self-inflicted. And left-liberal demands for equality, imposed "social justice" and diversity do not tackle this issue. One thing is very clear: those who respond to the necessity of more self-control will be healthier, but those who do not respond will lose in many ways.

It does not seem very likely that the long-term welfarists will respond very much. Theirs is now a deeply embedded culture. And so to have any chance of sustaining these poorest at any decent level of living we need to achieve a high productivity, high income economy, for sustainable growth. And we do need to tackle self-responsibility and reduce unnecessary demand in the NHS where we can. Especially so if we cannot do much to discourage an entitlement culture because the politics (and the BBC!) won't allow us to curb it very much.

Everyone should be paying less tax. Everyone should be taking more personal responsibility. Everyone should be making their own self-responsible decisions, with much more of their own money. And with a conservative, flat-tax economy as the basis for a booming economy. We most definitely do not need politics to be the threat that it has become to successful businesses.

I accept that during my administration we drifted too far towards governmental intervention, higher tax rates on income, and assaults on business. It has become worse under Milliband and Cable. Business needs a predictable and supportive climate in which to invest. It does not need micro-management from Whitehall. We have surely learned from the experiences of the French under Hollande, and our own under this Old Labour government. We must ensure that companies can expand profitably, and not keep after them. For it is they which create jobs, wealth- and tax receipts to pay for public services.

Indeed, the market contestability which is at the heart of good businesses should be spread to public services too. We need to reverse the direction of every of single policy ever even *mentioned* by Mr. Balls. *'Hoicks, Tally Ho!'*, as Facey Romford says!

We have only just begun to escape from the quicksand of the *unreflective* bigger state, for which I myself am in part responsible. I am partly to blame for not building much stronger public support for the free market economy and an enterprise culture. I am guilty of not doing the thinking, which I am trying to do now in retirement. Indeed, this is proving to be my main theme in these memoirs. This would have enabled me to undertake real NHS reforms.

But I let Clegg and Cable hold me back. They dragged the nation back against real change, like a pair of rusting anchors. And we allowed them to constantly reinforce such a consensus. But look where Clegg is now! The new Euro-Commissioner for Turkish Drains! Appointed by Milliband after losing that seat in Sheffield. And at £500,000 p.a too! Tax free, and pensioned, *a la* Lord Patterer. With Cable now the Deputy-leader of the once-again Relabelled New Old Labour Party, indeed!

As to the dear old NHS, you have only to look at the OECD reports on very poor outcomes for patients – worse every year for key diseases, compared with Europe – to realise that we desperately need real NHS reforms, based in a culture of enterprise, entrepreneurship and individual service.

Lord 'Owzat continues to make his inspirational speeches. But otherwise, alas, general ignorance of the working of the NHS is astounding. I am in good part to blame for this, I confess now. And I should have more carefully read Tony Blair's memoirs, where he stressed that he should have been much more radical and much earlier. Too much sand in the glass now, alas. That terrible English – phrase "Too late!"

But I hope that William can do it now. He has the 'dressing room' behind him, and the backbencher pack on his side – which I did not have for most of my years as PM. He should, too, make systematic use of our years of hard learning. For example, on patients' complaints. We wasted this key resource.

Economics remains a half-interest of mine – the results of your bullying, George! – even here under the swishing palm trees, with the healthy breeze, and with the restful sound of the surf. And my weekly package of news, which I review online, tells me of William's gradual recovery from the deflationary spiral that beset Britain under New 'One Nation' Labour. And which itself so undermined all NHS funding. Hardly helped by Mr. Birdnumb and his 'Back to Bevan' policies.

The whole economy soon got into a fix, of course. Vast capital flight. City of London pre-eminence lost to Frankfurt. 'Invisible-earnings' totally invisible. No banks, so no bonuses. Food shortages. Unannounced and often lengthy power cuts. Bread rationing. Queues everywhere. And I did warn what would happen if hordes of Tories voted UKIP. Let in Milliband and Kable. What did we then get? Low demand in the economy, which fed into lower wages, which produced falling prices, which produced more deflation. Which undermined all the new competitiveness which George and I did so much to enhance.

As on so much in the economy itself, with the NHS we stood at the cross-roads, but we took the wrong turning. And so we have plunged ever deeper into the darkness that surrounded us. We should have sought a leap into the sunlight. We wasted our years in opposition, and should have taken the advice of the Institute of Economic Affairs on the demand-side. Nick Gibb is quite right to remind us now, and to guide William.

But the NHS is now even more obviously living on borrowed time. Its results remain very poor. It is still 'process' focussed. It is still dominated by provider trade unions. Its culture is still statist, and with no-one taking any individual responsibilities for individuals in care. Yet in an age of personalised medicine the old hit-and-miss, inept, uneconomic, and clinically ineffective methods in a vast and unwieldy bureaucratic structure of shams and shibboleths will no longer do.

Taxes alone cannot fund it, either. We need real economic growth, and new ways to spread the funding burdens. Without growth the problems under Brown and after will seem like a ripple of a shrimp in a jam-jar. Under Milliband the deflation ogre came roaring home. We wanted falling inflation, and rising employment, but a long period of declining prices delayed household spending, hurt company profits, hurt wages, hurt the continued innovations of the markets.

Deflation, too, increased the real value of public-sector and household debt, which was yet another Balls-ish way to torpedo the modern economy. Alas, there is no sign that Milliband even now believes in the free enterprise economy, or in markets, or in labour market reforms, or in a slimmer public administration, or in consumer's making decisions for themselves.

Under Milkiband, the collapse of the housing bubble, falls in asset values, increases in personal and governmental indebtedness, all created enormous uncertainty about the future. So people cut back on spending and on investment, which itself produced lower sales, lower output, and lower employment. Firms were seriously short of cash-flow, demand was down, credit lines were restricted, future plans and investment were shelved, the entire economic environment became riskier. And government itself was fragile and misleading in its intrusive responses.

There remain the continuing scandals of medical errors. Of course, it is we politicians (and NHS managers) who – in the dumb public mind – are always being blamed for elementary doctors' errors. I confess that I take my share of the blame here. Again, a failure in public education. But the continued blaming of politicians and of local managers is, however, a serious misreading of what is going on even now. This remains an impediment to its rectification.

William's new NHS boss, the ultra-glam and very bright Ms. Silvikrin Portersmouth MP, must address this.

I am hopeful about the new government under William. The new health secretary will surely be supported by Michael Fallon, the very shrewd and safe new Chancellor of the Exchequer. By Michael Gove, the excellent new Foreign Secretary. And by the Education Secretary Nick Gibb – who is a very impressive and surviving Thatcherite who I ought to have promoted myself. IDS is proving a splendid leader of the Lords, which is no surprise.

Nadhim Zahawi is an outstanding Education Secretary, too – and he is putting up with no nonsense from the teacher unions. He had a successful business career before coming into Parliament, of course. We need many more like him. I suppose I'm glad too that Jesse Norman has been given a good job, although I could not stick the man. He should do well at Transport though. Knows cars. Edward Timpson another rising star. And Anna Soubry, of course.

I am glad to see, too, how brilliant Dr. Julian Lewis is proving as Defence Secretary after Hammond went off to be Ambassador in Washington. Julian and I did not usually agree with one another. But he has proved to be right on all the key issues in his special areas of expertise. Respected by the Service Chiefs. And still writing serious books. My bad mistake not promoting him much sooner.

The economic journalist Jeremy Warner has also proved to be an important accession as Chief Secretary to The Treasury. As has Fraser Nelson, who moved from editing *The Spectator* to chair the new Independent Bestpress Commission which will protect the free press. And, let us hope, finally reform the ghastly left-wing and wholly-biased leftie BBC and get rid of the license fee. As I wish I had done now. Gove would and could have done it. Lord Booth of Haywards Heath, too.

The doctors of course, remain a key problem for NHS reform. We can't do with them; we can't do without them. And they are thrilled that someone else is still being blamed for their negligence. The public mistakenly shoot at politicians and at managers. This passes the buck beautifully. The Royal Academy of Vested Interests, the Great British Whitewash Company PLC, the BMe-Me, and the GPs too, are happy about this. And they get away with it still as no-one is looking! Regular, systematic, local, specific inspections by *independent* medically qualified staffs? Not there even now.

But as one recent medical contributor to the *Daily Telegraph* website said:

"Doctors and nurses are very much part of 'the problem'. They are entirely clinically unaccountable – to taxpayers, to patients and to their own profession. Their 'leaders' (GMC, BMA, Royal Colleges) will not countenance such scrutiny – still less will they exact points, fines, punishment for the perpetrators of elementary clinical errors – which daily, nationwide, pass without professional remark".

"Patchy medicine continues. So called 'MOT' checks and revalidation for State health personnel are a smokescreen to avoid implementing rapid identification of simple errors on the wards and in GP surgeries. Simple errors by drivers, when seen, are daily and nationwide punished there and then. This is seen as a deterrent to bad drivers. There are clinical red lights driven through every day. Nothing happens to stop them."

Still, it's easier to shoot at No.10, and at local managers like old Stewed ["I will not resign!"] Bludgeon at St. Hilda's on the Hill. But it's not the managers and politicians who do the medicine on the wards. It's not them who make the clinical mistakes. The ones who make them are the doctors (and nurses). So it is important to make sure that the blame falls where it is due. And to correct, retrain, and punish where due.

It is the medical professionals who do or do not take the histories properly, order and assess the tests, liaise properly with the laboratories, and then advise the patient. It is not the politicians who do – or do not do! – any of that. So let us not let the professionals subvert the necessary controls over their slack practices by suggesting that the blame rests elsewhere than with the health professionals themselves.

We are not talking here about waiting times in A/E, or too few staff, or lazy management either. As Dr. Bill Pickering has shown us clearly, we are talking about simple medical errors, adverse ones made by professional staff every day. Of course, as PM I became used to the defensive claims that "If there were more doctors and less managers and more funding simple mistakes wouldn't get made." I do not believe it. The hosts of patient's complaints make my case.

I remind myself here – and my readers too – that there would be no work, no titles, no high salaries, no pensions, no social status for medical professionals if there were no patients! It is the patients who should be 'the top', not the docs. The politicians and the professionals are the base, on which good services should be built and respond to patients. They should not be the 'top'. But until patients can actually shift the money elsewhere to a preferred provider, power they will not have.

If the public is to be the "assessor" of the NHS, the "active regulator" (in Professor Sir Bruce Keogh's term), then this will only be real if individuals control money – so that they can express preferences in a way which will really count. If that had been in place how many would have walked away from the 14 NHS Trusts under special measures now??? Would they all have had to wait for the Francis Report on Mid-Staffs???

If enough individuals removed their funds, what would have happened with the NHS culture of poor information, weak chains of responsibility, process-obsessed staff, dirtiness, ill-trained nurses, absentee doctors, lack of compassion and concern, especially for the elderly? What would managers have to do to change jargon, bureaucracy, attitudes? And with someone in charge and who accepts responsibility? The Royal College of Vested interests may indeed decry Tesco, but Tesco is run to higher standards of concern for its customer preferences – and it would go bust if it was not so.

Of course, modern medicine is often terrific. Keyhole surgery, magic pharmacy, all that. But the rudimentary errors are different. They are about what every medical student is taught from the beginning. And it is when the basic rules are broken – no proper history taken; lab tests not done, or not followed up properly, patients not referred on swiftly and to the right person – that the damage is often done. It is these rudimentary errors which we have to tackle. And which the so-called and so-lauded new inspection regime is in my view absolutely not tackling at all.

Remember, dear patient. It is not the politicians who do or do not take the patient's history, do or not do the tests, study or ignore the lab. results. It is not the managers who do or do not do these things. It is the doctors! So: time to "get it"!

As to being PM, that was not all dross, of course. I loved being PM, actually. I especially liked the overseas visits. Loved going to Washington and to The White House and walking across Pennsylvania Avenue – if I was not entirely happy at staying at the government hostelry, which is called Blair house!

Moscow was always intriguing, if too much like Old Brown/Balls/Milliband Labour. I was always aware of what a dreadful graveyard that society was – how the whole Communist society itself was *the* prison.

As that shrewdly knowledgeable NHS columnist Facey Romford Jr. wrote, we need to keep reminding ourselves of what that society was like. An all-powerful state enforcing a monopoly system on behalf of so-called political values. And in the interests of some larger theoretical good. But political values which no one wants. And that itself only enforced in the Bolshevik state by brutal force and mass murder.

As Mr. Romford wrote, in the NHS we've still got such a terrible wastage of substance and energy. And that in a so-called free democracy! But as we've learned, a state monopoly system is always just one great deception. Conformist mediocrity. Endless repetition of a few prescribed and over-simplified ideas. But no bold investigation of new ideas. Imagination? Curiosity? Adaptive ventures? Trial-and-error initiatives? Action by people with executive ability? New ideas? "Dangerous" – is all that.

Then there is the oddity about New 'One Nation' Labour. Its leaders all socialists, but never say the word. They tried to substitute the words 'middle-class' for it. Leaders all FOR the people – ha! But they still will not give them any individual economic power as they are regarded as not fit to use their freedom. [But fit enough to Vote Labour?] Power only to be exercised by 'educated people', with the 'correct' perspectives. Acting in the interests of the uneducated masses. Otherwise, the people would never support this particular 'One Nation' elite and its ideas. The people themselves are not to have liberty until they are good and wise. Meanwhile, The Leaders will do it for them.

Seem to have heard this approach before. Marxigookery, Sovietism, Mao Tse-Tunged, Castroated, Klinnockleism, Prof.Hampsterites, &c. All the more reason why we must argue the case consistently for free markets and liberty.

Other regrets? If I had my time again I would not now set up the Prices & Incomes Commission under 'two-hand-bags' Mrs. Willitzers from the Socialisticised Cable's Department. Nor renamed the English Counties after those figures from Samantha's favourite children's stories. Nor opposed independence for the Isle of Wight, joining the Federation of Sark, &c. Nor appointed Viscount Benn as head of a new Industrial Favourites Commission. Nor let Lord 'Owzat make all those Monty Pythonesque speeches on the "World's Most Wonderful NHS." Nor voted for Muckitupistan in the Euro-Vision song contest. Nor sent John Selwyn-Gummerdrop and the Skiffling Daughters & Beefburgers as our entry. Nor let KG write our manifestoes.

As to the cricket… *Extract ENDS.*

Facey's Holiday Postcards, 1.
Give them the money!

17 February 2014.

Dear Roy,

Here I am fully suited at the dear old Lambton Arms. A good Yorkshire dinner, and excellent ale. Sent *Multum in Parvo* forward on the old puffing Durham & Cumberland County Rlwy train and rode *Gentle as She Goes* [previously known as *Buck-em-in-the-hedge* – Ed.] here myself. Now all well stabled and suited for the night. May be able to sell them on attractively. Gentle ladies horses perhaps. Eat fudge out of your hands.

And me now in the snug reading the latest from The Millkiband Kid. Aha! He shows how the political parties have merged into one anti-democratic whole. The Kid claiming that he will govern like Thatcher. Indeed! Well, no Tory has done so since. Blair did for a bit, but achieved little. Left it too late as he says in his memoirs. And just look at this – The Kid to give ordinary people more control over public services. In Committees!!! Well, that's alright then, isn't it???

This is, in course, the usual Klingfilm Fund meaningless guff. People to get more power in running hospitals and schools. By which he means more consultations! More Committees. More wasted time, debating an agenda set by managements. More official guidance by 'experts.' More of Prof Applecore and Prof. Hampster. More Astrologick wafflewhiffle. More local government interference. More 'activism.' More Millkiband chitter-chatter. With a tiny number of leftie nutter people appointing "patients representatives." Meanwhile, get back into your place in the queue!

WHEN will any politicians realise that the only *real* power for the individual – as the middle-classes perfectly well appreciate – is when the individual controls a personal budget by which to secure personalised care, and when there is a proper competitive market??? Then they can say, 'Thanks, but no thanks. I will go to an alternative provider.' So, give them the money! Then stand back and watch huge change! Give individuals real controls, with money which is mobile. Abandon the protection of the so-called 'public service' trade-unions and the medical vested-interests. Give up central controls. Trust the individual. Money is *the* solvent!

Likely? "Not likely!!!" as The Kid will say if ever in government! But we expect better from the Cameroons. Mmmm.

As to the weather. Well, wet indeed.

Your chum Facey.

PS. Have Just sent one of my grandsons a line from Smiles: "The object of the book briefly, is to re-inculcate…old-fashioned but wholesome lessons which perhaps cannot be too often urged, that youth must work in order to enjoy, that nothing creditable can be accomplished without application" – what I calls HEFFORT! – "and diligence, that the student must not be daunted by difficulties, but conquer them by patience and perseverance, and that, above all he must seek elevation of character, without which capacity is worthless and worldly success is naught." Smiles – he be the boy we should all be reading again!

Facey's Holiday Postcards, 2. Substance, or secret Masonic dimensions?

19 February 2014.

Dear Brian,

Had a great run with the Old Bozzles Hounds today. Fine scenting weather. Must have been 9 miles and four hours run if a minute. Fell upon old Foxie at Skimpledown Hills, just in time before dusk. An experienced and cunning old varmint he was. Now back in my bath, reading up on the news. Now who is this Sir Stuart Roses person who is to 'fix' the NHS? And what is this M&S? The earth-stopper here, Old Foggins Himself, says it's a place where customers have choices, pay their money, and bring the stuff back next day for something else.

Money talks, and all that. High street competition. Alternative suppliers. Costs that matter and are controlled. Buy on the net, and delivered locally. Smiles on the staff – actually W*elcoming* customers! *Jittery* with movement!

So how is this anything to do with the NHS, I asks myself. Isn't M&S a people-business? Whatever does Sir SR think he will be allowed to do by Lord 'Owzat & Co of the NHS? Beachcombing? Picking at a frozen seaside pool? Slithering on seaweed?

And do The Great Panjandrums at The Royal College of Vested Interests know about this? And at the Great British Whitewash Co PLC? Won't The Rt. Rev. Dr. B. Hogbin, GCSE be writing his *Mancunian Guardian* Toynbeeish articles again, in elliptical BMA-ese??? Here, little is said but much is meant and understood by the initiates.

So is this new project about change, or ambiguity? 'Empowerment', or merely 'consultation'? Curiosity, or expertise? Substance, or secret Masonic dimensions? The surface of things, or the substance? Revelation or concealment? Here, thought does not necessarily equal action.

I suspect that more will go missing than is ever found. Seems likely to be some initial fuss, then nil by mouth, then Nuffink done, then Sir SR back to the knickers counter, again. Sir SR to climb into C. S. Lewis's wardrobe, and hunt in vain for the secret doorway into the other world beyond? Who do you think *owns* this system? Eh?

I see the Tories plan to range a host of new Bills and legislation on our horizons. Well, dear old Smiles – Big Sam indeed – tells us that "…the value of legislation as an agent in human advancement has usually been much over-estimated. To constitute the millionth part of a Legislature, by voting for one or two men once in three or five years, however conscientiously this duty may be performed, can exercise but little active influence upon any man's life and character. Moreover, it is every day becoming more clearly understood, that the function of Government is negative and restrictive, rather than positive and active…reforms…can only be effected by means of individual action, economy, and self-denial; by better habits, rather than by greater rights."

Now, that's a handsome gee-gee I could ride to covers!

[to be continued this evening... on another card...]

PS. Having a lovely time, with all my annual re-read of favourite books. Dickens' *Our Mutual Friend*; Fred Hoyle's *Ossian's Ride*, John Christopher's *The Death of Grass*, C. S.Forester's *The Gun* and *Death to the French*; Evelyn Waugh's *Scoop,* and John Wyndham's *The Day of the Triffids*. Oh, and must do a bit of work, so have got with me Joel Mokyr, *The Enlightened Economy. An Economic History of Britain1700-1850* (New Haven and London, Yale University Press, 2009). And Surtees novels, in course!

Daniel Silva's new novel, *The English Spy*' is splendid. Lionel Davidson's thriller, *Kolyma Heights*, is a discovery. Must find his other works. Re-reading *Watership Down* now. Thank you, ancient Egyptians or whoever for inventing books!

Much more fun than the daily 106-page *Guaridna* public-sector jobs section!

Facey's Holiday Postcards, 3.
Make a muckle?

19 February 2014.

Dear Brian,

My advice to Sir Roses in one sentence – please pass it on: *Listen to Patients!*

He *might* be another Lord Ironsides. But my suspicion is that Sir Roses will be like Coleridge's sailors, locked in a power struggle with nature, finding old gods angry and vengeful, necessarily appeased if not vanquished. Or perhaps be like the Albatross of those seas, which were thought to embody the souls of dead sailors, but still baited, trapped and ill-treated before being released?

Or as Baudelaire says in his poem *Albatross:*

"This rider of winds, how awkward he is, and weak!
How droll he seems, who lately was all grace!
A sailor pokes a pipestem into his beak;
Another, hobbling, mocks his trammelled pace".

Or, Louis MacNeice:

"World is crazier and more of it than we think".

And how much nerve will politicians show with, a risky general election pending? How many guesses make a muckle?

As ever, Facey R.

Facey's Holiday Postcards, 4. All join hands and finish joint last together.

20 February 2014.

Dear Roy,

A by-day today. Not hunting. Too foggy for foxes. Too wet and cloggy in the quoggy meadows. Hounds eager, but do not want to lose any in the ditches. So, tucked up under a Scottish blanket in front of lovely, blazing log fire. With brandy. Reading the local rag, the *Daily Durham Denizen.* Which reports in its national summary that far down in the Soft Midlands there is something called Wolverhampton Council. Which has just let-go 2,000 staff. TWO THOUSAND? And this is only *some* of their staff! Whatever have that 2,000 been doing all this time? And what do the others – as yet uncounted – do?

This recession is a GOOD THING if it puts a stop to all this council-tykes never-properly-employed Sir Nicholson-like malarkey. I says. Monty could have beaten Rommel with fewer, didn't he? Beret and all.

Wonder if *any* of the 2,000 will get jobs in the private sector? Seems v. unlikely. Be on the dole forever, more like. Victims, eh? Unless employment is available at Featherbedding Mattresses of Sheffield, in Triffid Clugg's constituency.

'Course, bods might then need a sense of pace, urgency, customer-focus, hazard and risk in entrepreneurship, incremental change, all that economic stuff. For these former Wolverines it would be a bit like them playing dominos backwards, blindfolded, with the pieces daubed in Golden Syrup.

The Answer? Send for Bob Crow, c/o Silverbeeches Villas, Turks & Caicos Islands, for advice! Or advertise for him in the monthly *Which Strike? Your Practical Guide to Industrial Harmony* [Publisher, Lord Oeakegrotty. *[Who he? Ed].*

Once had a hargument with that Lordship. Me having private care not taking someone's place in the NHS queue, I insisted. I had joined a different queue entirely. And by doing so I had made a space for another bloke in the NHS queue, too. I'd paid twice as well, hadn't I? And a lot of spondulex as a higher-rate tax-payer. *Higher Rate Taxpayers Ahoy*, indeed! But should be tax incentives for more of us to do so. Come on George, get to it! And why can't see why the loonies can't see that it makes sense? Can't see it. Won't see it. Don't wanna see it! And so the queue grows, in which we are all to join hands and finish joint last together. Labour's idea of equality!

Will move on with the pack and the two horses tomorrow, to visit old Jogglebury. He does not know I'm coming. But I'm sure he'll accommodate me, stable the horses, and feed the hounds. Good chap he is. Might stay a while. See how the land lies. Trust all well with you.

As ever, FR.

Facey's Holiday Postcards, 5. Self-Help.

22 February 2014.

Dear Sir Roses,

Here is a sepia-picture of the old Kennels at Hamsterley, with the fast running fox on the weather-vane. *Tally Ho!* I only send it to those who I wish well.

It is, I trust, an antidote to what you are now discovering. That is, the happy joys of NHS group-thought, bureaucratic resistance to unpleasant warnings, the diversion of your own attention to a proper and thorough investigation of patients' complaints, and the usual inability to think outside the box of comfortable assumptions. What Thackeray once spoke of as the refusal to recognise "visible portents," and to connect the dots.

Incorrigibility rules, no doubt. And yet all this must be confronted and dealt with, just like any chronic disease. In course, to describe these complicated matters you will have first to disentangle all those threads that have been carefully woven to confuse, to mislead and usher you into a quiet corner.

Welcome to the murky world of NHS deception, masonic knots and twisted strands! As my old chum Johnno says, all this remains unlit to this day!

My holiday reading continues with the wonderful, shrewd, inspirational *Self-Help* by Samuel Smiles. A superb quote on every page. Should be a copy in every primary school classroom in the land.

Meanwhile, bring back Gove, all be forgiven!

Yours, in ever hopeful harness,

FR Jr.

Facey's Holiday Postcards, 6.
National Commission on *Not* Inspecting Care Homes?

4 March 2014.

Dear Roy,

Happy days trundling down the lovely east coast. Lots of care homes here. Made me think. Windy cliff-tops, awash with seagulls. Wondering why was it that those various National Commissions s'posed to be tackling standards on care homes did so little? Woz they told by Ministers that the job is to keep the lid on, NOT to take the lid off? Not to *find* trouble. No way, Jose. Dis is not zee jobee. But woz zee politics again? No CBE's and DBE's in lifting the roof, and *actually finding out* about the quality of care? So thank goodness for the *Daily Mail*!

Strikes me that when unannounced inspections happen now – oh, how rare they were once! – we do learn the truth, s'truth, Ruth. Can't have too much of that can we? Or can we?

As to politics internationalistically, I see that the Russians have been 'invited' in again, to Crimea and Eastern Ukraine just as they were to Hungary in 1956, to Czechoslovakia under Dubcek in the 'Prague Spring' crisis of 1968 – and arriving with tanks, as per usual, and not brass trombones. With big guns, not butter. With flame-throwers at the ready.

As KGBistical, as per usual. Only a dreamer could imagine that the Russians will ever let the Ukraine go. It is the bread-basket of the old Soviet Union, which still cannot feed its citizens. It will ever remain a hostage to the dictatorship by the USSR Stuffed – like the Baltic states – with Sovcitz, too.

Now I go to see tulips in Lincs. And Tennysonian hills. At least here the torturers do not knock on the door at four in the morning.

I'm out with the hounds tomorrow. *Yoiks!* As Jorrocks told us, "all time is lost wot is not spent in 'unting – it is like the hair we breathe – if we have it not we die – it's the sport of kings, the image of war without its guilt, and only five-and-twenty per cent of its danger"! That Blair should have left the foxes alone, and done that war properly the first time out.

As ever, your friendly observer chum.

Facey.

Facey's Holiday Postcards, 7.
Jobs for the boyos?

9 March 2014

Dear Lizzie,

In the Lincolnshire wolds today. Lovely sunny day, 63F. Sun blazing away, and can also see the moon shining above. Spring really here at last as saw first Brimstone and first Comma butterflies today. My personal test of springtime beginning. But a bit shocked by the *Sunday Times* Appointments pages. Well, MORE than a bit!

See adverts. Two bids for my spare time: The Bradford Teaching Hospitals NHS Foundation Trust wants a new chair. Pay is £55,145 p.a., for – what is it? – 10 days a month. Fancy head-hunters Gatenby Sanderson Board Practice paid, too, to find the bod. So add in their percentage. And this whopping £55k – plus zee expenses, too – for a non-executive Chair in an organisation that is never at risk, cannot go bust, has no competition and is under none of the disciplines of the market. Plus the OBE or CBE later for not making zee waves.

OR I could put in for a Trusteeship at The Altzheimer's Society. This being a really important charitable body, dealing with one of the most challenging of all issues. Unremunerated.

There are now over 800,000 people diagnosed with dementia in the UK, plus the many not diagnosed who are also suffering. And numbers set to rise to one million by 2012. Now…who has helped to develop this completely hoopla situation? Come On In Nye Bevan, Your Time Is UP!

Yours, in full cry, As ever,

Facey.

PS. Or I could put in for a Non-Exec. Director post in the Soviet State of Chesterfield. They want a non-exec for 3 days a month. But **only** paying £13,364 p.a. Why are they so mean? S'only taxpayers galore money. And why do some Trusts pay a Chief Exec. £150,000 to £200,000 and a Chair £55k, when no-one seems ever to be in charge of anything, and no-one takes any responsibility?

Facey's Holiday Postcards, 8.
No more Bennery!

17 March 2014

Dear Roy,

Has the time really come for me to entirely GIVE UP? The insanities of the world multiply. Who would have ever believed that people would actually vote [voluntarily?] to *join* the Soviet Union – as has just happened in the Crimea!

In course, it's not really a surprise, as the Soviet dictators over several generations flooded the Ukraine with Russian immigrants, deliberately diluting the Western-leaning Country, and so ensuring that in any future conflict they would be in control. Did the same in Estonia, Latvia, Lithuania as well. So not much of a democratic vote, was it, me-asks. Kruschev "gave" the Crimea to Ukraine, but he was only giving it to himself you see!

Note too in the news that Big Bob of the Rail Strikes and The Viscount Stansgate That Was are both now denizens of the Gulag in the Sky. Well, no tears shed for them two. Good riddance to both! Both would have happily imposed a Soviet tyranny on us. Labour camps, and the lot. Both denied State Funerals, too, it seems. But then neither did achieve their dream, of a British Crimea.

Meanwhile, see the Wonder Goal of the Decade, by the great Tomas Rosicky, 1-0 To The Arsenal vs. Spurs. So there is still hope for us all!

As ever,

Your Faithful Friend Facey.

Facey's Holiday Postcards, 9.
Whitewash galore!

12 September 2014

Dear Roy,

Here I iz at Canvey Island in the caravan, for my second holiday of the year. Borrowed from Lucy G. Just fancy!

Read about Manchester Dogs Fire. It has been revealed that all the unfortunate dogs had in fact come from Jupiter and Mars, on holiday. *None* were previously cruelly treated, or abandoned by the local Manchester people, as has been alleged. Not one. And so the money now being contributed is not guilt-money, said Alderman Chuffed Pakiwiggle, JP, leader of the Manchester Labour Group.

Also saw headline 'Wrong lung removed at Tunbridge Wells.' Today's report that over 300 serious errors on patients were made by Kent surgeons last year has produced an immediate response from The Great British Whitewash Co. PLC. "We have made certain that a porter is to be carefully examined and re-registered, in our Quality Control Programme", said Nursie Nursie Dixbungle, Chief Executive.

Shocked, too, that the girl-friend night-time murderer Pisstdorious was only sentenced to 120 hours voluntary time in an Oxfam shop, knitting booties.

Today's *Groggiaian* jobs-supplement, news section, says 'Judge Happlessdopeless Panderton, CBE announced today that she had never believed that it was credible and reasonable that the defendant should first have asked where his girlfriend was at 2.30 a.m. – in the bed? in the garden weeding? texting to her Auntie? – before blasting six shots through the bathroom door. Mr. Pisstdorious will however be very severely sentenced to work in an Oxfam shop, she stated. Meanwhile, he is free to holiday permanently in Malta. He has a new passport.

Did you see, too, that Milkiband suffers morning sickness? The New New Labour "leader" Mr. Mlikiband is suffering from morning sickness, it is said. He is pregnant with a new twice-daily policy. He has cancelled his monthly trip to Asda. Meanwhile, supplementary 'of-the-people' non-Blairite non-Brownite non-Balthsite leadership will be provided by Mr. A. Birdnumb [aged 7]. Laugh or cry?

More news tomorrow. As ever, FR, Jr.

Facey's Holiday Postcards, 10.
BBC speaks [like].

13 September 2014.

Dear Royo,

Further, noted Devious plan by Alex Pilchard. The Scottish Tsar-to-Be, Mr. A. Pilchard, has invited Cameron, Clegg, Brown, Prescott, and Milkiband to campaign in Scotland, in order to boost the "Yes" vote.

AND: 'Lord Paisley reports that God is Not a Roman Catholic.' At a séance this evening in Dublin Castle the late Lord King of Mumbledom [former N. Ireland Sec.] communicated with the other world, and reported that the late great and never-to-be-forgiven-for-being-right-all–along about-IRAthugs-Lord Paisley can now prove that God is CoE.

But if you want a real shock, *The Sun* says that the goalmouth footbooter Wayne Wookney is to learn English – to take new GCSE, reports their Sports Correspondent, Ms. Shuteye Dunnotherules.

Commenting on this development, a Mr. Ryan Gfiggs said, "Yerk nope hidea wunna da work. Me Ah Triedf Itt fer 9 yearers. Cdnuff dun Hit. Búnga lolly up wongkit drainphipe, c?" [See page 12, *The Sunday Sportie*].

I leave you with this one. BBC Scottish Editor reports on likely vote.

"Like, er, what, see what I mean, y'know." His annual salary is £267,000, plus pension and a new Mercedes car each year. And anticipatory dismissal bonus, too.

Remember what dear Jorrocks tells us: "There are but two sort o' folks i' the world, Peerage folks, wot think it's right and proper to do their tailors, and Post Hoffice Directory folks wot think it's the greatest sin under the sun not to pay twenty shillins i' the pound – greatest sin under the sun 'cept kissin' and then tellin."

Not Post Hoffice chaps, them BBCites. And more left-leaning than the Tower of Pisa. *License-Payers Ahoy!* Thank goodness for foxhunting!

Yours, in the saddle,

Facey Romford Jr.

PS. Big Sam says, ref the 19th century reformer Richard Cobden, that "…he had great perseverance, application, and energy, and with persistency and practice, he became at length one of the most persuasive and effective of public speakers…Sir Robert Peel said of Mr. Cobden, that he was a 'a living proof of what merit, perseverance, and labour can accomplish…'."

Take a bow IDS!

Facey's Holiday Postcards, 11.
Accident & Exit services.

23 July 2015.

Dear Lord 'Owzat,

Just back from Oz, now resting at Minshull Vernon, doing some family history. Pedigree, y'know.

I see that your gang was not Ukippered after all in the May General Election, and that you have your hands on the Seals of Office once again.

May I ask what you now propose to do about the shocking situation of the desperate sufferings of the very poor in the UK?

You know, only a small car, only two foreign holidays a year, only a small whopper-plazma tele, take-away grub only 14 nights a month, limited access to 2 crates of plonk per person per week, living in 6-bedroom council house rent and rates all paid by Town Hall, struggling along on £40,000 p.a. of benefits [plus supplements] and with only 9 kids paid for by the state, etc. etc.

Here's a truly shocking example of such dire poverty: how can it ever be allowed that a man like Frank Dobson, formerly Secretary of State for Health, can be *forced* to live in a Council house?

Similarly, the very recently and late poverty-suffering Lord Bob Crow of Rail Strikes, the RMT Union boss. *His* imposed social housing was surely a contributory cause of his mental suffering and of his early death?

And what about A&E [Accident & Exit] services? *The Sunday Times* informs me that overcrowding there is "killing thousands."

In "the best health service in the world" how can you allow such outrageous untruths to be published? Some Top Doc is reported to have claimed that it is now routine for Accident & Exit ambulance drivers to be diverted elsewhere from the most direct hospital, producing many avoidable deaths. And *daily*, too, it is said. Killing between 500 and 1,000 people a year. Can't possibly be true, can it, in our wonderful Big State System?

And this new official cancer report alleges that 30,000 people in the UK die unnecessarily every year due to our very poor services? So, over 20 years past, that's at least 600,000 poor souls.

I offer you the freedom of my pages in the first reprint of my book to dismiss all these ludicrous stories. We rely on you.

Yours, as ever, impartial,

FR, Jr.

PS. I'll be back.

Facey's Holiday Postcards, 12. The National Grocery Service.

25 July 2015.

Dear Secretary of State for Health,

I write from Skeggie. Still 'Very bracing.'

May I offer you an opportunity?

I see that the big grocery chains are talking mergers, and so reducing consumer choice.

Why not take the NHS into the grocery business?

After all, you have all the necessary experience.

You could build supermarkets to N£sd hospital specifications. You know about car parking, about local transport, about signposting and information-labelling in your surgical provision lanes, about queuing, about a complaints system, about NHS-lite, about weekend staffing, and about necessarily slow check-outs.

And so you could easily and confidently say to Tesgo or Muddlesons, "Hey, we've got an NHS like that. So why don't we get into the grocery business?"

They may well welcome your investment.

You could declare this "The Best Supermarket in the World!"

And send Lord 'Owzat to officialy open it.

Consider how well all our food, our choices, the quality, price and access would have been so much improved if the N£sd had taken over the failed mass-grocery business compulsorily in 1945 under Bevan. And if your Fabian "experts" had made all these irritating personal decisions on our behalf.

This was a major missed opportunity by the Welsh tyke in 1945. Should you not use your large majority to make the corrections now? Think of the willing customer support!

I remain, your friendly adviser, Facey R, Jr.

Facey's Holiday Postcards, 13.
Tax-free England?

26 July 2015.

Dear Chancellor,

If you really want to create a Northern Powerhouse – including my own beloved Hamsterley Grange, in course – and not just play with trains, why not declare every inch and acre of the country north of Birmingham a 100% Tax-free and a 100% Government Interference-free zone too?

No income tax, no VAT, no inheritance tax, no house-sales tax, no constant regulatory peskiness.

See then what happens!

This is already a successful city, but further north the economic expansion would be extraordinary.

Meanwhile I see that the *Grundiang* continues to re-define the English language. E.g., "Austerity" is to mean ""We cannot again spend the money which should never have been spent in the first place."

As to giving Greece another big bail-out, this is a big plastic Can't Pay Card too. *Kraut Taxpayer's Ahoy!*

Lastly, to the dear old N£sd again.

What's this in the papers about a fake locum doctor who worked illegally in *seven* different hospitals – treating *3,300 patients* in cancer, cardiology, surgery, transplant, and Accident & Exit? And no-one noticed…

'Course, how is the patient to know who is fake and who is "real" (*let alone any good?*) if hospital doctors and managers themselves can't tell – and if full information is not provided to us all on the lot of them?

Yours, respectfully (but prudently insured),

FR Jr.

Facey's Holiday Postcards, 14.
Stop press on Cancer services.

5 August, 2015.

Dear Roy,

I've been sent for review a typescript copy of a new book, *"Coming, Ready or Not. The Present, The Politics, and The Future of the NHS."*

Wonderful and very relevant read, and I see you mentioned a lot.

But there is are some deeply awful notes on Cancer Services, which I'm adding here.

The book says that the *Daily Telegraph* reported (31 July, 2015) both the wonder of a golf-ball sized artificial heart implanted for the first time, by a surgeon, Professor Stephen Schueler, at the Freeman Hospital, Newcastle-on-Tyne, and continued very poor cancer care.

But the newspaper also reported under the headline "Cancer patients only sent for tests after three visits to doctor." A quarter of cancer patients were dissatisfied with their care, and were losing faith in their doctor, said scientists from University College, London and the University of Cambridge. They studied data from 70,000 patients, and found that of the 60,000 people who were diagnosed by their GP, nearly 13,300 had been seen two or three times *before* they were referred for cancer tests. More than one in 10 felt that information had been deliberately withheld from them during their treatment.

Britain is eighth from bottom in league table comparisons of cancer survival in 35 Western countries, latest research shows. We are on a par with Poland and Estonia.

Almost half of cancers in the UK are diagnosed at an advanced stage, when treatment is less likely to work.

AND today, 5 August 2015, the *Daily Mail* reported that cancer survival rates in England lag well behind others in the West, despite millions being spent on diagnosis and treatment. Patients here are more likely to die of the six most common types of cancer than those in Australia, Canada, Sweden and Norway. In some cases survival rates are a third lower than the best performing countries. And even though there has been some improvement, researchers say that it will take years before government strategies can offer patients the best scans, drugs, and surgical procedures.

The study was undertaken on behalf of Cancer Research UK by the London School of Hygiene and Tropical Medicine. See the full research report published in the *British Journal of Cancer*. See *British Journal of Cancer* online publication 30 June 2015; doi: 10.1038/bjc.2015.164.

They looked at cancer survival rates for six types of cancer, in England, Australia, Canada, Denmark, Norway and Sweden. The result are truly shocking.

With the exception of Denmark, England's figures are the worst for all types. And especially so for lung-cancer where five-year survival rates are 12.7% in England, compared with 17.3% in Canada.

Only 20.7% of patients diagnosed with stomach cancer in England can expect to survive for five years, a third lower than the 27.9% rate in Australia. England lags more than a decade behind, the figures show.

For ovarian cancer the five-year survival rate is 35.2% – lower than that achieved by the other nations except Denmark in 1999.

For breast-cancer five-year survival rates in England have improved, from 81.1% in 2004 to 84% in 2009. This reflects major emphasis on the condition, and new investment. But even then the five-year survival rate remains behind the 86.2% of both Australia and Sweden.

Why is all this so? The reasons include patients being unaware of symptoms. Misdiagnosis by GPs is also a factor, and patients may not have been offered the most effective forms of surgery or the latest drugs. There is also much variation across the country.

The government has put aside £400m more for a drive to bring standards up. But other countries too will continue to improve, too.

What might have been so very different if the politicians and the doctors at Brighton and elsewhere had listened to the author of this new book in the 1990s? You may well ask!!!

As ever, your worried chum,

FR, Jr.

Facey's Holiday Postcards, 15.
Why not on the BleatBC?

6 August, 2015.

Dear Roy,

I know that you like puzzles…so, today I send a mystery for you to solve!

I see that *The Times* yesterday had a big bold headline: "Patients dying for want of drugs as Venezuela health system collapses." Whole structure kyboshed. Dreadful, avoidable sufferings and deaths. Wait months for vital treatment. No medicine, no chemotherapy, no radiography, nowt. Cancers which are curable not being addressed at all. Half of the 33,000 hospital beds unusable. Bloody chaos! Terrible sufferings, unrelenting.

This is what the late prezza Hugo Chavez, just the leading recent socialistical fantasist, did in providing free public healthcare for the poor. Half of the country's 15,000 doctors have fled abroad.

Why is none of this mentioned at all by the BBC? After all, Venez. is a famous exemplar of BBC-ite socialisticialism, is it not? A "socialist paradise"? Eh?

Public information not all it should be in Venez. it seems, either. *The Times* says that "The government claimed last year that there had been 36,000 cases of the potentially deadly mosquito-borne disease chikungunya. Independent health monitors put the figure at more than two million. A doctor who declared that there *was* an epidemic of the disease was branded a terrorist by new President Maduro, and an order was issued for his arrest. He, too, has now fled Venezuela Along with as many others as can get away. Not going to Cuba, either, I'll be bound!

Very sad to see that the great historian of the USSR, Professor Robert Conquest, has died here.

Genuinely very great man. But another one whose writings and warnings were ignored by the BB[USSR]C. He was scorned and ignored by academia, in course, but he turned out to be right about Stalin's Russia and his "socialism."

See Conquest's books, especially *The Great Terror. Stalin's Purge of the Thirties.* Released a month after fraternal Soviet tanks crushed the Prague spring.

Conquest said that an estimate of 20m deaths from Stalin's homicidal paranoia was certainly too low.

Conquest rightly was scathing of left-wing intellectuals, too – including G.B. Shaw and the Fabian Saintly duo Beatrice and Sidney Webb – for seeking to justify the Soviet Union under Stalin.

FACEY'S HOLIDAY POSTCARDS, 15. WHY NOT ON THE BLEATBC?

I wonder – oh, how I wonder! – if E.P. Thompson, E.J. Hobsbawm [CH!], Ralph Miliband, and the many other softly-cushioned-academical-Marxigooks like them ever *said that Conquest was right after all & in his life-time? Let alone that Corbynliner and his pro-Sov. Gang.*

Ask me another!

As ever,

FR, Jr.

PS. As the old nursery rhyme had it, *M... mourned for it.* And we might remind the politicians that it was *F... for fought for it!*

Facey's Holiday Postcards, 16. It beats them all! Death by diktat in the NHS.

8 August, 2015.

Dear Roy,

I'm on my walking tour of Bolt Head and the surrounds in lovely Salcombe in South Devon.

Exploring the coastline, the little coves and beaches (& the bistrolets!), and visiting old youth-hostelling pals. Found a really good house, with splendid views of this idyllic coast and sailing sky-blue bay. The scene itself saved by Operation Neptune in the 1960s. House is called 'The Anchorage.' Sleeps 8, with a little cottage in an orchard, too, for extra folks. So we could have a Christmas party of 12 here? You, her ladyship, etc. Just me and Woofie at present, and he after the squirrels! Found it on that site www.salcombefinest.com/holiday-homes. Take a peak.

Had meant to forget all about the N£sd. BUT I am so sorry. I am *so* upset. I have just read what must be one of the most shocking – but revelatory – stories about the set-up and its dreadful lack of mixed-funding ever told. I am aghast.

You know that a very close friend of mine died recently from inoperable lung-cancer – and I now find that a new drug could have been given to him and kept him going, but was not then allowed. He was diagnosed last November, died in April. Apparently, it had a trial, and worked so well (but expensively) that it is not yet licensed here. Get it in the USA, of course, but chum was too ill to fly. Get it in Europe now, too, but not here.

You cannot have it here – despite these other licences – even if you put your own house on the market and buy the drug yourself, to stay alive a bit longer. Barmy. And so cruel.

I could so happily run up to London on the GWR and deploy a howitzer on the NICE gang, *if* they can be found.

Stuff is called Nivolumab. Said to be one of biggest advances since chemotherapy. Doubles survival rates for many with lung and skin cancer. We've had successful clinical trials going on for ages. Then it got licensed here in June this year – but after my chum had died. And now, guess what, access to it has been stopped. *STOPPED!* I ask you! Don't we *want* people to live?

The thing is said to be likely to extend 12,000 UK lives a year. One of a new class of medications that teach the body to attack tumours. Brilliant. One of the class of drugs that that world-renowned cancer specialist Prof. Karol Sikora has long forecast, and which he has urged the NHS to fund properly. *But now it's a big N£sd No-No.* Costs around £6,000 a month, which is plenty. But it has almost doubled one-year survival rates for patients (like my mate) with advanced and inoperable lung disease. Isn't that what we want for them? Course, once licensed and used on a large scale here, price will drop, as ever.

FACEY'S HOLIDAY POSTCARDS, 16. IT BEATS' THEM ALL!

Here in June sufferers were able to get the drug free under a government scheme where manufacturers funded treatment. Otherwise, usual willy-wanky DoH waffling. BUT now even that funding deal has been stopped. Apparently because it has been granted a European license. *So, it works? Well, stop it then!*

NICE now has to decide whether or not to approve it. Approved long ago in USA. Now approved in Europe. So, well, we can't can we? Or not yet anyway. Likely to take months as the NICEITES shamble along.

AND meanwhile the Cancer Drugs Fund, which is meant to pay for treatments rejected by NICE [or one government outfit *versus* another!] is itself facing cutbacks due to over-spending. By "over-spending," of course, we really mean that the fund was too small in the first place. Can't have mixed funding, like the best care systems, can we? Oh no. Would be unfair. So the prudent saver is stuffed, as ever.

My take on this is that the drug works so well that a lot of people will want it, so the N£sd has had to say it can't pay. And nor can you! What a balls-up!

Meanwhile "A spokesman for the Department of Health [or Nuffsick] said: "We are taking ground-breaking steps to speed up access to innovative drugs."

By "ground-breaking" they mean getting a spade, digging up the garden, and burying the new drugs. Might as well scatter red poppies on the ground there, too.

If my next message is from the *Emigration Express Ship to Anywhere But*, you will know why!

As ever, your friend Facey.

Facey's Holiday Postcards, 17.
A question, with an easy answer!

11 August, 2015.

Dear Roy,

Lovely morning, spent in the sunshine, wandering across Sharpitor, round the cliff-edge on the precipitous and windy Courtenay Walk.

Tried to see the shadow in the water of the old beams of the long-ago wrecked ship in Start Bay. Water very clear, but no luck.

So sat on a bench reading the wonderful adventures of Rifleman Matthew Dodd of the Ninety-Fifth in the Peninsular War. In Forester's novel *Death to the French*. Title, no doubt, would not be allowed now by Mr. E.E.C. Cameron!

The retreating French in Portugal have to try to cross the Tagus. The mad plan is to build a pontoon across the half-mile of rushing water. The calculation is that they need 200 pontoons, most with four anchors. Ten kilometres of cable for the anchors for the pontoons. And the approaching roadway across the rocks has to be built, too. From scratch. Quite literally so. Two bridges to the roadway wanted, too. Have to be made from timber. In a bleak, rocky, very sparsely wooded countryside already stripped, burned, and battled bare by the long war in this bleak countryside.

A quote for you:

"'Have you got the timber and anchors and things?' asked Godinot, a little bewildered?

"'No', said the sergeant. 'But we have a good many houses in the town. We are to pull the houses down and use the joists. And we shall have to save the nails when we pull the houses down because we have no nails. And before we start pulling the houses down we shall have to make the tools to do it with, because we have no tools except a few hammers we have got from the farriers. But there is plenty of iron in the balconies. We have got to make hammers and saws and adzes out of that. And of course we have no hemp for the cables. We have got to make cables. There are three warehouses full of bales of wool. We have got to try ropes made of linen, or hay, or straw. Or we shall have to tie together every odd bit of rope the army can find in its billets. And there is no tar, of course, for the bottoms of the pontoons.

"I don't think General Eble has thought of a way round the difficulty of the tar. There is olive oil, however. Is there anyone who knows how to make a durable paint out of olive oil? I thought not. But they have begun experiments already down the road. If you sniff attentively you may be able to smell them.'"

"…This talk of building bridges to cross a half-mile river out of floor-joists appeared to their minds to take far too much for granted. The sergeant of sappers knew it, but he

FACEY'S HOLIDAY POSTCARDS, 17. A QUESTION, WITH AN EASY ANSWER!

could do nothing in the matter except change the subject."

Reminds you of....?

As ever,

FR, Jr.

Facey's Holiday Postcards, 18. To Zimbabwe, by postal vote at £3 a time?

24 August, 2015.

Dear Ken,

The season of Intellectual Aristocrats bidding to lead us, I note.

Consider this loony Marxigook the Very Antediluvianly Anciently Old Labourite, the anti-American, anti-NATO, anti-capitalist, anti-Monarchy, anti-Israelite, pro-IRA, pro-Hezbollah, pro-USSR, pro-TU bossdom, pro-unchanged 'public services', pro-politically-imposed "equality", pro-hyper-inflation-print-money-for-wheelbarrows bloke, this Outdated Icycle, this Venezulean Holiday Camper, this FU-economy-Ahoy-Chavezite, the Not-So-Savvy- Corbinliner & his McDuffer shadow-chancellor.

Well, old J.M. Keynes was right, wasn't he?

He who said that "the power of vested interests is vastly exaggerated compared with the gradual encroachment of ideas…soon or late, it is ideas, not vested interests, which are dangerous for good or evil."

So we may be going to become Zimbabwe, Mark II, by postal ballot, eh? At £3 a time.

Or as Comrade Binliner might say, 'There is no life without other people's wealth'?

AND, "It's All FREE!!!"

As ever.

Your very briefly depressable but ever hopeful chum, FR, Jr., who trusts the British people

PS. Higher-rate Taxpayer's Ahoy!

Facey's Holiday Postcards, No.19. Now let's price what really counts, eh?

20 October. Haircut day.

Dear Roy,

Ahab – now the Guvnment is really tackling THE critical issues! Plastic bags, indeed! That's the Dunkirk Spirit that is! That's how we beat the Nazis! That's how we remained an Island People! And Built THE EMPIRE!

Those infernalised bags. Now to cost those without a thought for the henviromumental 5 pees per bag. Aha! *That'll* show em!

But, what's this? Oh, shock, horror! I see in the *Scottishman* newspaper that there has been a sudden fall of 80% in the use of such plastic bags already. In a few days!!!

So *who says* that price is not an incentive, and that it makes *no* difference, then, eh?

And, being a hincorrible delinquent, I then ask myself what would be the impact if we did indeed charge people £10 to see a GP?

A fall in daft demand? A collapse of "Gimme the antiobotics & then I'll b***** off!"brigade? The snivels dealt with by an Aspro? The gammy leg examined by a pharmacisister, etc., etc? Doc morale, on the UP? Recruitment, on the UP? Energy for weekend cover, on the UP?

But, *can't* be done. *No way, Jose.* Not on your welly, Giorgio 'Osbornista. Remember the marginal seats. Cleggo will vote agin us. Corbynliner will make a mumbling speech about it to the Wiltshire Real Socialism is Coming Allotment Society [membership, 9]. Jobsworthik Vladimir Ulyanov McDonnell *[who he? Ed.]* will change his mind again, twice. Lord Oakegrotty *[not him again! – Ed.]* will volunteer to take untimely charge. The BleatBC will feature the horror story on every bulletin – between its adverts for itself – all day and night. With its usual discordant jangly "music."

So, no prices in the NHS. No, SIR! ["If it's free, I'll have two!"]. Don't be dopey, nopey. *WE* are the Party of the NHS y'know!

Next insteady in line for prices? A halfpenny tax on space at rural bus-stops, if standing. If a bus. If a day a week. If our majority in excess of 25,000.

THAT will cope with the deficit, that will! AND fund the undernourished NHS budget too!

Taxpayer's Ahoy!

As ever,

Your frugal friend, FR, Jr.

PS. Own a dictionary? Look up *"accountability."* Mine says "liable to account; responsible own actions." Ah, but that's not the NHS definition, is it? OH NO! In private sector, however, Volkswagen cheat on diesel emissions tests? Chief Executive resigns, promptly. Talk-Talk encryption cock-up on private details of millions? Begone, bosses! OUT! But…. Midstaffs NHS Scandal? Ah, different definition there, eh? Gone? On no account!!! Instead..."Move onto to other top NHS job, Double Pronto. Collect Big Pension as You Pass Zee Go. Kneel for Knighthood, too." Arise Sir Silent Communist Knight. Fair's fair, after all? Eh, what?

Facey's Holiday Postcards, No. 20. Thinking Cap Time?

Bonfire night, 2015.

Dear Roy,

Nasty wet day. Tucked in with tartan blanket on me knees, something to sup in beaker, prospect of cake nearby, old Jogglebury's Oporto to hand. Got me thinking cap on. Reading brilliant book by economist fellow, one Douglass C. North. Self-educatin' meself. Grammar-schoolink, if so to speak. 7-oakified.

Cheers me more than latest NHS cuttings. More cancer deezasters. More and More Frightfuls. Worser and worser results. Boss-docs still on weekend golf-courses. Juniors, all volunteers for this nicely paying status career, whingeing galore. *Socialist Shirker* magazine posters [propr. V. Redgrave & Co.] on the march. Co-op undertakers busier than ever. Me still trying to understand what's what, and why.

BUT I see that this chap North wrote that: "Obviously, competition, decentralized decision making, and well-specified contracts of property rights as well as bankruptcy laws are crucial to effective organisation. It is essential to have rules that eliminate not only failed economic organization but failed political organization as well. The effective structure of rules, therefore, not only rewards successes, but also vetoes the survival of maladapted parts of the organizational structure, which means that effective rules will dissolve unsuccessful efforts as well as promote successful efforts." Douglass C. North, *Institutions, Institutional Change and Economic Performance* (Cambridge, Cambridge University Press, 1990), p. 81.

Come on in leaking rowing-boat *NHS 1945*. Your time be HUP.

Grammar Schools Ahoy!

Yours, v. literally, FR, Jr.

NB. Facey now retires to the country, pondering his next opus, as the NHS Merry-Go-Round whirls onwards. And if <u>you</u> would rather get the best possible care, see <u>www.oecd.org/</u> and follow the necessary links. Don't ring Lord 'Owzat!

Afterword & Commentary, by *Soapey Sponge VII*.

This is an important book about the culture of health-care – and of public policy in education, too – in Great Britain.

I am most touched and grateful to my dear friend Facey for inviting me to write this Afterword and Commentary.

As you, the reader, will now have seen, the book sets out first principles for the better management and funding of essential public services. And for much better access to up-to-date treatments. It also endorses the critically important enhancement of self-responsibility in the individual as well as in those employed in "the system."

Facey believes in direct economic incentives, which we all know makes sense.

His often ironical and satirical work uses humour to make very serious points.

It is evidently well-informed and the work of an insider-outsider.

It tells many uncomfortable and hidden truths.

As a direct descendant of the original Frances Romford's own close friend, Mr. Soapey Sponge [on whose success in the gold-diggings our own family fortune is based], I am glad to contribute this note.

I am glad to say something of Facey's real life, origins, and times, which otherwise remain a mystery to many of his readers.

But who is he? I am not telling! Only a few people know his real identity. The nhsManagers.net site – where these episodes were first published – has been always been run by its originator, Mr. Roy Lilley. But the actual "Mr. Romford" has confirmed to me in person that he and not Roy is the author of the Facey Romford Papers. Roy, of course, has never suggested otherwise. And Roy's own daily commentary is invaluable and essential, as the best informed, liveliest, shrewdest and always current work on the NHS. He has quite enough on his hands! Facey's regular papers, however, also revealed much that you need to know as you consider the best basis for forward-looking and effective health services in the UK.

I write from my home in what the great and ever-living novelist Robert Smith Surtees called "Horseterylia."

Here, it has to be said, we are much more fortunate than you in the UK, with our creative and successful mix of public care, private insurance, and individual top-ups. If the UK does not copy, it's healthcare system will collapse. Or collapse further than it has already done.

As to what Facey has written, I am glad to affirm – which surely no one doubts? – what the novelist Arnold Bennett so rightly wrote to Siegfried Sassoon of the original, that "*Romford* is the real thing."

Like Surtees himself, our author has decanted real-life people into his articles, tales and anecdotes.

Here we see the world as it comes to the "ordinary" and often powerless, bewildered, and frightened individual.

It sets out many of these experiences of *everyday* NHS life in its many post-coded varieties.

We are grateful, too, for the picturesque details, which are so often left out of such accounts – save in novels.

Facey tells the story severely and persistently – and with his sometimes raucous humour.

The mixture, too, is employed both *between* the characters and *within* the characters.

The author is evidently a born story-teller.

He seems to have taken as much delight, too, as his evident heroes Charles Dickens and Robert Smith Surtees in conceiving such prismatic figures as Admiral Albert George Quincy Lascelles Vernon de St. Valery, The Lord Ironsides. Or Nursie Nursie Dixbungle, Chief Executive of The Great British Whitewash Company PLC. Or Grandmaster The Worshipful Sir Peter Coquille Albert Perceive Aloysius Gravities Cooke-Praster, CBE, a leading surgeon, and the deeply appalling "Jurassic" Johnson. This man, Mr. Augustus Melmotte-Jobber-Johnson, a 'political' doctor and long-term Woyal BMA activist is also notorious. Now aged 91 (or possibly more). Widely known in the profession as "Jurassic Johnson." Each really *tells* a story. Alas.

We may, however, delight, too in further revelations of such fictitious and absurd creations as these folks, or of Professor A. Hampster, of The Klingfilm Fund, London. And of The Rt. & Very Rev. Dr. B. Hogbin, GCSE, Bishop of St. Just, religious adviser to The Independent Labour Party. He is related to the Hoglebin family of Chessingfield-on-Soke and to the Hogblinkered family. The Very Dr. W. Hogblinkered, GCE, his relative, is also a religious doctor. All opposed to "change."

As we chortle, we should also fear!

No doubt representative, too, are Sir Snuffle Kettledrum CBE, President, Woyal College of Surgeons; Lady Gladyss Klinnockles of Income Augmentation, a life peeress; His Very Distinguished Grand Eminenceship The Lord High Grandmaster, The Worshipful Sir Pweeter G.G. Knatchbull-Bullknash, CBE, and The Very Hon. & Very Distinguished Surgeon and Very Life President of The Royal College of Vested Interests. Or Sir Extrasmuchsatisfied Perceval Nowtdunne, CBE, President, Woyal BMA.

Or even – surely fictitious, and rather far-fetched too? – The Lord Oakeshott [*who he? Ed*]. Then there is the obscure Baroness Sitting Bull of Emertonii, a constant appointee of sorts.

And, always representing the saner alternatives – the author's voice? – the pivotal and sympathetic figure of Sir Cyril Squoffington-Squogg, OBE, JP, Chief Executive of The Tower of London NHS Hospital Trust, London, E., and Bernice, his art historian wife. He a working-class boy made good.

Many of these characters are made probable by being, in the main, so ridiculous. There are few of them – save for the compassionate married couple the Squoffngton-Squoggs – who we can take to our hearts. Some, like Bumble, Fagin, Squeers, or Uriah Heap, we would not wish upon our worst enemies. But many of us meet the equivalent real life figures in the NHS every day!!! And they vote against us when they can.

Here they are all conceived with gusto and delight, all repetitive of vice or unpleasantness, or of failed if hopeful endeavours of different kinds. Many share the dual characteristics of arousing not only dread but amusement. And as the tales evolve they are made into something rounder and more complex than their Dickensian names imply.

The lavish use of grim settings is Dickensian, in course. The atmosphere of bureaucratic Chancery-lane muddledom which these reflect from the NHS is very telling. For example, The Great British Whitewash Co., PLC is in the frustrating and expensive tradition of the Circumlocution Office of *Little Dorrit*. Here, The Poltergeist of Probability is all-embracing.

As has been evident to the reader, this world of fantasy is indeed very vivid and very real. It is often necessary for the reader to be reminded that this is all fiction…*perhaps.*

All in all, Mr. Romford has succeeded in combining a comic with a serious rule. And by these means his characters – and the fundamental issues of public policy – are both animated and credible.

This approach – the presentation of character and by this means the dramatisation of the importance of the issues on which he focuses – gives Mr. Romford's work both significance and quality.

Here, hosts of dogs bark. [If entirely unheard at The Klingfilm Fund in London!]

Facey himself is a very agreeable companion, too, as we hunt the prevailing issues.

Notably, he is a man who sticks to his guns. He is like the immortal John Jorrocks, one who "keeps no cat wot don't catch mice!" And as JJ said, "'Arter all's said and done, there are but two sorts of folk in the world, Peerage folks and Post Hoffice Directory folks, and its the Post Office Directory folks wot pays their bills."

The Peerage Folks, conventionally, still make most of the decisions, however. *And for you!*

Our author, Facey Romford Jr., remains an anonymous but expert contributor to continuing debates about the NHS and the future of health and social care. He clearly has a strong sense of justice, and of duty to the deserving poor. But he does not wrap up issues in a sentimental Klingfilmy socialistical expertapotable knowebesti statistisickal haze. His Episodes, too, are as full of as rich a gallery of rogues, humbugs and noodles as Robert

Smith Surtees's own classic novels. He evidently detests shams and pretensions, and uncovers many which will be recognised in the NHS itself.

These anonymous contributions by Facey indeed stand in a grand tradition. For Surtees (who lived at Hamsterley Hall in the county of Durham but travelled widely – very sadly he died in the Metropole Hotel at Brighton in March 1864) himself combined an outer, public and an inner, hidden life. *He* insisted on writing anonymously, too. Indeed, he appears to have been in doubt that a Gentleman really ought not to own up to the fact that he used any of his valuable time writing novels, as Aubrey Noakes has noted.

Like Surtees himself, Facey Romford Jr. is evidently a diligent, busy, creative and indeed indefatigable and well informed original worker. He is a radical and economical interpreter and analyst of current events and a forecaster for the future. Like Surtees, to, he has a good ear for dialogue and is a born observer and satirist.

As Noakes said of the great novelist, "In my mind's eye I see him comfortably seated on his horse, wearing a scarlet coat and high, white cravat, observing quietly the antics not only of the fox, the hounds, and the horses, but the far more astonishing performances of the human race." We see Facey astride his charger.

Facey is, too, much less given to bobbing and bowing and curtseying amidst "the heavy fathers, the paterfamilias of the hunt" and "the complications of sheep" than might be thought proper by the Emertonicals. At least by the "great and the good" of the medical and political worlds. The directors of The Royal Academy of Vested Interests, the Great British Whitewash Co PLC, The BMA [or B-Me Me, as he dubs them], The Klingfilm Fund, &c.

Here, we see many NHS [or N£sd, as Facey calls it] examples of individuals who Surtees would have dubbed as Pomponius Ego [his name for Charles James Apperley, the hunting writer 'Nimrod.'] All of whom the novelist would have surely described, to lift his own words from another context, as "a landlocked, leg-tied tribe."

As Surtees noted, in his splendid novel *Ask Mamma (1858),* too, some such figures "ought to be preserved at Madame Tussaud's or the British Museum." As warnings. For example, Sir D. Nicholson of N. Staffs., the Communistical Silent Knight Pension King. But they should not be in charge of the NHS (or of a second-hand whelk stall).

Politicians and many in the NHS wait to see which way the policy fox will jump. Few offer any genuine leadership. But Facey looks ahead more clearly. He stays on the line, and regularly finds the fox. He is adept at staying in the saddle, too, however fast the pace, however muddy his breeches, whatever the roughness of the cautionary country over which he is set to ride. And, as our friend Surtees wrote in the Preface to his novel *Ask Mamma,* "It may be a recommendation to the lover of light literature to be told that the following story does not involve the complication of a plot. It is a mere continuous narrative of every-day exaggeration, interspersed with sporting scenes and excellent illustrations by Leech."

Like Surtees himself, our author's determination to publish anonymously allows us to say that he has not written for personal effect. Indeed, much of what follows is "painfully gentlemanly" – if sometimes 'rum' in the extreme and enacted in "chancery-like darkness" – to borrow briefly again from Surtees.

Mr. Romford evidently offers much informed knowledge. Internal evidence in the Episodes suggests that he has been involved in the NHS at least since c.1990. He is declared in his writings to have been a senior non-executive on more than one NHS board, both locally and nationally. He is evidently a competent historian and an economist, who has apparently held local and national NHS office. He clearly knows his way around Whitehall and its in-grown politics. But no CBE-hunter, he is honest, fearless, opinionated, and well informed. And, seemingly never intimidated, either by people or by ambition.

As to policy, he is an advocate of empowering individual patients with money, using tax-based funds for an individual healthcare account for each of us. He believes that it is vital to introduce price into the system. He would have spent his years, if a politician, making the case for liberal, adaptive, capitalist markets – which every leading Conservative politician since Thatcher [Boris, and perhaps George O, excepted?] has thus far failed so to do. There is, however, no other way to deliver better care. And only by financially empowering individual patients can we capture the millions of messages about what individual and different people want from the services, and are prepared to finance – either by tax, insurance, or personal top-ups.

There is, too, no other way to use economic incentives to encourage self-responsibility.

And to improve management and quality.

There is no other way to discipline demand.

And to sort individual preferences, thus efficiently and effectively distributing scarce resources by price, markets, and willingness to fund.

Facey Romford Jr. might be thought by some to be a Grand Vagabond. An aware Insider-Outsider. And/or an Amiably Eccentric Old Gentleman. But he certainly tells us much about the hidden world of the NHS, for which we all have to pay, and not just financially. As Professor Brian Edwards has pointed out, there remain many "dark corners" of the NHS indeed. Here, as was said in the 19th century we should "Cut the cackle and come to the 'osses."

This is, then, an insightful, an unusual, and important book. It not only offers a wide-ranging, thoughtful, knowledgeable and detailed forensic analysis. It offers a template for thought about the daily events of the NHS as they unfold before us. For Facey has the creative and unusual gift of being able to express complex issues in ways which help us to understand them more clearly.

Several of his pieces would have made excellent instalments of *Yes Minister*. Like these, Facey's are original, funny, yet also in the main factual even if creatively composed. Of course, he knows that the NHS does good to many – *if you can get it* – but his key points include that it does not achieve what it could do if there were competitive changes. Meanwhile, the services are too often condescending, lacking in empathy and compassion, too often devastatingly awful, and too often shockingly complacent.

The NHS is an Amphitheatre. It is full of very varied images and people, like Frith's *Railway Station* and his *Derby Day*. But it is comprised, too, of many farces. Here, the topics on which Facey focuses normally include the special agenda of vested-interests posing as the national interest – politicians, medical trade unionists, and bureaucracies. Those that Nobel Laureate Professor Milton Friedman dubbed "the iron triangle" of self-interest. Those which economic theorists have called "rent seekers." Facey suggests ways in which the payers of the bills (those noticed by one of our heroes as *"Taxpayers Ahoy!"*) can begin to get an equivalent for their money.

One other attractive feature of these Episodes is that Mr. Rumford is evidently in touch with contemporary literature and culture, whatever his age. He is, too, a supporter of *The Arsenal*. [But, as Facey would have said here, *"Isn't everybody?"*].

These essays then offer many important insights into those inner sanctums of government, Whitehall, and the management of public services which affect the lives of every one of us.

Facey, as one would expect, has his own 'hobby-horsical' tendencies, in particular concerning incentives, economics, and individual behaviours.

He is usually *going the pace.* BUT he does always stop at every hedge and ditch to see how it all looks.

A good deal of his works were thus written in the saddle and at speed, ready for the moment – like many of Anthony Trollope's novels, written on train journeys. This urgency and currency itself is perhaps amongst their value, even if they are sometimes a little raggedy at the edges. They compare well, in style and format, with Thackeray's *Roundabout Papers*, too, which says a good deal. Facey, however, gives no hint that he has ever read them. There is, too, something of the Dickens in his playlets – a living sense of the galactic profusion and oddity of it all. Something of the bewilderment of chaos of Sterne, too.

As to the name…the anonymous author has seemingly taken the name Facey Romford [adding the Jr.] from the timeless novels *Mr. Sponge's Sporting Tour* (1853) and *Mr. Facey Romford's Hounds* (1865) by Robert Smith Surtees (1805-64). It will be recalled that both were originally published anonymously. And that the original Facey, a loveable rogue, set himself up as a freelance Master of Foxhounds.

The drawing of the original Facey which we reproduce as our frontispiece is by the great John Leech (1817-64), the master illustrator. My own ancestor, Mr. Soapey Sponge, of course features strongly there.

In the novels the self-important do not often receive what they view as their due. There again, as in the NHS itself, many of consequence no doubt feel that their self-considered importance is not yet properly attended to by our author. Very Emertonical. A key lesson of the novels is the ability of people to be so inclined as to deceive themselves. And *en masse*, too. So, the economic and social lessons of the Episodes which follow in this book. Here, like the first Mr. Romford, our Facey can settle on and hunt a scent. He never loses the line nor tramples on his hounds nor takes a fence only to land in a great yawning ditch big enough to hold himself and his horse.

The original great sportsman, the first Mr. Francis ['Facey'] Romford Esq in the novels, was well known as a man who "liked to be doing." And so those familiar with the marvellous novels of Surtees will have already considered Facey Romford's background "in the detective style." They will know how that original Mr. Facey Romford was himself anonymous in pivotal and significant ways. They will have seen Mr. Romford in his adventures, including his notable "meet" at the tenth milestone on the Larkspur Road with the Countess of Caperington.

They will have recalled that Mr. Romford and his wife, the delectable, plump, lisping and handsomely bonneted former Miss Cassandra Cleopatra Watkins (of the fine landed mansion at Dalbery Lees, near Pickering Nook on the provokingly slow new mid-Victorian Union Railway), were eventually blessed with twins when living in Melbourne, Australia. And so the reader may well assume that our Facey Romford Jr is indeed a direct descendant of that happy couple.

Such, if it were so, would be typical of the original Mr. Romford, himself having been successfully mistaken for the great but absentee person of the same name, the true owner of the great Abbeyfield Park and Beldon Hall, JP, DL, patron of five livings, his crest a Turbot sitting upon its tail on a Cap of Dignity. Indeed, the reader will recall the *posse comitatus* at the wrong Mr. Romford's heels.

Thus, "our" Facey Romford, Jr would be the ultimate inheritor of the First Melbourne Bank of Romford and Sponge [now, in 2015, known as The Sharpitor Bank of The Commonwealth], which the original Facey opportunely established in the gold rush in 'Horseterhaylia.' That is, with his *allegedly* very doubtful friend, my ancestor Soapey Sponge (the runaway husband of Lucy Glitters as was, known in the novel as Mrs. Somerville, the original Facey Romford's actress friend and his pseudo-sister). If this is so then there is a story within a story here, and the name on these Episodes might not be a non-de-plume at all!

The pair who went to Oz set up in handsome premises in Collins Street East in the very elegant centre of classical Melbourne in an open market frontier society. And Facey's descendant may, too, have inherited the successors to the pack of hounds which the duo in due course let run in Australia. In the Bank the original Facey will no doubt have by then abandoned his usual foxhunting clobber – a slouching brown wide-awake hat, a dirty ditto suit of health-coloured Tweed, ditto waistcoat, and a pair of rusty-looking lack-lustre Napoleon boots – for a smarter and confidence-building suit and cravat, the equivalent of a proper hunting redcoat.

The original Facey Romford, as his readers well know, "could go across country like a comet", a dashing and fearless rider. If "our" Facey Romford, Jr is indeed the successor in the family name and fortunes he may, indeed, have returned from Australia and somehow inveigled himself into the 21st century mastership of the handsome house known as Beldon Hall, in Doubleimupshire once so colourfully occupied by his 19th century predecessor on behalf of the unfortunate absentee and unwittingly generous The Right Honourable the Lord Viscount Lovertin himself. And on this doubtful basis have seen himself mistakenly appointed in the English Midlands or in the North East as a non-executive director – *even a Chairman?* – in the NHS? And from thence, onto some national offices and advisory roles in Whitehall and in think-tanks too?

If so he will certainly have shown courage in the job. Our readers will well know how Surtees saw *his* Mr. Romford as Master of the Larkspur Hunt, so brilliantly mounted on a high-couraged bay (supplied on 'tick' by the notorious horse-coper Mr. Goodhearted Green, aka "Sir Roger Ferguson, Bart.", of Bagnigge Wells Road, Islington).

Facey regarded *any* danger at a discount, riding powerfully and confidently with great skills amidst ragged blackthorn, briar-tangled and prickly close-looking gorse, broom and fern – and across every kind of difficult fence, gate and wide ditch, in angular woods and grassy dells. In the Hawkworth Hills, in Rockwoodside, in Tarring Neville Park, and beyond. Alongside the Dukes and their grooms and huntsmen, with the cattle-jobbers, the horse-breakers and copers, the auctioneers and the fat farmers, the 'airdressers, the soldiers and the County Court bailiffs, the young and old bucks, as well as the glittering actresses and the doubtful tuft-hunters.

How his successor came to ride so well on such an unpromising turf as the NHS itself, and hunt this problematic, clod-ridden, muddy, briar-strewn and unpromising country, is, however, just about anybody's guess.

Especially with him lacking the necessary £sd. And when, to borrow words from Surtees himself, so much of that road remains "in a very indictable state of repair."

But the present is, perhaps, not the moment for further speculation as to the authorship itself, but the time for the fuller enjoyment of his writings.

For, as Surtees says in concluding his novel *Ask Mamma*, "…let us leave our hero open. And as we have only aimed at nothing but the natural throughout, we will finish by proposing a toast that will include as well the mated and the single of our story, as the mated and the single all the world over, namely, the old and popular one of 'The single married and the married happy!' drank with three times three and one cheer more! HOO-RAY!"

Or sound the cry! *Tally-Ho! Holloa Away!*

[Signed]

Mr. Soapey Sponge VII,
Private Executive Chambers,
The Sharpitor Bank of The Commonwealth ,
Collins Street East,
Melbourne, Victoria,
AUSTRALIA.

4 July, 2015.

PS. Taxpayer's Ahoy!

Also recently published by EER

'Coming, Ready or Not!'

The Realities, the Politics, and the Future of the NHS.

Reflections on the potential of consumer power to renovate health care.

John Spiers

Lately, Visiting Professor, School of Humanities and Social Studies, University of Glamorgan.

Formerly Member of the Board of the National Care Standards Commission, of the executive of the National Association of Health Authorities & Trusts. Also Chairman, Brighton Health Authority, Brighton Health Care NHS Trust, the South East Thames NHS Management College, & The Patients Association.

Previously a Senior Visiting Fellow & Head of Health Care Studies at the Institute of Economic Affairs, London. Founding Chairman of Civitas, & a founding member of the Advisory Council of' Reform.

With a foreword by Professor Philip Booth, Editorial & Programme Director, Institute of Economic Affairs, & Professor of Insurance & Risk Management, Cass Business School, London.

This radical new book by a leading commentator offers a way-out from the current – and rapidly worsening – crisis of healthcare provision. It urges that vast changes are coming – *ready or not!* – and that urgent reforms are vital if the NHS is to deliver its founding values.

We cannot afford to waste more years without acting. New policies require wider funding. Competitive purchasing. Competitive provision. And individual self-responsibility. Without urgent changes the bank will soon be broken. And the NHS is already no longer "fair."

The author seeks ways to ensure that the promises made by and for the NHS can be reliably delivered to all, as a personal, individual, timely, intimate and safe service. He is concerned with the underlying principles and the actions necessary for successful change.

Professor Spiers here encourages politicians to make the clear argument – with conviction, eloquence and persistence – for the liberal free capitalist market. For this does more for 'ordinary' people than any other social mechanism. It can provide the solutions we need. Yet it remains a major deficit in our provision of good healthcare.

This is an important alternative to the received default position – surprisingly, still accepted by Conservatives as well as by the left – that the state-monopoly, solely tax-funded NHS is the best approach to care. Yet it remains unlike any system adopted anywhere else in the world. We need to ask why. And to examine the alternatives now.

The funding problem is especially acute – and chronic! We need to examine how France, Germany, Switzerland and Australia cope much better and with a mixed structure. The alternative of insisting on 1% annual efficiency savings, where NHS Trusts are already under-funded and seriously over-spent, is unpersuasive. And doing the same for less cost inevitably requires more rationing.

NHS Executives already have to find £22 billion of savings in the current year from its £115 billion budget. The model is clearly broken. And meanwhile, public demands increase, life expectancy increases, opportunities and effective but costly new drugs multiply, as do patient expectations. The dangerous train is coming fast down the track! This carefully-argued book offers direct individual economic incentives as the mechanisms by which to release individual economic power in the hands of all consumers, with individual tax-based Health Savings Accounts introduced, and with tax incentives to top-up too. This more flexible and more broadly-based model can provide more efficient and more reliable care. By this means self-responsibility can be radically improved too. Patient fund-holding can thus put the less well-off in the same position as the middle-classes, to the benefit of all. And also encourage better ways to live, in taking more care of your own health.

This is a significant new work which is addressed to consumers, and to politicians and civil servants in Whitehall – where the author has much personal experience of working within the NHS, advising at Prime Ministerial and Ministerial level. And it speaks, too, to the greater world beyond, where the author has served as Chairman of one of the largest Health Authorities, an NHS Hospitals Trust, the NHS South East Management College, and The Patients' Association.

edwardeverettroot@yahoo.co.uk

Public Policy Series, No.1.

Hardback ISBN: 978-1-911204-03-9
Paperback ISBN: 978-0-954-2075-19
eBook ISBN: 978-0-954-2075-95

Acclaim for other works by Professor John Spiers.

Who Decides Who Decides? Enabling choice, equity, access, improved performance and patient guaranteed care.

"Wonderful read. As John Spiers shows, in this sprightly, erudite, concise book, when you ask the right questions, you get the right answers. He asks what a patient-centred health care system would look like and comes up with novel and pragmatic answers." – Professor Regina E. Herzlinger, Harvard Business School.

"John Spiers detailed yet fluent book demonstrates how we can achieve better healthcare for all." – Professor Philip Booth, Institute of Economic Affairs.

"[he] has the gift of presenting complex ideas clearly. This makes this book a challenging offering to current public policy debates." Professor Michael Connolly, University of Glamorgan.

ISBN-13: 978 184619 276 0

Patients, Power and Responsibility. The first principles of consumer-driven reform.

"If we are to get out of the current rut in healthcare delivery we need visionaries to point the way. This book is an inspirational guide to a potential way forward." Professor Karol Sikora, University of Buckingham.

ISBN: 1 85775 924 9

Both titles published by Radcliffe Medical Press, Oxford.

TO BE PUBLISHED IN SEPTEMBER 2016

This Will Only Hurt A Little!

Achieving Patient Benefit and the Reform of Clinical Practice.

Dr. William G. Pickering

Cloth ISBN: 978-0-9542075-4-0
e-book ISBN: 978-1-911204-01-5

320pp.

Foreword by Dr. Phil Hammond, author of *What Doctors Really Think*, &c., and the star of TV series *Trust Me, I'm a Doctor.*

This trenchant and expert book by an experienced doctor – who has worked both in hospitals and in general practice – advances the urgent case for an independent medical inspectorate to stop a host of avoidable errors which damage patients.

Dr. Pickering draws on his many years of practice and on his later career as an expert witness on behalf of plaintiffs, to marshal both arguments and detailed evidence which support the need for major changes.

To prevent many avoidable clinical errors and to enhance clinical practice we urgently need a local and independent body in every region, free from the NHS 'brotherhood' of vested-interests yet staffed by clinicians. These local inspectors would all investigate *all* clinical practices. They would do so on a regular, normal, week-by-week basis. And thus help to prevent very many everyday errors which do so much damage to patients, and which are usually both costly and unremarked, and often disastrous to patients.

As Dr. Hammond says: "It was a brilliant idea. It was strongly resisted by the medical establishment.

"Dr Bill Pickering was a huge influence on my thinking over 15 years, and along with the Bristol whistleblower Steve Bolsin and Bristol parent Maria Shortis (now Maria Von Hilldebrand), he was the most lucid thinker about patient safety that I was privileged to meet.

"Steve demonstrated the urgent need for NHS staff to be able to speak up about NHS failings without fear of persecution, and the duty of managers and regulators to act on this. Maria lost her baby at Bristol and yet started a wonderful charity called Constructive Dialogue for Clinical Accountability, whose focus was on culture change in the NHS towards an honest, open and trusting relationship between users and staff that was truly accountable. But it was Bill who had the best idea on how to achieve this.

"Although elements of it appear in the CCQ hospital inspectors and the new whistleblowing guardians. Bill's idea was much simpler, leaner and quicker – and in my view would've been more effective. Instead of sending 80 inspectors to hospital at huge expense to invade a hospital periodically, have a lean team locally placed and charged with continuously monitoring the concerns and experiences of patients, carers and staff. This would use the frontline of the NHS as a smoke alarm to nip problems in the bad and prevent them becoming disasters. It would also dismiss vexatious complaints quickly."

ALSO FORTHCOMING

Wray Vamplew, Emeritus Professor of Sports History, University of Stirling; Visiting Professor, Manchester Metropolitan University; Special Projects Editor, International Journal of the History of Sport.
How the game was played. Essays in Sports history.

Asa Briggs, Formerly Master, Worcester College Oxford; Vice-Chancellor, Sussex University; Chancellor, The Open University.
First and Last. Reflections on Time, Place, and History.

John Sutherland and Johanna Marie Melnyk. John Sutherland is Lord Northcliffe Professor Emeritus of Modern English Literature at University College, London. Dr. Melynk is an independent scholar.
The 'Prince of Puffers'. The Life and Works of the Publisher Henry Colburn (d.1855).

C. Stephen Yeo, Formerly Principal, Ruskin College, Oxford.
Alternatives to State Socialism, The History of Cooperation. A 3 volume set.
Volume 1. *Victorian Agitator, George Jacob Holyoake (1817-1906): Co-operation as 'This New Order of Life.'*
Volume 2. *A New Life, The Religion of Socialism in Britain,1883-1896 : Alternatives to State Socialism.*
Volume 3. *Class Conflict and Co-operation in Nineteenth and Twentieth Century Britain.*

Peter Burke, Emeritus Professor of Cultural History, Emanuel College, Cambridge.
Secret History, from Renaissance to Romanticism.

F.M. L. Thompson, Formerly Reader in Economic History at University College London; Professor of Modern History at Bedford College; Director of the Institute of Historical Research, University of London, and President of the Royal Historical Society.
English Landed Society Revisited

NOW AVAILABLE

Serious About Series. American Cheap 'Libraries', 'Railway' Libraries, And Some literary Series of The 1890s.

John Spiers
Senior Research Fellow, Institute of English Studies, School of Advanced Study, University of London; Professorial Fellow, London Metropolitan University.

ISBN: 978-0-9542075-3-3.

Second edition. Published 5 November 2015. Includes illustrations of 25 series, 16 in colour.

Paperback, £30.00.

x + 1-107pp. 211 x 148mm

The History of The Book series, No.1.
This is the innovative, trail-blazing enquiry into the importance, range, and history of the publishers' series in America and in Britain, by the leading expert in this field.

From the introduction: "Wherever you look, wherever you live, whichever publishers' catalogue you open, whichever integral advertisement in a book you consider, whatever your interests, there is the series. There seems to be no issue, no concern, no topic, no theme, no adult, juvenile or specialist subject, no way of seeing, thinking about or commenting upon the world which does not have its 'series.' Every series carried its 'messages' and implied advice, targeting specific readers and market segments....It is fundamental to publishing in every continent."